L. W. Green

MEMOIR

OF THE

LIFE AND CHARACTER

OF

REV. LEWIS WARNER GREEN, D.D.

WITH A

SELECTION FROM HIS SERMONS.

BY

LE ROY J. HALSEY, D.D.,
PROFESSOR IN THE THEOLOGICAL SEMINARY OF THE NORTHWEST.

NEW YORK:
CHARLES SCRIBNER & CO.
1871.

PREFACE.

In publishing the present volume, containing a selection of Dr. Green's Discourses, with a Memoir of his Life, the purpose has been twofold: first, to place in the hands of his numerous friends and pupils, some suitable memorial of one whom they greatly loved and admired; and secondly, to preserve for the wider circle of the public, and especially of our young ministry, the record of a life singularly devoted to the great work of education, and blessed of God in the varied spheres of its influence. He lived in an eventful period of the American Church, and filled successively many important positions in the central and western portions of our country. It has been thought, therefore, that some monument of this kind was due to his memory, and that hundreds of his friends and pupils, in all parts of the land, who had heard his living voice, would gladly welcome a volume of his strikingly original and elevated discourses.

Our great and good men, especially at the West, live, labor, die, and are too soon forgotten. The writer of the Memoir has felt that it would be a service to the ministry, to the church, and to the country, to place on record, along with these discourses, some fitting tribute to a man of God, who served his generation well, and who had attained to a purity and elevation of character not often surpassed. Amid the feverish excitements in which we live, the retrospect of a life so consecrated to God, so lifted above the murky atmosphere of earthly pursuits and ambitions, may come like an inspiration from a purer world to teach us the value of things unseen and eternal. It was a life eminently distinguished as one of thoughtful contemplation, and, at the same time, intensely devoted to work, and to all active, practical duty.

The sermons of this volume are now published for the first time. They had never been prepared for the press by their author; and they are, almost without exception, what his own hand marked them—"unfinished sketches." They are selected from a large mass of similar manuscripts. Gifted in extemporaneous delivery, and able to recall any trains of thought which had been once mentally composed, he was accustomed to write only an outline of the intellectual and argumentative portions of his discourses; and then to trust himself without writing for all the emotional and exhortatory parts. This will account for the fragmentary character of some of the sermons, and for their apparent want of pointed application at the close. Though it was in the unwritten applications and perorations that he often rose to his highest excellence of thrilling and impassioned eloquence, still enough remains, in these uncompleted productions, to reveal many of the striking characteristics which distinguished him as one of the most original, impressive, and powerful preachers of his day.

The estimate here given of Dr. Green's ability, both as a teacher and a preacher, is based upon the testimony of many competent judges among his contemporaries. It will doubtless commend itself as just, to such readers as may have enjoyed his instructions or heard him in the pulpit. The writer has not aimed to eulogize, but to present a true picture of the man and the minister—avoiding the extreme of an over-estimate on the one hand, and that of saying too little on the other. At all events, it is a satisfaction to know that the sermons are before the reader to speak for themselves; and from them, though that powerful living voice can no more be heard, he will be able to form his own estimate of what the lamented author preached, and how he preached.

CONTENTS.

CHAPTER I.

DANVILLE, 1806—1824.

CHAPTER II.

DANVILLE AND PRINCETON, 1824—1832.

CHAPTER III.

DANVILLE, 1832—1840.

CHAPTER IV.

ALLEGHENY, 1840—1847.

CHAPTER V.

BALTIMORE, 1847—1848.

CHAPTER VI.

PRINCE EDWARD, 1848—1856.

CHAPTER VII.

LEXINGTON AND DANVILLE, 1856—1863.

CHAPTER VIII.

DANVILLE, 1863.

CHAPTER IX.

CHAPTER X.

CHAPTER XI.

SERMONS.

LIFE AND CHARACTER

OF THE

REV. LEWIS WARNER GREEN, D.D.

CHAPTER I.

Danville, 1806—1824.

Birth.—Parentage.—Early Education.—Maternal Influence.—Orphanage.—Judge John Green.—Schools and Teachers.—Studies at Dr. Lewis Marshall's.—Classical Attainments.—Conversion and Profession of Religion.—Dangerous Illness.—Recovery—Deep Religious Impressions.—Transylvania University.—Centre College.—Graduation.—Fondness for Philosophical Investigation.

LEWIS WARNER GREEN, of whose life and labors it is proposed to give an outline, introductory to a volume of his posthumous discourses, was born on the 28th of January, 1806, in a midland county of Kentucky, near the town of Danville. He was the twelfth and youngest child of Willis Green and Sarah Reed, who were married at that place in the year 1783, while Kentucky was yet an almost unbroken wilderness and the few settlers about Danville still dwelt in rude forts. This, it is said, was the first Christian marriage ever solemnized on Kentucky soil. Both parents were of Scotch-Irish descent. They were born and reared in the Shenandoah Valley of Virginia, where their ancestors had long resided, closely connected by marriage with some of the most prominent families of the State.

His mother, Sarah Reed, was the daughter of John Reed, a man of fine personal appearance and of superior intellectual and moral endowments. At an advanced age Mr. Reed removed with his family of ten children from his home on the Shenandoah to the vicinity of Danville. He was, in fact, one of the early pioneers of the place, and left, at his death, a family highly distinguished for intelligence, social position, and moral worth—his six daughters being all remarkable for personal beauty, and his eldest son, Thomas Reed, rising to political eminence as a senator in Congress from the State of Mississippi.

His father, Willis Green, was the son of Duff Green, and grandson of Robert Green, who had been one of the early settlers of the Shenandoah Valley. Willis Green, when quite a young man, catching the spirit of adventure, left his paternal home in the Mother State to try his fortunes at the West. Having obtained contracts to locate land warrants in Kentucky, he set out with his surveyor's commission and instruments, and plunged at once into the pathless forest. Arriving, at length, in the region of Danville, he selected a beautiful sweep of land adjoining the farm of the old fort, which he cleared and named "Waveland," from its gentle undulations. Here, meeting and marrying Sarah Reed, he settled down for life and built the family homestead. Here his twelve children were born. And here, also, he died at the age of fifty-one, after a well-spent life, during which he had served in the Legislature of the State, and filled other important civil offices. He was a man of tried integrity and practical wisdom, whose Christian principles and rugged virtues were powerfully felt in the new and forming society around him.

Of this sterling Christian stock, and under these circumstances, so auspicious for the development of a noble character, the subject of this memoir was born, and here he received his earliest impressions. He was the child of faith and prayer. From his infancy he was devoted by his Christian mother to the work of the ministry. Upon this child of promise, this son of her declining years, the very Benjamin of her heart, she lavished the whole wealth of her strong and loving nature.

Gently, prayerfully, and hopefully did she perform the faithful mother's part and sow the seeds of instruction and sacred influence in the young heart. During the few years she was spared to him she lost no opportunity of impressing his opening mind with a sense of religious things, thus early leading him along that path which he was afterward to tread, and preparing him for that career he was destined to illumine by a life of consecration to God.

But her instructions were of short duration. When but five years old he was deprived of a father's care; and at seven this loving, faithful mother was also summoned to the skies. It was not, however, until her life-work of lasting impressions had been successfully accomplished on his young and plastic heart. Her own life was a beautiful illustration of the truth she sought to inculcate and its lessons were not soon lost upon the thoughtful child. Her death wrung his heart with anguish. But her sweetness of temper, her patience under suffering, her unmurmuring resignation to the will of God were indelibly engraven on his memory. Like seeds in genial soil, they sprang up and bore fruits in subsequent years. To her death he was accustomed, through life, to trace back his first serious impressions on religion. The saintly influence of her character lingered in his memory as that of some tender and sympathizing guardian angel. To that influence, and to the seeds sown by her faithful hand, during the first seven years of his existence, he never failed to attribute, under God, whatever fruit of good or of usefulness his subsequent years may have borne.

Seldom has a mother's influence over a son, though brief in its opportunity, been more signally crowned with blessings after she was gone. It is another added to the many examples of that living power which flows from a faithful mother's influence, and shows how God answers prayer and rewards faithful toil long after the heart has ceased to pray and the hands to labor. In the toils and conflicts of life, amid the darkest hours of doubt and temptation, he loved to think of her as some blessed visitor from heaven, who had been permitted to smile upon him for a few brief years, as if to allure to that better world and lead the way. From every struggle with the tempter, and from every scene of discouragement and trial, he arose with a stronger confidence in his mother's God and a warmer love for that faith which he had first learned at a mother's knee.

His early orphanage, depriving him of both parents, threw him into the family of his oldest brother, Judge John Green, who became his guardian. He was a gentleman of high character adorned by many noble virtues; and he felt the kindly interest of a father in the education of the orphan brother now committed to his care. Though in later years Judge Green became a devoted Christian—two of his own sons afterward entering the ministry—his views at that time were somewhat tinctured with the prevailing skepticism of the period. About the opening of this century a phase of unbelief, originally imported from France and indorsed by Mr. Jefferson and other prominent statesmen, had taken strong hold upon many of the educated minds of our country, particularly in Virginia and Kentucky. Religion found few advocates among the more elevated classes. Still, there were some shining examples of evangelical piety. Conspicuous among these was the wife of Judge Green. She was a lady of rare accomplishments, both of mind and manners, and of the most lovely Christian character. In her own household and in the social circles around her she threw the whole weight of her influence on the side of evangelical religion, and used all the means within her power to check the prevailing worldliness and ungodliness of the times. Dr. David Nelson, who, in subsequent years, became pastor of the church of Danville, remarked of her, that she had probably done more than any other person in Kentucky to stem the current of infidelity and irreligion and to mould the society at Danville into that evangelical character for which it became distinguished.

Into this home of refinement and culture, presided over and adorned by so much that was attractive in piety and womanly influences, the orphaned boy was now brought; and here he spent the greater part of his youth. While there was much to develop and stimulate his opening mental faculties in the associations and companionships of such a family, there was not wanting that gentle guiding hand of Christian love, which might take up the work where his mother's hand had left it, and carry forward the religious training which had been so well begun. In this noble Christian lady he found a friend and his second religious teacher. To her example and influence he was indebted for many of the elements and impressions that entered into the formation of his character and at last prepared him for the great work of life. If she had done no more, this alone would have been an object worth living for—that from her home circle, and through her humble yet potential influence, had been given to the church three ministers to preach the Gospel of God.

As a child his manners were singularly shy among older people. His serious, thoughtful turn of mind would have very much isolated him from his young and more boisterous companions, but for another characteristic equally strong—his fondness for out-door sports and the exuberant joy which he felt when partaking of them with his boyish associates. An enthusiastic love for books, amounting almost to a passion, developed itself very early. At an age much younger than is common with boys, he acquired a knowledge of the Latin and Greek languages, read Virgil and Homer in the original with delight, and became as familiar with their scenes and heroes as with the things of every-day life. He had the advantage of a thorough drilling in these tongues under the instructions of Mr. Duncan F. Robertson and Mr. Joshua Fry, two of the most famous teachers and scholars in that part of the country. No boy of his years, probably, ever studied the Greek and Roman classics with a keener relish or a higher ardor. He lived in the world created by their genius, caught the inspiration of their great thoughts and the glow of their sublime imagery, fought over their battles, mingled in their sports, sailed over seas and stormed cities with their heroes, kindled with the eloquence of their orators and sages, and felt his whole soul dilated, refined, and ennobled by the high and loving communion.

When thirteen years of age, with his brother Willis, a boy of fine promise, two years older than himself, he entered a classical school at Buck Pond, in Woodford County, Kentucky, taught at that time by Mr. W. R. Thompson, at the residence of Dr. Lewis Marshall, in whose family the boys boarded, and afterward by Dr. Marshall himself. This was regarded as the best classical academy then in Kentucky. Here were educated many of the men who afterward rose to the highest distinction in the State. Among all the young and brilliant minds here gathered from different quarters, and brought into daily contact for the purpose of instruction under the eye of these accomplished linguists, none appeared to greater advantage for native talent, and all those traits of character which boys admire in each other, than the brothers Willis and Lewis Green. The latter was pronounced by Dr. Marshall one of the finest classical scholars who had ever been under his tuition. His natural quickness, his ardent love of study, and his thorough training by his former teachers, Fry and Robertson, enabled him to sustain himself with ease in classes composed of boys much older than himself. In his eager pursuit of classical knowledge, and in hearty appreciation of its beauty and power, he was the noblest Roman of them all.

With unabated ardor he pursued these studies about two years at Dr. Marshall's, finding in Mrs. Marshall another warm-hearted and devoted Christian friend and counsellor, who felt a deep interest in his welfare, and cherished for him a strong attachment through life. During these years his progress in study was rapid and satisfactory. But during this time two events occurred, which probably, more than mere intellectual growth or attainments, contributed their influence to future years in the formation of his character and the shaping of his destiny.

The latter part of the first of these years was marked as a period of religious awakening in the school and through the neighborhood. Quite a number of the pupils and others became deeply interested in the matter of their salvation, gave satisfactory evidence of conversion, and made a public profession of their faith in Christ. Among these were both Willis and Lewis Green. They were baptized and received into the communion of the Pisgah Church in March, 1820, the one being then about fourteen and the other about sixteen years old.

During the second year of their stay at Dr. Marshall's a malignant fever made its appearance in the school, and raged for a season with great violence. The two brothers fell under its power, and soon became dangerously sick. After a brief illness, Willis breathed his young spirit into the bosom of the Saviour he had loved and trusted. The younger brother, after a hard struggle for life, protracted through weeks of suffering, at last rallied sufficiently to be carried home to Waveland.

Here, however, a relapse ensued, and again there seemed little hope of his recovery. But the disease was at length subdued. Through a convalescence of months he came up slowly from the gates of death. Not in vain for him had been that long gaze into the grave, that calm scrutiny of himself in the light of eternity. Not in vain was the loss of that gifted brother, so endeared to him by nearness of age, similarity of taste, and close companionship in the sports, the studies, and the experiences of childhood. The impressions made upon him were as deep and lasting as life. Loud and distinct now sounded that call to the Gospel ministry which had rung in his ear ever since he had knelt at his mother's knee, and learned from her sainted lips to cry, "Our Father." But the preparation was not yet complete. Other trials and deeper experiences awaited him. A fuller insight into his own unworthiness, clearer views of Christ and his all-sufficiency, were needed before entering on the vocation to which he aspired with such awed and trembling expectancy.

His health being at last restored, he was sent to the Transylvania University, in Lexington, Kentucky, then under the administration of Dr. Horace Holley. After completing the studies of the junior year in this institution, he was transferred to Centre College in Danville, then just organized by the Presbyterians of Kentucky, and placed under the presidency of Dr. Jeremiah Chamberlain. The reason for this change was that the Presbyterians of the State, becoming dissatisfied with the infidel principles of Dr. Holley, had withdrawn their support from Transylvania, and determined to build up an institution at Danville. Here he spent his senior year; and having now completed a full collegiate course, he graduated with the first class of Centre College in 1824, at the age of eighteen.

An insatiable thirst for knowledge and love of reading led him into paths of both philosophical and classical study not often trodden by youthful students. Every thing having a connection with the subject of his studies, or in any way throwing light upon them, was read voraciously, and incorporated with his accumulating stock of knowledge. The study of the human mind, its structure and capabilities, possessed from boyhood a wonderful charm for him. To the close of life he pursued these investigations. With the single exception of the contemplation of God's revealed truth, he believed there could be no higher and nobler employment of our faculties than in the study of the human mind. While still a college student, the writings of the Greek and Roman sages were perused by him with the ardor of discipleship. By this early and familiar contact with the acute and powerful thinkers of other ages, a living energy of thought was infused into his mind, which marked all his public discourses. The reader of the sermons in this volume cannot fail to see how full his mind was of images of beauty and sublimity, and how rich in treasures of wisdom and philosophy derived from the inexhaustible store-house of classical antiquity.

CHAPTER II.

DANVILLE AND PRINCETON, 1824—1832.

Choice of a Profession.—Deep Experiences.—Conflicting Plans and Purposes. —Becomes a Student of Law.—Then of Medicine.—Settles on a Farm.—Impediment of Speech.—His Marriage.—Death of his Wife.—A Final Decision.—Preparation for the Ministry.—Studies at Yale College.—At the Theological Seminary in Princeton.—Recollections of Dr. Boardman.—Testimony of Dr. Judkin.

THE time for a decision as to his great life-work was now drawing near. With the young man no problem is more important, and at times more perplexing. Thus far he had been sedulously disciplining his mental powers, and treasuring up, against the day of need, that elementary knowledge which was to give edge and temper to the weapons of life's warfare. But at the same time, the spiritual part of his nature was undergoing a deeper and far more important discipline. Though converted at an early age, his faith was subjected to almost every form of assault devised by the great adversary of souls for their destruction; but from each dark abyss of doubt and despair into which he was plunged, it emerged brighter and stronger, and with a firmer grasp upon the Rock of Ages.

The wisdom of God, in suffering him to pass through this fiery ordeal, he recognized in subsequent years, when called to administer consolation to others in similar trials. His experience in these spiritual conflicts had given him wonderful sympathy and patience with those who, harassed with doubts and tormented with fears, hesitate to receive without question the faith of their fathers. With an awed and subdued sense of his great deliverance, he acknowledged the divine goodness and mercy which preserved him from making shipwreck of the faith once delivered to the saints. And thenceforward it became, not only the most powerful, but the most vital and real of all realities to him.

He was now emancipated from the doubts and anxieties that had long tortured him, and his freed soul had found perfect rest and peace in the assurance that he was a child of God; that Christ was indeed very God, and that the Scriptures contained the sure and infallible truth of God on all the deep questions of man's nature, duty, and destiny.

But the hour for the choice of a profession brought with it temptation and trial in a new form. A purpose which had been maturing with each year of his life, from the early period at which he began to reflect, and which no degree of gloom or despondency could long unsettle, now developed into a burning desire to preach the unsearchable riches of Christ. He was the centre, however, of far different hopes and expectations. His determination to commence at once his preparation for the duties of the ministry met with persistent discouragement. The Bar and the Senate had attracted most of the talent of the State. Among worldly people no other position was considered a fit theatre for young men with abilities above the ordinary range. Some of his nearest relatives, at that time unconnected with the church, shared largely in this prejudice against the pulpit, and exerted all their influence to dissuade him from his purpose.

On a former occasion, while the brothers were yet little boys at school, the remark had been made to some of the ladies of the family, "I want you to understand, that you may take Lewis and make what you please of him: as for Willis he is entirely too smart to be turned into a preacher." When, however, in a few brief years, the favorite, and as was then supposed more gifted boy, thus destined to worldly distinction, after giving his testimony to redeeming love, was called away to a better world, the purpose was then formed for the remaining brother, that no reproach of the cross should bar his road to fame. Every argument that could be adduced from his extreme youth and inexperience of the world, and from the illusory character of things unseen and spiritual, was employed to shake the purpose which Lewis had so long cherished, and was now ready to put into execution. He too, it was thought, had talents too bright to be wasted upon the visionary work of the pulpit.

For a moment he yielded to the persuasive voices which whispered to him of fame and fortune and gratified ambition. In deference to the counsel of friends he loved, and of his young companions in study, he concluded to prepare for the legal profession. He entered the office of his brother, Judge Green, and applied himself to the study of law with the assiduity which characterized all his pursuits. But he soon found that his heart was not in the matter. Conscience upbraided him as one who was flying from duty. His soul was a constant prey to unrest. Unable to prosecute a profession which had become thoroughly distasteful to him, in little less than a year he abandoned the law, and commenced the study of medicine with Dr. Ephraim McDowell at Danville. If he might not enter the race for distinction, here was at least a road to usefulness. But from this also he soon turned in utter weariness. He felt that it was not his vocation. His heart was not in it. He could not pursue it with enthusiasm. His soul had been smitten with the early love of a nobler mission, and could not be satisfied with the husks of earthly pursuits, while hungering for heavenly sustenance. It was not that other pursuits were unimportant. It was not that the loftiest Christian virtues might not adorn all honorable secular occupations. But his mind had long been filled with a great purpose, and he could not rest till it was accomplished. The remembrance of his early dedication by his mother, God's providential dealings with himself and those around him, and his growing convictions of duty obtained the mastery. "Woe is me if I preach not the Gospel!"—this became the burden of his life.

There was one circumstance in his personal history which must be mentioned in connection with his difficulties as to the choice of a profession. For this, probably, as much as any opposition or discouragement he encountered from others, contributed to his indecision at this time. When a little fellow, just learning to talk, he was accustomed to amuse himself by mimicking a nurse, who stammered dreadfully, until the pernicious habit became fixed. It does not seem to have cost him much uneasiness, until he began seriously to think of a profession, when he was overwhelmed with a sense of his misfortune. He at once applied himself to the reparation of the evil, with a determination which successive and most mortifying failures could not conquer nor discourage. And although each fresh effort seemed to leave his utterance only the more hopelessly defective, the conviction that he could and would overcome it was abiding. No remedy was left untried, yet with hardly a gleam of improvement. When excited by debate in the rival societies at school or college, the hesitation would disappear, and his fluency on such occasions is said to have been remarkable. But the slightest confusion or embarrassment would almost deprive him of the power of speech. His first public effort is said to have been painful in the extreme, both to himself and to the friendly audience he attempted to address. He rushed from the house in an agony of shame, and few who witnessed that painful exhibition were so sanguine as to hope that those stammering lips would yet open in streams of fervid eloquence. Distressed but not disheartened by this mortifying failure, he persevered until his efforts at elocution were crowned with complete success. But he was ever after extremely sensitive on the subject, so much so, that no member of his immediate family ever ventured an allusion to it.

In February, 1827, he was married to Miss Eliza J. Montgomery, daughter of the Hon. Thomas Montgomery, of Lincoln County, Kentucky. She was a young lady of piety and excellence, and great loveliness, to whom he had been attached for several years. She was already in an advanced stage of consumption, and knew that her days were numbered, but she yielded to his desire that the rite might be performed which would give him the privilege of ministering to her steadily declining health. After his marriage he settled upon a part of his paternal farm, and abandoning every object that had hitherto engaged his thoughts, devoted himself to soothing her passage through the dark valley. She lingered a little longer than two years, and expired with the words upon her lips: "Bless the Lord, O my soul, and all that is within me bless His holy name."

Her death revived, in all their force, convictions of duty that had for a time been lulled into repose. Powerless now were the arts of the tempter, in vain his cunning devices to induce any further delay in the fulfilling of resolutions already too long deferred. God had led him, now, for the second time through the deep waters of affliction, and he came out chastened and refined by the sorrow. He recognized the hand of God, he heard the distinct call of his Providence, and he was ready for the consecration. His deep sense of unworthiness for the awful trust of the ministry, the probable estrangement of friends, the embarrassment that might arise from his impeded utterance, all yielded to the superior claims of duty, and he went forward under the guidance of an all-wise Providence, with that calm unquestioning faith which ever afterward enabled him to commit every interest, whether of this world or the next, without reserve to Him who careth for us. He determined now finally and fully to forego all prospects of worldly distinction, ease, and affluence, and to give his life to the Gospel ministry.

In accordance with this decision, he entered the Theological Seminary at Princeton, New Jersey, in the year 1831, and devoted himself with his accustomed ardor to the prescribed studies of the course. Before entering the seminary at Princeton, however, he spent some time at Yale College, giving his attention to the study of the Hebrew language, and such other departments as had a special reference to his preparation for the ministry. He studied at Princeton through one session and part of the second, but did not remain to complete the course, in consequence of an urgent call from Kentucky. One of his classmates at Princeton, Dr. Henry A. Boardman, referring to the period in which they were thus thrown together, speaks of him in the following terms:—

"I recall him as a man of genial temper, and frank, cordial

manners, of recognized and very marked ability, a ready and effective speaker, in no sense a cipher, but an earnest true Christian man, who could not fail, if spared, to make his influence widely and beneficently felt in after years. His rare gifts commanded the highest respect of his fellow-students; and those of us who knew him well, cherished him as a friend worth having. It was a matter of regret with me that I had no opportunities of renewing my intercourse with this admirable man after we parted at Princeton. He deserves to be held in remembrance by the church."

An idea of his character and bearing at this period may be gained from the testimony of Dr. David X. Junkin, who was also his fellow-student: "In the seminary, Mr. Green assumed at once the position of a student, and in his class that of a man of mark. He was regular in attendance, and his recitations were always thorough, evidencing careful study. In the 'Oratory' exercises he was distinguished as a thinker and writer of superior promise. He grasped old thoughts with a fresh and original hold, and bore the reputation of an independent original thinker. The tone of his piety was decided, and his conduct always dignified and consistent. If in his piety there was less of heat and enthusiasm, there was more that was the result of fixed, matured, heartfelt conscience-controlling principle. His prayers in the social meetings were characterized by much humility: he seemed to prostrate himself before his God. In social life he was genial, dignified, and attractive; although at first, and to strangers, there might seem in his manner a slight degree of *hauteur*. This, however, was the result of a bearing natively or habitually dignified: for he was one of the finest gentlemen, in his social manners, with whom I have ever met. There was in the expression of his countenance a lofty benignity, and in the *pose* of his tall, erect, and slender form, an unconscious dignity, that at once arrested attention."

"In the social circle," continues Dr. Junkin, "he was peculiarly interesting. His genial manner, his rich conversational powers, his sprightly, yet barbless wit, his stores of information, his original way of putting things, and withal his entire freedom from the frailty of monopolizing conversation, made him one of the most agreeable companions with whom it has ever been my privilege to visit or to travel. I esteemed him one of the best preachers of my contemporaries in the seminary. There was at the beginning of his sermon a slight indication of impediment of speech, but it soon disappeared; and he proceeded, slowly at first, but warming with his subject, until often a torrent of eloquence was poured forth. His tall, erect form, his long arms and slender fingers, and his fine commanding *pose*, all combined to make his attitudes and gestures, while speaking, impressive and effective. His style, like that of most extempore preachers, had a tendency to the diffuse, but never, when I heard him, to such an extent as to impair its vigor and eloquence. He was a noble man—a fine specimen of the high-toned, dignified, Christian gentleman."

CHAPTER III.

DANVILLE, 1832—1840.

Opening Years of his Ministry.—Licensure and Ordination.—Professorship in Centre College.—Anecdote.—Punctuality.—Skill in Teaching.—Style of Preaching.—Second Marriage.—Voyage to Europe.—Studies and Attainments Abroad.—Travels and Acquaintance.—Return to Danville—Call to Shelbyville declined.—Professorship in the Theological Seminary at South Hanover.—Professorship and Vice-Presidency in Centre College.—Presidency of Transylvania University declined.—Colleague Pastor at Danville.—Emancipation.

In August, 1831, Mr. Green, while pursuing his studies at the East, was elected Professor of Greek in Centre College. This appointment, which, if accepted, would have cut short his theological course, he thought it best to decline. But a year later, August, 1832, he was elected Professor of Belles Lettres and Political Economy in the same institution. This second call from his Alma Mater, he accepted. He had not completed the full course, as intended, at Princeton; but the position offered him was one which, while opening an important sphere of usefulness, would also enable him to pursue his theological studies to advantage.

After a year spent in this double occupation, he was licensed to preach the Gospel by the Presbytery of Transylvania, at Harmony Church, Garrard County, Kentucky, October 4th, 1833. He was ordained to the full work of the ministry, by the same Presbytery, at the same place, October 6th, 1838. Not having accepted any pastoral charge, and having been absent in Europe nearly half the time since his licensure, while the other part had been devoted to teaching, he was not ordained until the latter date, and only a short time before his election to a professorship at South Hanover. This portion of his life, from 1832 to 1840, interesting in its bearing upon his subsequent career, must now be more fully described.

On leaving the seminary at Princeton, in 1832, the young Professor of Belles Lettres and Political Economy entered at once upon the duties of his department. It was a position well suited to his tastes and studies. He threw into it the whole energy and enthusiasm of youth, and soon became one of the most popular and successful instructors ever connected with the institution. He possessed, in an eminent degree, that scholarly ardor which wins the admiration of young men, and that courteous urbanity of manner which attracts them to the high-toned gentleman; and with an unusual facility in imparting what he knew to others, he made the work of instruction as agreeable as it was important. The impressions made upon his pupils were as lasting as life. They all became his friends. Few teachers, if indeed any, have ever been more admired, and more warmly loved. One of his pupils at this period, Dr. W. W. Hill, of the Bellewood Academy, now widely known himself as an accomplished teacher, writing after his death, bears the following testimony to his excellence, which doubtless expresses the estimate of many others: "My acquaintance with Dr. Green commenced just thirty years ago. I was then a boy at college, and he was a teacher. He very soon won my heart. I saw, boy as I was, that he was a high-minded, honorable, and true-hearted man, whom it was safe to confide in, and about whom there was no sham. My views of him never changed; I have always said that he was the second-best teacher I ever sat under. Dr. Addison Alexander I always ranked first, and Dr. L. W. Green second; and you will better appreciate the compliment when you remember that such men as Dr. A. Alexander, Dr. Miller, Drs. John and William Breckinridge, Dr. Young, and Dr. Hodge were among my highly honored teachers."

An anecdote is related which will serve to illustrate the prompt punctuality of the young professor. He insisted on absolute punctuality on the part of his pupils, and made it a point of honor and duty never to be behind time himself. On one occasion, having a distance of several miles to go, and having been necessarily detained, he found he had barely time, though on horseback, to reach the college before his hour of recitation. Before starting he had loosely slipped forty dollars into his pocket. On nearing the place, he discovered that in his rapid ride the money had dropped out, and he knew that it must be lying somewhere on the public road; but rather than go back and be behind time with his class, he determined to meet them promptly at the hour, go on with his recitation, and look for the money afterward. When he returned it was gone; but he felt that punctuality was worth more than forty dollars, and he could better afford to lose the money than to lose his prestige of professional promptness.

Thorough, accurate, and systematic in his own studies, rigidly conscientious in the discharge of every duty, and feeling that whatever was worth doing at all was worth doing well, he was just the man to give to his class-room the precision of a military drill, and to make his pupils feel that study meant work. He knew how to be gentle, and how to be severe. There was every thing to encourage, to stimulate, to inspire boys who could be moved by the love of knowledge and of moral excellence. But for the idle, the careless, the vicious, he had no place; and when he found that they could neither be stimulated by good counsel nor won by love, his policy through life was, to send them home to their parents.

His duties as a college professor did not, however, altogether supersede ministerial work; he loved to preach, and felt that this was his highest function. He preached almost every Sabbath, sometimes in Danville and its vicinity, and sometimes in distant parts of the State. His preaching was from the first distinguished by many of those characteristics which at a later period were very strikingly developed. A fervid eloquence, a whole-hearted absorption in his theme, and a sort of electric influence over his auditory marked all his pulpit performances. He carried an earnestness of spirit into all his efforts, a directness of application in all his arguments and appeals, which gave to truth a cutting power, and could not fail to arouse the attention of even the most lethargic hearers. The young preacher seemed to have struck upon a new vein, to have found a new path, and to have swung himself loose from much of the dry routine, the dead formality, and the stiff conventional common-places of the pulpit. Thoroughly master of his subject in all its bearings, kindling with emotion as he advanced, his diction teeming with images of sublimity and beauty, he poured out things new and old from the treasure-house of his well-furnished mind, while every sermon seemed but the spontaneous outburst of thought and feeling. The fire thus kindled was quickly communicated to his hearers; the attention was fixed, the imagination excited, the conscience aroused, the heart melted and subdued, under a style of preaching which at once fed the mind with knowledge, and attracted it by the charm of a true pathos. It was the fire of passion; but at the same time it was the sober reasoning of the coolest logic.

From the commencement of his ministry he seems to have adopted the extemporaneous delivery, and he adhered to it through life. But his matter was always the result of careful preparation. It is evident from the dates of his extant manuscripts, that almost all the writing of sermons he performed during life was the product of the first ten years of his ministry, though he rarely used notes of any description in preaching, even during this early period. In subsequent years his sermons were almost exclusively the result of a purely meditative process. His command of language was very perfect; his mind teemed with thought and imagery; and he had no difficulty in recalling in perfect order any train of thought he had elaborated in the study. This rare power gave to his sermons at once the exactness of written composition and the graceful freedom of extemporaneous speeches.

In April, 1834, he was again married, taking as his life's companion Mrs. Mary Lawrence, daughter of Mr. Thomas Walker Fry, of Spring House, Kentucky,—a lady eminently qualified by education and natural endowments to sympathize fully in all his plans of study and contribute to his usefulness and success in life. Later in the same year, a purpose which had been for some time maturing was also carried into execution. For some time past he had been anxious to avail himself of the libraries and theological lectures of the great German universities. Impelled by his early and unabated thirst for knowledge, and eager to obtain a wide and thorough cultivation of his powers for the work of life, he longed to stand in the presence of the great scholars of Europe, to sit for a few years as a disciple at their feet, and to drink in the inspiration of theological truth at the very fountain-head of genius and learning. The young professor and the popular preacher would be all the better furnished to train the rising youth of Kentucky and to plead the cause of classical education and Gospel truth in the West, after he had visited these seats of wisdom and held converse with the mighty masters there.

Accordingly, leave of absence for two years from the college being granted with that view, he sailed from New York in August, accompanied by his wife, and after a voyage of three weeks in a sailing vessel, arrived at Liverpool on the 15th of September.

While abroad, he devoted himself with special interest to those branches of knowledge which had a direct bearing on the chosen work of his life, which would best prepare him to be an effective preacher and an accomplished instructor of the young. Religion and education were the two poles on which every thing revolved. Biblical and Oriental literature, archæology, theological and historical science, the French and German languages, with the wide range of general literature and natural science, formed the subjects of his daily reading and of his profound investigations. He attended the lectures of the leading scholars at the German universities and formed a personal acquaintance with Neander, Tholuck, Gesenius, Hengstenberg, Ullman, and others. While in England, he visited, with Mrs. Green, the great universities and a number of ancient towns and castles, spending about two weeks in London. He then went directly to Berlin, where he spent the first winter, attending the lectures of Neander and Hengstenberg. On leaving this country he had taken letters of introduction from Henry

Clay, Dr. Charles Hodge, and other prominent gentlemen well known abroad, and going as a professor from an American college, and at the same time accompanied by his wife, he found easy access to the best circles of Berlin. Their sojourn, in a social point of view, even aside from its advantages for study, was exceedingly pleasant. They visited on friendly terms, or met at social gatherings, many of the most distinguished persons, the Baron De La Motte Fouqué, Baron Alexander Von Humboldt, Roediger, Schultze, Von Weltzien, Wilke, Professor and Chief Justice Von Gerlach, the Von Blankenberg family, and others; from a number of whom, on coming away, they received in German or English, tokens of regard in brief notes and letters, which have ever since been preserved in the family as pleasant mementoes of the visit.

The summer vacation was spent in travelling through the south of Germany and Switzerland; and, being provided with letters from their Berlin friends, they found everywhere an open door, with much to see and enjoy. The second winter was spent in Halle, where he pursued his studies under Tholuck, Ullmann, and Gesenius, forming an intimate acquaintance with the first. From Halle he went to Bonn, and gave special attention to the study of Arabic, Syriac, and Chaldaic, under the instruction of distinguished Oriental scholars. But, after some months, Mrs. Green's health declined and they thought it best to return. They came through Belgium, and spent six weeks in Paris.

From the various letters and other memoranda of this pleasant sojourn in Germany we take a single paragraph as illustrating the affectionate regard in which Professor Green and his wife were held by their German friends. It is from the pen of the learned and evangelical Dr. Tholuck, with whom he kept up a correspondence after coming home, and is in a letter addressed to him in December, 1835, on hearing that, instead of going back to Halle to resume his studies there, as was his intention, he had decided to return to America :—

"DEAREST FRIEND: How much have I been longing for news from you We are not accustomed to speak out our feelings here so fully, else you would have been convinced that there dwells in my heart a warm and sincere friendship for you, such as is not felt for many of your countrymen. For this reason it was the more painful to me to learn that you would return to us no more. With much sympathy do I hear of the new afflictions to which the Lord has subjected you, and of the apprehensions you feel concerning your wife. You will do me a great pleasure if you will let me hear from Paris or America in regard to yourself and your beloved wife. To our friend, Dr. Hodge, bear with you across the sea the salutation of my constant and sincerest love, and you yourself will be accompanied by my prayers. You are an Israelite without guile, and as such I shall always bear you in my heart. This spiritual communion we have, unhappily, much too seldom enjoyed. I remain forever yours, united with you in the Lord. "A. THOLUCK."

After about two years spent abroad, during which he had made large accessions to his theological and literary stores, he returned and resumed the duties of his professorship at Danville. He was now an accomplished linguist, surpassed by few of his years in this country, an educator in full sympathy with his work, and eager to raise the standard of classical and collegiate education at the West. His quickness and facility in the acquisition of learning, his unwearied industry, and his enthusiastic ardor in study had all conspired to bring him a full return for the time spent abroad. He had seen much, thought much, learned much, in the two years, and he returned laden with rich fruits. Above all, he returned uncontaminated with that subtle and pretentious infidelity and rationalism with which he had been in such close contact in Germany. His observation there had but served to strengthen the grace of God that was in him and to intensify his love for all the old evangelical doctrines of the cross.

His professional duties at Danville were agreeable and acceptable; but other fields of usefulness opened around him. In the fall of 1837, having spent a Sabbath at Shelbyville, Kentucky, and preached in the Presbyterian Church of that place, he was invited and urgently pressed by the Session to become the pastor. But, having an important position in the college, he thought it best to remain where he was, although a pastorate had many attractions for him, and the congregation at Shelbyville opened a wide door of usefulness.

In 1838 he was elected to the chair of Oriental and Biblical Literature in the Theological Seminary, at that time connected with the college at South Hanover, Indiana, and afterward removed to New Albany. He received this appointment from the Synod of Kentucky, which had engaged to endow a professorship in that institution in concert with other Synods, north of the Ohio, that had undertaken to found and sustain the school. This seemed to be a position, in many respects, congenial with his tastes and studies. He accordingly accepted it, not feeling that he ought to decline a call coming thus as the voice of his brethren through the Synod. Resigning his professorship at Centre College, and leaving his family at Danville, he repaired to South Hanover, and entered upon the duties of his chair in the autumn of the same year. Dr. James Blythe was then President of the College, and Dr. John Matthews his colleague in the theological department. He continued at his post during the session, hearing two recitations a day in Greek and Hebrew and delivering two or three written lectures a week, which, with preaching on the Sabbath as opportunity offered, gave him, as he expresses it, "as much as he could do well, and no more." In a letter to his family, written soon after he went to Hanover, he mentions an amusing incident: "On last Sabbath I went to preach—knocked down the pulpit and fell over with it. Fortunately it was quite low and neither received any harm. In about one minute all was right again, and I went on as if nothing had happened. I am getting pretty well under way; the students are coming to understand my method of teaching, and to value it, I think. The devil has made, I am convinced, a special attempt to destroy me since I received this appointment, and my feet had well nigh slipped. But I hope I am now over the arts of the adversary." The fall of the pulpit some interpreted as an evil omen—that he would tear down the institution, then not firmly established. But it is rather to be taken as an indication of the lively style and energetic delivery of the young preacher.

His connection with this institution was, from the first, somewhat of the nature of an experiment. It was doubtful whether the seminary, greatly in need of funds, could be carried on sucessfully, at least in its present location. He had not been long at Hanover before an effort was made by influential gentlemen at Lexington, Kentucky, trustees of Transylvania University, and others, to induce him to return to Kentucky and accept the presidency of that institution, which was then vacant. It was thought by these gentlemen, that the placing of him at the head of the university would be the means of restoring it to the favor of its original friends and founders, the Presbyterians, and of thus insuring that success which had been wanting since the time of Dr. Holley. But he was a loyal alumnus of Centre College, too long identified with its welfare, and too thorough-going a Presbyterian withal, to think of doing any thing that might injure the rising institution at Danville, around which the Presbyterian Church of the State had now rallied. After some personal interviews, and in answer to repeated letters on the subject, he said, that so long as there was any prospect of the success of the seminary at Hanover, he felt it to be his duty to remain in that position; and that he would do nothing which could in any way injure the Presbyterian Church in her enterprise at Danville. He, accordingly, declined the appointment, and continued through the session at Hanover.

In the spring of 1839, having completed the duties of the term at Hanover, he was recalled to Danville, under influences which seemed to make it his duty to return. He was elected vice-president of Centre College, with the department of Belles Lettres and Political Economy under his control, Dr. John C. Young being president. He was also elected Colleague Pastor, with Dr. Young, in the Presbyterian Church of Danville, it being arranged that they should supply the pulpit on alternate Sabbaths. Here a wide door of usefulness opened before him. It was one of the largest and most influential congregations in the State—a congregation that had been accustomed to the eloquence of Drs. Gideon Blackburn, David Nelson, and other gifted preachers.

Stimulated to their utmost exertion by all the associations of the place, past and present, surrounded from Sabbath to Sabbath by large and appreciative audiences who hung with growing interest on their lips, filled with high professional ardor, as well as with that higher inspiration which comes from a view of God's glory and the worth of souls, these comparatively youthful but gifted preachers soon rose to an excellence and effectiveness of pulpit ministrations not often surpassed in the annals of the Western pulpit. "No man," says one who knew him well, "ever entered upon the peculiar work of preaching the Gospel with a keener ardor, or with a sublimer view of its self-sacrificing joys." His peculiar temperament, his well-disciplined mind, his far-reaching sympathies, his natural gifts of oratory, added to a form of personal piety as remarkable for its tenderness as for its stern sense of duty, seemed to mark him out for the successful preacher and the laborious sympathizing pastor. And it was with the greatest possible relish that, after the weekly duties of the lecture-room, he addressed himself to the Sabbath work of preaching the Gospel.

We may form an idea of the character of his pulpit ministrations at this time from the testimony of John A. Jacobs, Esq., of Danville, who had known him from boyhood. "Lips, which in youth could scarcely utter a single sentence without the most painful stammering, poured forth for many years a most copious stream, sometimes a torrent, of thought, now profound, and now soaring to the utmost bounds of human imagination, clothed in language apt, accurate, ornate, and sometimes gorgeous in expression. His manners were affable and kind in the highest degree, though, like most men of high genius, he was susceptible of great excitement, and liable to occasional waywardness. It was, however, the effervescence of intellectual fervor." Taking a retrospect of his whole ministerial and educational services through life, and associating his name with his co-laborers on the same field, Drs. Nelson and Young, Mr. Jacobs remarks: "The West, I am sure, and, in my judgment, the whole land, has not produced in the generation that is now almost past, three greater men. Their names, memories, and services ought to be transmitted to distant posterity."

Toward the close of this period, in the prospect of leaving Kentucky to settle in a free State, Professor Green emancipated all the slaves he had inherited or possessed in his own right. He had desired to do this some time before, and to send them to Liberia through the Colonization Society, but they were unwilling to go. He was at no time an Abolitionist, in the commonly received sense of the term. He was, on the contrary, decidedly opposed to any sudden and violent abolition from without. But he was an early and warm friend of the colonization cause, and he greatly desired to see Kentucky relieved from the incubus of slavery, and the condition of the colored race bettered by some scheme of gradual emancipation, originated and carried forward by the State itself. He had, accordingly, from the first, sympathized fully in the views of his uncle, Judge Green, Henry Clay, and other leading men of the State, who organized the first party and made the first movement in Kentucky in favor of emancipation. Nothing would have delighted him more than to see his native State adopt some practical plan of taking her place among the free States. And so strong were his feelings on the subject, that unable to send his slaves to Africa, and unwilling to leave them in bondage, he emancipated them all on the soil, to the number of twenty-five or thirty.

CHAPTER IV.

Allegheny, 1840—1847.

Election to a Professorship in the Theological Seminary at Allegheny.—Testimonial as to his Ability.—His Colleagues in the Faculty.—Inaugural Address.—German Philosophy.—Growing Reputation.—Literary Addresses.—Lectures on Popery.—The Title of Doctor of Divinity.—Standing and Influence as a Preacher and Instructor.—Various Calls.—Testimonials from Dr. R. L. Breck.—From Drs. Wilson and Allison.—From Dr. McGill.—From Dr. David Elliott.—Seven Years' Work.

In May, 1840, Mr. Green was unanimously elected by the General Assembly of the Presbyterian Church, to the Professorship of Oriental Literature and Biblical Criticism in the Western Theological Seminary, at Allegheny, Pennsylvania. This was a position, for which, by all his previous studies and attainments, he was well fitted, though at the time but little over thirty-four years of age. Recognizing it as the call of Divine Providence to a wide and inviting field of usefulness, in which he might hope to spend his energies with best advantage to the church and her rising ministry, he accepted the appointment, removed with his family to Allegheny, and entered upon the duties of his office at the opening of the session in the autumn of the same year.

It will serve to show what reputation the young professor had won at Danville and throughout the West, to present here the testimonial of one of his contemporaries. It is from a letter of the Hon. C. S. Todd, afterward United States Minister to Russia, written at Cincinnati, under date, April 21, 1840, addressed to Rev. Dr. David Elliot of the Allegheny Seminary, in reply to inquiries as to the character and qualifications of Mr. Green to supply the place of Dr. Nevin in the chair of Oriental Literature in that institution. "I seize the first moment to say to you, that the reputation of Mr. Green in this respect is eminently high. He has been professor in Centre College for several years; was during last year one of the theological professors at South Hanover, selected by the Synod of Kentucky, and was for several years at one of the universities of Germany. He is an eloquent divine and a most accomplished scholar. He is now adjunct pastor with Dr. Young at Danville, and a professor in the college: but I doubt whether he would be induced to change his location."

His associates in the faculty of the seminary, during the most of his time at Allegheny, were Drs. David Elliott and Alexander J. McGill. His work here called into exercise all the treasures of his cultivated intellect, and enlisted the deepest and holiest feelings of his heart. And for the next seven years—till his resignation and retirement in 1847—he gave himself up to its demands with unabated ardor. At his inauguration in 1840, he delivered an address, afterward published, which was very favorably received, not only by the community, but by the Synod of Pittsburgh, then in session in that city. It was replete with sound practical views on the subject of Biblical interpretation, and did much to extend his reputation through the church, as a safe interpreter and as a scholarly and eloquent writer.

The following sentences from the graceful opening of that address will give the reader some idea of the unaffected modesty of the man, as well as of his meetness for the important work to which the voice of the church had here called him: "Though not altogether unaccustomed to address my fellowmen upon subjects even of the deepest and most momentous interest, yet the novelty of my position, will, I hope, excuse any degree of embarrassment which may be apparent on the present occasion. Surrounded by faces entirely new to me; invited by your kind confidence, while yet personally unknown, to occupy an important and responsible situation in your theological institution; though yet a stranger, welcomed as a brother among you, I should do injustice to my own feelings, did I not express my deep sense of the unmerited kindness which has called me hither, of the weighty obligations I am about to assume, the solemn responsibilities inseparable from the station I am called to occupy, and my own deeply felt and candidly acknowledged incompetency for the full and adequate performance of all the arduous duties of the station. Nor can I deem it inappropriate to the occasion to express before the patrons of the institution my views of the nature of that office —of the duties it enjoins—of the qualifications, intellectual and moral, which it requires. Not as though I had attained, or were already perfect, or even expected to attain the full measure of those large and various qualifications which I shall attempt to describe, but that you may understand what are my views of an excellence which it should be the constant effort of the Christian theologian to attain, and toward which every student of theology should be taught, from the commencement to the termination of his course, to aspire and to struggle."

In this masterly address he takes a wide survey of the whole field of Biblical interpretation, showing the true province of reason, the relation of science to religion, the connection of Revelation with the works of God, the essential qualifications of a true expounder of the Divine Word, and the dangers arising from the rationalistic and infidel theories of the German theologians and philosophers, into which he had gained so clear an insight while abroad. And he closes with an earnest and powerful appeal in favor of a new and native American exegesis, which, while using the results of German investigation, yet independent of German authority, shall be founded on the solid basis of a pure devotion, a sound orthodoxy, and a sober Anglo-Saxon common sense. The key-note of his argument may perhaps be learned from the following suggestive paragraph:—

"The transfusion of German philosophy and exegesis into the American mind would be at once the indication and the cause of disease, in the system so transfused, and in the mind which had stooped to be its passive recipient. You cannot support the life and health of one man by injecting into his circulation the blood of another. The foreign ingredient would be poison and fever to his system. You must give him nourishment and let his own digestion supply vital warmth, sensibility, motion. And as every man, so every nation has an individuality of its own, and, to be vigorous and healthy, must be independent, self-nourished, and self-developed. An American exegesis, therefore, and, as founded upon and supported by it, an American theology, are as clearly indicated and as imperatively demanded, both for ourselves and for the world, by the peculiar circumstances of our age and country, as an American general literature, American policy, political constitutions, or any other product of that novel and extraordinary combination of political, social, intellectual, and religious elements, which, variously operating on and blending with each other, at once signalize and constitute American character."

The number of students in the seminary was small and his compensation inadequate. But there was a good prospect of increase, and the work was one in which he delighted, especially as he found constant occasions for the exercise of his ministry in the pulpits of the city, and in the neighboring churches. His reputation as a preacher and lecturer rapidly rose, and went abroad through the country. His services were in such demand that scarcely a Sabbath found him unemployed. In 1840 he received the honorary title of Doctor of Divinity from his Alma Mater, Centre College. In 1842 he was invited to deliver an address before the Literary Societies of Jefferson College. He delivered similar addresses in subsequent years at La Fayette College, Easton, Pennsylvania, and at the Miami University in Oxford, Ohio. Through his whole career he was called on for many services of this kind, which he rendered cheerfully when in his power to do so. In 1844 he received an urgent request from the Secretary of the Board of Education, to present the cause of ministerial education at the West, in a sermon at the meeting of the General Assembly in Louisville, Kentucky, that year. In 1845 he received from Dr. William S. Potts, of St. Louis, an urgent overture to accept the pastoral oversight of a new church, a colony from his own, just formed in that city. But this proposition, with others of the same kind, he declined, on the ground that his services were needed in the seminary, and that he could not leave a position to which God, by the voice of his Church, had called him.

Between the occupations of the study and the lecture-room,

regular preaching at home and calls from abroad, Dr. Green was kept incessantly employed during all the year at Allegheny. This activity he enjoyed. During this period his mind became deeply interested in the position and claims of the Papal Church, which was attracting much attention at the time, and, at the solicitation of prominent gentlemen in Pittsburgh, he prepared and delivered a course of public lectures on Popery. The series extended to six in number, and they were delivered in weekly succession, partly in Dr. Herron's church and partly in Dr. Riddle's. They excited an interest which drew increasing crowds to the end of the course, filling the houses to their utmost capacity. In these lectures he often spoke from an hour and a half to two hours, in his most animated style, pouring out the treasured results of his reading and reflection, and making a profound impression on the public mind. "These lectures," says Dr. Elliott, "delivered without notes, added greatly to his reputation as an eloquent orator and a skilful controversialist; and, although they were never published, the impression made by them on the public mind did not soon pass away." He afterward preached before the Synod on the same subject. The newspapers of the city gave full reports of the lectures, and he was urged by his friends to write them out and publish them, but no vestige of them is found among his writings.

The following interesting account, by one who was for a short time under his instruction as a pupil, will aid us in forming an estimate of his character and influence while at Allegheny.*

"Occasionally I had heard Dr. Green preach in my boyhood, but my personal acquaintance with him began in 1845, when I became a student in the Western Theological Seminary at Allegheny. His reputation in Kentucky attracted a number of students from that State. The seminary was in a prosperous condition, and of the young men then gathered there a number have since become eminent in the church. Dr. Green was at that time in his early prime, and perhaps at the full height of his popularity as a teacher and as a preacher. As a professor, his thorough and elegant scholarship, his enthu-

* Rev. Robert L. Breck, D.D., of Richmond, Ky.

siasm in his work, his high-toned, serious piety, and his affectionate interest in the personal welfare of his pupils, commanded the highest respect and veneration of the students. He was subject to occasional depressions and disturbances of equanimity. Sensitive, impulsive, transparent in his feelings, unable to conceal any strong emotion, and scrupulously exact in his notions of honor, he sometimes hastily censured with severity what he thought unbecoming conduct, and sometimes misjudged acts done in ignorance or thoughtlessness, rather than in transgression of exact rules of propriety. Issues or ruptures, however, were not frequent, and seldom or never long continued, as his own kindliness of nature, and the universal esteem entertained for him, were too great for them to last.

"In the class-room he was interesting, full, and sometimes eloquent. Being under his instruction during a session, afterward a student at Princeton, and later, in my more mature years, admitted to renewed intimacy with him, I retain a high estimate of his rare learning and qualifications as a teacher of students for the ministry. As a linguist he had few equals in our country. In criticism and exegesis he excelled. And probably no American scholar was more thoroughly acquainted with every phase of modern metaphysical philosophy, or had, with more acute discrimination, chased down infidelity through the different philosophies of Continental Europe. At the time of which I write, the doctor did not often preach. When, however, it was known that he was to preach for any of the pastors of Allegheny or Pittsburgh, the house was generally crowded to overflowing. His efforts were not always equal. But he sometimes rose to the highest and most impressive eloquence, which those who ever heard him in one of his happier moods will never forget.

"In private and social life Dr. Green was one of the most charming of men. Gentle, affectionate, playful, brilliant, he won the heart while he entertained. He lived at this time some three miles below the city, on the bank of the Ohio, where he dispensed a wide and elegant hospitality. The *élite* of both the neighboring cities were frequently to be found in his house. In the enjoyment of those charming assemblies his pupils were often invited to participate. They all, no doubt, retain most agreeable and vivid memories of them. Dr. Green's character was marked by the simplest and most unmistakable piety. And this gave it its highest charm. No one probably was ever in his presence an hour without the conviction of a rare spirituality and godliness permeating his thought and life."

Another of his former pupils at Allegheny, afterward associated with him at Hampden Sidney, and now of Augusta, Georgia, Doctor Joseph R. Wilson, gives a brief estimate of his excellence as an instructor, a preacher, and a man, in the following terms:—

"It was my good fortune to enjoy his instructions in Hebrew, and in New Testament Greek exegesis. Surely there never was a more admirable teacher. His scholarship was as profound and as comprehensive as it was minute and exact. His whole method of imparting knowledge, his skill in drawing out the utmost resources of his pupils, his enthusiasm in dealing with truth, the impression he made on his classes of an equal greatness of mind and heart, his flowing geniality, mingled with all the elements of needful authority, rendered the hours of recitation wonderfully pleasant and profitable. Then, when he mounted the pulpit, that mellow voice, elastic enough to accommodate itself to all the demands of his singular oratory, that gesticulatory warmth, that glitter of illustration, than which nothing could have been more brilliant, that patience of reasoning, attended by an appropriate urgency of exhortation—all this, and much that cannot be described, no one, who heard and saw, is able to forget. Socially, too, he was a great favorite; he shone in conversation, and enjoyed good company almost as much as he contributed to its enjoyment. His standing at Allegheny, in the esteem of all, was as high as possible. He was regarded as a man of genius and a man of God."

We have an interesting account of Dr. Green, at this time, from still another of his former pupils, Dr. James Allison, editor of the *Presbyterian Banner*, who, writing from Pittsburgh, March 21, 1870, says:—

"He made a strong impression upon all with whom he met, as a scholar, a thinker, a preacher, and a genial Christian gentleman. Immediately after he had entered upon the duties of his professorship in Allegheny, his power for good began to be recognized, not only by the students, but also by the ministers and churches, and the community generally. His services as a minister were eagerly sought and highly appreciated by benevolent societies, by literary institutions, and by his brethren on sacramental occasions. There are many still living in this city and vicinity who recall, with gratitude, the effect produced on them by his powerful sermons. He was not merely a preacher for scholars, but also for the common people. We have listened to him in Providence Hall, at Jefferson College, when professors, students, and the people who earned their bread by the daily toil of their hands, heard with breathless attention, and were alike profited. Wherever he went to preach, the people in the city or in the country, among the polished or the plain, in great crowds attended. In a wonderful degree he had the faculty of addressing the understanding, employing the reasoning powers and touching the heart at the same time.

"As a professor in the seminary," continues Dr. Allison, "he will never be forgotten by his students. At the very first he met them with a warm grasp of the hand, looked them in the face with a kindly eye, and made them feel

2*

that he was their friend. He was not satisfied with meeting them in the class-room, but went to their private rooms, talked with them individually, that he might learn their peculiarities and gain their confidence, and pray with them. He sought not merely to cultivate their intellects, but also to train their hearts. He seemed to consider, and rightly too, that the General Assembly appointed the professors in the theological seminaries to be instructors in sacred learning, and also, for the time, the pastors of the students. Rarely was a student at the seminary more than ten days before receiving a visit from Dr. Green, which he never forgot. To the class-room the doctor always came fully prepared; and he expected the same of the students. With the indolent he had but little patience; but he delighted to encourage the studious. In the Greek and Hebrew languages he was a master; and he employed all the wealth of this learning to the elucidation of the Messianic Psalms and Prophecies in the Old Testament, and the Epistles to the Romans and Hebrews in the New. He held up to our astonished vision truths and beauties we had never seen before. He showed us how to enter the mine of Divine truth, explore its wonders and mysteries, and gather up its precious treasures. For the word of God he had the profoundest reverence; it was sufficient for him to know that a doctrine or duty was plainly taught in the Bible; and then he accepted it with the greatest readiness and held it with the firmest tenacity.

"He fully understood the teachings of the German Rationalists, and had sat at the feet of some of the greatest of them; but he rejected their doctrines with abhorrence. He could not endure them. In interpreting Scripture he was an independent thinker, and followed no man or school blindly. While he accepted the doctrinal system in all its extent, as set forth by Dr. Charles Hodge in his Commentary on the Romans, he by no means agreed with him in the interpretation of every passage, and believed that the doctor did not do justice to his own general system of doctrine, in some of his interpretations, while he at the same time failed to bring out the full meaning of the original Greek. While in the Western Theological Seminary, Dr. Green had also charge of the department in which Butler's Analogy was a text-book. We have often thought that his great powers appeared to better advantage here than anywhere else. The keen logic and scientific knowledge which he brought to the elucidation of that celebrated work were the wonder of all who listened. His lecture on the first chapter I have always considered one of the most remarkable productions to which it has ever been my privilege to listen. Afterward, at the request of the late Rev. E. P. Swift, D.D., the Hon. R. C. Grier, late Judge of the Supreme Court of the United States, and others, he threw this lecture into a popular form, expanded it considerably, and then delivered it in a series of sermons, which were heard by vast crowds in the First Presbyterian Church of Allegheny. I am afraid that neither the lecture, nor the sermons which sprang from it, were ever written. If this should be so, the church and the world are the poorer on this account."

After speaking of his fine historical knowledge, his deep interest in all the great movements of the times, and of the profound impression made by his lectures on Romanism, already referred to, Dr. Allison adds :

"Nowhere was Dr. Green happier than in the social circle, to which he was always welcome. He enjoyed the society of his friends, and they delighted in his companionship. He could be mirthful or serious; could listen to others or entertain others. He had a warm heart and was a hater of all meanness and selfishness. But it was especially when in the company of theological students that his fine qualities would shine out. He was ever ready to encourage the timid, to gently repress the self-sufficient, to impart information to those seeking it, and to make them acquainted with books and men. His students reverenced him as a professor and loved him as a friend. When he left to become a pastor in Baltimore, it was felt that the seminary, the church, and the entire community had suffered a heavy loss."

Rev. Dr. Alexander T. McGill, who became associated as a professor with him in the seminary in 1842, says: "I was won to him at once by his cordial and cultivated manners. Within the first hour of my acquaintance with him an impression was made of his character which was never changed by subsequent intimacy of observation as a friend and colleague. A beaming intelligence, transparent candor, and impulsive imagination revealed the man just as I knew him five years afterward when we parted, and just as I remember him now after many years and many comparisons in my intercourse with colleagues. The perspicacious mind of Dr. Green saw the future of the seminary more brightly at that time than any other man connected with its interests. If his patience had been equal to his foresight, and he could have brooked, without fretting, the delay and vexation through which any institution of great and permanent value must rise from such a depth of discouragement, he would have been signalized as the best builder that seminary has ever had among men. His ability, scholarship, and eloquence were unquestionable. His affability and radiating kindness of heart, with captivating power of conversation, everywhere attracted men and won the attachment of students."

After referring to some of the petty annoyances and discouragements incident to his position, which weighed heavily on his spirits and led him to resign a professorship which might have been one of life-long eminence and usefulness to his generation, Dr. McGill adds: "He was not appreciated as a preacher among the rural churches as he was in the cities, owing mainly to the academic taste which had never been governed by a pastoral experience and the indifference of his mind to prevailing forms of sermonizing. His vivid imagination, classical allusions, and impassioned declamation were lost at times on people accustomed to the homiletic measure and proportion of heads and particulars, according to the fashion of the pulpit so long prevalent in that Scotch-Irish region. I have never ceased to regret the retirement of Dr. Green from Allegheny, and the consequent shifting of his mind to other and miscellaneous labor—no more returning to the department he was so peculiarly fitted to fill by his learning and genius alike. A commentary from his pen, having the sparkle and emotion he was wont to combine with sound judgment in the exegesis of God's word, might have delighted the church, and occupied the place of much that is dull yet salable on both sides of the Atlantic in the prolific fields of exposition. His memory is cherished as that of an honorable colleague, a noble friend, an able and faithful minister of Christ."

In further illustration of his influence, character, and work while at Allegheny, we have the following testimony from the pen of the venerable Dr. David Elliott, who was one of his colleagues in the seminary:—

"In his public performances Dr. Green was very unequal. Sometimes he was eminently forcible, brilliant, and impressive, carrying his audience with him in rapt attention. At other times he failed of so happy a result. This was owing chiefly to his variable bodily temperament, which had much to do with his mental operations, elevating or depressing them according to its peculiar condition at the time. He was constitutionally impulsive. But he was a man of generous impulses—kind, liberal, a lover of good men and good things, ever ready to do his part in whatever tended to advance the cause of Christ in the sphere in which he was called to labor.

"In his intercourse with his brethren in the ministry he was remarkably cordial and free from that petty jealousy by which some men, whose aspirations all centre in themselves, are led to disparage the character and standing of others. Upon such conduct he looked with perfect loathing. His character was formed on the higher and more ennobling principles of the Gospel; and, as a Christian minister, he was deservedly held in reputation. As a professor he had a well-stored mind and great readiness in communicating. I have good reason to believe that he was a skilful and acceptable instructor. His retirement from the seminary, which he had so faithfully served for seven years, was greatly regretted by the friends of the institution. But having received a call from the Second Presbyterian Church in the city of Baltimore, his convictions of duty led him to accept the pastorate of that church and to resign his professorship."

Testimonials like the foregoing, from his colleagues, pupils, and others, might have been greatly multiplied. But these are sufficient to illustrate the character of the teacher, the fidelity and zeal which marked his labors, and the lasting and blessed impressions made upon the successive bands of young men trained under his instruction at Allegheny. The seven years spent in this high and sacred work of Biblical interpretation may be regarded as among the most important and useful of his whole life. The successive classes of young men trained in part by his faithful teaching at Allegheny and prepared for their great life-work—some of them filling important positions in the church, some in distant stations preaching Christ to the heathen, and some, their work being ended, already entered upon their rest above—if they could join their voices, would, doubtless, all attest the singular fidelity, devotion, skill, and earnest zeal of the beloved instructor. As we shall now follow him, step by step, through his subsequent career—honorable and useful as that career was—we can almost sympathize in the regret felt by his colleagues that he should have left a position for which he was so nobly furnished, and in which his labors had been so blessed by God and so useful to the church.

CHAPTER V.

BALTIMORE, 1847—1848.

Resignation of Professorship at Allegheny.—Removal to Baltimore.—Preference of the Pastoral Work.—Labors in the Second Presbyterian Church.—Congenial and Useful Employment.—Failure of Health.—Dissolution of Pastoral Relation.—Noble Testimonial of his Church.—Poetical Tribute.

DR. GREEN resigned his professorship in the Theological Seminary at Allegheny in October, 1846; but he continued to give instruction through the session until February, 1847, when he removed to Baltimore. He had received and accepted a call to the pastoral office in the Second Presbyterian Church of that city—a congregation which had enjoyed the ministrations of a number of very eminent men, among them Dr. John Glendy and Drs. John and Robert J. Breckinridge. His health had become somewhat impaired at Allegheny by long continued application to study; and it was thought that a change of location, as well as a change of employment, might be the means of restoration.

But the prevailing motive with him in making such a change was his long cherished and growing desire to devote himself fully to the work of preaching the Gospel in a settled pastoral charge. Of a genial, social disposition, full of benevolence and sympathy, he possessed many natural aptitudes for the work of a pastor. But, besides this, his soul had ever turned to the functions of the working ministry with the greatest possible relish; and he was constantly concluding that both his duty and his happiness demanded that he should devote himself to the high service of the preaching office. Thus far, through all his professional life, he had been a teacher. He felt more and more that he ought to be a pastor, that preaching ought to be his chief work, and that his life would not be complete until he had entered on this service. Had he consulted his own inclination he would have done this at the beginning of his ministry. His fine pulpit powers, as shown in his first sermons, and his popular, engaging manners seemed then to point to the pastorate as his proper sphere of labor. The leadings of Providence and the calls of duty, however, had urged him forward on a different path, and he threw himself heart and soul into the work of education.

But now, at the age of forty-one, and after a ministry of fourteen years, chiefly devoted to the teaching office, he felt that the long-looked for opportunity had arrived of giving himself fully to preaching, and he accepted what seemed to be the clear call of duty to go to Baltimore. The position was all that he could have desired, as furnishing at once a delightful residence for his family, and a large and growing field of usefulness, demanding all his energies.

From the first Dr. Green's preaching—fresh, original, impassioned, and peculiar as it always was—attracted much attention in the city, and was attended by crowded audiences. "He talks Homer and the old Greek and Roman poets and philosophers, and every thing else, here in Baltimore," said a resident of the city to a visitor who was anxious to hear him, "and he mixes it all up with religion and makes people listen to him. But he is not a revival preacher. He makes flights into the clouds, and you will wonder how he is going to get down. But, I reckon, you will be gratified to hear him. He is a gentleman. He is just fit for college boys." It is not strange that he should know how to preach to college boys and all other youth after having taught and preached to them fourteen years.

But, pleasant as were Dr. Green's surroundings in Baltimore and acceptable as were his ministrations to the people of his charge, it soon began to appear that his strength was not equal to the task he had undertaken. Frequent spells of nervous prostration and a general running down of his physical system admonished him that he must seek a change and give up, for a season at least, the much-loved work of the pastorate. After a continuance of a little more than a year and a half of this delightful relationship, he came to the conclusion to ask for its dissolution and so announced his intention. It is seldom that a pastoral relation is sundered with more cordial good feeling on both sides. The following beautiful testimonial of respect and affection, creditable alike to the people and the pastor, is worthy of being placed on permanent record :—

"At a congregational meeting, held, agreeably to regular notice from the pulpit, in the Second Presbyterian Church of Baltimore, on Wednesday evening, 4th of October, 1848, Rev. J. C. Backus, D. D., was called to preside as Moderator, and James George was chosen Clerk. The meeting was opened with prayer, by the Moderator, when the following preamble and resolutions, offered by Elder Wilson, were unanimously adopted; and, on motion of the Hon. W. F. Giles, it was ordered that an attested copy of the same be presented to the Rev. Dr. Green in the name of the congregation :—

"*Whereas*, In the Providence of God the health of the Rev. Dr. L. W. Green, the beloved pastor of this congregation, has become so much impaired as, in his judgment, to render him unable any longer to discharge the laborious duties of his official station, in consequence of which he has given notice to the congregation that he would apply to the Presbytery of Baltimore, at its next stated meeting, to be held in this city on the 10th of October inst., for a dissolution of his pastoral relations to this church and congregation. And, whereas, this meeting has been called for the purpose of taking action on the subject, either by opposing the dissolution, which it has a constitutional right to do, or by uniting with Dr. Green in his application to effect it. Therefore,

"*Resolved*, As the sense of this meeting, that under all the circumstances of the case, it is clearly the duty of this congregation to acquiesce, however painful, in what seems to be the will of God in the premises; because any opposition on the part of this congregation would, doubtless, be regarded by the Presbytery as selfish and unkind, especially after the repeated declarations made by Dr. Green both in public and private that his strength was unequal to the task; it is therefore deemed inexpedient to interpose any obstacles to the dissolution.

"*Resolved*, At the same time that it is with feelings of the deepest regret that this congregation looks forward to its separation from a pastor so able, so beloved, and so faithful; a pastor whose labors among us have been owned and blessed of the great Head of the Church; a pastor by whose conciliatory efforts peace and harmony have been happily restored to this congregation, which was greatly agitated when he took charge of it by repeated disappointments and from having been so long without a stated ministry.

"*Resolved*, That this congregation deeply laments the affliction with which its beloved pastor has been visited; and while it offers him its kindest sympathy and condolence, would, at the same time, respectfully assure him that its members, in their humble prayers, will not fail to implore Almighty God that he would, in his infinite mercy and goodness, be graciously pleased to restore him to wonted health and usefulness, and that he would greatly bless and prosper him in his new field of labor.

"*Resolved*, That this congregation heard, with profound satisfaction, the declaration made by the Rev. Dr. Green, at the close of the morning service of last Sunday, namely, that there was no other cause, either proximate or remote, but that of ill-health, which had induced him to ask for a dissolution, and that the relations between himself and the members of the congregation were of the most amicable nature. This declaration will greatly tend to alleviate the pain of separation.

"*Resolved*, That the Rev. Dr. Green be, and he is hereby respectfully requested to remember this congregation at the throne of grace, and pray that brotherly love may continue; that we may be kept from strife, division, and disunion, and that God would direct us in the choice of an under-shepherd, whose labors he will own and bless; a man after his own heart, to go in and out before us, and to break to us the bread of life.

"*Resolved*, That Mrs. Green, by her many amiable qualities, has greatly endeared herself to the members of this congregation; that they view the necessity of being separated from her society with the deepest regret, and they will ever remember her with the kindest and most affectionate feelings of respect and regard; nor will they forget to pray that the choicest of Heaven's blessings may continually rest on her and her dear children.

"Attest, JOHN C. BACKUS, *Moderator*.
SAMUEL GEORGE, *Clerk*."

It was not merely in words that the church expressed their appreciation of his services. Dr. Green had subscribed a thousand dollars toward the erection of a new edifice which his church were then proposing to build; but, in consideration of his failing health and consequent removal from the pastorate, the trustees came forward and voluntarily released him from this obligation. During his residence in Baltimore he was invited on two different occasions to visit New York for the purpose of delivering addresses before the anniversary meetings of the American Tract Society. He was a warm friend of this society, and on both occasions rendered it valuable service by the enlarged views which he presented of its usefulness and by his earnest vindication of its claims against prevailing misrepresentation.

The following beautiful lines, written by a lady of Baltimore, and sent to him with the unknown signature of "Miriam," soon after he entered upon his work in that city, will serve to illustrate both the spirit of his preaching and the interest with which he was heard during this brief pastorate :

"Ambassador of Christ! how fearlessly
Thou liftest up the voice to publish forth
The tidings of salvation to the lost
And ruined sons of men; how earnestly
Dost thou entreat the thirsty soul to come
And drink of that fair river which makes glad
The city of our God. Oh! with what love
Dost thou beseech the weary, sin-sick soul
To accept the invitation Jesus gave—
'Come unto me, ye heavy-laden, come,
And I will give you rest.' With what a voice
Of thunder dost thou set the terrors forth
Of God Almighty's law, and seek to rouse
The slumbering sinner from his deadly dream
Of false security. How gently, too,
Dost thou encourage those who tremblingly,
As following after God, whose faith is weak,
Yet by the pure word strengthened, will grow up
Unto the Christian's perfect stature. One
There is, less than the least of all who love
The blessed Saviour, who will long rejoice
In having heard those glorious Gospel truths
By thee set forth, and in the faith built up,
And strengthened by Almighty grace, will run
With greater zeal along the heavenly road.
May God be with thee, champion of the cross!
And crown thy labors with immortal souls.
And when thou hast thy hallowed work fulfilled
On earth, and gone to thy reward above,
Then mayst thou shine in glory as the sun,
And as the brightness of the firmament,
Forever and forever; then shall praise,
High, holy, pure, be given to Him who sits
Upon the throne, and to the Lamb who died
And lives again, glory for evermore."

CHAPTER VI.

PRINCE EDWARD, 1848–1856.

Election to the Presidency of Hampden Sidney College.—Intercourse with the Professors.—Portraiture by Dr. Foote.—Restored Health.—Extended Labors.—Scholarships.—Successful Administration.—Influence on the Students.—Style of Preaching.—Anecdote.—Method of Discipline.—Account of it by Dr. Dabney.—Testimonial of Dr. Wilson.—Various Calls.

DR. GREEN had not been long in Baltimore, before the attention of the trustees of Hampden Sidney College, and other prominent members of the Synod of Virginia, was turned to him, as a suitable person to fill their vacant presidency. The college had been for some time much depressed; but its trustees and faculty, with commendable zeal, were carrying it for ward without a president, until a competent one should be found. It was a time-honored institution, and from its origin could boast a succession of distinguished names on its roll of presidents. Samuel Stanhope, and John Blair Smith, Drury Lacy, Archibald Alexander, Moses Hoge, Cushing, and Maxwell had each in turn adorned its headship, while in its faculty had quietly labored some of the best instructors in the State, and among its alumni were found many names eminent in the annals of the church and the country.

In the summer of 1848 he was invited to Prince Edward, and delivered an address before one of the societies of the seminary at the time of the college commencement of that year—making a very favorable impression on all who heard him, as to his ability and scholarship. Rev. Dr. Foote, who was present and heard him for the first time on that occasion, describes his appearance, and the effect produced, in the following terms:—

"His countenance wore the expression of one who had been sick, and might be unwell still; a slight flush of anxiety passed over his face, as he looked around over that collection of Virginia people, a fair specimen of the

Ancient Dominion, of which he had so often heard, of which he was himself a Kentucky offshoot. It was announced that Dr. Green, of Baltimore, would address the young men. And who is Dr. Green? Ah! it was whispered, he is from Kentucky, has held places of honor and trust, and has sought the advantage of the climate east of the Alleghanies for his health, wasted under intense application. There never was a time that Virginia did not turn with interest to a son of her fair daughter Kentucky, and sometimes, like other grandparents, show greater partiality than to her home-born children. That he was a little nervous, his spirit a little restless, as he met the face of an assembly, gathered from the *élite* of the land of his ancestry, only won the attention of the auditory. Almost as matter of course that auditory listened with profound attention, and at the close of his address gave him a place among the men to teach and guide the hearts of the community, especially the young. My sympathies were with him from the first. His motions were quick, his thoughts flowed rapidly, and yet he had command of a spirit evidently excitable, fiery, and fearless. There was a philosophic composure thrown over all the excitement—perhaps I should have said Christian calmness—but I use the word philosophic in its best sense."

The trustees and other prominent friends of the college, a large number of whom were in attendance on the exercises, and some of whom had known him before, felt that he was the man for the place. He was accordingly soon after elected with cordial unanimity; and in the autumn of the same year entered upon the duties of the office. His inaugural address, however, was not delivered till January 10, 1849. He was now in a situation, in many respects, congenial with his tastes and aspirations. Though in feeble health he was yet in life's meridian; and he had much to stimulate and encourage him. He was on the soil of his ancestors, and had been received with a generous, warm-hearted welcome, which made him feel from the first that he was among friends, not strangers. He had an important work to do, in raising again the fortunes of the embarrassed college, and he had the hearty co-operation of many earnest workers on every side.

He soon grasped the problem of its success. He knew its history, and he saw at once what it needed; and cheered by the prospect, he devoted all his powers of body and mind to its welfare. Frankness, cheerfulness, and confidence marked his intercourse with the professors; he sought their co-operation in all important matters, and made them feel from the beginning, that he was a friend, and would rely upon them for counsel and action. Though he had a large experience, and strong convictions of his own, on most educational questions, yet he came not as an innovator, but as one who sought to build on the broad foundations already laid. He let it be distinctly understood that he expected entire unity of purpose and action between himself and his colleagues; that their honor was his honor; and that in the prosperity and success of the college they should all alike find their surest reward. Dr. Foote, who was an eye-witness of this delightful harmony, which continued during the whole period of the presidency, has placed on record the following tribute to the moderation and wisdom that marked his official relations:—

"The honorable purposes expressed at first were carried out to the full by Dr. Green on his part, and by the professors on their part. Such a thing as private piques and jealousies was never known. He evidently sought and seized upon opportunities of honoring his professors; and they were always ready to mete out to him in full measure, confidence and co-operation in their daily duties, and in those extra ones that were often thrown upon him. He never stepped out of his way for any kind of popularity, and never gave expression to any feelings but gladness when honor was done another. Alive to the approbation of good men, he never thrust himself forward on any occasion. After I became sufficiently acquainted with him to know him, I never saw him brought forward, but I could see by the flush on his cheek and the quiver upon his lip, and the quick glow of his eye, that he felt his position for good or for evil, and that his soul was agitated with a desire to do or say the right thing in the right way. Even before he began to speak, if I looked upon his face, he enlisted my favor. It was evident that his soul was alive to the subject. It made no difference whether his flights were even or uneven, fitful or continuous, there was that earnestness and modesty combined, that at the close of each sentence, made me wish to hear the next. A deeply sensitive man himself he could appreciate the feelings of others, and sympathize with speakers who were in every thing antipodes to himself, except in honesty and earnestness."

When Dr. Green went to Hampden Sidney, he considered himself entirely broken down in body by his labors in Baltimore, and remarked to a friend, that he had come there to die. To his mind, at that time, the most inviting feature in the position was the rest and quiet offered him. But the change, country air, congenial occupation, and the approach of middle life restored him so that he went away a healthy man. And he soon found himself under returning health, almost as busily engaged as ever in the ministrations of the pulpit. His preaching was acceptable and frequently called for. Besides repeated calls for his services in different parts of the State, he took his turn regularly with the Professors of the Theological Seminary in preaching in the chapel of that institution, and was also frequently invited to preach in the College Church of the village, of which Dr. Benjamin H. Rice was then pastor. Wherever he went an effectual door was opened to him. He felt that he was useful, that his labors were blest of God; and that he was appreciated by congenial brethren who loved and honored him. It was one of the happiest periods of his life. He mingled freely with many of the leading men of the State, who gave him not only their approval but their cordial co-operation in his efforts to restore and elevate one of their oldest colleges.

And in this important work he had the satisfaction of feeling that his efforts were not in vain. His administration continued through eight years, during which, under his vigilant and judicious discipline, every thing moved on with precision, harmony, and a good degree of success. The number of students increased, the funds were augmented, the annual commencements became more interesting and more largely attended. He spent his vacations in advancing the cause of the college, and attended the meetings of Presbytery and Synod, obtaining scholarships, and securing students. His presence everywhere created new interest in the college, and his felicitous manner of presenting the twofold object of his mission, the education of youth and the salvation of men, interweaving the two as indissoluble, drew attentive audiences wherever he preached. And seldom did he preach without producing a favorable impression for his cause. With the co-operation of his faculty and the trustees, the course of studies was gradually enlarged, and the standard of scholarship raised, so as to meet the wants of the public and preserve the relative position of the college among the more liberally endowed State institutions. The students themselves caught the enthusiasm, and the ardor of pursuit in literature and science diffused a joyousness over the whole college precincts.

Rev. Dr. R. L. Dabney, who became Professor of Theology in the seminary at Prince Edward, a few years after Dr. Green took charge of the college, speaks of him and his administration in the following terms :—

> "He was a cordial and hospitable neighbor; an exceedingly animated and agreeable companion, and a firm and enlightened friend of our seminary and faculty. Dr. Green's interest in Hampden Sidney was warm and sincere. He was a valuable acquisition to the college. When he came, its literary and financial state was bad; the faculty small and nearly starved out; the endowment almost exhausted; there were about twenty-seven students, and these in an insubordinate condition. With the zealous support of Professor Charles Martin (still a member of the faculty), he restored the finances, chiefly by a scholarship scheme. Two efforts made by Mr. Martin, whose enterprise and energy were invaluable, and other agents, added about eighty thousand dollars to the permanent endowment. The faculty were sustained, and the number of students ran up to a hundred and thirty-five, or even a hundred and fifty. There was also a great increase in their order, diligence, and manliness."

Besides the important aid of Professor Martin in maturing and carrying forward this scholarship scheme of endowment, he found also in Rev. Dr. Jesse Armistead an efficient and successful coadjutor. He also gave his own personal attention to the work, spending his vacations in raising funds on that plan. One secret of his success, through all these efforts, was in the fact that he had the hearty co-operation and sympathy of the leading men around him—his own faculty and trustees, the professors and directors of the seminary, and other members of the Synod. In the life of a good man there is no sweeter reward and no keener stimulus to exertion than to feel that God blesses his labors, and that his brethren appreciate and sustain him. This encouragement he had in a high degree during his whole administration in Hampden Sidney.

An incident is related of him at Hampden Sidney, which serves to illustrate at once the pungency of his preaching and his faithfulness in dealing with the pupils committed to his charge. After preaching one morning, he was followed to the gate by a student, a special favorite, who abruptly accosted him thus:—"Good morning, Dr. Green, you are no gentleman, sir. I always believed you were a gentleman until this morning." "What do you mean, C—," he replied, calmed in an instant by a glance at the face of the agitated youth. "I mean, sir, what I say, that you are no gentleman, for no gentleman would insult another as you chose to insult me publicly in your sermon just now. You know that every word of it was meant for me, and you had no right to expose me to the whole congregation." "My dear C—," said he, "I was not thinking of you at all; that sermon was written and preached ten years ago in Kentucky." This assurance pacified him instantly. The doctor carried him into the house, had a long talk with him, and had the happiness afterward of seeing him a hopefully converted man.

He was well fitted, as the Baltimore preacher expressed it, to preach to college boys. "I did not wonder," says Dr. Foote, speaking of this period, "that his students loved him, and loved to hear him preach. He added to and filled out the charming variety on College Hill." He chose subjects interesting to the young, and presented to them the results of deep study and protracted thought in a pleasing elocution His fancy was lively, his imagination glowing, and his heart warm; and their own hearts and minds were deeply interested in his sublime thoughts and forcible conclusions, which seemed to them to re-echo and apply the profound logical discussions they had heard in the class-room. His own high sense of honor and gentlemanly bearing incited the students, in happy emulation, to the cultivation of the kind, the noble, the elevated, in their social intercourse. They were constrained to look upon him as a friend. His disapprobation was grief to the offender, and he was unhappy till reconciled. He put his students upon their sense of honor; appealed to whatever was manly in their nature, and sought to govern them by the principles of right and duty revealed in the word of God.

His discipline was kind, paternal, and skilful. "His method of management" says Dr. Dabney, "was to discard petty surveillance, to treat the students with cordial confidence while they seemed to behave with propriety, and as soon as a chap seemed slack in recitations or morals, to send him back to his parents summarily. As the institution received no tuition fees (scholarships having superseded them) the faculty were not restrained from applying the knife promptly, by any sensitiveness about the pocket. When any outrage was committed by an unknown student, Dr. Green had a very adroit way of trapping the real culprit. A conference with his colleagues, with an examination of recitation marks, and other indications, would lead to a guess as to which students were likely to be engaged in pranks. And they rarely guessed wrong. The faculty would meet in private conclave and send for the suspected party. Dr. Green addressed him very respectfully to this effect. "You know, Mr. B., that such an outrage has been committed. We lament exceedingly to be obliged to say, that the circumstances point to you. But such is our confidence in your honor, that one word of disclaimer will relieve our minds wholly, and we shall hasten with great pleasure to make every reparation in our power for an unjust conclusion." Mr. B. would probably scratch his head, hesitate, look sheepish, and end by saying that he could not speak that word of disclaimer. Dr. Green knew that if he lied, the students would expel him. "Well, then," he would answer, "Mr. B., the faculty find themselves constrained to recommend that you return to the parental control," and the next morning's stage would carry him away, bag and baggage.

We have an interesting account of his work at Hampden Sidney from the pen of Dr. Joseph R. Wilson, already referred to,—who was, at the time, associated with him in the faculty of the institution.

"The good work he accomplished there it would be hard to overrate. He found the college not very flourishing, he left it in a high state of prosperity. The whole purpose of his soul was given to the interests of that institution. He left nothing undone or untried which promised to promote its welfare. In this position he showed that his rare qualities as a disciplinarian were excelled only by his eminence as an instructor. His knowledge of human nature, and his conspicuous goodness of heart, together with the attractions of his personal intercourse, admirably fitted him for dealing with boys. He possessed that disposition, both merciful and just, which enabled him to win their love, while administering the severest reproofs. And as the presiding officer of our faculty, he was every thing that could be desired; never overbearing, never selfish, never exacting, never coarse, but always superior; he won our hearts at the same time that he commanded our respect and confidence. His reputation soon spread abroad; and every year it spread more widely. No college president ever enjoyed a purer fame. The fact is undeniable that Dr. Green was a really great man, and had his bodily health been as robust as his mental energies were strong, he would have become illustrious. As it was, he left behind him, in Virginia, a name free from blemish, and for commanding, positive excellence, well deserving of being held in grateful remembrance. The cause of education in the Old Commonwealth will forever remain his debtor. There, too, the cause of religion owes more to his influence than it does to most men of his day. Altogether he left a mark which cannot be easily obliterated."

Scarcely had Dr. Green become fully settled at Hampden Sidney College, with returning health, before efforts began to be made to draw him to other fields of labor. The friends of Jefferson College, at Cannonsburg, Pennsylvania, even before he left Baltimore, had made an overture to place him at the head of that institution; and they renewed it again during his residence in Virginia with still greater zeal. But though his own college had opened with less than thirty students, while Jefferson had two hundred and fifty, and though Dr. A. B. Brown, the former president, in repeated letters urged upon him the claims of the latter institution; yet feeling that he was where God had placed him, and that he must not despise the day of small things, he cheerfully declined all further propositions, and determined to abide in his lot and work on. Even as late as 1855, a very inviting overture was made to him to return to Kentucky, and settle among his old friends and kindred, as Pastor of the First Presbyterian Church of Danville, then vacant by the removal of Dr. William M. Scott to Cincinnati. But this he also declined. On several other occasions, as will be seen in the next chapter, he came to a similar conclusion as to his duty at Hampden Sidney; and it was not until he had labored on for eight years, and saw his beloved college on the high ground of prosperity, that he could feel himself at liberty to leave it.

CHAPTER VII.

LEXINGTON AND DANVILLE, 1856—1863.

Positions Declined.—Predilections for the West.—Strong Call from Kentucky. —Resignation of his Presidency at Hampden Sidney.—Presidency of Transylvania University.—Scheme for a Normal School.—Inauguration.— Auspicious Beginning.—Disappointments.—Resignation.—Called to the Presidency of Centre College.—Inaugural Address.—Joint Pastorate in Danville. — Successful Administration.— Trials and Conflicts. — Testimonial.

ON the organization of the Theological Seminary at Danville, in 1854, Dr. Green was the first choice of his ministerial brethren in Kentucky for the chair of Biblical Literature in that institution; and he would, no doubt, have been unanimously elected to it by the General Assembly had not influential members of the Synod of Virginia, the friends of Hampden Sidney College, interposed to retain him in the important position he then occupied. He was a Western man, and had never ceased to feel the most lively interest in the cause of education and religion at the West. He was a Kentuckian, and his residence at the East had in no degree abated his attachment to the people of his native State. All his sympathies and predilections would have strongly drawn him to a position so important and honorable as a professorship in the new seminary located in the bosom of the Kentucky churches. But the call of duty was urgent at Hampden Sidney. The friends of that institution prevailed, and the appointment was not made. He had also, in 1853, promptly declined being re-elected to a professorship in the Allegheny Seminary, on the ground that he could not leave Hampden Sidney. Still earlier, in 1850, he had been the first choice of the Synod of Kentucky to fill its professorship in the Theological Seminary at New Albany, which position he had been strongly urged to accept, but had declined on the same ground.

In the lapse of years, however, another call came to him from Kentucky, which he felt it to be his duty to accept. It seemed to open a door of extended usefulness, not often opened to any man, and he felt that through it he might, in all probability, accomplish the greatest work of his life. In 1856 the Transylvania University at Lexington, the oldest collegiate institution in the State, was re-organized by an act of the Legislature of Kentucky, and in connection with it a normal school for the education of teachers was established, as an indispensable auxiliary to the common school system of the State The normal school was itself to be a part of the university, forming one of five schools or departments, each having its appropriate course of instruction, but all under the direction of the faculty and trustees of the university.

It was a noble scheme. It looked as if Kentucky were about to step forward on the high-road of popular education, and to illustrate, in a new way, the fact that the schoolmaster is abroad in the land. At the head of this important and most promising movement the friends of education in Kentucky desired to place a man of acknowledged ability and experience. The choice fell on Dr. Green, whose learning, practical skill, and enthusiasm in the cause of education, all singled him out as the man for the place. He was accordingly elected president of the institution. His old friends—many of them among the most prominent men in the State—urged his acceptance. Some visited him in person to press the call. He was induced to make a visit to Lexington and see the field for himself. The visit was almost an ovation. Everybody urged him to return to his native State and take a position which—thus placing him at the head of its whole educational system—would put it in his power to do incalculable good for all time to come. Such a call he could not resist. Returning to Virginia he resigned the presidency of Hampden Sidney before the close of the session of 1856. Rev. Dr. R. L. Dabney, of the Theological Seminary, agreed to take his place as temporary instructor and graduate the Senior Class of that year.

He removed to Lexington in August, and on the 18th of November was inaugurated President of the Transylvania University and the State Normal School. On this occasion, in presence of a large concourse, Governor Charles Morehead, ex-officio President of the Board of Trustees, addressed him in these words of cordial welcome: "On behalf of the trustees, whose organ I am, under whose control the institution has been placed, and by whom you have been unanimously elected president, and may I not add also, on behalf of the State of Kentucky, whose most cherished institution is sought to be promoted, I welcome you back to your native State, and with a heart glowing with honest pride with the anticipation of triumphant success, I congratulate you on the enlarged sphere of usefulness which is open before you." To this kindly greeting Dr. Green responded, in words of deep emotion, that for sixteen years he had been an exile from his native State, in no dishonorable exile it was true, but still that he had always looked upon Kentucky as his home, and it was with the most intense delight that he now girded himself for the loved work of instructing her youth, and training them for usefulness and honor. His whole address, delivered on the occasion, was heard with rapt attention. It was one of his happiest efforts, abounding in noble, patriotic sentiments, and just views of the teacher's province, responsibility, and duties.

He entered upon his work at Lexington with his accustomed zeal and energy. There had been much dissatisfaction and discouragement previous to his arrival. But he at once infused new life into the institution, and inspired its friends with the highest hopes. Through the fall and winter he was kept exceedingly busy, maturing his plans for the Normal School, and preparing to carry forward the great work, while from Sabbath to Sabbath, not only at Lexington, but in other adjacent places, he preached to large and delighted congregations. His pulpit ministrations at this time were, in ability and eloquence, equal to any of his life, and were universally admired. This was especially the case with a lecture on the "Immortality of the Soul," which he delivered in many places with great effect, but of which nothing remains among his manuscripts. Every one was delighted with his administration of the institution. In his letters of this period adverting to the fact that some people had already begun to predict that they should do a great work, he says—"But I do not wish to be high-minded, but fear, and gratefully accept what God may mercifully send. Our number is about 125 or 130, as many as I desire to start with." A month later, he writes—"I think I am giving universal satisfaction, and the college moves on beyond all expectation. But I have had first, great anxiety, and since, rather too much applause." During these months also he set to work, and secured the co-operation of the ministers and leading men of the place, in a movement in behalf of the Temperance cause, delivering an able lecture on the subject.

But this auspicious opening was destined to be followed by disappointments of which no one then conceived. By one of those strange freaks, or follies, of legislation, from which our country has never been entirely exempt, the wise and noble work thus begun was all reversed by the succeeding Legislature. This is not the place to discuss the causes, or reveal the influences that led to so unlooked-for a result. Suffice it to say, that the appropriation was withdrawn, the law was repealed, and the project of a Normal School, in connection with university education abandoned. Seeing that the great object for which he had come to Kentucky, and on which he had labored in hope for nearly two years, was thus nipped in the bud, and that now there could be little prospect of raising Transylvania University into a first-class institution, after all the changes and disappointments of its past history, Dr. Green felt himself at liberty to retire from the position, and accordingly resigned the presidency in the winter of 1857, on the passage of the bill which destroyed the Normal School.

He retired as one who felt that no responsibility of the failure rested on him or his friends. He had accepted the high trust in good faith, had girded himself for a great and good work, and, in the brief space allotted him, had accomplished enough to show what he could have done, if opportunity had been given. No part of his life had been more marked by activity. Young men had been drawn from all parts of the State. The annual commencement had never been attended with better success. And his whole instruction in the university, as well as his preaching, had elicited the admiration of all classes at Lexington. He was invited to preach in the churches of all denominations in the city, where large audiences gathered to hear him from Sabbath to Sabbath; and in the afternoon of each Sabbath he preached in the chapel of the university. In no sense had he failed. But through causes over which he had no control, his beloved State had failed to secure a great boon.

Dr. Green was elected President of Centre College, August 6, 1857, and on the 1st of January, 1858, entered upon his appropriate duties, with strong hopes of usefulness and success. It was a position in every respect desirable, and one for which his mature experience and his well-tried abilities amply qualified him. It seemed to be a special distinction of Providence, and an omen of much good for the future, that he who graduated with its first small class, should now return, so richly furnished, to take charge of it as president. His inaugural address was delivered before the Synod of Kentucky, at its meeting in Lebanon, October 14, 1858. Like all his inaugural discourses it was scholarly, sound in sentiment, eloquent in diction, and full of practical suggestions of great importance.

Centre College had thus far held an important place among the educational institutions of the West. For a quarter of a century, and almost from its foundation, it had stood as the leading college of the Presbyterian Church in the West. Under the long and faithful services of Dr. John C. Young—Dr. Green's immediate predecessor at Danville—the institution had been greatly prospered, and had risen to a position of commanding influence in the church and in the country. All felt that in Dr. Green it had secured a head worthy to succeed those who had gone before, and competent to conduct it to still higher success. And it cannot be doubted that, but for the disasters of the civil war which soon broke out, and almost disbanded its students, such would have been the result. As it was, he was destined to labor on, amid trials and discouragements, for five years, until death arrested his useful labors.

In addition to the duties of his presidency, Dr. Green soon became actively engaged in pastoral work at Danville. In April, 1858, Dr. Alfred Ryers and himself received a joint call to the Second Presbyterian Church of the place, and were associated as colleagues in the pastoral care of that congregation. Here he preached with his usual power and success for several years, until the church edifice was destroyed by fire, and the congregation was left without a house of worship. Afterward the two congregations worshipped together in the building of the First Church, of which Rev. Dr. Yantis was at that time pastor, and with whom, after awhile, he also became associated in preaching—officiating on alternate Sabbaths until his death, though not installed as pastor of that church.

During the first years of his administration, the college made steady progress, the number of students becoming greater than it had ever been before, and the funds being also much increased. But this prosperity and all his plans of usefulness were sadly changed on the breaking out of the war. As the crisis came on, and party lines began to be more strongly drawn, he found difficulties and discouragements which had not been anticipated, and which severely tried his spirit. Though the prospect for the college was satisfactory and encouraging, for the times, still he felt the want of that hearty co-operation and appreciation of his services which had so cheered and sustained him at Hampden Sidney. It was under such impressions that he penned the following lines to an intimate friend, "I long for quiet and leisure for nobler objects, and am more than half prepared to make my own definite arrangements to retire from the field, when the college shall have become what they call great, and devote my latter and best days to study and writing in the vicinity of some foreign university. Six years, I think, will bring three hundred students to the college.

When these six years of toil and conflict are accomplished, what think you? May I retire? I ask your opinion seriously, but in entire confidence."

Nevertheless, "bating not a jot of heart or hope" in the high endeavor to discharge his whole duty, he stood at his post and worked on, steadily and perseveringly amidst increasing toil and conflict even to the end. The times were out of joint, and even good men were unable to see eye to eye; but God was on the throne, and he felt that no true work and labor of love would lose its recompense. "How we love to remember that kind old man," says a pupil of these last years, "as with his hair fast whitening, and even then enfeebled step, he used to come through the Campus in the morning, and, with smiles of recognition, the affectionate clasp of the hand, and an anxious inquiry for our health, reply to our early salutations. With bowed head and dignified step he marches down the aisle to his chair, his eagle eye scans each answering countenance at roll-call, and each absentee is marked for censure or excuse. After reading some impressive lesson, as only he could read, from the pages of Holy Writ, how eloquent was his prayer for the spiritual and eternal welfare of his boys—how earnestly did he beseech God, that he would forgive the many impenitent among us, make us sensible of our condition, and turn all hearts heavenward! With what fervor did he ask that teachers and pupils might be rendered faithful in the discharge of their respective duties, that the seed might here be scattered by diligent sowers, and falling into good ground, in due season bear fruit a hundredfold!"

There was a singleness of aim in all the great purposes of life, and he was true to it to the last. He had worked on different fields, and often far asunder, but in every office he had filled, whether as an educator or a minister of God, the grand purpose of all his exertions, the uniform pursuit of his life, had been to disseminate among his fellow-citizens, and especially among the educated youth of his country, a taste for solid and sanctified learning, to carry education into religion, and religion into education, and to give to each its proper elevation in the public esteem, to reclaim the young men of his generation from all low and sordid interests, from all selfish and unhallowed ambitions, and to fix their minds on objects of a nobler, even an immortal character. This was the key-note of his life, and he was true to it to the last.

"Oh! be it ours at life's blest close to stand,
Scarred though it be with sorrows, still erect
In harness to the last, raising our heads,
In the one battle-field, aloft to Thee!
Scourged, chastened, purified, and hearing now
The inner voices chanting victory!
Like some old warrior chief on his last field,
Dying with upturned face, and in his ears
An army's songs of triumph, heedless all
If so be the stern fight is won at last,
And his flag flies victorious in death!"

CHAPTER VIII.

DANVILLE, 1863.

Last Sickness and Death.—Multiplied Labors.—The Church and College.—Cause of his Illness.—Incessant Work.—The Closing Scene.—His Last Sermons.—Increased Spirituality.—Intense Sympathies.—Letters on the War.—Ministry of Love and Consolation.—His Funeral.—Burial.—Resolutions of his Church and of the Faculty.

DR. GREEN died as he had lived, in the midst of work. His last illness, which was sudden and of short duration, lasting less than a week, found him at the post of duty, and with all his armor on. He was filling an important and ever-widening sphere of usefulness (all feeling that he was the right man in the right place), dividing his time and energies between the duties of instruction in the college, the preaching of the Gospel, and the numerous calls of duty to the sick and dying around him—when the summons came. Never, perhaps, in life had his work been more pressing, his duties more multiplied, his preaching more acceptable, and his whole intercourse with those around him more blest of God, than during these last days at Danville. And when he fell in the midst of these useful labors—his eye undimmed, and his natural force unabated—being but in the fifty-eighth year of his age—many were the hearts far and near, that deplored the loss. How soon, and how suddenly was the strong staff broken and the beautiful rod.

He was taken sick on Thursday and died on the Tuesday following—May 26, 1863. It was soon after the terrible battle of Perryville, near Danville, when the college and the churches of the place were turned into hospitals for the sick, wounded, and dying soldiers; three thousand of whom, from first to last, were brought there to be cared for. For days and nights his time and strength were devoted to the relief of the sufferers—visiting the sick, ministering to the dying, burying the dead, and giving comfort and counsel to the living, and at the same time carrying on his instructions in the college, and preaching on the Sabbath. It was too much for his highly wrought sensibilities. His physical system was overtaxed, and fell an easy victim to disease in the almost pestilential condition of the atmosphere then prevailing at Danville—his own residence being very near the college, which had been used as a hospital by one army or the other for many months.

On Thursday morning he was making a call at the house of a friend, and complained of chilliness. The lady, observing his pallor, offered to send him home in her carriage, but he declined, saying that the walk in the fresh air and sunshine would warm and revive him. His family were not at home, but one of his daughters, reaching the house about fifteen minutes after him, was met at the gate by a servant who begged her to hurry in, as he was very sick. Physicians were summoned at once, and quickly arrived; but he was already in a congestive chill. It was a mortal illness from the first. That evening he became delirious, and all through the night, and the next day and night, he was in extreme agony. A second chill on Friday was followed by paralysis, and he sank into a state of unconsciousness, from which he could be aroused only a few moments at a time. Says the daughter who describes the scene: "I think he must have had conscious intervals. I begged him if he knew me to press my hand; instantly his fingers closed on mine, and for a moment he was convulsed in what seemed to be an effort to make himself understood. Just at the last, when no one supposed him conscious, some one mentioned his absent wife and daughter, who were hurrying home but could not reach him. His eye missed them; one tear trickled down his cheek; it was wiped away; another came; it was all he gave to earth. His face during the last day and night was peaceful as an angel's, and in the morning of the resurrection will hardly wear a more heavenly expression."

He was often urged by his family to leave Danville, at least for a time, and get away from the poisoned atmosphere he had been so long breathing; for they saw that he was not well, and was reeling under double burdens. To the expostulations of friends and the remonstrances of physicians he made but one reply--he felt himself in no danger, his duty required him to remain at his post, the interests of the college demanded his presence, especially as two of the professors were gone. The exercises of the college were never suspended, though the building was used as a hospital. It mattered not how great was the excitement in the town, he still went on with the work of instruction, even supplying the place of the absent teachers. He also continued to preach, although his clothing would be drenched with perspiration after every effort; and to teach, though often so unwell as to receive his classes in his bedroom. Insensible still to his danger, he remarked but a few days before his sudden and fatal attack, that his brain had never in his life been so clear and active, and that the only effort required in preaching was to check the rush of thought long enough to clothe it with expression. It is evident that the feverish, excited condition of nerves and brain in which he had been living for more than a year, the state of tension in which his system was kept by the troubled condition of the country, and the heavy draughts made upon his strength, proved too much for the delicate frame, and he fell an easy prey to the malaria.

Instead of spending his vacations in quest of that rest and relaxation which his system required, he had invariably kept himself at work even when changing from place to place, either raising college endowments, or pleading the cause of education before the public, or preaching as opportunity offered. As a consequence, preaching, talking, writing, travelling in behalf of his work, formed a part of his regular summer recreations. He enjoyed little of the repose needed to recuperate the exhausted energies of so nervous a temperament. Not that he was ever unduly urged to exertion of any kind; on the contrary, so warm and tender was the interest he excited, that every influence was employed to induce him to treasure his strength. His activity both mental and physical was so great, that he did not in fact know how to stop, and had never trained himself to the habit of taking refreshing rest. Work had become the law of his being, and he would continue to work till he sank from exhaustion. This was the case to the last. The warning example of others, and the repetition of violent attacks of illness produced no effect. He was deceived as to his own strength. He would not have wasted life, had he seen what he was doing. To no man was earth more beautiful, life, with home, and kindred, and friends, and country more dear. He did not know that the spirit had triumphed over its frail tenement, and was chafing to be free. He imagined all was well, because his mind was so clear and worked so vigorously. And the stroke that felled him was so quick and sharp, that no time was given to be undeceived.

Every thing around him contributed to the heavy drain upon his mind, his thoughts, and his sympathies. While his own heart was troubled and saddened almost to breaking at the prospect of a still further protraction of the dreadful civil war, he was the comforter to whom sorrowing friends and neighbors turned for consolation in those dark sad days. Only a few days before his illness, he called to see a lady who was in deep distress; and when struck with his feeble and tired appearance, she inquired, "How are you, this morning, doctor?" "Faint, yet pursuing, madam; faint, yet pursuing;" was his characteristic reply. The answer seemed but a fitting epitome of his life. "About this time," says his daughter—the one who was with him in his last illness, and shared so deeply in all his thoughts and feelings, "I attended with him the funeral of an old friend, and remember, during the prayer offered by another minister, the pang that shot through me, as my eyes unconsciously rested on the face of my father. He was sitting with his eyes closed and his head thrown back and resting upon the folding doors that separated the rooms. Who will be next? flashed through my mind. I did not think of *him* in that connection. I only saw there was too little of the earthly in his countenance, and too much of that which, resting on it as a halo of spiritual beauty, lured my mind to another world; and it gave me pain; I could not tell why. But the thought that he would be taken so soon could find no entrance to my mind."

It is interesting in this connection to notice the tone and character of Dr. Green's pulpit ministrations, as he approached the terminus of life. From the very opening of the war, there was a marked change in his preaching. It savored less of the things of time, and more of the great things of eternity. Onward through the stormy days of 1862 and 1863, even to the close of life, it became more and more spiritual, more and more evangelical and pungent. He preached as one standing on the borders of the eternal world, awed, subdued, and chastened by the judgments of the Almighty which were abroad in the land. His office as an educator had led him through life, to preach much in behalf of great temporal interests, education, the advancement of learning, philosophy, science, literature, liberty, and the well-being of the common country. But now his thoughts were chiefly bent on the grand essentials of the cross, and the necessity of a holy life, and preparation to stand before God. At the time of his death he was engaged in delivering a series of discourses on the Last Judgment. The very last sermon he preached was on the text, "Stand in awe, and sin not," which well defines the general tenor and aim of all his sermons during these closing years of his ministry.

Fools rush in where angels fear to tread. But this good man, humbled, appalled, and overwhelmed by the judgments of the Almighty upon his beloved country, and upon the people whom he had labored so long to elevate and bless, now set himself to the task of preaching to them the unsearchable riches and the consolations of Christ. The exceeding sinfulness of sin, God's hatred of and determination to punish it, Christ the strong tower of defence against all human calamities, Christ the Rock of Ages in whose cleft the bleeding hearts around him might find safety; Christ the great Physician of souls, the tender Shepherd, the gentle Saviour, the living friend; Christ the shadow of a great rock in a weary land, the refuge from the windy storm and tempest; Christ, when there is sorrow upon the sea, and the troubled waters cannot rest—became the ceaseless and all-absorbing burden of his message. "Not often," says one who heard him at this time, "do we listen to such tender entreaty, to such melting appeals, to such thundering denunciation of sin, and such searching of the heart, laying bare its secrets as by sheet lightning, and flashing through the soul some awed sense of its actual depravity. And through the whole, it seemed as if this earth was not his home. Even then his pure soul was pluming its pinions for the heavenly flight."

His letters to his family and friends during this period, were filled with remarks upon the war and the condition of the country. With a full foresight of the evils which were coming, he counselled moderation and forbearance, one toward another, and sought to prepare all hearts for the worst by drawing them more closely to Christ. In a letter to a brother minister written only a few months before his death, describing the fearful calamities of the times, he says—"What shall the Christian minister do? Bow in awe, in penitence, in deep sorrow and compassion for his race, in earnest prayer, and humble trembling trust, before God. Pity—sincerely, tenderly, forgivingly pity—the madness of the people; partake none of their mutual hatred; love and pray for all; preach Christ more than ever. Surely, it becomes us now, as ministers, more than ever to preach Christ and him crucified, solemnly, earnestly, affectionately, simply, exclusively, seeing the time is short." To an absent daughter, he writes in the same spirit. "I think much and anxiously about you; but what a blessing it will be, if these passing troubles lead us to cling closer to the cross and the Saviour. It is not easy to withdraw our minds from the merely worldly view of the calamities, national and individual; but it is possible, and I often get a more solemn view of God's providential government, and the dreadful evil of sin, from these than from any other source. But then, there is a sweet peace in feeling that we are in his hands, and that all his purposes toward us are love. I was filled with deep horror at the sentiments expressed, by men of all classes, on the cars and at hotels. Ruthless vengeance, total extermination, they say, is becoming the general feeling. 'It is working admirably,' said a man, 'toward that point.' God sometimes allows such fiendish purposes to prevail: but never without tenfold retribution. Amidst these horrors present and prospective, let us flee to our sure refuge, until these calamities be overpast."

In a letter to his daughter written a few months before his death, and in the prospect of seeing Kentucky soon the seat of war, he writes—"In this awful visitation we must recognize the hand of a righteous and terrible God, and bow in penitence and reverence before him, pitying our poor fallen race, and trembling in view of His judgments when abroad in the land. What may fall on any of us at any time no man can foresee. To one who abhors and pities the madness of both parties, and sees in the success of either, only a different form of ruin; silence and sorrow are the only course left open. Pray for this land bleeding by the wounds her own sons have inflicted, and for the church distracted and rendered worldly, and sinners perishing without thought of God. Let these scenes be but sanctified to make us better and wiser."

In letters to his wife, written about this time, he unbosoms his feelings still more fully, showing what position he occupied, and with what spirit he sought to discharge the sacred functions of his ministry, even to the last. To Mrs. Green he writes, "Civil war in Kentucky is now, I fear, inevitable. We ought to realize its enormous evil and sin, but not exaggerate them; above all, not aggravate them, in our own circle, by partaking in its passions, or irritating, uselessly, either of the parties. All reasoning in such cases is folly; we must accept the situation and be concerned only to do our duty. Of the terrible times which are coming, and are even now come, I think Christian duty, and ordinary Christian feeling and discretion, suggest the following plain and undoubted principles for the guidance of our course. First, very solemnly (and the more solemnly the more calmly) realize the full measure of the evil that is upon us, and stand in awe, deep awe and reverential submission, before God; and thus prepare to stand in our lot, and serve our generation, according to the will of God—quietly, prayerfully, cheerfully. I am persuaded we have seen but the beginning of evil, and if there be any substance in us, by grace or nature, now is the occasion to exercise and prove it. Let petty troubles and grievances real or imaginary be forgotten, or spurned away, amidst these appalling dangers to all. Second, partake not at all in the passions of either party. Both are wrong in many points—altogether wrong in their mutual hatred. But a mad bull would not be more impervious to reason, or more ferocious in his resentment of any interference, than both, and with equal sincerity. For each can make good a long, black catalogue of wrong things done by the leaders or zealots of the other side. Pity, forgiveness, wonder, sadness, and sincere sympathy with all the sufferers on either side, are the only emotions which one untainted with the poison can properly feel. Things must now run their course; and it is the most childish imbecility to fret or repine, or attempt to influence that course. Amidst much that I could have wished otherwise, yet I cannot but consider the men who adhere to the Union, and the repeated decisions of the majority of our people, as the safest and best. But do not argue, do not resent, all are mad. There is but one thing left for me, for us—to soothe by gentleness and love these asperities of feeling; to learn and lay to heart the stern but necessary lesson God is teaching us, and so to adorn the doctrine of the Saviour, that when (if in our life) these calamities are over-past, we may have the love and confidence of all."

The foregoing extracts, which might have been largely increased, will be sufficient to illustrate his sentiments and feelings as he beheld the dark clouds of war gathering thicker and thicker over his beloved country. If ever an American bosom beat with a pure and lofty patriotism it was his. Next to his devotion to the church of God was his attachment to this land of his birth. But ere these portentous clouds were broken, his tried and sorrowing spirit had passed to a world where sin and sorrow are unknown.

If it be indeed the crowning glory of the just, that his path shineth brighter and brighter to the perfect day, that blessed and glorious distinction was his. It was a source, not only of gratitude, but of sweet delight to his family and friends, to know that the purity and elevation of his character shone resplendently in the extreme hour of test and trial. When Kentucky was convulsed with dissensions in every church, every neighborhood, and almost every family, to a degree of which the united North and united South knew but little, that wisdom which cometh down from above, which is first pure, and then peaceable, gentle and easy to be entreated, shed its mild radiance over the closing days of a life ended in storms. Shaking from himself the dust of the strife, and girding on afresh his spiritual armor, refusing to echo the violence of any party, and letting his moderation be known to all men, he went in and out amid the fierce partisans, calming the bitterness, and softening the asperities of faction, and curbing, not ministering to, the conflicting passions of an excited community, comforting the bereaved of all classes, soothing the suffering and afflicted, and arousing the souls around him to some vivid conception of the awful judgments of God. Such was the work—such the blessed ministry of love and mercy in which this great and good man spent his last days on earth, wore his life away, and fell as the true soldier of Christ would ever wish to fall, a martyr to duty.

The funeral services at his death were held in the First Presbyterian Church of Danville, attended by a large concourse of citizens, and the students and faculties of the college and theological seminary. An appropriate and eloquent discourse, from the text, "I have fought a good fight, I have finished my course, I have kept the faith," was preached by the Rev. Robert G. Brank, of Lexington, in which, after recounting the distinguished services, the varied learning, the shining virtues and eloquence of the deceased, the preacher made a touching application to the members of the church of which he had once been pastor, and to the students of the college over which he had so lately presided. Rev. Wm. J. McKnight, the acting pastor of the church, also took part in these funeral services. At the conclusion of these impressive solemnities at the church, an immense procession of persons in carriages, on horseback, and on foot, followed his mortal remains to the grave, all the business houses of the place being closed. His body was laid to rest in the cemetery at Danville, there to await the resurrection of the blest. To the college, to the church, to the community, to the State, the loss was great, to his family irreparable. But to him the change was eternal gain. "And I heard a voice from heaven, saying unto me, write, Blessed are the dead which die in the Lord, from henceforth, yea, saith the Spirit, that they may rest from their labors, and their works do follow them."

A few weeks after his death, a public meeting of the Second Presbyterian Church of Danville, of which he had been pastor, was held to express their sense of the bereavement, and their grateful appreciation of his services. A minute was adopted, which after reciting the principal events of his life, and the several offices he had held, in different parts of the country, closes with the following paragraph and resolutions:—

"Few ministers of the Gospel in our country have held so large a number of important, useful, and responsible positions. It is to be especially noticed that he abandoned those previously occupied, to accept one still more important, only at the call of the Synod to which he belonged, or that of the General Assembly, or of the trustees of the public institutions in which he spent the greater part of his life in the service of education, both secular and theological. Therefore,

"*Resolved*, 1st. That in the death of the Rev. Lewis W. Green, D. D., the Presbyterian Church of the United States has lost one of its ablest, most honored, and most useful ministers—one who had spent a whole life-time in the service of the educational interests of the church, and the training of young men for the Gospel ministry.

"2d. That the congregation mourn his loss as an able, faithful, and eloquent preacher of the Gospel, and as far as his official duties permitted, a sympathizing and diligent pastor, ever ready to administer comfort to the afflicted, and instruction to those needing or desiring it.

"3d. That they tender to his family their tenderest sympathy and condolence for his death, especially under circumstances so peculiarly trying and painful."

The following paper from the records of the college may be subjoined, as serving to show the estimation in which he was held by his colleagues of the faculty.

"At a meeting of the Faculty of Centre College, held May 28, 1863, the following Preamble and Resolutions were adopted:—

"*Whereas* an all-wise though mysterious Providence has seen fit to remove from us, by death, the Rev. L. W. Green, D. D., for nearly six years the President of this institution; therefore,

"*Resolved*, That in this dispensation of Divine Providence we recognize the will of Him, whose ways are not as our ways; whose path is in the great waters, and whose footsteps are not known.

"*Resolved*, That in the removal of the Rev. Dr. Green from the superintendence of this institution, Centre College has lost one of its oldest and warmest friends; one who had devoted himself to the furtherance of its welfare as, next to the preaching of the Gospel, the great work of his life, and one whose labors, during the brief period so suddenly terminated, had been eminently successful in the promotion of its interest.

"*Resolved*, That Dr. Green is entitled to the grateful remembrance of the friends of Centre College for the wisdom with which, especially in the time of trial through which the institution has recently been called to pass, he guided its course amidst surrounding difficulties; and for the cheerfulness with which he undertook and discharged duties that doubled his labors as an instructor—labors which, we fear, must have overtasked the energies of his exhausted frame.

"*Resolved*, That while we profoundly feel the loss which the College, the Church, and the Community have sustained in the decease of Rev. Dr. Green, we cherish also the conviction, that, released as he has been from a life of labor, cheerfully undertaken and faithfully performed in the service of God, ours only is the loss and his the infinite reward.

"*Resolved*, That we tender to the family of Dr. Green the assurance of our deepest sympathy in their sudden and sore bereavement; while we pray that the God of all comfort would sustain them with the consolations that transcend all human sympathies.

"*Resolved*, That a copy of these resolutions be transmitted to the family of Dr. Green."

CHAPTER IX.

Review of his Public Services.—Estimate of his Preaching.—Prominent Traits of Character.—His Fervor.—High Sense of Honor.—Conscientiousness.—His Beneficence.—His Learning and Eloquence.—His Excellence as an Instructor.—Influence as a College President.—Testimony of Dr. Dabney.—His Strong Points.—His Elevated Tastes and Studies.—His Love of Books.—His Religious Devotion.—Personal Appearance.—His Polished Manners.—Easy Address.—Tact in Conversation.—Ministries of Love and Mercy.

The foregoing narrative of Dr. Green's career will be sufficient to show in what demand his services were held by the public, and what reputation he had won, both as a preacher and a practical educator. His career began and ended at Danville, but between its opening and its close it had swept a wide compass of useful labors. He had strong personal aptitudes and affinities for the pastoral office, and loved above all things the work of preaching the Gospel. But God had led him through a long period into fields of labor where teaching, rather than preaching, was his immediate business. With the exception of his brief pastorate at Baltimore, for thirty years he was constantly engaged in the active service of instruction, either as a professor or as president of some institution of learning. During all this time, he never ceased to exercise the appropriate functions of his ministry. Few men preached more. And when he did preach, it was on the essential doctrines and duties of the Gospel, which he pressed with all his might on the consciences of men. Considering the amount of time he spent in the work of teaching, and considering also the state of his health, which was never robust, his ministry was a laborious one; and it cannot be doubted that it was the means of turning many to righteousness.

But it was chiefly through the responsible positions he occupied in colleges and seminaries that he exerted, both as an educator and a minister, his most important influence upon the church and the country.

By all who knew him, he was regarded as one of the strong men of the church, competent to represent and defend her, whether from the pulpit or the press. His learning was accurate and extended, the result of careful reading and constant reflection, early begun and long continued. Far more than is usual in the ministry, he ranged beyond the limits of professional study, keeping himself fully abreast with the science and literature of the times. Whenever he preached he was listened to with rapt attention by crowded audiences, especially by the educated classes, and by young men, who were attracted by the originality and grandeur of his conceptions, the startling boldness of his imagery, and the enthusiastic ardor of his manner. He was a man who could do nothing by halves, could say nothing by halves. His convictions of truth and duty were all positive—all clear, settled, immovable. The truth with him was all and every thing. When he took his position on any subject, he was ready to maintain it against all the world. His moral courage was of the highest order, because founded on the most intense convictions of truth. He had much of the *ingenium perfervidum Scotorum.* No man perhaps ever held his opinions with a firmer grasp, or expressed them in a tone of more absolute assurance. There was an elevation of tone, a certain loftiness of view, a range and grandeur of thought, in all his public performances, and even in his daily conversation, which indicated a mind in perpetual communion with the great things of God's salvation.

These and other striking characteristics, with his large sympathies, his gospel unction, and his impassioned, extemporaneous delivery, rendered him at all times a popular and much admired preacher. All who heard him, recognized at once a man of superior intellect, and a minister not unworthy of his high vocation as God's ambassador. He had an inexhaustible flow both of thought and diction. His style was diffuse, classic, ornate, and full of those forms of expression which marked the play of a vivid imagination. His mind teemed with images of grandeur. His fertile, brilliant fancy, revelling, as with a poet's or an artist's eye, on scenes of sublimity and beauty, gave a gorgeous coloring to his language, and at times seemed almost to overshadow his other faculties. By some, this was regarded as a fault, and as scarcely in keeping with the simplicity of the pulpit. A severe critic can no doubt find something to disapprove on this score in his published sermons. But it must be borne in mind, that the lofty and gorgeous diction which marked his pulpit performances, was in harmony with the magnificent themes which he handled, and the wealth of thought which he lavished upon them. We can forgive a fault of mere taste, when it stands in the presence of so many substantial excellences. They are but spots on the sun. In the language of one who knew and loved him well—"He was a man of genius, of learning and piety, eminently a good man, though subject to the defects and faults of fervid genius and brilliant fancy.

Nothing perhaps was more prominent in the whole career of Dr. Green, than his high sense of honor, his superiority to every thing mean and selfish, and his large-hearted beneficence. He sometimes failed to be appreciated by the selfish and ambitious, just because they could not comprehend the purity and elevation of his motives. They thought him an abstractionist or a visionary, only because he was living so far above the range of worldly men. Yet his extreme conscientiousness and adherence to principle, never unfitted him for the practical duties of life, or interfered in the least with the genial flow of all those social and domestic virtues which made his intercourse delightful to all his friends. He was as practical as he was conscientious. He lived in the world, though not of it, and far above it. Faithfulness to God as a steward, the most uncompromising faithfulness in the discharge of duty, even in that which is least, was one of the cardinal virtues of his life. When he was a mere youth, his scrupulous honesty displayed itself, in causing twenty dollars to be returned to a man from whom an agent had purchased a horse for him that much below the value. Having inherited an estate which he regarded as a competency, he determined, after entering the ministry, to devote the whole income received from the church for his services, to beneficent purposes. This decision he carried out with faithful exactness. When necessity compelled him to use for private purposes any part of his salary, he would in the following year or years refund through some channel all that had been thus temporarily appropriated; and so well did he balance his accounts with his Master, that a few months before his last illness he informed one of his children, that of all he had ever received in the world, whether from a salary or other sources, one-half had been given in one form or another to the church. This large and long-continued beneficence, as unostentatious as it was unusual, demonstrates how unselfish and complete had been his consecration to God.

By his scholarly culture, his enthusiastic zeal in the cause of education, and his impressive eloquence in the pulpit, Dr. Green was eminently fitted to fill the position of president of a college. He had the important gift, essential to all successful educators, of imparting his own enthusiasm to his pupils. He took large and exalted views of truth and duty, appealing to every manly and noble sentiment, and clothing his thoughts in a style of sublimity and beauty well calculated to strike the ingenuous minds of youth. The fine play of his prolific imagination, the bold, free, extemporaneous delivery, the rich exuberance of his matter, rendered his preaching as well as his lectures exceedingly attractive to his students. He loved his high vocation as a minister of God; he also loved and magnified his office as an instructor of youth. In enthusiastic ardor for the higher learning, in the ability to communicate that ardor to the minds of others, and in his warm fellow-feeling for the young, no man in our country has perhaps ever excelled him. His pupils at Hampden Sidney and at Danville loved him like a father. And the secret of their affection was that he regarded and treated them as if they had been his sons. He won the good, he both conquered and won the bad, by kindness. He well expressed his theory on this point, when he once asked, concerning the qualifications of certain teachers, whether they could love a boy in all his badness? These diversified gifts and attainments—his great thoughts, lofty diction, impassioned oratory, intense convictions, bold imagery, strong enthusiasm, accurate scholarship, wide range of reading, deep earnest voice, and ready willingness to enter into conversation, and pour out instruction on almost every branch of science, literature, and art—altogether, made him one of the most entertaining of men to those who were under him in the capacity of learners. In the teacher they always found the sympathizing friend and the genial companion. In the preacher they beheld a living model of high Christian character, of every generous liberal sentiment, of every manly and noble virtue. Few college presidents have ever been more sincerely loved, more ardently and reverently admired by his *alumni* than Dr. Green. They saw in him only the great, good, and true man, whose highest aim was to train them for usefulness here and immortality hereafter.

Rev. Dr. R. L. Dabney of the Union Theological Seminary, Virginia, speaking of the time he was President of Hampden Sidney, gives the following estimate of him: "As a teacher, Dr. Green was undoubtedly able, animated, and successful. He aroused and elevated the faculties of his pupils. As a preacher, he was often very eloquent. He always preached without written preparation. His style was ambitious, and his elocution ardent. He more often fell short of his full force (when he did fall short) from this cause; namely—his ardent disposition led him to enlarge too much on the introductory parts; so that he consumed his time and strength, and was sometimes obliged rather to huddle up the more important parts near the close. But his preaching was often truly fine."

The strong points in Dr. Green's character, both as a man and a minister, shining out in all his intercourse with God and his fellow-men, and distinguishing his whole public and private life, might be summed up in the following: an intense consciousness of his responsibility to God, a realizing assurance of the shortness of life, the nearness of eternity, the existence of heaven and hell, a stern and uncompromising sense of duty on the ground of principle, and an overflowing tenderness, sympathy, and love for every thing around him—his family, his pupils, the people of his charge, the whole brotherhood of mankind. His wealth of affection, of all gentle, generous, and kindly feelings, was equal to his wealth of thought. As a pastor and an educator, he was to all under his care a father and a friend; while in his own domestic circle, no man could more fully exemplify the sacred relations and endearments of the Christian home.

One feature, already adverted to, in Dr. Green's character that impressed itself upon every one who came into daily contact with him, or even conversed with him or heard him preach but once, was the peculiar elevation of his mind. He seemed to live and move in an atmosphere of great ideas and of noble sentiments. He had a keen eye for the sublime and beautiful in nature, in art, in revelation; and his enjoyment was exquisite, whether gazing in his lonely walks on the wonderful works of God in nature, or holding converse in his study with the mighty dead of other ages through productions of human genius, or, rising still higher, to communion with God as he contemplated the unsearchable riches of the sacred word. It is difficult, by any mere description, to give to one who did not know him, a just conception of this uniform elevation. In the pulpit, the moment he began to speak, he lifted his hearers above the level of the common-place, and they felt that they were on a new track and higher ground. The topic might be old, but the method was new: the argument, the illustration, the handling all new. In conversation, especially with scientific persons who could appreciate the subjects, his thought and diction assumed the same elevated cast. And in such discussions he found intense enjoyment.

Nowhere, however, did he find a keener delight than when alone in his study. There, surrounded by his books, he thought out and prepared those trains of argumentation and appeal which were to be reproduced in the pulpit and the class-room, and occasionally to appear in his educational and religious discourses. His study was a sanctuary consecrated to thought, consecrated to communion with his books and with God. He handled a book with the tender carefulness of a mother handling her child. It was an object of love, almost of reverence. He never marred its fresh beauty. Though deeply and often studied, there was nothing save an occasional pencil-mark, to indicate that it had ever been opened. There were probably few better private collections in the country. His library comprised more than three thousand volumes, selected by himself with much care, and consisting largely of German, French, and choice classical works, with the standard English authors in science and literature.

But the fire that glowed so ardently in this sanctuary was not kindled at the altars of human genius and learning alone. He was a man of prayer, and held daily communion with his God and Saviour. He had learning, he had eloquence, but above all he had piety, kindled and sustained at the cross. He had the heart of love, the unction of the Divine Spirit. It was consecrated talent that gave power to his life and ministry. In a sermon on the parable of the talents, he struck the key-note of all his preaching, and all his educational labors, in the following emphatic words: "If in this land of unfettered freedom and overflowing prosperity, there be one necessity more urgent than all others, it is the demand for holy talent, the necessity for consecrated learning. It is that men should rise up on our soil, strong in native intellect, rich in acquired learning, filled with the spirit of the Lord, to walk boldly forth over the whole field of human science, gathering its scattered riches, digging deep for its precious ore, and from the Babel of discordant opinions drawing fresh materials to build up in new glory the temple of the Lord."

These were not words that should serve merely as a sign-board to direct others. They were words of which his own life was the illustration. He preached and practised the Bible doctrine of consecration in its integrity. We have already seen and noted his struggles with the spirit of worldly ambition, how first one and then another cup of hope and expectation was dashed from his lips, before he could make the surrender which conscience demanded. But from that time no part of the price was kept back. The decision was unreserved, complete. Life, health, substance, all he had, and all he was, gold, frankincense, and myrrh, whatever is costliest and most pleasant, all were brought to the feet of Jesus. And now looking back over his laborious, faithful, and sometimes tearful life, so fraught with patience and self-sacrifice, so chastened by suffering, so subdued to the humility of the Gospel, and so elevated to its grandeur, we may say of him without sacrilege, that the zeal of God's house hath consumed him.

In personal appearance Dr. Green was a man of medium stature, erect and well proportioned, though rather spare in flesh, of unpretending manners, with bright dark eyes, a highly intellectual face, his dark hair slightly waving and revealing an expansive brow. His countenance, except as it was lighted up in the glow of animated conversation, and the pleasant and playful pastimes of social and domestic life, which had an unusual charm for him, wore an expression of gravity and profound meditation, as of a man whose mind was habitually engaged on the grand themes and problems of human knowledge. This was his aspect in the repose of silent and thoughtful study. But he could easily unbend and disport himself. In the bosom of his family, when conversing with his children or intimate friends, and in the social circle, when stimulated by the presence of cultivated people, his face would light up as with a gleam of sunshine, his eye twinkle with humor, and his whole conversation would sparkle with flashes of wit and joyousness. On rising to speak also before an audience, his countenance was often flushed with the intense excitement of his intellectual and moral powers. In the progress of discourse his whole form and features seemed to glow and dilate to the utmost, under the kindling emotions which filled and fired his soul. On such themes as man's immortality, and the redemption of the cross, when excited by the presence of a large audience, he often preached like one inspired.

Dr. Green was a noble type of the gentleman, and that in the highest and best sense of the word. He left this impression on all who knew him. And there was another characteristic about as strongly marked. He was a noble type of the Christian. It is in no spirit of mere eulogy that this statement is made. All who ever came in contact with him long enough to see what he was, and were themselves capable of appreciating such qualities, know that the statement is the simple truth. There was a tone of gentility and refinement in his address, which gave him easy access to ladies and gentlemen of the highest social standing, and attracted such persons to his friendship and to his pulpit ministrations. Wherever he lived—in Pittsburgh, in Baltimore, in Virginia, in Kentucky—and wherever he travelled, he mingled freely with the leading people of the country, and found associates in men of science, in members of the learned professions, and in the statesmen of the land, not less than among his own brethren of the ministry, and other classes of society. And as to the depth, earnestness, and sincerity of his religion—probably there never was a man who could doubt it, unless it was himself. To any suggestion of unworthy means or ends, his invariable reply was in these simple but weighty words, "Honesty—humble, downright, pious honesty—is the only pledge of success, I mean permanent success."

In the intercourse of society, Dr. Green's manner was polished and affable in the highest degree. His kind feeling and his easy pleasant address, enabled him to approach all classes of people, and he lost no opportunity of doing them good, by speaking a good word for his Master. With a deep insight into human nature, and a nice sense of propriety, he at once won upon the good will of the persons he met, and ere they were aware he had them engaged in a conversation about spiritual things. Among his happiest traits was the wonderful facility he possessed of bringing the subject of personal religion home to people without giving offence. The subject was so familiar to him, that he would introduce it, and press it in the most natural and pleasant manner imaginable, without a shadow of the stiffness and effort that so often embarrass attempts of the kind, made with the best intentions. Even in promiscuous society, if the opportunity presented itself, the tact with which he would turn conversation into that channel was so remarkable, that it seemed as if nothing else could have been expected of him, and that it was the most natural and proper thing for him to talk on the subject, and would be for everybody else if equally gifted. His fine address gave him great ascendency over the young, and was especially useful in his intercourse with the gay and worldly. Having mastered them with their own weapons of wit or logic, the gravity and earnestness with which he would urge his advantage, never failed to leave a deep impression of the man and his religion, and very happy were the results in many instances of this way-side preaching. He was often grieved and surprised at the reluctance of professing Christians to dwell on these topics. He used to say that the very mention of heaven seemed to scare some very good people almost out of their senses.

Another beautiful trait of his character was that which shone forth in his visits to the house of suffering and sorrow. He had known what it was to wrestle with doubts and fears and manifold temptations, and from his own deep experience, he knew how to comfort the mourning, the despondent, the tempest-tossed soul. A son of thunder in the pulpit, when denouncing God's law against iniquity, he was equally a son of consolation at the bedside of the suffering and the dying. That deep spirituality which diffused itself through all the associations of life, and permeated his whole nature as a vital, controlling principle, made itself felt with wondrous power during seasons of bereavement and affliction, in instructing, sustaining, and comforting the weak, the wavering, the bereaved, and the dying. Many a sinking saint, many a broken-hearted mourner, many a conscience-stricken and trembling sinner, did he cheer in the hour of anguish, and inspire with new hopes by his fatherly counsels, his earnest prayers, his faithful presentation of Gospel truth, and his voice of sympathy and love. And never during his whole earthly pilgrimage did these characteristics appear in greater perfection than during those last sad days at Danville, when he went the rounds of his daily ministries of mercy among the sick and dying, telling of the love of Jesus, and pointing the trembling soul to that heaven to which he himself so soon ascended. His last days were his best and brightest—having least of earth, and most of heaven. His career, in its ending, was like the setting sun, which, large and full-orbed, shines with its softest loveliest light as it leaves the world.

CHAPTER X.

Dr. Green in his Family.—Members of his Home Circle.—The Husband and Father.—Intensity of his Affections.—Picture of Domestic Happiness.—Description by Dr. Foote.—Mrs. Green.—Poetry.—Education of his Daughters.—Religious Character of his Correspondence.—Beautiful Letters.

Thus far we have contemplated the character of Dr. Green chiefly as it appeared in his public and official relations. After tracing his early history, and his introduction to the ministry, we have seen him successively in the pulpit, in the professor's chair, in the pastoral office; and have pointed out his work as a preacher, as a theological teacher, and as president of three different colleges.

But any account of such a man would be imperfect without bringing into view those qualities which found their development in the more private relationships of life. It is not idle curiosity, but a natural and useful instinct, which prompts us to follow a good man into his domestic retreats, to look in upon the home circle, and see how he appeared to those who knew him best. Where dwellest thou? was an inquiry made even of the Master. In the present case there are ample materials for a full and distinct portraiture of Dr. Green's whole interior life, as it manifested itself in his daily intercourse with those nearest him, in the innumerable courtesies and graces that distinguish the Christian father, husband, and friend.

His immediate family consisted of his life's companion and two daughters, who all survived him. He had never lost any children. No man could have been more blest in his household. From the first he felt the deepest interest in the education and the spiritual welfare of his daughters. His letters to them, when absent at school, are filled with advice and direction about their studies, and breathe most earnest prayers for their salvation. Though he had them trained in the best schools of the country, he was himself, to a degree not often equaled, their intellectual instructor and their spiritual guide. And he had the unspeakable joy of seeing them both at an early age members of the Presbyterian Church.

It was, indeed, in the sanctuary of home, when surrounded by his family and friends, that Dr. Green's character shone with peculiar lustre. His house was his Eden, and he threw over it the joyous radiance of his own loving nature. His children grew up to be his companions, and he entered into their feelings, sports, and studies with all the tenderness of parental affection. Nothing could exceed the intensity with which he loved them, and the attachment with which he bound them to himself in return. That intense and sacred affection with which, from infancy, he had cherished the memory of his sainted mother, when he became a husband and a father, seemed to be the very type and measure of the feelings which clustered around all the loved ones at home. His studies, his letters, his prayers, all bore witness to the fervor of his love for those whom Providence had committed to his care. Those gentle graces and virtues which in all his intercourse in the wider circles of society made him the agreeable companion and the whole-hearted friend, assumed their intensest glow and wore their most graceful drapery in the home circle, and made him the life and joy of his household.

We may not intrude too far into the sacred sanctuary of domestic life, even to draw a picture of more than usual loveliness. His private letters when from home, to the different members of his family, reveal a tenderness of love, a watchfulness of affection, a deep solicitude for each one's salvation, a skill in counsel, a fidelity to God and truth, and a mature and heavenly wisdom which show their author to be one of the noblest and best of men. One passing glimpse, however, of the home circle and of the loved ones there, we may, without impropriety, give. It is in the descriptive words of an intimate friend who was a frequent visitor at his house during the period of his presidency of Hampden Sidney College, and who thus reveals the interior workings of his heart:—

"For a long time," says Dr. Foote, "I was doubtful which ruled strongest in his heart, the desire of excellence, or the affections: and I am not sure that I ever settled that question. I know that often, very often, he startled me by the strength of both these ruling powers, in a nearness that forbade their separation, even in thought. And then, where in earthly things lay his heart's treasure: where next, after the Lord of Glory, whose love and fear reigned strongest, as I thought—where was the casket of the most precious jewel? In his domestic circle was evidently his greatest joy. And where then? When his daughter just in girlhood glided in, in her simple attire, and modest mien, and artless nature, his eye, cheek, his hand, if not his voice, whatever might be the stage of our discussion, revealed the unutterable fondness of his heart. 'Surely,' I have said to myself, as the vision passed before me like Jesse's son, 'this is the priceless jewel.' Then again, when the little one—there were but two—came in, sometimes toddling carelessly along, sometimes running in glee, and sometimes gravely and carefully imitating her mother's step and air, the inimitable air and manner of loving kindness with which he would bend to her—kiss and raise her to the settee, and listen for a moment if she had any message for him, and drop a word or two—'Oh, there,' I have thought, 'is the little nestling that has gone into the inner treasury.' And then again, when all three were present, the mother and the daughters, the manly complacency with which he looked upon and listened to the wife and mother, there was no doubt she reigned queen in the happy family."

Dr. Green was greatly blest in the chosen companion of his life, and he felt that whatever degree of happiness and success had attended his pathway was largely due to her influence. In hearty sympathy with all his plans and purposes, capable of entering fully into all his views and feelings, and endowed with those attributes of character which win respect and friendship, Mrs. Green not only contributed largely to his influence in every field of his influence, but by taking upon herself the chief burden of all domestic cares and responsibilities, enabled him to accomplish an amount of study and of professional labor which otherwise would have been impossible. The parting tribute of the Baltimore church shows in what loving appreciation she was held as a pastor's wife. And it is on record that in every sphere of his educational labors his home had always been a centre of attraction and of pleasant social intercourse to his students. She delighted in every thing that could gratify his tastes and contribute to his great work. Both at Hampden

Sidney and at Danville her house was the home of young men, often several at once, studying for the ministry, and without the means of self-support; and whatever additional burdens this entailed were cheerfully borne by her for the common good. At Allegheny Seminary, as well as at Hampden Sidney College, students that were sick were taken to their house and kindly nursed until restored to health.

The following little effusion, penned by Dr. Green soon after his marriage, and at a time when he expected to visit Europe unaccompanied by Mrs. Green, reveals the depth and tenderness of feeling with which he contemplated the separation:—

"When on the bounding wave I ride,
Or gaze upon the calm, blue sea,
How sweet to have thee at my side,
And whisper all my thoughts to thee.

"When far from country, friends, and home,
And all that are so dear to me,
In pensive solitude I roam,
How sweet to have one smile from thee.

"But if I still must go alone,
Whene'er my thoughts may wander free,
And evening shades come gathering on
To tell me I may think of thee,

"At sunset, from some Alpine height,
I'll gaze far o'er the western sea,
And proudly think that parting light
Will rise in glory soon on thee.

"And while in distant lands I rove,
Though friends should all forgetful be,
I know that thou wilt faithful prove,
And kindly still remember me.

"And think you I could ever slight
Those fond affections fixed on me?
Or ever cease, by day or night,
To think and speak and dream of thee?

"And when before God's throne on high
I raise my voice and bend my knee,
My fervent prayer, my earnest cry,
My first, my last, shall be for thee."

Twenty-nine years of uninterrupted domestic happiness—during which she had been his helper and his counsellor, sharing every thought and feeling of his heart, the devoted wife and the honored mother—attested the wisdom of his early choice, and illustrated the sacredness of that relation which he thus essayed to describe.

As his daughters grew up, and were separated from him at school, he followed them with his tenderest affections, and his correspondence teemed with lessons of wisdom and experience. "The love of human applause," writes he to one of them, "is essentially an unhealthy stimulus to the human mind. The severe love of truth and knowledge, the calm repose on God, and solemn sense of duty—these are the principles that give at once stimulus and steadiness to all our energies. "Character," writes he to another, "Christian character, is fixed principle, a firm will controlling momentary impulses, self-conquest, victory over self. Character is our own, reputation comes from others. The former is the only sure mode of gaining the latter, and they usually go together. Wit, wealth, beauty, elegance, modesty, kind affections, generous and magnanimous impulses, education, accomplishments, all are of small avail for happiness or usefulness without character."

The letters which were constantly passing between Dr. Green and his loved ones of the home circle, whenever they were separated from one another, are models of ease and elegance, of the most sparkling vivacity, and the deepest spirituality. It was one of the pleasures of his life to hold this correspondence; and he was unhappy if it was long interrupted. It is not necessary to draw largely here from these treasures. It will suffice to present a few brief extracts, simply as illustrations of their style and spirit, showing how he could mingle instruction with his most playful thoughts, and with affectionate tenderness seize every occasion for the inculcation of the great truths of religion. Under date of April 27, 1839, while he was absent at his work in South Hanover Seminary, he closes a letter to his wife at Danville with the following allusion to their first-born daughter, then an infant:—

"But as for that little angel—train her up for God, and dedicate her anew to Him daily: and if she be indeed *very lovely*, stand ready to have her transplanted to her proper place at any moment; for who knows the day or the hour? Let us thus learn to consider God's mercies as loans; and while we rejoice in the blessing, let our exultation be subdued by a consciousness of the uncertainty of all human possessions. I feel it would be a desolation to lose her, an agony to see her suffer; but my love may turn to idolatry. Remember we have transmitted to her a fallen nature, and the elements which form the rainbow may become a thunder-cloud. Nothing but God's grace can save her." As this daughter grew up, one of his letters to her, accompanying a copy of "Mrs. Hemans" which he had bought for her, closes with a quotation which he thus beautifully appropriates—"I have tried to adopt and apply it to my first-born.

" 'I give thee to thy God, the God that gave thee,
A well-spring of deep gladness, to my heart!
And precious as thou art,
And pure as dew of Hermon; He shall have thee,
My own, my beautiful, my undefiled,
And thou shalt be His child.'

Heathen poetry has nothing so touching, or indeed so truly sublime, because heathen life had no feeling like that of a Christian father and mother. Oh! that my J—— and L—— may be his children. You see, my dear daughter, how my pen runs on. I sat down to tell you that I had reached this place, and cannot withhold my feelings from the greatest, best interests of my children. My watch says, almost ten; everybody has retired; and stillness prevails over all the grounds. It is the time for parents to bless their children, and commend them to God—the time for all of us to commit ourselves to our

Father in heaven. May sweet rest, and thoughts of love, and trust in God be yours, my wife and daughters."

In another letter to the same daughter he says—" The love I bear you is beyond expression, and how much my own happiness is involved in the dutiful reception of that love on your part, you cannot *now* understand. Such love is inseparable from a watchful and anxious care, and possibly in my feeble health, I may indulge that anxiety too much. Yet it is a world of danger to the young, to all. Forgiveness is a word that seems too solemn for a mere man to use; and yet, I remember, it is used in that prayer, which our Saviour has taught us—'Forgive us our trespasses as we forgive those that trespass against us.' And be assured that if an earthly father can so freely and joyfully forgive and forget, how much more freely will your Father in heaven forgive and pity. Do not fear then to approach the mercy seat of that eternal love, in comparison with which all human kindness is absolute indifference; and let your confiding faith in your earthly father's love and sympathy, teach you the nature of that filial confidence with which you may come to our Father in heaven. Seek His face, my daughter, and learn how freely Jesus can forgive. Oh, taste and see that the Lord is good. Write me very soon, and believe me, with increased tenderness, your affectionate father."

Many of these letters to his daughters were written on the Sabbath, and introduced with the remark, that while it would be a sinful violation of God's holy day to devote any part of it to worldly business, pleasure, or correspondence, yet it is a sweet and blessed privilege to talk to one another, by tongue or pen, of the goodness of God, the glory of heaven, and the love of that blessed Saviour who on this day rose from the dead, and wrought out our salvation. And in this spirit he wrote many a long letter, filling up the intervals between public preaching, by thus lovingly conversing with his absent children about Jesus and the things of His kingdom.

The following passages are from a letter addressed to both daughters, from the Virginia Springs, in 1850:—

"Improve your voices, my dear children. You cannot take a piano or harp along with you as you travel, but you have a much superior instrument, which may be improved almost without bounds, and is far superior to any stringed or wind instrument of man's invention. This you can always take along for your own entertainment and your friends. Love your home, learn to make it happy to yourselves and your dear mother. There is nothing in this world so sweet and so sacred as home. The thought of it now is worth more to me than all the transient enjoyment of company, and all the glory, even, of this mountain scenery.

"To-morrow is God's holy Sabbath. How will my daughters be employed? Early awake—dressed—cheerfully employed in all the morning duties of the Sabbath? Your father will be engaged in prayer for you—will you pray for yourselves, and for him? that we may be spared to each other long below, and meet again in heaven? You can hardly think of your father as taken from you; yet, my dear children, you must learn to view this as a certain reality. It will only make us love one another more tenderly, and begin our heaven here below. It is now late, and I am glad I have the opportunity of closing my first week in the mountains in talking with you. Let my accounts of you be such as a father loves to hear, and may we meet in peace and health, and long live in love—love to God and one another."

From the letters to Mrs. Green, which abound in expressions of the most tender and devoted affection, we give, in this connection, a single paragraph:—

"You seem to fear that I have some special annoyance—by no means, I have every comfort which a man can have, whose heart is five hundred miles out of his body. I have just received yours of the twelfth, and thank you a thousand times for it. Glad to see you are well and cheerful. Trust in God, for we shall yet praise Him. Is there nothing in signs? The brightest sun, the purest and most bracing atmosphere, the happiest faces all around, seeming to rejoice with me at the news from home? 'Well and busy'—then happy. Thank God and take courage. With a thousand anxieties and a thousand cheerful anticipations blended strangely together, I remain, your ever affectionate

"L. W. Green."

The following beautiful extract is from a letter to his second daughter, written from Danville in 1860:—

"My dear L——: It is now nine o'clock, Sunday night. I am just from the church, and though I have only a few moments, I cannot refrain from dropping a line or two to my own darling daughter. I had laid off a long letter for this afternoon, but the prayer-meeting appointed for three o'clock, at which I was requested to officiate, interfered. The sermon by Dr. Yantis was from a precious text, and well handled: 'Fear not, little flock; it is your Father's good pleasure to give you the kingdom.' I could not but think of my little L—— as a lamb in that flock, and remember the promise of the Good Shepherd, that He will bear the lambs in His bosom. If He bears you, where is the danger? What power can harm you? If on His bosom, how near His heart! How gently softly, tenderly, with His own Almighty arms, and on His own bosom of infinite and eternal love! And then He bears you to a kingdom, beyond all earthly kingdoms, and that even a heavenly! 'And it is the Father's good pleasure.' Who can resist it? It is a part of His own infinite blessedness to save sinners; and there is a good pleasure, not a malignant pleasure as in inflicting misery, but a good, kind, benevolent pleasure—a good pleasure consistent with His holiness, justice, goodness, truth, with all His attributes. All are harmonized, all are magnified and made honorable in the salvation of His people. He can be just and justify the ungodly. Blessed thought—that the same arms of infinite love are stretched out over all the world, and embrace this night my L—— and J—— as well as those at home. Sweet be your rest, my daughter, as you lie there folded in those arms, so gently, so tenderly, so omnipotently, on that bosom so warm in its bleeding love. Good night, my daughter, under the canopy of that 'good pleasure,' and may our last good night on earth be as full of cheerful hope, the precursor of a brighter morning."

To these passages we subjoin one other extract, in a different vein, written to the elder daughter in 1855, while at Hampden Sidney, an illustration of that intellectual cultivation and companionship which existed in the home circle.

"I ran off to hear Everett at Petersburg. An accomplished rhetorician, not a great orator (*sit venia verbo*), nor great man, *me judice*. But he was unwell, and did not do justice to the language or thought. A few magnificent passages no doubt, 'where affection rises into reverence, and reverence melts back into affection,' in our contemplation of Washington. As an orator he lacks vivid emotion and electric power; as a philosopher, profound thought. As a moralist and conservative patriot, his sentiments are beautifully correct and happily expressed. 'But as a work of art, was it not complete and perfect?' said a gentleman to me. Granted, *in a sense*, yet this is my objection. The *summa ars* is *celare artem*. I heard all through the scratch of a polished pen, not the music of the spheres, or any of the sublime voices of nature or of human passion. I saw the graceful step of a Knight of the Garter, or a Lord of the Bedchamber, not the massive form or gigantic stride of a Hercules. The beauty of a garden is not the grandeur of a forest. You can trim a hedge and train a honeysuckle, not the oaks of the forest. A beautiful experiment by Dr. Doremus cannot rival the whole gathered thunders of the tempest and the storm. It is artificial electricity, not lightning and thunderbolts.

"Now is not there a piece of criticism for you? And late at night, too, with the March winds howling around, the great oak at my window now bending sullenly before the storm, then lifting its head as in defiance, and throwing its brawny arms abroad to meet the full fury of its foe; the black gaunt clouds drifting silently over the sky, are driven careering before the tempest, while ever and anon a bright star is seen through the parted clouds, and the deep heaven of heavens beyond, serenely solemn, speaking amidst the voiceless midnight of immensity and eternity, of God and immortality. How strange, that even when we begin in jest, we close in earnest. I meant to amuse myself with Mr. Everett's fondness for the 'stars,' and behold I am running on as one moonstruck. For

"'Ye stars, ye are the poetry of heaven!
And in our aspiration to be great,
We claim a kindred with you; for ye are
A beauty and a mystery, and create
In us such love and reverence from afar,
That fortune, fame, power, life have named themselves a star.'

They that turn many to righteousness shall shine as the stars for ever and ever. But O Lucifer, son of the morning, how art thou fallen! Such genius, such aspirations to be great! Such total ruin to himself and others! A great star fallen upon the waters—burning as it falls—and its name was wormwood—the rivers and fountains became wormwood, and men died of their bitterness.—See *Rev.* viii. 11–13.

"But, my dear, the night is far spent, physically as well as morally, the day is at hand; let us look to Him who is 'the bright and morning star,' that through the tender mercy of our God, the dayspring may visit us from on high. Good night, my daughter, and may our last night on earth, be followed by a glorious morning. Affectionately, YOUR FATHER."

CHAPTER XI.

His Writings.—Unpublished Sermons.—Inaugural Discourses.—Literary and Educational Addresses.—Lectures at the University of Virginia.—Adverse Criticism.—Method of Preparation for the Pulpit.—Estimate of his Preaching by Dr. Brank.—Estimate by Rev. W. G. Craig.—Closing Tribute from a Lady.

THE sermons contained in the present volume are now published for the first time, and of course without the author's revision. Written, as they were, with no view to publication, and prepared, not for the eye of the critic, but for the ear of a popular assembly, they should be judged rather by the impression they were calculated to make on his hearers than by any abstract standard of perfect written composition. Though necessarily incomplete and fragmentary, they yet retain enough of original, striking thought, and enough of the speaker's fire, to be read with interest and profit, especially by those who ever heard the living voice that uttered these magnificent periods. Besides their intrinsic excellence, as containing the grand things of God's salvation, and of man's duty and destiny, they possess the additional value of completely revealing the speaker's own heart and life. They show what he preached and how he preached; the range of his subjects and his method of handling them; what he depended on as the rock of his salvation, and by what principles he aimed to live and die. By his wide circle of friends they will no doubt be welcomed as a noble monument to his excellence.

But, during his life, Dr. Green was called, on special occasions, to deliver quite a number of inaugural discourses and other literary addresses, which were for the most part prepared with much care, and published at the time of their delivery. One of these, his inaugural address at the beginning of his professorship at Allegheny Seminary, has already been referred to as a production of great excellence. His inaugural address on assuming the Presidency of Hampden Sidney College in 1849, written in his characteristic style of boldness and vigor, is a masterly defence of the higher collegiate education, replete with sound, practical sense, and abounding in passages of eloquence and power. In 1842 he delivered an address before the Literary Societies of Jefferson College, Pa., on the Philosophy of History, or the Development of God's Plan in the Progress of Nations, embracing a wide range of thought, and an amount of historical information not often found in a single discourse. In the winter of 1850–1851 he delivered, at the University of Virginia, two lectures on the Harmony of Revelation and Natural Science, with special reference to Geology. This was one of the ablest productions of his pen, and was published, with a series of similar lectures by other prominent ministers, in a volume entitled "Lectures on the Evidences of Christianity." The two lectures occupy more than sixty octavo pages, and were intended to bring into view the different opinions and theories of all the prominent modern writers on the subject. They show a vast range of reading and research in the wide fields of natural science, as well as in the more special province of the theologian. Every page gives evidence of the profound thinker and the man of learning. After his return to Kentucky he delivered two other inaugural discourses, both of which were published—one in 1856, as President of Transylvania University and State Normal School, and the other in 1858, before the Synod of Kentucky, at his inauguration as President of Centre College. In each of these he discusses with great fulness and power, that subject which, above all others, he had mastered—education—primary, collegiate, and professional—in all its relations and bearings. The lofty patriotism breathing through these admirable discourses, their sound, practical principles and noble views, excited much attention at the time, and called forth letters of commendation and encouragement from some of the most distinguished educators in America. One other address, at the dedication of the Caldwell Female Institute in 1861, at Danville, in which he well describes woman's true sphere, education, and mission, completes the list of his published writings.

The inaugural address before the Synod of Kentucky was republished by Dr. Van Rensselaer in *The Home, the School, and the Church*, the year following its delivery, under the title of the "American System of Collegiate Education." The lecture before the University of Virginia was also published in *The Southern Presbyterian Review.* It gave rise to some adverse criticism at the university. Dr. Green delivered it in his usual style of animation, without the use of notes, and was heard with great interest by the students. But he advanced certain opinions which were regarded as erroneous by some of the professors, and as misrepresenting the position of scientific men on the subjects under discussion. He was requested to modify or omit these views before the lecture went to press: but this he declined doing, and the lecture was published as delivered. He had taken much pains in the preparation of it; and, in a private letter to a member of his family after the publication, refers to it in the following terms: "It contains in a popular form the best and largest results of natural science—the views of all the great men about the universe. Its most peculiar view on the certain temporary extinction of suns, and the possible and probable suspension of light in our own sun, was stolen, reprinted in Boston, and circulated over the West and the nation; and the editor who stole and used it as his own, assures me that it has given universal satisfaction at the North; and it was considered by him as fair plunder as any other contribution to human knowledge."

It may serve to illustrate the interest which the lecture, on its delivery, had excited among the students, to state that, at the next commencement following it, he was invited to deliver the annual literary address before the four societies of the university, which service he performed in a style acceptable to all parties.

Some of Dr. Green's sermons were written out with great care, at least so far as he wrote them at all: for his habit was to leave parts of them to extemporaneous delivery. Occasionally heads of discourse would be jotted down ; sometimes a skeleton reduced to writing, but it was seldom carried to the pulpit, and if produced there, proved a source of embarrassment rather than of help. On one of the few occasions toward the latter part of life, in which he ventured to use a manuscript, he was trammeled in the delivery. His usual method was to preach without manuscripts of any kind. His health not being very vigorous, and the manual labor and confinement of writing costing him much pain and exhaustion, he wrote very few discourses of any kind after the first ten years of his ministry. His sermons were thoroughly elaborated in the study by a process of mental composition which gave them the accurate diction and the rich consecutive thought usually attained by writing. And even without this previous preparation, his mind was so full of material, and so gifted with ready invention, that he would gather fresh impulse and new wealth of imagery and illustration from the very inspiration of extemporaneous speaking. To a friend, who was once deploring the loss of productions worthy of being preserved, he replied, that it cost him hardly an effort to recall any train of thought he had once mastered in the order of its development, and that at some day of leisure he purposed to put his reflections on several subjects into permanent shape. Unhappily the gift itself proved fatal to the purpose, and only encouraged his unconquerable aversion to the pen.

But whether written or unwritten his discourses were always delivered with freedom and fire. It was not in his nature to speak without animation. Animation is, indeed, too cold a word to describe his manner. It was with the intensest energy of soul and body. The whole man in every faculty and organ was engaged. His sermon was a great battle for God and truth ; and he fought it with all his might till the conflict ended : and often the victory was won. His sermons were characterized by long and elaborate periods ; but they were constructed with exquisite euphony, and uttered with distinct articulation and telling emphasis. His mind, teeming with the grand themes of revelation—God and a risen Saviour; life, death, and immortality; heaven, hell, and a judgment to come—needed only the stimulus of his own deep emotions to rise to the very highest scores of eloquence and power. On some of these occasions he would retire from the pulpit like a soldier from the battle-field, completely exhausted and faint by the excessive heat of the action. There are people in Kentucky who are accustomed to speak of certain of his sermons, heard long ago, as the greatest they ever heard. In a beautiful and appropriate discourse at his funeral by Rev. Dr. Brank of Lexington, this peculiar fervor of his oratory is referred to. After speaking of his genius and learning, and his many noble excellences as a man, an educator, and a pastor, Dr. Brank remarks: "His preaching was sound, able, fervent, and eloquent, riveting the attention of his hearers with the beauty and splendor of his imagery, and thrilling their hearts with the tenderness and power of his appeals. His style of oratory was peculiar to himself, and impassioned beyond almost any thing I ever witnessed. His mind loved to soar, to rise above the common tracts of thought; his imagery was often magnificent; his soul seemed to be all on fire, and his words came burning from his lips as coals from a furnace. It was not merely his voice that spoke, but his eyes, his lips, his whole countenance; his whole body seemed to be moving, trembling, palpitating in unison with the high thought of his mind, laboring to give it expression, and to urge it upon the attention of his almost breathless hearers. But few men in our church in the development of pulpit oratory have gained a wider or a more deserved reputation."

We have aimed in this imperfect sketch to give at least some approximate conception of the life, labors, and character of a true man of God, whose memory is still fresh in many hearts, and who contributed much to the collegiate and theological education of our country. His praises are in many of our churches, and his name will long be cherished in many households of our land. But his sermons will probably be his best memorial. From the manuscripts extant, they might have been swelled to twice or thrice the number here published. These, however, will be enough to recall him to his friends, and to give others some idea of his excellence. No man could hear him preach even once, or engage in conversation with him—and no one can read these sermons we think, without seeing that he was a thinker, a scholar, and a worker, a man of gentlemanly bearing, of noble impulses, of large views, of warm charity, and loving heart. We have aimed not to eulogize, but to present his life and character in the very light in which he was seen by his friends and contemporaries. The appreciative pen of one who had many opportunities of hearing him, has drawn the following graphic portraiture of his appearance and style, as in his happiest moods he stood in the pulpit and poured forth his masterly discourses :—

"As he spoke, his person, singularly erect and commanding, seemed instinct with life in its supremest emotion; his eye, soft and mellow in repose, would kindle as he summoned his powers for some lofty effort, until it sparkled and shone, and burned like a flame, now lustrous with the light of rapt affection, now gleaming with the glow of some grand imagination, now piercing like an eagle's as he rose to the height of some fiery denunciation of sin or untruthfulness. We never saw such an eye. It was the shining through of the fires that burned within. In its keen and vivid flashes it announced the coming thought; men sat entranced beneath its fascinations, and acknowledged the supremacy of its power. The intellectual force and vivacity of his character sparkled on his face; his voice rose with the demands of the effort; his utterance became rapid, his gestures impassioned, yet the very embodiment of grace, and as his whole mien assumed the commanding posture of an authorized ambassador of the Most High, we have rarely heard a man, either in the pulpit, on the stump, or at the bar, who surpassed him in moving eloquence, or who might lay a better claim to the rank of a master of the human heart. By the structure of his mind, and the delicacy of his physical constitution, he was necessitated, as it were, to those internal processes by which the very depths of his own soul were sounded until its fearful competency for suffering as well as for enjoying was fully realized. As a result, he could tread those remote and mysterious paths which take their dark way through the profounder consciousness of the soul with a steadiness and fearlessness of step rarely equalled; and many instances might be recorded of happy relief afforded to doubt-pressed and storm-swept souls, by the keen and satisfactory analysis of their troubles in his public discourses.

"But this hasty outline would be incomplete, if mention was not made of his exceeding tenderness when he would come to speak of the comfortable things of the Gospel to the children of the covenant. His own views of the unfathomable depths of God's loving heart were the most profound and touching that the writer has ever heard presented, and no man was more successful in drawing souls under the very shadow of his wing. How wonderfully could he speak of the peace of the Gospel! Beautiful is the sea after a storm, with the rays of the sun sparkling upon its dancing waves, or the calm mild beams of the moon sinking into its impenetrable depths. So is the soul after the storm of doubt and passion has passed, settling to rest in the peace of the Gospel. So he was accustomed to speak. It is said that in the last year of his life, his preaching was more and more permeated with this tenderness, as the horrors of civil war broke loose upon his hitherto happy people, causing them to taste the bitterness of life. There never beat a tenderer heart than his; and that thoughtful tenderness to-day brings tears to the eyes of many of his friends who will pass by the claims of his genius, to dwell with subdued affection upon his almost womanly tenderness. One of his most frequent epithets in speaking of Christ was—'the Gentle Saviour;' and yet the fire and passion of his nature was such, that the lightning would gleam from his eye, and the thunder might be heard in his voice."*

It will form an appropriate conclusion to our task, to present one additional testimonial. It is the graceful tribute of a young lady who met Dr. Green, for the first and last time, the year before his death, and here recalls the impressions, agreeable and lasting, made by that passing acquaintance. Nothing perhaps will better illustrate the character of the man, as he appeared even to strangers and in his unofficial and least guarded aspects, than this genial and graphic memorial.

"Some months ago, it chanced that in carelessly turning the leaves of a borrowed volume, I discovered, with deep emotion, the unlooked-for autograph of its former owner, Lewis W. Green. This abrupt presentation of a name which, sacred to memory, had long been embalmed in my heart, overwhelmed me with proud, and now pathetically tender remembrance of my brief acquaintance with its possessor.

"It was my fortune to spend the summer of 1862 at a water-cure in Cleveland, Ohio; and there, some time after my arrival, Dr. Green also repaired for the benefit of his health. As I was passing down the hall the day after he reached the Cure, I was attracted by the sound of an unfamiliar voice leading in the customary morning devotions of the place; and entering the

* From a sketch by the Rev. W. G. Craig, of Keokuk, Iowa.

parlor, I heard from Dr. Green the parable of the Pharisee and the Publican. 'The Pharisee,' said the reader (in a voice whose penetrating sweetness I shall never forget), 'The Pharisee stood and prayed thus with *himself*.' This novel and strikingly suggestive accent on *himself* was the first illustration I received of the doctor's truly characteristic power of impressing his own original and appreciative genius upon the most familiar subjects which he touched; so that not infrequently the useless and unvalued bullion of thought was first prepared for service when freshly conceived by his vigorous mind, and stamped with its own image and superscription. A stranger in the midst of strangers, he unconsciously sat that morning for a portrait, which, like the pictures of Cimabue, was drawn on a golden ground, and though some of its lines have been effaced from my protecting memory by the resistless wear of six long years, yet the original glow by which it was surrounded still sheds its unfading radiance on my heart.

"A form above the middle height, somewhat spare, but well proportioned; an eye as keen as an eagle's, relieved by a mouth as sweet as a child's; a broad and lofty forehead, strongly developed in the regions of ideality and reason; a complexion of that peculiar sallow hue, so often noticed in men who have ever toiled in the intellectual vineyard, the whole face combining with rare attractiveness, vivacity and dignity, sensibility and self-command, delicacy and power. Such is my recollection of Dr. Green as he appeared at that time. His carriage and gestures were distinguished by a native grace and dignity; and the united charms of his manner and conversation I have never known surpassed.

"Affable to all, he appeared that summer to delight especially in the society of intelligent and sprightly women, whom he successfully rivalled in their own peculiar powers of tact, graphic description, and graceful courtesy. The lightning of his wit attracted and electrified his audience, but it was lightning still, and could on needful occasions, repel the claims of presumptuous pride, and paralyze irreverence and folly. Still it ever seemed his choice to conquer by persuasion. The Greeks have enriched their mythology by the fable of Bacchus' invasion of India. The joyous warrior, we are told, in common with his followers, disguised his hostile aims by wreathing his spear with vine leaves and concealing its barb in a cone. The moral of this fantastic tale Dr. Green appeared to have mastered, for none better understood how to adorn his weapons, and by the guise of peace to secure a victory.

"One of his most amiable characteristics was the ready tact with which he understood and attracted the young, a power in most cases sufficiently explained by the habits of his professional life, and the enlarged sympathies of a profound and liberal mind. In instances, however, which his experience had multiplied, and in some of which I am personally cognizant, nothing short of a secret susceptibility of temperament (which needs only to be known, to suggest a resemblance to Lavater's) could account for the ease with which he deciphered the hieroglyphics of feeling, and perused unassisted the past history of a life.

"In general society Dr. Green displayed the most versatile and attractive powers. His discriminating, but pointed satires made him a dangerous foe in a war of wit; while to the attack of others, he presented a burnished shield which not only dazzled the enemy by its lustre, but from its brilliant and polished surface turned aside all missiles; yet in the gayest badinage, he was never betrayed into that meretricious brilliancy which society esteems and cultivates, and which is so pre-eminently superficial and untrue, that it may be assumed with equal ease by men of widely differing merit, as the bubble and the rainbow are embellished by the same colors.

"The personal influence which he soon acquired with all whom he knew at the Cure, I would have deemed incredible had I not myself been a witness. It is a fact, however, which was then generally observed, that cards (which had been before his arrival the usual evening amusement) were almost entirely abandoned during the period of his stay. As a preacher I shall not venture to judge of the full scope of his powers, since the only sermons which I heard from him were extemporaneous efforts, delivered before the inmates of the house and the neighboring families. My memory, however, still vividly retains the impression of his fluent rhetoric, his captivating fancy, and his touchingly tender exhortations. If Dr. Green had been like many clergymen, his conversations might have thrown some further light upon his style as a speaker, but he judiciously disarmed the prejudice of the worldly by simply living his religion, while he confined his preaching to the formality of sermons. The religion, however, with which his soul was interpenetrated and controlled, continually escaped from his tongue in forms more enticing than precepts, as unasked the exquisite perfumes arise from the heart of a flower.

"Thus far I have only described him, as he must have appeared to all, and my heart importunes me in vain for her own individual shrovetide. The homage of memory, the gratitude of years, the awakened aspirations of a life, shall alone attest the reverent and tender affection with which he inspired me."

SERMONS.

L. W. Green

SERMONS.

I.

THE RESURRECTION OF CHRIST.

LUKE, xxiv. 34.—"The Lord is risen indeed."

In the days of Augustus Cæsar appeared a man of singular and extraordinary character. We have no description of his person considered certainly authentic. Yet there is one of very ancient date, which informs us that there was, in his whole countenance and manner, that amazing union of elevation and meekness, of gentleness and dignity, which characterizes all his recorded acts, which painters have, in vain, attempted to transfer to canvas, and for which neither history nor fiction has ever found or formed a parallel.

Born a Jew, he surmounted all the narrow prejudices of his age and nation, and looking abroad, over the face of human society, with a large and liberal survey, took the whole world as his theatre of action, and all of human kind as his brethren. An unlettered peasant, he despised at once the traditions of the elders, the learning of the rabbins, the subtlety of the lawyers, and the authority of the priests; and resolved to reform and revolutionize the whole moral and religious system of his people. Trained in no school of philosophy, yet did he teach a purer and more perfect morality, a more exalted and spiritual religion than could be collected from all the volumes of all the heathen philosophers together. Sprung from an obscure but reputable family, he claimed to be of the royal lineage of David, to be the Messiah of the Jews, the King and Saviour of Israel. Yet when the people welcomed him with enthusiastic acclamations and offered him a crown, he spurned it contemptuously away, and said, the kingdom he had come to establish was not of this world, but a kingdom of peace and holiness and truth.

The period of the world at which he appeared was one of momentous interest. It formed an era in the history of our race. It was the transition state of human society from its ancient to its new and better form. The intellect of man had done its utmost. Philosophy had long since degenerated into scepticism. And centuries of proud reasoning had terminated in universal doubt. The cheering belief in the immortality of the soul, in the existence of one supreme, presiding Deity, in the reality of moral distinctions and moral obligations, had passed away from the creed of the cultivated classes, and was fast losing its hold upon the popular mind. And society, without any fixed principles or authoritative guide, might well be compared to some stately vessel broken loose from her moorings, and cast out in a dark night on a tempestuous ocean, without a pilot to direct her course, or one twinkling star to guide her wanderings. Amidst the darkness and universal gloom, passion seized the helm, and all man's present happiness and virtue were wrecked, along with all his future hopes. Political freedom was lost amidst the universal crash, and the Roman emperors, sensual, beastly, cruel, vindictive, tyrannical, were only incarnations (embodied representations) of the spirit of their age—of that degraded and brutal spirit which, amidst the turmoil of the times, threw the basest of human beings to the helm of human affairs. The annals of the world contained no parallel to the enormities which are recorded by the Jewish and Roman historians of this and the succeeding age.

Such was the condition of the world when, in a distant province of the Roman Empire, in an obscure corner of his native land, this bold and original adventurer conceived and avowed the stupendous design—stupendous in its nature, its extent, its results—of revolutionizing the whole moral, religious, and social condition of the habitable globe, of casting down into the dust its magnificent temples and venerated idols, of overturning its consecrated, time-honored institutions, and, on the ruins of all that was old, erecting a new dominion of his own, whose extent should be bounded only by the limits of the earth, and its duration measured out by the long lapse of her revolving centuries. But if the conception was vast, what shall we say of the accomplishment? All human prejudices were arrayed against him, all earthly power was exerted to oppose his progress. The Jew and the Gentile, the priest, the magistrate, and the people, the emperor, the philosopher, and the fanatic—with learning, eloquence, and argument—the tongue, the pen, and the sword, all were engaged in the war of extermination waged against his system. He fell himself a victim to the power and malice of his foes, yet did his religion survive. It advanced with amazing rapidity from the province of his birth to the city of his death, was diffused over the civilized world, planted itself in the Imperial city, entered the palace and the senate chamber, and soon mounted the throne. And now, after the lapse of eighteen hundred years, the systems of philosophers have passed away and are forgotten. Jerusalem and her magnificent temple are buried in the dust. Rome, the Eternal city, she that was called the *almighty*, the Goth, the Vandal, and Hun have long since trampled under foot. Yet does the faith of the despised peasant of Judea live in the memories and affections of millions of his followers.

Yes, amidst the lapse of ages, the decay of systems, the sack of cities, and the wreck of empires, does she still survive. No decay is stamped upon her front, no dimness beclouds her eye; but there she stands, strong in the vigor of an immortal youth, and her brow is trimmed with the laurels she has won in the many battles of the many generations that are past. She stands, the religion of every civilized nation under heaven, and numbering among her advocates the mightiest names that adorn the annals of our race, that have shed a lustre upon literature and science, upon arts and upon arms—a Newton, a Bacon, a Locke, an Addison, a Boyle, and last, though not least, the soldier, the patriot, the statesman, the admiration of all nations and the father of his own, the immortal Washington.

But if the events of his life were wonderful, still more astonishing were the circumstances that attended, that preceded and followed his death. And we propose to present this day before you a portion of that evidence, which leads us to believe that the faith of eighteen centuries is not founded on a fable; but that the "Lord is risen indeed." And, surely, if there be in all history a single page, which for its singularity and importance deserves the serious and scrutinizing investigation of every reflecting man, it is that which records the strange event that formed the turning point in the faith of nations, and still continues to influence so extensively the whole moral, social, and civil condition and destiny of our race.

We remark, 1st. That he foretold his own death, the time, place, circumstances, and results; and promised his disciples that he would rise again, and thus vindicate his claims as a teacher sent from God.

So numerous and so various are these predictions, that the only difficulty lies in selecting from them all such as shall appear most striking. They were delivered in public and in private, before friends and foes, at distant intervals of time, and under every variety of circumstances. Now they are suggested by a hint or an allusion, now casually introduced into conversation upon some other subject, now formally stated and explained for the instruction of his disciples. As he stood in the temple, and the Jews asked for a sign, he said, "Destroy this temple, and in three days I will raise it up again;" and again, "No sign shall be given to this generation but the sign of Jonas, the prophet, for as Jonas was three days and nights in the whale's belly, so shall the Son of man be three days and nights in the bowels of the earth." (John, ii. 19; Matt. xii. 40.) Again, descending from the mount of transfiguration, "he charged his disciples to tell no man what they had seen till the Son of man was risen from the dead." Again (Matt. xvi. 21), it is said, "From this time forth began Jesus"—clearly indicating something habitual—"to show unto his disciples how that he *must* go up to Jerusalem and suffer many things of the chief priests and scribes and be killed, and *be raised again the third day*." In Luke, xiii. 33, he says distinctly, that he would die at Jerusalem, "for it is impossible that a prophet perish out of Jerusalem." Still more minutely do we find all the prominent circumstances of his death predicted in Matt. xx. 17-19: "And Jesus going up to Jerusalem took his disciples apart, and said unto them, Behold, we go up to Jerusalem; and the Son of man shall be betrayed unto the chief priests and unto the scribes, and they shall condemn him to death, and shall deliver him to the Gentiles to mock and to scourge and to crucify him: and the third day he shall rise again."

Observe how many circumstances are here minutely specified: 1st, That he should not be seized openly, as he taught in the temple, but should be betrayed; 2d, Not to the Romans, who were to condemn and execute him, but to the priests and scribes; 3d, He was to be delivered to the Gentiles, and not stoned by the Jews, as their law required in every case of blasphemy; 4th, To be mocked and scourged; 5th, To be crucified, contrary to all the Jewish customs; and 6th, To be condemned by the Jews, though executed by the Gentiles; they were to try and condemn him first for blasphemy, and then prosecute him on a charge of treason and sedition before the Roman governor.

Now it was natural to expect that death would terminate his career, and that the doctrines of this crucified malefactor would soon become extinct. Such was the hope of his enemies, and such the fear of his former friends. But the eye before which all time lies equally revealed, beheld, in the distant future, a far different prospect. He predicted that the very means employed for his disgrace and ruin, would only redound to his glory, and multiply incalculably, through all ages, the number of his followers. Just before his death he exclaimed, "The hour is come that the Son of man should be glorified;" and again, "And I, if I be lifted up [on the cross], will draw *all men* unto me;" "Verily I say unto you, except a grain of wheat fall into the ground and die, it abideth alone; but if it die, it bringeth forth much fruit;" thus, by a beautiful analogy, pointing forward to that glorious harvest which should spring up from his grave and bring forth fruit unto eternal life.

But it is useless to multiply quotations. Those who have even only a general and superficial acquaintance with the New Testament, cannot fail to remember that his own death and resurrection were not only the subject of frequent conversation, from the commencement to the close of his ministry, but that they were openly avowed by him as the very end and object of his existence—the great purpose for which he came into the world. He was introduced by John the Baptist at first as "the Lamb of God that taketh [or beareth] away the sin of the world;" and the last hours of his intercourse with his disciples were spent in celebrating a most affecting memorial of his approaching death and sufferings, in which he represents his "blood as shed for the remission of sins." The prophet Isaiah had long before predicted of the Messiah that he should be "brought as a lamb to the slaughter," that he should bear our sins, be wounded for our iniquities, and bruised for our transgressions. To this the Baptist referred when he pointed to the Saviour and said, "Behold the Lamb of God that beareth the sins of the world." And to this the Saviour undoubtedly alludes in the solemn language of the final supper. Indeed, his own death forms an *essential* and *inseparable* part of his religious system. It is not only interwoven with the other doctrines of that system, but it is the foundation of them all. It is the very substance and essence of his whole doctrine—the grand peculiarity which distinguishes it from every other. Without the propitiatory death, and sufferings, and resurrection of the Saviour, in what would Christianity differ from any other enlightened system of morality? If, then, this extraordinary person had any plan at all, his own death and resurrection formed an essential part—nay, were the very centre and substance of that plan.

Now this is the point of our argument. We humbly conceive

that this fact is altogether inexplicable on any possible theory of the Saviour's character, except the Christian theory. We care not what hypothesis you adopt—whether you consider him an ardent enthusiast who really believed himself divinely commissioned from on high; or an artful impostor, endeavoring to delude others for his aggrandizement; or a wise and benevolent man, elevated above the prejudices of his Jewish faith, yet conforming to them all as for the benefit of others, practising a species of pious fraud on the community, whose welfare he sincerely desired to promote. On either hypothesis the facts are equally inexplicable. Now we do not feel disposed to deny or conceal the fact, that there was much in the circumstances and the spirit of the times well calculated to excite the imagination and stimulate the passions of an ardent enthusiast. We learn from various sources, from Josephus and Tacitus and Suetonius, that there existed then, and from Virgil and Cicero that there existed some time before, a universal expectation of some mighty prince, who, issuing from Syria or Judea, was to subdue the world. Such a conqueror the Jew expected to behold in the person of the long-looked-for and predicted Messiah; and accordingly of the many enthusiasts or impostors who assumed that character in the latter days of the Jewish commonwealth, we are informed by Josephus that there was not one who did not deceive himself, or attempt to impose on others, with the vain promise of divine interposition, for the purpose of temporal deliverance and worldly glory for his chosen people. Under such enthusiasts the Jews were ever ready to enlist by hundreds and thousands to fight the battles of the Lord. And so strong was their confidence in the expected deliverance for Israel, that even in Jerusalem's last extremity they followed one of these enthusiasts, who promised them deliverance in the temple, and six thousand perished miserably in the flames that consumed it.

Now, if Christ had been such an enthusiast, he must have partaken of the spirit of the age; he would have dreamed of victory and glory, of temporal deliverance for Israel, of a wide, extended dominion over the heathen. To break the Roman yoke from off the neck of the nations, and bear the lion of the tribe of Judah aloft over the Roman eagle, would have been an enterprise congenial with such a temper. But surely, of all conceivable events, an ignominious and painful death for himself, the cowardly flight and cruel sufferings of his disciples, would have had fewer attractions for such an imagination. That would be indeed a strange enthusiasm which, during a whole life-time, could regale itself most enthusiastically with the delicious anticipation of torture and disgrace, which should make this the object of all its efforts, the consummation of all its desires.

But perhaps he was an impostor? Neither will this hypothesis agree with the acknowledged facts of the case. An impostor endeavors to impose a falsehood upon others for the purpose of promoting some selfish object of his own. Now, was it ever known, is it even conceivable, that any man should coolly and deliberately devise a system of which his own death—violent, excruciating, disgraceful—was to be the prominent part, the very centre and consummation of the whole? We say that in all his labors and exertions there must be some object. But did any man ever employ his whole life in deliberately devising his own death and disgrace? Again, whatever was his scheme, he must have wished it to succeed, and could never voluntarily have placed its success upon an issue which he must have known would unmask his imposture, expose and explode the whole. For the sake of illustration, suppose there were some strange impostor here, endeavoring to palm some new system on our belief, and we should propose to him, deliberately to suffer death, and then promise, that if he would rise again we would embrace his system. What impostor would accept such a proposition? Yet this is the very proposition which the Saviour again and again presented to the Jews. If, then, he was an impostor, he deliberately and voluntarily did that which must necessarily unmask his imposture and prevent his success forever. That is, he was an impostor, who, after all, did not desire to impose.

But was he an amiable and benevolent man, wielding the

prejudices of his countrymen for their own improvement, and promoting virtue by a pious fraud? Now we pause not to show how utterly inconsistent this supposition is with our Saviour's whole character, with the high and solemn earnestness of his whole nature. It is by far the most plausible of the three opinions, and that usually adopted now by enlightened and philosophic unbelievers. Yet we must be permitted to say, it involves a moral impossibility. It is not impossible that such a man should die a martyr to his opinions, and thus leave behind the strongest testimony of the sincerity with which he held them; but it is impossible that he should expose all his pretensions to a test which, from its very nature, must inevitably eventuate in his own disgrace, and involve his doctrine and his followers in universal contempt. He must have known that he could not rise. Now observe, if he did not, all was lost. Whatever might have been his purpose, it failed, certainly, necessarily, hopelessly, forever. All the labors and sufferings of his whole life had been in vain; all the good he had already done was lost; all he hoped to do was resigned —nay, voluntarily thrown away on an experiment, which he must have known would fail; and all this without a motive—causelessly, senselessly, madly. Why did he not die as did the great and holy men that had gone before him, a martyr to his principles, and leave his bright example a glorious legacy to coming generations?

If, then, his scheme was not purposely suicidal, if it was no part of his design to thwart his own designs, prosecuted sedulously through his whole life, he could never have proposed a test of the truth of his pretensions which *must* eventuate in their complete and disgraceful overthrow. There remains but one possible opinion, that he really believed his own predictions, and met death voluntarily in the confident expectation that he would rise again; and if he really believed this, his belief must have been founded on the inward consciousness of his own high power to lay down his life and to take it again. Now the minds of men are so differently constituted that we cannot determine how this species of evidence may appear to most of you; but to my own mind it comes with a force of probability amounting almost to a moral demonstration.

2d. He really was crucified and buried, and on the third day his body was missing. These are the admitted facts—admitted by Jew and Gentile. That his body had disappeared from the sepulchre is evident, from the fact that it was not produced by the high priests, when, soon after his death, they were charged with his murder, and his resurrection was boldly proclaimed by St. Peter.

Now, but two suppositions are possible. (We must draw our own conclusions from the facts.) He either rose again by his own power, or his disciples stole him away, and knowingly palmed a falsehood on the world. Against this latter supposition of the infidel much may be urged which appears like solid and convincing argument. Consider the character of the disciples, and the circumstances of the case. It was the feast of the Passover, and the thousands and ten thousands and hundred thousands of the Jewish people (for Josephus informs us that at the feast which preceded the fall of Jerusalem two millions were collected there) were gathered, not only from every corner of Judea, but from every portion of the habitable globe. They had brought with them, as an offering to the Lord, their cattle, their sheep, their goats. The city would not contain them all, and with their families and flocks they were encamped in the suburbs of the city, in the numerous fields, gardens, and vineyards that lay around. It was the full moon, and in the clear atmosphere of an eastern climate, all was as distinctly visible as by the light of day. The sepulchre was situated in one of those gardens that lay under the walls of the city; and around it were spread out the tents of the pilgrims that had come up thither to worship in the holy city. It was sealed with the broad seal of the Roman government. It was guarded by the bold and watchful soldiers of a Roman cohort. For the priests had gone to Pilate and said, "Sir, we remember that this deceiver said, while he was yet alive, After three days I will rise again." (Matt. xxvii. 63.)

Thus carefully was the sepulchre secured. That seal it was

treason to break. To slumber on his watch was death to the Roman soldier. There lay the dead impostor, cold in his sepulchre of stone. It was a bold and dangerous attempt to pass, at dead of night, amidst all those crowded tents, evade the vigilance of a Roman guard, and steal away the body especially committed to their care. Who should roll away the stone? Of sixty soldiers trained to endure all the hardships of war, and accustomed to all the severity of Roman discipline, it was scarcely possible that all should sleep at once. But if all were asleep, how lightly does the soldier slumber at his post, leaning on the top of his spear? How readily does he start at the slightest sound—the bark of a dog from a neighboring tent, the sound of a sheep bell, the lowing of a cow, the rustling of a leaf, the crackling of a stick beneath the cautious and stealthy tread of the nocturnal adventurer? Nay, the sighing of the wind, as it passeth over the neighboring mountains, and among the vines around, might wake that soldier from his stolen repose. And then detection was unavoidable, and on detection death was certain. Now, who are those bold and daring men, skilled in all the stratagems of war, trained to endure its hardships and brave all its dangers, who shall, under the broad moonlight, thread those crowded tents, elude the vigilance of sixty Roman soldiers, and steal away the very object they had been sent to guard? A few poor fishermen. It was but two days ago, and they all fled at the very sight of danger; and the boldest among them, with cursing and swearing, denied that he had ever known this man. Dispirited, chagrined, hopeless, at the death of their leader, would they have dared to attempt so dangerous an enterprise? And if they had attempted it, where was the prospect of success? The supposition is in the highest degree improbable.

But this improbability rises into impossibility on one side, and moral certainty on the other, when we consider, *First.* They had no inducement falsely to assert the resurrection of the Saviour, but every inducement to the contrary. No inducement! If any, what? You say, "a thousand deceptions and impositions daily occur, and so, probably, it was in this case." We have often wondered that men can go to the verge of truth and yet not see it. Men who can pass from individual facts to the principles on which they depend do not see that this is only confirmation of our argument.

We care not whether you take it up historically or philosophically; dive into the bosom of man, or read the record of his acts. It is equally apparent, that amidst all these various deceptions there is one principle at the bottom: that in every case recorded in history, or conceivable by man's mind, deception has originated in some selfish motive,—pride, hatred, interest of some sort. So that expatiate as you please over the whole field of human deception, we accompany you with pleasure, knowing well, that as you accumulate fresh instances of human depravity you only add strength to our argument; and each excursion brings back new materials to build up the bulwarks of our faith, fresh illustrations of the truth—that human acts are guided by human motives; and in the whole catalogue of crimes none can be found without motive, in the gratification of some known desire, passion, or propensity of man.

We challenge any one to say what motive was possible in this case. Mr. Hume endeavors to evade argument. How? By saying, "We are not bound to account for every act of every devotee." Granted. But we do not ask you to enter the mind and say which of various possible motives may have prompted certain acts, but only to show that, of all these motives, some may possibly have operated—that deception was not impossible in this case according to the known laws of human action. We say it *was*. And we return to our question: What motive had they to deceive? Wealth, honor, ease—all these were jeoparded; nay, certainly lost; and it is no dogmatism to say, that where poverty, disgrace, persecution, were certain consequences, the opposite advantages could not be the motive of action.

This leads us to observe, that not only was there a want of motive, but, *secondly*, every motive was in the opposite direction. If Christ rose not, he was not the Messiah, but an impostor, who, grossly, shamefully, deliberately imposed on them and involved them in his own disgrace and persecution. Hope deferred maketh the heart sick; but hope mocked, confidence betrayed, turns into bitterest hatred. And as they thought of their blighted hopes, could they laud their deceiver? Nay, risk life, and all life holds dear, to advance his glory? Transport yourself for a moment to that age and country, become a Jew in hope and in feeling, and tell me whether you could have lauded and loved a Messiah who had thus deceived you and blasted all your hopes of glory?

Hence the disciples were really slow to believe, cautious to examine. One had to thrust his hand into His hands and side. Again. It was to lose all things with the remotest prospect of any gain. Throw yourself into their position. A few individuals, ignorant, unknown, without wealth or connections, or eloquence or power—helpless as children, they had hung upon their leader; timid as women, they had fled at the first approach of danger; and they were now surrounded by priests flushed with victory, and their appetites whetted by the taste of blood, whose malignity slew their leader, and was ready to devour them also. If they had formed a combination to deceive, the very soul and life of the conspiracy was gone. If deceived themselves before, the delusion had vanished at his death. Whatever might have been their scheme, that which was dangerous before had now become desperate. The work of destruction once begun would certainly go on. They who cursed and crucified the living and wonder-working prophet, would scarcely worship the crucified malefactor. The exaltation which the Jew expected for his Messiah was to a throne of princely dominion, not to a cross between two thieves. To those who know the inveteracy of early prejudices, the bitterness of religious fanaticism, the desolating fury of that fiery zeal which thinks to do God service by slaughtering his creatures, it is scarcely necessary to remark, that defenceless followers of a crucified leader could hope for safety only in retirement and silence; and to renew his claims was to brave persecution and death in their most horrid forms.

But perhaps they expected a better reception by the world. No. Their prophetic master had foretold distinctly the extent and kind of their sufferings. Yet with these consequences full before them, the very men who had abandoned him in dismay when alive dared all danger in attestation of his resurrection. The fury of the mob, the power and malice of the priests, were unheeded, and they went forth proclaiming him "Lord of Life and Glory" in the streets, in the temple, before the Sanhedrim. They were beaten, and thanked God for the honor. When imprisoned, the jail resounded with their songs of exultation and praise. And at last a life of ignominy, suffering, danger, incessant toil, was terminated by a death whose horror we shudder to recite. But they rejoiced to endure in testimony of their fidelity to Him, the despised and crucified, the risen and exalted one.

Ah! some strange influence must have issued from that grave thus to give vigor to the nerveless, and manly courage to the timid, and cause him, who just before trembled at a woman's voice, and with cursing and swearing denied his Lord, now boldly to teach in the temple, and fearlessly denounce the high priests in their own Sanhedrim. Now what was to be gained, let me ask, by such a procedure? Much, if stripes and imprisonment and persecution and universal hatred and derision be indeed a gain. And what was to be lost? Nothing, if property and character and life be of no value. But if they suffered much from the bigotry of their own countrymen, they endured still more from the fierce intolerance of the heathen. Christ foretold this, St. Paul said, "In every city persecution and bonds await me." And the Acts of the Apostles is but the record of the labors and sufferings of the Apostles. But we need not refer to Christian histories; enough is related by heathen writers. We are informed by Tacitus that *thirty years* after the death of Christ, a vast multitude of Christians were in Rome, and suffered persecution. And the philosophic historian remarks, that, though Nero's charge was false, they were "a pernicious superstition, and deserved the severest punishment." Pliny and Trajan, the most amiable of philosophers and best of emperors, agreed that the Christians ought to be punished, at any rate, for their obstinacy in adhering to their faith. What, then, had they to expect from the malice of interested priests and a fanatical populace? Ten persecutions by imperial authority, bloody and desolating, followed, while the hatred of the heathen populace was perpetual and universal. Suetonius, Juvenal, Martial, all confirm the same.

Since such was the spirit of Jew and Gentile, and such the sufferings they endured voluntarily, we may surely say, that in attesting the resurrection of Christ they lost all earthly good, without the slightest prospect or possibility of earthly gain. Now we make bold to say, that it is not only in the highest degree improbable, but absolutely impossible, that men should thus expose themselves to the certainty of utter ruin, in support of a known falsehood, which they, after all, have no interest to support. It supposes the utter subversion of all the principles of our nature. It is not only impossible, but self-contradictory to assert, that any human being would thus act, not only without any motive, but against all motives. This would be conclusive from the case of one person. But the argument acquires (if possible) additional *cumulative* strength, when we remember the numbers engaged in this supposed conspiracy to deceive the world—twelve, one hundred and twenty, five hundred; many of whom, if not all, must have known the deception; and any one of whom, at any time, might have gained, not mere exemption, but rich rewards, by exposing the fraud. Yet no bribery could ever buy the secret, no skill detect it, no torture wring it out. And though many were thus forced to renounce the Saviour, none ever dreamed of exposing what did not exist to be exposed.

It is easy to conceive the value which would be attached by Jewish or heathen priests to a secret which would crush at once this new and growing sect. Even supposing a combination to have been formed with the vain hope of personal advantage, it must have soon appeared how hopeless was the enterprise, and the bond of mutual interest which bound them being broken, they who began with deceiving the world would certainly have ended with betraying one another. The argument then is cumulative. "Honor among robbers," may be alleged in reply. But this confirms our argument. It is only a sense of common interest. And thus, if you look on society on every side, the highest and lowest, you will find but two levers which move all things—interest and moral sense. But every principle of self interest was against the Apostles' course. They must then have been guided by moral principle. Here, then, we plant ourselves, and think our position impregnable, and say, that without an utter and inconceivable subversion of all the principles of human belief in ourselves, and of human conduct in others, it is impossible to doubt the sincerity and truth of their testimony to the resurrection of Christ.

II.

THE SIN AND FOLLY OF ATHEISM.

PSALM liii. 1.—"The fool hath said in his heart, There is no God."

IN nothing does the difference more strikingly appear between the truth of God and the opinions of men, than in the comparative estimate which they make of the wisdom and folly of human character and conduct. He is the wise man, according to the maxims of this world's philosophy, who sagaciously devises and vigorously executes some scheme of secular aggrandizement—who, whether he aims at distinction or at wealth, coolly and comprehensively surveys the various causes which may promote or thwart his interests, and, neglecting all secondary objects, skilfully employs his own resources and dexterously guides the feelings and passions of men around him, to promote the one great object of his wishes and his efforts. And it is easy to perceive, when such an individual mingles in the common crowd of his fellow-citizens, from the respectful deference with which his opinion is always asked, and the close attention with which, like the response of an oracle, the reply is listened to, that he has closely marked the course of trade, or diligently studied the passions of men, or has successfully applied his observations to the extension of his fortune or his fame.

Or perhaps his mind has moved in a wider circle and comprehended larger interests. The sagacity which might have advanced his personal wealth or ambition, may be employed about the interests of his neighborhood, or, taking a still wider range, may embrace, in its capacious grasp, the interests of a state or an empire. He may have read all history and studied all philosophy. He may be deeply versed in the science of government and human nature, and be intimately acquainted with the present relations and conflicting interests of the most distant countries. He may bring light from the past to shine upon the present and illumine the future, and in the darkest hours of a nation's peril this pilot of the state may guide the vessel safely through a stormy sea, till she reaches the destined port and swings securely from her moorings. And it is in just such a case as this, when the greatest of earthly efforts has accomplished the greatest of earthly objects, and obtained the greatest of earthly rewards, that the difference most manifestly appears between the wisdom of this world and that which cometh from above. The name of a successful statesman is upon every tongue, and the praise of his wisdom is proclaimed by every voice; and as he is charioted along in splendor, the opening crowd joyfully greet his approach, and man presses close upon his neighbor, that he may hear the accents of his lips, or exhibit some testimony of his cordial admiration.

And yet, in the midst of all this admiration from man, there may be that in the character and conduct of this universal favorite which stamps upon him, in the eye of God, marks of the most egregious folly. And, even as he would look with contemptuous disapprobation upon the contracted views of some simple peasant, whose thoughts all centring on the present moment and the present spot, never look onward to the future interests of a wide-spread nation, thus may He, who sitteth in presiding dignity over all worlds and comprehendeth eternity at a glance, laugh to scorn the imaginary wisdom of the man whose mind never ventured away from earth to hold communion with heaven, whose views are limited to a few short years of a fleeting and uncertain pilgrimage, who neglects his best and highest interests for the sake of a temporary gratification, who is wise for time but not for eternity. Of such a man, however exalted in station, however ennobled by birth, however adorned wlth learning, the Bible says he is a fool. The fool, then, who is spoken of in the text, is not the man who reasons feebly and acts injudiciously in the common affairs of life, but he who neglects the one thing needful, who has not the beginning of wisdom, which is the fear of the Lord. Of such it is said—of every sinner it is said—that he hath said in his heart, There is no God.

I can see neither necessity nor propriety for the criticism which would change the translation and make it read, The fool hath said in his heart [I wish] no God. To say in the heart, to believe with the heart, to love with the heart, indicate the reality of the internal feeling in opposition to the external profession. The doctrine seems then to be simply this: the sinner—the fool—every sinner, whatever may be his verbal profession, does, in reality, say in his heart, does in his soul cherish the belief, the hope, that there is no God. And it is this hope, this secret, almost unconscious impression, which emboldens him in sin. And this is the doctrine that we shall endeavor to confirm, to illustrate, to enforce, and to apply to-day.

There are some who say not only in thought, but in their words, There is no God. There are some who can open their eyes upon this fair and beautiful world which God has made, can enjoy the rich blessings of his hand, and even riot upon his bounties; can look abroad with admiring gaze upon the vastness and magnificence of this great creation, beholding everywhere the traces of boundless wisdom and benevolence; and yet can turn away from this grand and glorious exhibition with their heart untouched and their mind unexpanded, and say, with fearless hardihood, There is no God. They see everywhere innumerable traces of design, but deny the existence of a designer. All nature teems with life and happiness and joy, yet they deny the existence of a living cause of all this happiness. All without is beauty to the eye, and music to the ear; and all within is admirably adapted to receive delight from external nature. It is but to look and all is loveliness; it is but to listen, and all is melody. He enters upon a world which is already fitted up like a great mansion to receive an expected guest, who is likewise exquisitely adapted to occupy the mansion prepared for his residence. The air which surrounds him is just fitted to expand his lungs and to communicate the principle of life and heat to his flowing blood. The earth on which he treads is just suited to produce food, which his system is just suited to digest and to carry through the intricate machinery of tubes and canals to every part of the body, giving flesh to the muscles, hardness to the bones, sensibility to the nerves, and incessant, never-sleeping energy to the beating heart. Yet he denies the existence of a power which could create this mysterious dwelling-place, and so harmoniously adapt, in every part, the living inhabitant to his earthly habitation. There are those whom God has richly endowed with the gifts of nature and the advantages of fortune, who employ the high capacities of their nature against the author of these blessings, who reason shrewdly and argue gravely to prove there is no God ; who think, by the ingenious array of logical syllogisms, to overthrow the government of the eternal God, and, by a pointed sarcasm or an ingenious witticism, hope to cast the thunderer from his throne. But he that sitteth in the heavens laugheth them to scorn; the Almighty holdeth them in perfect derision.

Now, we are accustomed to look on the atheist as a monster of iniquity, and few of us can feel the slightest sympathy with one who openly denies and contemns the existence and attributes of God. But it is one of the strangest marvels of the human heart, which is a world of iniquity at best, that the very sins which we shudder to name we do not hesitate to commit, the very thoughts and feelings which we would not for the world avow, even to ourselves, we secretly cherish and openly manifest in our daily conduct. And thus it is that while there are very few avowed atheists in the world, there are many real ones; while there are few in word there are many in deed. And the doctrine of our text, if we do not altogether mistake the meaning, is, that a real, deep-seated, practical atheism is at the bottom of all the wickedness of men. Upon the authority of God's word, and the authority of every man's conscience, we make the charge this day against each sinner, that he is, for every purpose of a real and practical belief, an atheist before God; and we pray you to consider how fearful is your condition if, instead of being almost Christians, as some of you may hope you are, you shall be found to be far from God and hope, and in nothing practically different from the atheist you abhor—if you shall be found, after all your self-gratulation and all your complacency, to be so far from true religion that you have not received, in honest sincerity, the very first elements of religious belief. As for you who plume yourselves upon the purity and elevation of a philosophical deism, while you avowedly reject the revelation of the Bible, what is your condition, if it shall be true of you as well as others, that with all your high pretensions to a pure theology, there is in reality and truth no fear of God before your eyes, no belief of God in your hearts, no service of God in your lives. Is there any value in words without ideas, in professions without practice, in opinions which have no influence upon conduct?

That we may establish the doctrine of the text, and bring home upon every conscience the conviction of its truth, we only ask that we may be permitted to reason on this as on every other subject, from the known laws of human belief, and the observed phenomena of human conduct. Appealing fearlessly to every individual present for the truth of our assertion, we say that the general course of human conduct and the general current of human feeling are much the same as if there were no creator of the universe, or none who cared for the affairs of men. It is a proposition too plain to be doubted, almost too obvious to be advanced in argument, and yet too often forgotten in our reflections, that all the conduct of rational beings is influenced necessarily by their real opinions. You cannot introduce a new truth into the mind without affecting the feelings or influencing the conduct. Let us take an instance which is not our own, and where we can exercise our unbiassed judgment. It was a doctrine of the Epicureans that the gods existed, but that they dwelt apart, in great indolence, regardless of the interests of this lower world. Now, suppose that a new idea could be added to their views of truth, and that instead of a god afar off, reposing in motionless dignity, there had been brought before their view a god of love, of mercy, of active benevolence, ever active and deeply interested in the affairs of men. Is it possible that these new ideas should really be received and adopted by the mind of any man without at all affecting his feelings or his conduct?

Suppose there was a world of intelligent and active beings, like ourselves, professing the same social feelings, the same ardent passions, the same mutual interests, the same mental and physical organization, as ourselves, with no knowledge of a God. We can readily conceive, that there would exist among them, the same pursuits, the same affections, the same play of social sympathies, the same gentle and the same terrible emotions—hatred would burn as fiercely, love would glow as warmly, and the whole machinery of human society would move onward as it does with us, upheld by the play of the natural principles implanted within us to counteract and regulate each other. Law would punish crime and public interests would form a public opinion to control the intercourse of life. The more and less amiable, the more and less respectable would form, as they do with us, divisions of their society. Now, suppose that the knowledge and real belief of a holy and Almighty God were introduced among the inhabitants of this world—would it have no influence upon their feelings and their conduct? Would it not become one element, and a mighty one indeed, of all their actions? Would it be possible to introduce into the minds of intelligent beings a set of ideas entirely different from all they possessed before—ideas relating to objects the most important to their interests, the most elevating in their nature, addressed to their fears and to their hopes, appealing to all their strongest emotions, involving their whole happiness for time and for eternity—without producing any corresponding change in their feelings and conduct? The very supposition is absurd. And why is not this corresponding effect produced upon us? Why do we live and act and feel just as if there were no God in the universe, or as if the knowledge of his existence were concealed from us?

There would be nothing necessary, to change the whole face of human society and the whole current of human affairs, but to bring down upon every human bosom the deep conviction of the existence of God and a true conception of his awful attributes. Could I bring home to your minds this day the presence of the Holy One of Israel, his awful majesty, his infinite purity, his all-embracing greatness, the fierceness of his hot displeasure against sin, the keenness of his searching glance, those eyes which like a flaming fire pass to and fro through the earth, penetrating the hypocrite's disguise, detecting the formalist's heartlessness, and gazing with clear and unimpeded vision on the dark pollutions of the sinner's bosom—could I lift the veil which separates the seen from the unseen, and show you that majestic presence which fills this house, encircles this assembly, pervades each bosom, lays bare each thought and purpose—would it not bring down each proud imagination, subdue each rebellious thought, and bring the mastery of a deep and breathless reverence to bear on every emotion and feeling? But I see a hand you cannot see. I hear a voice you cannot hear. And it is because, having eyes, you see not, having ears, you hear not, understand not, believe not, that you shall die in your sins, O sinner! and where God and Christ are you can never come.

Let us take a few cases out of many which present themselves to our view upon the surface of every-day society, and see whether we may not recognize the same fundamental atheism which is charged by the text against all the sons and daughters of Adam. Let us pass through human society, in all its orders and gradations, and notice the operations of our common nature in each, from him who grovels in its lowest state, to him who shines the wonder and the envy of thousands upon its highest pinnacle. Let us visit the abodes of wretchedness and crime, where the victims of justice, the outcasts of society are reserved for long confinement or for speedy punishment. There lies the chained murderer. He was a man of blood, fierce and fiery passions have burnt deep upon his face the marks of crime. His last crime was perhaps his greatest, and deep remorse now overclouds his brow, while savage and malignant passions send forth gleams of more than anger from his stern eye. When he whetted the knife for his unsuspecting victim, when he tried its temper sportively amidst his hardened comrades, when he spoke of blood, of human blood, and his eye flashed wildly at the thought of his sweet revenge, when he approached with slow and stealthy pace to the appointed spot, and crouched in breathless silence to leap upon his prey, when his dagger gleamed in the twilight and met a brother's heart—did he then believe that there is a God, who ruleth in the heavens and heareth the voice of blood when it crieth from the ground? One believing apprehension of his existence, his greatness, and his presence, would have quelled his angry passion, the upraised dagger would have fallen harmless at his side, and the man of blood, rebuked by the majesty of the Almighty, would have stood abashed and humbled in his sight.

Let us rise one grade in the scale of moral being, and behold the drunkard and the gambler—men who would shudder at the crime of murder and spurn the charge of atheism as a calumny. Is it possible for any man who witnesses their midnight revels, their reckless disregard of all the warnings of conscience, their horrid desecration of the tenderest and most sacred ties, their violation of the most solemn duties and inhuman trampling under feet the most binding obligations—is it possible to believe, that the mind which is the dwelling-place of such desperate passions, and the perpetrator of such horrid crimes, does at the very moment entertain the strong belief, that there is a God who beholds and will reward?

Did he, who won from the infatuated husband the last mite which remained to supply the wants of a dying wife and her perishing children; did he, who to gratify his lust for gaming, reduced his family to beggary and want; did he, who gave himself to be a slave to beastly drunkenness, destroying his own rational powers and involving an innocent family in his disgrace and ruin; did he, who laid his snares for the young and unsuspecting and allured them onward in the same career with himself to the same hopeless destruction—did any of these believe, in their inmost souls, that there is a God, who will take vengeance on iniquity and sin, who will hear the cries of the distressed and afflicted, and will visit on every sinner, with tenfold fury, the recompense due to his transgressions? Could they delight in the sin which they knew was to be so speedily punished? Could they roll, as a sweet morsel under their lips, what they knew would turn to gall and wormwood and deadly poison in the system? No, they have said in their hearts, There is no God. They have said, Who is the Lord, that we should regard him? They have said, "He is altogether such a one as ourselves." "He doth not observe, he doth not consider." And because sentence against an evil work is not executed speedily, they have asked, Where is the promise of his coming? and their hearts have been fully set within them to do evil.

Even among those whom the amiable and courtly moralist is most disposed to treat with kindness and with deference, who move in the walks of refined and elevated society, and by the gentleness of their manners, and the cheerfulness of their spirits, cast a life and buoyancy over all around them—may there not be found, with all their amiable traits, a carelessness of God, an indifference to his favor, which carries home upon them too the charge of atheism in the sight of God. Behold the young man, as he enters upon life, panting for distinction, keen in his pursuit of knowledge, or his love of pleasure. The bloom of health is upon his cheek, the buoyancy of youth is in his spirits, the frank and unsuspecting confidence of youth is developed in all his movements. He commends himself to the approbation of man, for he abounds in all those qualities which are useful and agreeable in human society. But we ask if, amidst all this anxiety and effort to commend himself to man, he has one single anxiety, makes one single effort, to commend himself to God? Would his conduct be at all different, would not his feelings be the same, if the name of God were erased from his memory, and the notion of God blotted out from his understanding, as the thought of God undoubtedly is from the whole current of his reflections?

We know not a more engaging spectacle than that alluded to before, unless it may be that of one who has just passed the tempestuous season of his youth and escaped the shipwreck of the passions, who retains all the ardor of youth without its violence, all the sensibility of passion without its wild excesses, whose feelings have been regulated by experience and not destroyed, who has mellowed into ripeness without losing the freshness and fragrance of his first young emotions. Now, we care not how highly you exalt such a character as this, and cast around him the dazzling drapery of a thousand virtues which exist only in the imagination of his warm admirers—we are willing to admit the truth of all your fancy dreams; nay, so satisfied do we feel of the perfect certainty of our position, we would lend our feeble aid, if necessary, to fill up the outline your fancy has already sketched. Let his bosom be the home of the gentlest and loftiest emotions, and over all his intercourse with men let there be diffused the charm of a winning gracefulness which, flowing unstudied from the heart, reaches the hearts of all, and gathers to itself a still higher tribute than that of admiration, even the unbought affections of all around him—the purest of patriots, the firmest and truest of friends, the tenderest of parents, the kindest among all his acquaintance. Let him unite, in his single person, all those public and private excellencies which men admire and exhibit to the world—the fairest specimen that has yet been seen of our fallen nature. Yet against this man so endowed by nature, so improved by education, so enthroned in the hearts of those around him, so encircled with the halo of those virtues which men admire, do we bring the same sweeping charge, as against others, of utter alienation from God, and a practical renunciation of his existence and his government. Nor can we at all perceive how, if the whole population of our globe were composed of such individuals, it would at all affect the truth of our position. The possession of certain relative and social feelings toward men, which we admit, does not certainly prove the existence of certain other feelings toward God.

The inhabitants of a State might cast off the authority of our Union, or a distant province might reject the dominion of an emperor, and yet, amidst the very leaders of this rebellion, there might be exercised all those relative and social feelings to which we have alluded. There might be a chivalry which defied all danger, an honor that was never tarnished, a patience that endured every privation and labor and suffering, a high enthusiasm which endeared to all the inhabitants of their province and their state; and yet toward the government against which they have rebelled there is certainly no feeling of regard, no recognition of its authority. And even so may there be all these various exhibitions of what is amiable and agreeable and admirable among men, while there is no recognition of God whatever.

I could point you to the metropolis of a polished nation where education and fashion have combined to cast over female society a vivacity, a brilliancy, and a charm, not elsewhere known; and yet in the most polished circles of that gay metropolis the doctrines of atheism are taught by female lips, and the astonished foreigner is told that he is still in the shackles of priestly domination, and that his reverence for Deity is the last relic of an exploded superstition. Now we ask you if all the vivacity of her conversation, all the gracefulness of her movements, all the bright intelligence of her sparkling eye, will at all disprove the assertion of her lips? And does she not stand before you by her own mouth, a self-convicted atheist? But which carries with it the greatest weight—the conduct, or the language? And those two gay and thoughtless devotees of fashion and of pleasure, who circle side by side in the maze of the dance, and dwell, with wrapt and senseless admiration on the splendors of the theatre, and, in every other way that human folly has devised, endeavor to waste together the day of their probation—we say not, that there is no difference between them, but we say that it is rather nominal than real, that it is more in word than in reality: and we appeal to your own sober reason to decide, whether, if the difference be important, it be not all in favor of that one who, denying altogether the Divine existence, treats the whole as a delusion, and against her who professing to believe it, as the most solemn and important truth which has ever burst upon the human mind to enlighten and exalt it, yet treats it all as the idlest superstition, gives it no place in her thoughts, no hold on her affections, no influence on her conduct, and thus adds to the folly of atheism, and the folly of worldliness, the guilt of hypocrisy.

And here we would turn aside for a moment to notice that charge which is so often brought against the professors of Christianity—that they are the exclusive hypocrites of the day, and that, though there may be something of virtue in the church, in it especially is found an abounding vice, which, by its meanness, casts all others in the shade. Now to all that infidels or worldly men may say against the inconsistency of many professing Christians, we yield at once our most hearty and unqualified assent, and we say let hypocrisy die the death, whether it be transfixed by the brandished spear of truth, or perish under the poisoned arrows of a malignant infidel. And to the infidelity of our own and other times we must yield this passing homage, that its sarcasm and its petulance have often aided the cause of truth and helped to weed out many errors in doctrine and in practice, that it may aspire to this dignity in common with other beasts of prey, that it lives by feeding on vermin more noxious than itself. But not only would we root out hypocrisy from the church, we would also banish it, if possible, from the world. And therefore would we allude to a species of hypocrisy universally prevalent among worldly men, which, to the eye of impartial observation, wears a still more revolting aspect than any that is witnessed among professed Christians. There are those who deride the revelation of God's truth as a feeble and idle fabrication, and view the believers in its doctrines as ignorant and misguided zealots. They assume the air of superior wisdom, and assert the possession of a higher, purer, and more philosophical theology. To them the book of nature is transparent on every page. All the mystery which is thrown over the dealings and character of the universal Father is dissipated by that clearer light which comes to them from the skies, and chases away from their minds the darkness and the mists of a gloomy superstition. However it may be with others, they, at least, are privileged to walk in the clear sunshine, to breathe the pure air of a more exalted region, to expatiate in the freeness of their untrammelled spirits over every field of large and elevating thought.

Now, to such we would only say, you who have so much more worthy and exalted views of the Creator's character should certainly be, of all men, the most profound in your reverence, the most ardent in your affection, the most faithful in your obedience, the most unwearied in your service, the most submissive to his dispensations, the most frequently engaged in holy contemplation of his character, and wrapt in humble and delightful admiration of his glorious perfections. To you the motives are still stronger than to any other for rising superior to all sensual pleasures, and all selfish interests, and, borne upward as you are on stronger pinions, you well might soar to higher flights of virtuous exertion. But, alas, for the philosophy of Deism, the very mention of what you should be is the bitterest of sarcasms upon what you are. The very language of devotion is unknown in your vocabulary, the habit of meditation upon God is the farthest of all others from your practice. Among all your other busy and restless thoughts, the thought of God seldom ever mingles, or, if it come at all, is hastily expelled as an unwelcome intruder. The name of God seldom falls from your lips; when it does, it is only that its sacredness may be profaned by some horrid imprecation, or some trivial oath. When, in the society of some Christian friends, the name of God is mentioned with reverence, and his praises meekly spoken, does it not sound in your ears like the strange language of some unknown land? And would it not appear the dreariest of all possible conditions to be confined for life to society such as this, with which you have no community of thought or sympathy of feeling? And now we ask you whether, in the whole universe of God, there can possibly be found a more palpable and shameful contradiction than that which is exhibited in the conduct of the man who has so much regard for God in words and so little in reality, who professes so much love and admiration for a being of whom he seldom or never thinks, who acknowledges a benefactor and yet feels no gratitude, has a father and exhibits no filial affection, a sovereign and shows no obedience, who boasts of all the light of day and yet has all the chilliness of night, and the beautiful display of all his boasted and philosophical religion is only the frost-work which has grown up amid the coldness of his own abstracted speculations, and disappears before the heat of passion, or is trampled under foot in the bustle and haste of worldly business, and the conflict of worldly interests?

And now, having endeavored to illustrate and to confirm, by various examples, the doctrine of our text, we would direct your attention to one important deduction that may be drawn from the whole, namely, the importance and reasonableness of the doctrine of justification by faith. It has been for centuries the habit of superficial reasoners to deride the doctrine of justification by faith, and to dwell, even to nauseousness, on the indifference of human opinions, and the absurdity of judging man by his internal principles instead of his outward conduct. Now in opposition to all such declarations, we might plead, did we need aid of authority to sustain us, the opinion of the most acute philosopher and most eloquent historian of our age —a man who stood alike pre-eminent at the bar, in the senate, and in the literary circles of Great Britain—the late accomplished Sir James Mackintosh. Speaking of the doctrine of justification by faith, as avowed and defended by Luther, and especially his doctrine "that men are not made righteous by performing actions externally good, but must have righteous principles in the first place, and then they will not fail to perform virtuous actions," he calls it "the principle which is the basis of all ethical judgment, by the power of which he struck a mortal blow at superstition"—a proposition equally certain and sublime—the basis of all pure ethics—the cement of the eternal alliance between morality and religion. It is founded, indeed, on a profound and thorough knowledge of the human heart, and the secret springs of human actions.

As a man thinketh in his heart so is he. His character is always decided by his prevailing views and opinions. Place before you the finest possible specimen of human nature, a man the most energetic in his conduct, the most vivid in his emotions, and deprive him one by one of all his opinions; let him cease to believe that there is kindness in the smile which beams upon him from the countenance of his friend, that there is heat in the fire upon his hearth, that there is nourishment in the food upon his table, and do you not perceive that as you strip him gradually of all his opinions and belief, you likewise divest him of all his feelings and principles of action, till he stands at last before you a statue, mute, motionless, unfeeling, with all the organs of speech, and all the capacities for vigorous action and strong emotion, but dormant now and undeveloped for want of their natural and appropriate stimuli. Now, suppose you wished to arouse this breathing statue from the listless apathy into which he had sunk, would you not just seek to open the only avenue by which feeling could reach the heart, and which had just been closed—the avenue of an assured belief of all the truths which he had doubted? And as each new truth flashed home upon his mind, would you not expect to see the glow of a new feeling on his cheek, and the movement of a new impulse on his whole frame, and would not this harp of a thousand strings vibrate harmoniously to every ray of light that beamed in upon it from without, as did that fabled harp of old which, though untouched by human hands, sent back the softest music when touched by the first beams of the rising sun? If then a change must pass upon the human heart before we can be saved, if we be altogether dead in sins as the Bible represents us, if we need the introduction of some new affections and dispositions into our characters, it must be accomplished through the introduction of some new truth, and this truth can neither enter into the mind or influence the feelings or character or conduct without being believed.

There are two problems to be solved, and only two, with respect to man's salvation. First, to make it consistent with God's law. And this has been done by the substitution and death of the Saviour. The second, to make it consistent with man's character, and this can only be solved as it is done in the Bible. He can only be sanctified by faith or an honest belief of the truth, unless indeed you can find some other way of promoting moral purity and worth than through the influence of moral truth, or some way for this truth to operate without being received into the mind and cordially believed. If faith were indeed as some conceive, a mere set of notions, having no connection with feeling or action—did the Bible connect the salvation of man with the belief of certain dogmas which have no relation to his happiness or virtue, were not faith an active, living, practical principle that worketh by love and purifieth the heart—then it would all be absurd enough. But since the connection is obvious and indissoluble between the belief of men and their whole character; since no man acts without an object, which he believes to have both existence and value, nor feels but in view of something which he believes deserves the exercise of feeling, we conceive that the doctrine of justification by faith is no absurdity in morals, but is only the particular application of a principle which is universally true. Indeed, the very conception of a religion which did not require the exercise of faith would be a contradiction in terms. It would be a system of belief which was not believed, a system of truths not received as true.

But in vain does the fool say, that there is no God. He is contradicted by all without and all within him, by the whole animated and the whole inanimate creation. Does he commune with his own heart upon his bed, and in the stillness and solitude of night does he seek to hear the still soft voice of conscience? From his inmost spirit there comes a voice which neither hesitates nor doubts, but says with undoubting assurance that there is a God. Does he ask of the wise and good of every age? With united voice they testify to the existence of a God. Does he seek to know the universal opinion of mankind? From the East and from the West, from the North and from the South, from the burning Equator to the frozen Poles, from every savage tribe and every nation of civilized and enlightened men, from every people and kindred under heaven there comes one long and loud response, like the voice of many waters, and the sound of mighty thunder, saying, There is a God that ruleth in the heavens. Does he turn to the works of nature and question them? Nature, through all her provinces has but one answer. The lowly valley with its verdant covering and its garniture of flowers as plainly declares his existence and his greatness as the mountain which lifts its head on high with its mighty forests waving for centuries untouched upon its summit. It is murmured by the rivulet, it is whispered in the breeze, it is thundered on the storm, and when Ocean lifts up his voice on high, and wave calleth unto wave, the roar of his ever-dashing waters is only the deep and majestic chorus to that universal hymn of praise which swells from land and sea, from hill and valley, from the untrodden desert and the cultivated field, by day and by night, unceasingly, to the Omnipotent Creator.

And do not the heavens declare his glory and the firmament show forth his handiwork? Yes, there is a voice which comes to man from those far distant worlds, and they tell him that the energy of Almighty power has not been exhausted on this single world, and that wherever they have travelled, yet in the greatness of their way, as they have swept by other planets and other systems in their dizzy flight, they have ever been guided by an eye that slumbereth not, and upheld by an arm that is never wearied, and that in those regions of immeasurable space which no eye of man has ever reached and no telescope of man has ever brought within the field of human vision—there are the footsteps of the Creator visible, and that over the boundlessness of this unseen and illimitable empire has he poured forth with unsparing hand the riches of a goodness which knows no limit, and manifested the greatness of a power which is infinite and inexhaustible. But regardless of all this concurring testimony of nature, amidst this joyful symphony of all creation, the voice of the atheist is heard, in peevish and querulous accents, murmuring forth : No, there is no God. It is not surprising then that he who denies and contemns the existence and the attributes of God should find little sympathy among the rest of mankind, that he is regarded with unmingled abhorrence, and considered as one of those rare and stupendous monsters of iniquity whom we seldom see, whose very existence, we are often prone, for the honor of our nature, to deny.

Now we have not the slightest wish to lessen in your minds this natural abhorrence for the principles and character of the speculative atheist. Nay, believing as we do that it is both natural and just, we would desire to see it increased and rendered permanent, to see it pass from a mere sentiment to a warm emotion, and from an emotion to a principle of action, extending to atheism of every form, whether exhibited by ourselves or others, avowed by the tongue or by the conduct, or lingering in secret concealment in the recesses of the heart.

III.

WHAT WAS FINISHED IN THE DEATH OF CHRIST.

JOHN, xix. 30.—"He said, It is finished: and bowed his head, and gave up the ghost." (John, iv. 34, xvii. 4; Luke, xii. 50, xviii. 31; Acts, xx. 24; 2 Tim. iv. 7.)

How much of solemn and touching interest is often contained in this brief expression, It is finished! We stand by the bed-side of one endeared to us by a thousand tender recollections of the past, and doubly endeared by the sufferings of the present, and the mournful anticipations of the future—a child of sorrows, lingering through months of tedious disease, quietly, with lamblike resignation, enduring the visitations of a father's hand; and when death, whose slow approach we have long observed, at last seizes the extremities, and, advancing onward a triumphant foe, storms the citadel of the heart, we exclaim, with a melancholy satisfaction, It is finished! The conflict is passed. The struggle at last is over. The suffering spirit is released, and, far above all scenes of earthly sorrow, reposes in the presence of the Lord.

We hear of the death of some benefactor of the race, distinguished by his self-denying labors, his eloquent appeals, his patient sufferings for the benefit of man, and we say, It is finished! The fatherless have lost a friend, the poor a protector, the oppressed an advocate, the world an ornament. He is gone; his loss is irreparable, and hallowed be his memory. But his virtues shall live in the hearts of men, and his blest example be fondly treasured up as a model to admire and to imitate. Some man of ambition, some aspiring politician or successful warrior, passes off from the scene which he had long filled and agitated; and we say again, at last, It is finished! The mighty is fallen; ambition has reached its goal. In the full tide of his success has he been arrested; blasted are all his hopes, frustrated his schemes, "dimmed his bright eye, and curbed his high career." And thus ever, in proportion to the tenderness of our mutual relations, the depth of his sufferings, the nobleness of his nature, the largeness of his plans, and the wonderfulness of his achievements; as he has excited our affection, our sympathy, our gratitude, our admiration or esteem, do we comprehend the full meaning of that expression, It is finished! And it is only when the fond heart gathers up its recollections, and memory recalls the traces of a character at once so tender and so noble—all that he was to us and to others, to our country, to the world, to the past, the present, and the future—that we sink beneath the weight of our emotions; and mournful and startling, as the toll of midnight death-bell in pestilential city, is the sound, It is finished!

But never before were these words so full of meaning as in the mouth of the crucified Redeemer. Never was friendship so ardent as his to mankind. Never was love so tender, designs so large, accomplishment so glorious. His love was a brother's, his compassion a God's; his designs, formed in eternity, embraced two worlds; his victory was over death and hell, over principalities and powers. His throne is exalted far above the heavens, and around it are gathered uncounted millions of those who were redeemed by his love out of every nation and kindred under the whole heavens. We have said there is a fulness of meaning in the language of our text which is found nowhere beside. Do you doubt it? Behold that meek and patient sufferer on the cross, and hear him say with his expiring breath, "Father, forgive them, they know not what they do." Do you doubt it? The blackening heavens roll onward as my witness. Do you doubt it? The bursting rocks thunder it in your ears. Do you doubt it? The dead spring from their graves to rebuke your incredulity, and the trembling centurion unconsciously exclaims, Truly this was the Son of God. Let us then contemplate the words of our text without hoping or attempting to exhaust their full meaning, and inquire,

What was then finished? And we say,

1st. His state of humiliation and suffering was finished.

2d. All that prophecy had predicted, and types had prefigured, and hope had longed for, was accomplished.

3d. The glorious work he had come to do was completely finished.

1st. His state of humiliation and suffering was finished. If we had been informed that a messenger should visit us from heaven, how various would have been our expectations. How different from all these expectations was the actual condition of our Saviour. He took no angelic form, but was made in fashion like a man; he wore no robe of light, but was wrapped in swaddling clothes, and laid in a manger. His first appearance was not in the world's metropolis, but in a distant and subjugated province. His countrymen were a despised and outcast tribe. Of this distant province and this outcast tribe he chose not the most conspicuous city, or the most distinguished relatives. His native town was one of the obscurest villages of Judea, his relatives came of the humblest among the people: a carpenter his reputed father, and his birthplace a stable. The course of his life corresponded to its humble commencement. He was a man of sorrows, and acquainted with grief, despised and rejected of men, and we turned, as it were, our faces from him.

That life which began in poverty was closed in ignominy by a death that was as agonizing as it was disgraceful, the instrument a cross, his companions two thieves. He had left the throne of his glory and come down on an errand of unutterable love. And how was he received? Was he greeted with the loud welcomes of the race he came to save? Did the grateful multitudes gather around him to catch those lessons of wisdom, and to hear those tones of grace and mercy which fell from his lips? They collected, indeed, often around him, at one time to entrap him in his words, at another to feed on his bounty, or to be healed of their diseases. And even when they listened to his teaching, their corrupt and sensual hearts revolted at its pure and exalted spirituality. Their pride rebelled against his just rebukes, their hypocrisy trembled at his keen exposures, and now they exclaimed, This is a hard saying, who can bear it? None. Do not we well say, thou hast a devil and art mad? Even they who were the chosen companions of his ministry, whom he had selected from the world to be the depositories of his doctrine, the witnesses of his resurrection, the honored heralds of his great salvation to a guilty race, how slow to comprehend the sublime truths which he revealed, how slow to believe the promises he gave.

There is implanted deep in human nature the yearning desire after human companionship and human sympathy, the felt necessity for the mutual interchange of thoughts and feelings, for hearts that swell with emotion like our own, and minds that can comprehend and appreciate our character, to whom we may communicate our hopes and fears, our plans of usefulness and our views of duty, our sober reasonings and our waking dreams. Nor can we conceive a condition more melancholy than that of him who, elevated too far above those around him in intellect and feeling, seeks in vain for sympathy among all his fellows, and finds that the whole cast of his mind and current of his feelings is irreconcilable with theirs. That his high enthusiasm is, with them, another name for madness, his lofty conscientiousness is stigmatized as hypocrisy, his aspirations after nobler objects and high attainments denounced as ambition. And when from the uncongenial society around him he retreats into the sanctuary of his own bosom, and in the privacy of his retirement holds converse with God and nature and his own chastened soul, he is considered as one possessed with an anti-social and gloomy spirit.

Now the Saviour possessed in all their energy the innocent emotions of our nature, and especially those most warmly cherished by lofty and generous minds. With him to feel was to communicate, to know was to teach, to mingle with men was to go forth in all the ardor of his emotions, approving what was right, condemning what was wrong. When he looked upon the young man who had kept the commandments, he loved him. When he beheld the hypocrisies of the Pharisees he groaned with anguish, and denounced their wickedness in terms expressive of the deepest detestation. To one thus constituted, in whom all that is lovely and noble produced a thrilling delight, and all that is base and low excited a loathing inexpressible, how painful must it have been to mingle, even, with the best and purest of mankind. He had mingled in the society of heaven, he had lain in the bosom of his Father through untold generations, he had rejoiced in the glories of that upper world, in that mysterious and unfathomable intercourse between the Father and the Son; and now, a voluntary exile from the court of heaven, a voluntary participant of an inferior nature, he was to mingle with those whose every feeling was fastened to the dust, to pity the weakness and blindness and ignorance and vanity of the best, to endure the hypocrisy and fraud and angry violence of the worst. How did his holy soul groan beneath the weight of this affliction? And how often did his feelings burst forth in earnest expostulation? To his apostles often did he complain of their stupidity and blindness. At one time he rebukes their unbelief: "Oh, fools, and slow of heart to believe all that the prophets have spoken;" "Are ye so also without understanding; do ye not know, neither perceive?" And again, "Oh, ye of little faith, how long shall I be with you; how long shall I endure?"

But what language shall express the deep emotions of holy indignation which he felt when witnessing the cool and artful hypocrisy of the priests and elders? These were the lesser evils which darkly tinged the whole current of his life, and were the prelude to those keener agonies which immediately preceded its final close. When we speak of that we have not felt, we speak at random, and no human mind can at all conceive, or human tongue express the agonies that wrung the Saviour's soul in the hour of his last great conflict. There is an awful mystery around the subject that shrouds it from human view. We know, indeed, that he bore our sins in his body on the cross. But what is this—the burden of our sins? We may have felt its weight upon our consciences; we may have seen its temporal punishment in the persons of others, or felt it in our own. But what is this to the far more exceeding and eternal weight of anguish which presses on the soul hereafter? And what are the sins of an individual to those of a world? Ah, he was mighty to save, who bore the burden of our sins, and he travailed in the greatness of his strength; yet did the pressure of our heavy guilt force from his agonized frame great drops, as of blood, and wring, thrice wring, from his resigned and patient spirit that earnest prayer, "Father, let this cup pass from me"—this cup of salvation for a race, this cup of bitterness for me, let it pass away. We know that he who was one in essence with the Father cried out upon the cross, "My God, my God, why hast thou deserted me?"

But how little do we know of the mysterious and fearful meaning of that dying cry? Did the Divinity leave that human nature to bear unaided and alone the whole penalty due to sin? And what is the condition of one deserted by God? What darkness gathers around his soul? What desolation overspreads his nature? What despair sickens his heart? What torture racks his frame? Ah, we shall never know the full meaning of this cry, until perdition shall disclose its terrors, and reveal in that world of woe the condition of those whom God has deserted forever. Now these agonies were over, the last drop was exhausted from the cup of trembling and wrath, the Saviour, about to leave this world of humiliation and suffering for enjoyment of his rightful glories, might well exclaim in triumph, "It is finished."

2d. All that prophecy had predicted, and types prefigured, and hope had longed for, was now accomplished. For four thousand years man was a prisoner of hope, shut up to the glory that was to be revealed. During this long period the whole creation longed and sighed for that deliverance which was to come. This hope of a coming deliverer is found stamped on the literature, and interwoven with the institutions and habits, and the traditions of the most distant nations, from the remotest times.

The sense of guilt and ignorance and misery, on which the necessity and desire for such a Redeemer and Instructor was founded, expressed itself in the sacrifices, the self-tortures, the penances, the pilgrimages, the ablutions which have been universal among mankind. This feeling was confined to no portion of the globe, and no condition of society, but was experienced alike by the civilized and the barbarous, by the peasant and the philosopher. Whether this expectation be the obscure recollection of some traditional prophecy, I care not to inquire. If not it is something more conclusive still. It is the universal voice of nature, the prophecy primeval within us, not written on paper, or on stone, but engraven by the Almighty's hand on every heart. It is the universal yearning of man's heart after some expected and necessary good. It is the appetite which points to the proper food. It is the want which indicates a certain supply. It is the adaptation which necessarily supposes the use.

And tell me now, ye who have studied man, is there in his whole physical, moral, and intellectual constitution any thing superfluous? Is there any universal desire for which God has not prepared a gratification? Any want, for which there is no supply? Any adaptation, without a corresponding use? Has God taught us in our very nature, to hunger and thirst after righteousness, and does he supply no bread of life? Does he hear the young ravens when they cry for food, but disregard the longings of man's immortal past? And to what, I pray you, is this universal desire and expectation adapted, for what purpose given, unless to prepare us for that Redeemer who at last was revealed? To preserve, to strengthen, to increase, and to render more distinct this universal desire and expectation of the race, was the great object of the whole Jewish dispensation. To him pointed all the types, of him testified all the prophets. He was the substance of all the shadows, the fulfilment of the whole law. Did the innocent lamb die an offering to God: it was to point to the Lamb of God slain from the foundation of the world; it was to testify that without the shedding of blood there could be no remission of sins. Did the scape-goat upon which the people's sins had been confessed flee away into the wilderness to be seen no more: it was to signify that our sins should be borne away by one who was able to sustain their burden, and that they should rise up no more in judgment against us. Was the whole of that complicated and expansive ritual kept up from generation to generation: it was that each successive generation might look away, through the shadow, to him who is the substance. Did prophet after prophet rise and pass away: it was that from age to age the evidence might increase in quantity and clearness in favor of that mightier prophet who was still to come.

To prepare for his coming was the design of the whole providential government of God: to this end served the whole Mosaic law, the august succession of prophets, the mighty revolutions of empires and kingdoms. How do we love a time long expected, long foretold, long prepared and prayed for. This time the prophets all desired to behold; Abraham beheld it from afar and rejoiced in the sight. This was the true "seed of the Patriarch in whom the world was to be blessed." Moses looked forward with delight to the time when Judah's departed sceptre should rest on Shiloh's head and the gathering of the people should be to him. Isaiah, Jeremiah, David, all the prophets, foretold in burning strains the approaching king and ruler, and desired earnestly to witness the realities of those wonders which they had all predicted. And now all this was completed. What was so much desired, predicted, hoped, prayed for, all, was accomplished, not one prophecy that concerned his person, his office, his sufferings, had failed. However contradictory some might appear, in him they were reconciled; however minute, in him they were precisely fulfilled. Large were the hopes that men had cherished, large the blessings they anticipated from the coming of this deliverer; and these hopes were expressed and these blessings described in language of the most dazzling splendor. Those hopes were surpassed, those blessings exceeded. His origin was far nobler, his nature more exalted, his kingdom more extensive, his designs more magnificent, and the accomplishment more glorious, than hope had pictured or language had portrayed. Man looked for some superhuman deliverer; he who came was Divine: for some mighty ruler; his throne is the heavens, and the earth his footstool, and to his dominion there is no boundary, and shall be no end. Deep was the interest felt by heaven and earth in the accomplishment, and anxiously were the eyes of men and angels directed to the hour when it should be said at last, "It is finished."

His birth, which prophets had long announced on earth, angels proclaimed aloud from heaven; and the exalted spirits who appeared with him on the mount of transfiguration spoke of his decease which he should accomplish at Jerusalem. The appointed hour had now arrived, the preparation of centuries was completed, the desire of all nations had come: the seed of the woman, who had bruised the serpent's head. Earth's hopes were fulfilled, heaven's designs accomplished. In this hour of deep and solemn interest, when hell was pouring forth the last vials of its fury, and all heaven looked on in amazement, amidst the shuddering of nature, the blackening heavens, the bursting rocks, the opening sepulchres, the Saviour cried out, "It is finished." Well might the sun veil his face from that spectacle of horror, well might the astonished centurion exclaim, "Truly this was the Son of God."

3d. The glorious work he had come to do was finished. That was no message of trifling import which the Saviour came down to bear: that was no work of inferior moment which he came down to execute, for which he put forth the greatness of his strength, for which he lived a life of humiliation and suffering on earth, for which he sweat great drops of blood, and offered up his soul to the agonies of the cross. In all the works of God there is a characteristic majesty, and on this there is the impress of his hand. He came not to create a world of matter, but to redeem a world of immortal spirits: not to bestow temporal blessings on an empire or a kingdom, but eternal happiness on the untold millions of Adam's fallen race.

If it was great to create, it was greater still to redeem. If the morning stars sang together and the sons of God shouted for joy, when of these heavens and this earth it was said, "They are finished," what notes of higher ecstasy and far diviner joy must have resounded through the upper sky when the heavens and new earth, in which dwelleth righteousness, were completed; when the great scheme of man's redemption was finished; when the Saviour with his last dying breath sent from his full soul the cheering annunciation, "It is finished!" when the attending angels bore aloft the rapturous tidings, and heaven's high portals opening wide uttered soft music as they proclaimed aloud, "It is finished," and the spirits of just men caught up the sound, and, gazing in each other's faces as they thought of earth, re-echoed, with a loud enthusiasm unknown to angels, "Glory to God. It is finished," and God the Father accepted the atonement, and smiling on this work of love, said likewise, "It is finished."

This earth had long been in bondage to sin and Satan. Idolatry, impurity, and misery had darkened and polluted it. A daring and high-handed rebellion had overspread all its borders. Darkness covered the earth, and gross darkness the people, and the last ray of light and comfort from on high, which might have cheered man's desolated heart, was shut out by a dreary and hopeless scepticism. The Saviour had come to bring life and immortality to light, to overthrow the power of the Evil One, to cast down the idols, to establish a new government of peace and holiness and love on earth, to transform rebellious subjects into peaceful citizens of his kingdom, to people heaven from earth, and to bring down to this lower world those heavenly principles which create happiness above.

And, oh, what must have been the delight of his holy soul, when he saw that the object of his mission was accomplished, that his work was finished, finished beyond defeat, finished with naught to add. When, from the cross on which he hung, he looked with prophetic vision through the long, long lapse of ages, and beheld the innumerable multitude of the redeemed, the ten thousand times ten thousand from every nation and people under heaven, their garments washed white in his blood;

and their souls rescued by his sufferings, how triumphantly might he exclaim, "The mighty work is finished! The fatal stroke has been given to the kingdom of darkness. The barrier between God and man has been broken down, the claims of the law fully answered. Now God can be just and justify the ungodly; now Heaven is reconciled to earth, and all its richest blessings are freely offered to the lowest of earth's children. It is finished!"

Yes, for you, O Christian! nothing is wanting. It is perfect in all its parts. The garment of righteousness, in which you will be clothed, needs no addition or improvement. The Saviour having loved his own, loved them on to the end. He drank the cup of bitterness to the dregs, he wrought out a plenteous redemption. For you, O sinner! it is finished. Nothing will now be added. This is God's last great effort to redeem you: his finished salvation. "What more could I do for my vineyard, which I have not done, saith the Lord." And now, how shall you escape if you neglect this great salvation? Heaven's inexhaustible treasury hath been exhausted; the Son of God hath come to purchase your salvation; and what will you more? If after all this, "you neglect him who speaketh to you from heaven," there is no more sacrifice for sin, but a certain looking for of judgment and fiery indignation, which shall consume the adversaries. This is the only salvation and you must accept this, or perish in your sins.

But let us remember, my friends, that to each one of us, the hour shall come when it shall be said of him, "It is finished." A deadly mortality shall seize upon our vitals, and the symptoms of death shall gather fast and thick upon us; the difficult and impeded breathing, the low and fluttering pulse, the dim and glazed eye wandering aimless in the socket, the mind now sinking into stupor, now waking into fierce and convulsive life —while vain are the remedies of physicians, and fruitless the lamentations of friends. And at last, when death's agony is over, they shall say of us as they have said of others, "It is finished." Of that careless sinner now trifling away his day of grace, it shall be said, "It is finished;" and of that haughty scoffer, now heaping up wrath against the day of wrath, and soon perhaps to experience the realities he now derides, shall be said, by those who watch around his dying pillow, "It is finished." The agony is now over; it was fearful to behold: one last convulsive effort did he make to struggle against death, as man grapples with his mortal foe: but it is finished.

Then to his long account at last
With many a groan that spirit past.

But all is not finished there. It is appointed unto man once to die, and *after that*—what comes? Annihilation? No, would you accept it as a boon? But *after death* the *judgment*. You may disregard the judgment of man, you may stand before his tribunal and challenge scrutiny into all the actions of your life. But can you defy the scrutiny of the heart-searching and reins-trying God? Dare you stand before his bar and assert your perfect and unsullied purity in word, thought, or feeling? Alas, will you add insult to injury, folly to sin, and madly rush upon the vengeance you have wickedly provoked? And for you, O Christian, shall soon be finished the cares, the anxieties, the temptations, and dangers of this life. On you shall open the unseen glories of the world above. But let us remember, likewise, that then will close all our opportunities for usefulness among our fellow-men. And as we contemplate this day the death and sufferings of the Lord, let us determine to devote our whole selves to him who has done all for us; who shunned no suffering and spared no expense, that we might be saved. And may we all be able to say, with the apostle, at last, "I have fought the good fight, I have kept the faith, I have finished my course; henceforth is reserved for me a crown, which he will give me in that day."

IV.

THE ANGELS INTERESTED IN MAN'S SALVATION.

I. PETER, i. 12.—"Which things the angels desire to look into."

THE most ignorant man in the community will believe that a stone, thrown from the hand, will fall to the ground, because this is an occurrence which he has often observed, and which has thus become familiar to his mind. By directing his attention to the subject, he may be easily induced to admit, that the tendency of the stone toward the earth depends on some power in the earth, attracting it toward itself. But if you attempt to extend the principle further, and apply it to other parts of the universe; if you tell him, that the same principle of attraction which draws the stone to the earth, and whose operation he may observe in every moment of his life and upon all the bodies around him, operates likewise upon the remotest parts of God's universe, keeps the stars in their course, and binds the whole creation together, as in one bond of universal harmony, you present to his mind a train of thought, which is new, unusually strange, entirely without the sphere of his accustomed contemplation, and you will find it extremely difficult to persuade him that you are not endeavoring to practise upon his ignorance, or yourself laboring under the melancholy influence of that "much learning, which maketh men mad."

He never doubts, indeed, the existence of the world in which we live, or of the busy inhabitants which teem upon its surface, and waste their frail and feverish existence in the pursuit of its idle pleasures, and still more idle and unsubstantial honors; but he never dreams that there may be other worlds, crowded with other inhabitants; that every star may be a sun, and every sun the centre of a system as large as that to which our world belongs; and that throughout the immensity of space, wherever the hand of the Creator has spread the evidences of his almighty power, there he has placed intelligent, immortal creatures, to gaze with rapture on his works, to relish their beauties, and admire their sublimity, and to adore and love the wonderful Being from whom these glories sprung. Now we are accustomed to smile at the simple wonder of some, or the hardy incredulity of others, among the uninformed, when these majestic truths are presented to their minds, founded, as we know they all are, upon accurate observation and rational analogy, and some of them upon the solid basis of mathematical demonstration. But among those who feel their pity and their mirth excited by this resolute incredulity, this dogmatical scepticism of the ignorant upon astronomical subjects, there are not a few, who exhibit the same disposition, in the same degree and proceeding from the same causes, upon a different but much more important subject.

The unlettered man rejects the truths which have just been enumerated, because he does not know their evidence. He sets them down at once as absurd, merely because they are uncommon, because they do not lie in the beaten track of his usual thoughts, or observations. On the same principle the infidel proceeds. He doubts the existence of a future world and the truth of all that has been revealed about it, because he does not understand the evidence in its favor: he rejects it peremptorily as absurd, because he has never seen it; because it introduces his mind to a train of thought and feeling which is uncommon; and to him it appears unlikely, strange and incredible. He believes that there are other material worlds beside the little globe on which we live, and possibly admits that they may be inhabited. But the existence of angels and their holy employments in worshipping God, and ministering to man, he utterly denies. That principle of attraction, which binds the remotest parts of the universe together, is admitted by him, as an important part of his astronomical system. But the opinion that there is a great principle of moral sympathy, which attracts the moral universe together, and excites an interest for the welfare of moral agents even in the most distant parts of the creation, he brands as the idlest fantasy of a disordered brain. While he gazes with intense interest upon the motion of worlds which are at an immeasurable distance from our earth, he thinks it the highest absurdity to suppose that there may be other beings in other worlds, watching with thrilling and anxious concern the actions of moral agents upon this; and while he gladly employs the telescopic glass in examining those stars, which are invisible to the naked and unassisted eye, he proudly rejects as useless and absurd those lights which the Gospel has provided to aid our feeble reason—that moral telescope, which has been kindly offered us, to extend our vision to the future and invisible world.

Now the existence of angels is not in itself intrinsically more improbable than the existence of men. That their knowledge should be superior to ours is not more remarkable than our superiority to brutes; and their sympathy with us is not more incredible than our sympathy in the sufferings or the joys of inferior beings around us. The text asserts that the angels desire to look into these things, which concern man's salvation—the great plan of redemption which extends pardon to guilty rebels, and elevates fallen and ruined beings to happiness and heaven. That these are the things referred to in the text may be readily seen by examining the context. The expression in the original is still stronger than in our translation, "Which things the angels anxiously long to scrutinize closely or accurately." The interest which is felt by the angels in the affairs of this world is represented, in other parts of Holy Writ, as being ardent and intense. There is joy in heaven, and among the angels of God, over even one sinner that repenteth. And here we are told that they anxiously scrutinize, strive to understand, the plan of salvation and closely watch its gradual developments. There is nothing at all incredible, that God should take some interest in the happiness of those beings whom he has created; or that those holy, intelligent beings, who partake largely in his character, should feel a certain portion of the same interest. But it does seem remarkable that one little world should so strongly excite the interest, and attract the anxious attention of those high and holy beings; and we may surely be permitted humbly to inquire, why it is that "the angels so anxiously desire to look into the things" which concern mankind.

And may we not say that it is because the condition of our world is singular and unexampled, and the method of God's administration over us, being suited to our condition, is likewise uncommon. The angels are spiritual beings—great in power and vast in their capacities of thought and feeling. The whole creation of God is doubtless spread out as one great map before them, over which their immortal minds may expatiate forever, gathering each moment fresh stores of knowledge, and discovering new sources of ethereal happiness. What is the ardor of their activity, and the intensity of their enjoyment, we may learn faintly to conceive, from observing the operations of our own feeble and contracted minds. Even man, polluted and distracted as he is by impure and ungovernable passions—hampered and fettered as he is by a load of flesh which bears down the immaterial spirit in all its loftier aspirations, and sinks exhausted beneath its highest efforts—even man, when the soul is excited to its most vigorous exertions by the love of knowledge, or elevated to its highest ecstasy in the contemplation of God's sublime and wondrous creation, or expanded to its broadest comprehension by the boundless love of a risen and exalted Saviour, can send forth thoughts that wander through eternity, and think and feel unutterable things.

Those bright intelligences no doubt enjoy a wider field of observation, a loftier elevation of feeling, and a more exquisite enjoyment than we are able ever to conceive. To us this little world is a world of wonders, and always affords to our feeble minds new subjects of wondering inquiry during our short and transitory existence. But to them the whole is unfolded, and it is a universe of wonders, a boundless field of inquiry for an undying mind, an inexhaustible store-house of pure and ever increasing felicity. On every part of this great universe is stamped some feature of the Almighty's character. It is as one great mirror to image forth his glory, to reflect his praise. Over every portion of it has he cast a gorgeous magnificence, an enchanting beauty, an awful sublimity, which overpowers the mind of an intelligent being, and subdues the spirit to the stillness of mute, reverential homage. And we may well suppose, that in some other worlds there may be greater displays of almighty power than in ours. He may there have built up greater wonders, and pencilled brighter beauties, and in the minds of its rational inhabitants, as well as in the material scenery upon its surface, may have offered to the eye of contemplation a more lovely and more magnificent spectacle.

But there is that in the history of our globe, which is of far deeper and more enduring interest than all the beauty and all the magnificence which are spread in such rich and boundless profusion over the other works of God. It is to the universe what Palestine is to our earth—a land of marvels: small in the space it fills upon the chart of nature; but wonderful have been the events transacted on its surface; and deep and breathless has been the interest which those events have excited. We have reason to believe that, of all the unnumbered worlds which are spread over the immensity of space, there is none, except our earth, that has broken loose from its allegiance to the Almighty; that through the wide extent of God's magnificent creation universal happiness and peace prevail. The smile of the common Father rests upon his obedient children, and the voice of humble gratitude and filial affection is wafted to the throne of the Eternal from his intelligent and happy offspring. But amidst this delightful scene, brightened all over with the beams of the Creator's favor, there is a little spot which lies beneath his frown, and is darkened by the visible tokens of his fierce displeasure. Amidst this general symphony of happy and unfallen beings, a sound is heard, it is the voice of wailing, the shriek of agony, the stifled groan of unutterable woe. One portion of God's happy family has cast off his mild and paternal government, has wandered far away from the community of holy beings, and though it still revolves around his sun, and retains its station in his heavens, remains only by sufferance—a blasted, scorched, and withered thing, the abode of misery and crime.

There is in the feeling mind a pleasing sympathy with joy. But our sympathy with sorrow is far more deep and permanent. And if upon this globe there was but one instance of suffering and affliction, we might more easily understand the nature of that interest which attracts the angelic minds from the sublimest and loveliest scenery of creation to gaze upon this world of solitary and unexampled misery. Unhappily we are but too familiar with pain in all its shapes. We are surrounded by it on every side; we feel it in ourselves, and often still more acutely in the persons of beloved and endeared friends; till at last we have learned to meet it without surprise and sometimes to bear it without impatience. But suppose we had only seen one instance of pain and misery upon earth; that wherever else we turned all was peace and happiness, every countenance was lighted up with pleasure, and every eye was bright with exquisite enjoyment; but by some mysterious dispensation of a mysterious providence, the single individual alluded to was pressed down by the weight of some overwhelming calamity, his body racked by the most excruciating torments, and rendered loathsome by disease in its most disgusting forms, while his mind was crushed and blighted beneath the awful visitations of heaven—frenzied by the sufferings of the present moment, and haunted by the hateful remembrance of the past, and the still more dreadful anticipation of the future.

If such a scene of suffering were the only one on earth, it would be considered the most remarkable phenomenon that ever appeared to excite the sympathies and attract the notice of mankind. In all the glories of the material world and all the happiness of its living inhabitants there would be nothing found to stir so deeply the feelings of our nature. The traveller would turn aside to gaze upon it as one of the world's wonders; the philosopher would visit it to observe and meditate; the man of sensibility to sympathize, and, if possible, to soothe. And when the tale of his sufferings was told in distant lands by the returning voyager, the pale cheek and the quivering lip and the eye bedewed with tears, would reveal the power of that sympathy that swelled and trembled in the bosom of every hearer. Now this world is among the other worlds of creation what this single individual would be among the numerous inhabitants of the earth—a solitary example of suffering misfortune, concentrating all the attention and all the sympathy of others upon itself.

It may be thought that the sufferings of fallen angels should form an exception to the generality of this remark. But it seems almost superfluous to dwell upon the difference between the condition of those ruined spirits of darkness, shut up in eternal night, and the unhappy posterity of Adam who, though seduced by their malicious art, are prisoners of hope, and many of them heirs of eternal life. There is certainly a point in the progress of depravity where pity is converted into abhorrence, and all our sympathy for the suffering recoils at the hopeless and abandoned hardihood of the devoted sufferer. Where this point may be it is not for us to decide; but of this we may be certain, that the devils at least have passed that point, and while their sufferings are intense, they are unnoticed and unpitied, too. So that for all the purposes of argument or illustration it is just the same as if their existence and their sufferings had never commenced, or were all unknown to the rest of the creation. The devils are shut out from the whole brotherhood of intelligent beings, and from all the sympathies belonging to it, by the malignancy of their hatred to all that is good or lovely in creation. Man still belongs to that great society of beings, fallen and polluted as he is. And the very frailty of his nature, and the depth of his misery, when connected with the hope of his amendment, excite a trembling interest in his welfare, and an anxious solicitude for his restoration, which may be likened to the feelings of an upright and virtuous man toward a licentious and ungodly brother, whose vices he abhors and whose wanderings he laments, while he prays and agonizes and hopes for his recovery.

But besides the peculiarity of man's condition, so well calculated to excite curiosity and the deepest interest, there is something singular in the method of God's dealing toward him, which could not fail to engage the attention of angelic minds. When there was war in heaven, and the haughty spirits of archangels rebelled against the government of God, the arm which had created was stretched out to subdue them. And those who were not contented with the happiness of heaven were immediately driven away into everlasting darkness. When man joined the standard of that dark rebellion, and with faculties more limited, and powers less sublime, defied the Omnipotent, and spurned his just authority, the power which was exerted to crush rebellious angels was employed to save unhappy man; to repair the injury he had done himself; to raise him from the ruins of the fall and exalt him to such a union and intercourse with God as in his unfallen state was probably unattainable. This whole condition was extremely singular. He was a prisoner of hope; a condemned, but reprieved rebel; a sinner upon whom the penalty of sin was still unexecuted. The whole history of man was one continual wonder. The scenes were changed, and event succeeded event; but every new scene was stronger and more wonderful than that which had preceded it. Empires rose and fell, cities were built and demolished. Armies met in the shock of battle, and the blood of thousands was poured upon the plain. The mighty men of earth contended for conquest and for crowns; the philosopher reasoned, the poet sang, the prophet swept his lyre with holy energy, and poured from his rapt soul the burning language of inspiration; and all conspired to hasten on the accomplishment of God's purpose toward man—the great development of his wondrous plan. At last that hour arrived for which all other hours were made. And the angelic hosts beheld the Lord of life descending upon earth, lying in the manger, sojourning among men, dying upon the cross, going down into the grave, and then arising and ascending into glory.

Upon us the record of these events, all wonderful as they are, produces but a transient impression. We have heard them from our infancy. They form a part of our most common thoughts. The idea of a Saviour is always united with that of God, and the works of creation and redemption are associated in our minds as the different exhibitions of the same glorious character, as wonderful in mercy and in love as he is in Almighty power. But if we had stood among the angelic hosts and gazed with them upon the new-born creation—if we had wandered with them over all the universe of God and seen, as far as created eye may see, the immediate revelations of his glory, till the mind was overwhelmed with the view of his boundless perfections, and lost in that mighty field of contemplation spread out before us--if we had always had him present to our minds, arrayed in all the dazzling glories of his divinity, as the self-existent, eternal, unchangeable, almighty Jehovah, dwelling in light inaccessible and full of glory, reigning in heaven, and ruling over earth, establishing empires and crushing them at his pleasure, creating worlds and upholding them by his power—then we should feel indeed how wonderful, how singular, how passing strange, that condescension was, when the Eternal Son became the babe of Bethlehem, and God himself was manifested in the flesh. Great must have been that design which brought him down to earth, and well does it deserve the admiring scrutiny of men and angels.

The method of God's administration upon earth is different from that which appears in heaven, or in hell, or in any world with which we are acquainted. In heaven all is love and happiness. In hell all is wrath and misery. Upon earth there is a mingled state of being and of character; and the administration of the moral governor is accommodated to the condition of his subjects. It is this mixed state of existence, this alternation of virtue and vice, of happiness and misery, which has so much perplexed the minds of thinking men, which has shaken the believer's faith, and confirmed the atheist in his folly; and it is this, we may suppose, which has attracted, in part, the attention of superior beings. The love which bestows happiness on virtue, and the justice which inflicts merited punishment on crime, are characteristics of Deity, inseparable from every conception of his nature, and exhibited whenever there is vice to be punished and virtue to receive enjoyment. Such love and justice are simple qualities of a perfect mind, everywhere exhibited and easily understood. But the love which is exerted toward the sinner, the justice which falls on the head of a mediator, the love and justice united, which punish the crime but save the criminal, which gently chastise the offender that he may cease from his offence, which substitute the lamb when they cannot dispense with the sacrifice—such love and justice are displayed, as far as we know, only upon earth.

When we remember, then, how anxiously the angels gaze on every new exhibition of the divine character—that heaven and earth, and all that them inhabit, the great universe itself, with all that it contains of sublime or beautiful, glorious or lovely, are only admired as exhibiting his character and manifesting his glory—we cannot be surprised at the interest which angels feel in gazing on this wondrous exhibition, which has been given in these last times, through the plan of redemption, of the height and depth and length and breadth of that love of God which passeth understanding.

The language of the original, which represents the angels as anxiously prying into the plan of redemption, seems to indicate that the very mysteriousness of that plan, the unfathomed and unfathomable wisdom contained therein, is one cause of their constant attention to it. The pleasure of discovering new truths, of whatever kind, is one often experienced and well understood among thinking men. And when, in addition to their novelty, the truths discovered are of a pleasing and elevating character, the satisfaction arising from the discovery is greatly increased. The ardor in the pursuit of knowledge is proportioned to the enjoyment we receive from it; and such is the nature of the mind, that, when its powers are really excited in the investigation of truth, difficulties which would otherwise appear insuperable vanish before it; and curiosity is stimulated by the obscurities which would otherwise repress it. We might compare the anxiety of the angels to scrutinize the plan of redemption, to the solicitude with which an aspiring and indefatigable student pores over some massy volume where he knows are all the treasures of ancient wisdom, or some knotty problem which lies in the pathway of science, and whose solution leads on to a thousand unknown truths. How does he struggle with the obstacles in his way, and summon all his powers to carry on the contest. Though often foiled, he never despairs; he never doubts the existence of the truth he has not been able to discover, but returns repeatedly to the investigation, till at last his efforts are crowned with complete success. So it may be with angelic minds. There may be, there are, mysteries to them, and we are taught in our text to believe they are diligently employed in scrutinizing that part of God's plan which to them appears mysterious.

Nor is it inconsistent with any rational view of the happiness of heaven to suppose that the inhabitants of that world feel, like ourselves, the desire of knowledge and the pleasure of acquiring information. The spirit is essentially and intensely active; its home is in the midst of mighty thought and lofty contemplation, and there is a high-breathed pleasure in the very pursuit of knowledge and the victory over difficulties that cannot flow from any other source. It is the perfection and not the weakness of spiritual beings, that they long insatiably after knowledge, and that this longing is at once the source of their highest efforts and most exquisite enjoyments. I would not be understood as countenancing the opinion that all mysteries may be investigated and understood by either men or angels; nor that it is either wise or proper to waste, in the contemplation of truths which are plainly incomprehensible, those faculties which are given for far different purposes. Yet if the knowledge of angels is not all intuitive, it must progress by repeated steps, and that which now seems mysterious may hereafter wear a different aspect. The gradual development of God's plan may cast new light upon his past administration, or the frequent contemplation of it, as developing and already developed, may open up new views of his holy character and ever blessed government.

In the creation of the world his power and creative wisdom were wonderfully displayed; in its redemption the same power and wisdom are displayed, united with a love and compassion, a tenderness and mercy wonderful and divine. In the heavens and the earth, in the sun, moon, and stars, we may see displayed, in everlasting characters, the existence and many of the attributes of God. But it is in his intelligent and moral creation that we see the brightest specimens of his creative wisdom; and it is in his moral government that we find the most interesting subjects for thought and examination. How great is the wisdom of that scheme which offers life and happiness to man, we may learn from the folly of all other schemes devised by human ingenuity. All are self-contradictory or defective. On all, the difficulty presses with irresistible power, how shall justice be satisfied and the sinner be saved? In the Gospel, mercy and truth have met together; righteousness and peace have kissed each other, and now God can be just, and the justifier of the ungodly who believe in the Lord Jesus Christ. On the Gospel plan the sinner is saved from all his sins: the very method of salvation is a method of purification; and the voice which says, "thy sins be forgiven thee," says likewise, "go and sin no more." If the morning stars sang together and the sons of God shouted for joy, when the world was created, light was brought out of darkness, and from the confusion of chaos there arose a scene of smiling loveliness and beauty, well may the angels rejoice together, when by the same almighty power similar effects are produced in the moral world. Order and harmony, peace and happiness, spring forth from that chaos of warring elements, that abode of vice and misery, the depraved unregenerated heart of man. And if it be admitted that the living and immortal beings around us are of greater dignity and importance than the material world which we inhabit, then will the grandeur of the great plan of salvation appear in its proper light, and the wisdom which devised and executed it, will be acknowledged as that which was hidden in Christ, from the foundation of the world ; and this scheme of condescending mercy will be honored as that last great exhibition of himself, by which God designs to be known to his intelligent creation, to which all his other works are tributary, and in which all finally meet.

Let us observe now, First, What a view this subject gives us of the character and employments of angels and the happiness of heaven.

The happiness of heaven does not consist in the passive reception of pleasure. In other parts of God's Word we are told that the angels are ministering spirits, swift to do God's will; "that his ministers are a flame of fire." They are frequently spoken of as going on errands of kindness to men, and their very name of messenger indicates the activity of their engagements. They are said to have shouted for joy at the creation of the world, and still to feel a deep interest in the welfare of its inhabitants. From this we may fairly presume that they are acquainted with the condition of the various portions of the universe, and are accustomed to employ their minds in observing their situation, and as far as possible rendering them service. Let no indolent and useless man suppose that he could enjoy the society of heaven. All is life, activity, and feeling there, and his dull repose would be constantly disturbed by the zeal of its inhabitants. The cultivation and the exercise of benevolent and kindly feelings, seems to be one of the chief employments and most delightful duties of heaven. Let no man then, however lofty his intellect, or extensive his requirements, however pressing or important his business may be—let no man, upon any pretence whatever, neglect the cultivation of benevolent feelings. To weep with those that weep, and rejoice with those that rejoice, to sympathize readily and deeply with our fellow-men under all the trials of this changing world, to deserve and to receive their sympathies in return, is a luxury which kings might envy, did they know its sweetness. Real benevolence of feeling is at once the strongest evidence and the loveliest ornament of a truly elevated mind. Let us learn, too, from the example of angels not to despise any of our fellow-men, however weak in intellect, low in station, or degraded in vice. They sympathize with us in all our pollution. Shall not we do good to all our fellow-men whenever an opportunity occurs? It cannot be improper here to remark how closely the truths of divine revelation agree with the purest dictates of enlightened minds. The heathen Elysium and the Turkish paradise are represented as the abodes of sensual enjoyment or indolent ease; but the heaven of the Bible is the home of the spirit, its pleasures are spiritual and pure, its employments are worthy an immortal nature, and constitute at once its duty and its happiness.

Let us observe, in the Second place, the justice of God in the condemnation of the sinner. If no salvation had been offered to man, if no light had shone upon his darkness, no hope had beamed upon his ruin, if he had been left ignorant of his origin, his nature, and his destiny, and, thus groping his darkling way along the journey of life, had stumbled through inadvertence or wandered from the path, his misery would have excited the sympathies of all benevolent beings, and abhorrence for his crimes would have been forgotten in pity for his sufferings. But light has come into the world, and men have loved darkness rather than light. "Nature with open volume stands" to instruct the ignorance of man, and the volume of God's great revelation has brought life and immortality to light. The dictates of reason have been forgotten amidst the tumult of the passions. But the precepts of revelation have been heard sustaining its authority. The silent instruction which is given by the works of God, and which falls like the music of the spheres upon the mind prepared to hear it, has been unheeded amidst the bustle and agitation of life. But a voice has come from heaven, to arrest the attention of mankind; and the monitor within, which no tyranny can awe and no neglect can silence, still is heard in the darkness of night and the stillness of retirement, bearing solemn witness to truth. Without the Bible, all would indeed be darkness; and this miserable world of ours, as it wheels its annual round in the system with its sister planets, but separated far away from the moral system of the universe, might be compared to some stately vessel which the storm had separated from her companions, and, broken loose from her moorings, had cast, with all her precious cargo, in a dark night, on a tempestuous ocean, without a pilot to direct her course, or a twinkling star to guide her wanderings. But while all is darkness without and all is misery within, while she is tossed by the tempest and shattered by the billows, and the last hope is fast turning to despair, the eye which is directed to heaven beholds a star shining brightly through that darkness. It is the Star of Bethlehem! pouring its own calm and heavenly radiance across those troubled waters and pointing to that heaven of eternal rest. Oh, who would not look to it as the star of hope, as the harbinger of peace, as the messenger of mercy!

But such is not man. That star has shone in vain. The Sun of Righteousness has risen to enlighten the world, but many have turned their backs upon his brightness, and, enjoying his reflected light, have boasted of the acuteness of their natural vision, and denied the existence of the great luminary they refuse to see. Oh, how shall they escape, who reject this offered illumination, and love their darkness, with all its misery, better than the light and joy and peace of the Gospel! The scheme of salvation which has been offered to men is such as it became God to reveal and man to accept. There are those indeed among our dying race, who think it wholly unworthy of their serious attention, who neither deign to study its character or investigate its evidences. But how shall they excuse their folly or their pride, who despise the revelation that God has given, and angels desire to look into—a revelation which he has stamped with his own broad seal of authenticity, and which they have delighted to study, as the most glorious exhibition of his character? And how shall the sinner excuse his heedless indifference about his own salvation, when the angels of heaven are so deeply concerned in the happiness of man? It surely aggravates his guilt and must add awful horror to his condemnation—that his sins have been committed in spite of the warnings and entreaties and sympathies of the highest and holiest beings in the universe—that he has cast away from him his brightest hopes and trampled under foot his lofty destinies.

It too often happens that we have to observe among our fellow-men a species of conduct which will serve to illustrate our argument. We often see a young man, bright in promise and buoyant in hope, hastening at the commencement of life into those paths of dissipation and folly which destroy alike his present happiness and future prospect. And while the mind contemplates with pain the melancholy wreck of what he was, and turns away in disgust from the thought of what he is, does it not serve to aggravate his guilt, when we remember, how he disregarded a father's warning and a mother's prayers, how he destroyed the happiness of a family whose happiness was bound up in him, how he proved false to all the bright hopes and fair expectations of his friends, to his own early promise and high capabilities!

Precisely analogous to this is the condition of man. Possessing large capacities for happiness and moral improvement, the sympathies of God and angels are enlisted in his favor. Eternal happiness is presented for his acceptance, and eternal misery is the awful punishment of his guilt. All heaven is anxious for his welfare. God himself gives his Son for his salvation; the angels are ministering spirits, that minister unto him, and with trembling solicitude observe every step of his career. All hell is awake and smiles with horrible delight at the prospect of his ruin. He is placed, as it were, upon an elevated theatre—the object of continued observation to invisible and innumerable beings. With every thing to stimulate him to duty, should he prove insensible to his great responsibilities, should he forget his rational and immortal nature, and fall from the high station which God designed him to occupy, great must be the fall thereof, and upon his own head the guilt of his own destruction.

V.

PAUL'S ZEAL FOR ISRAEL, AND ITS LESSONS.

ROM. ix. 1–5.—I say the truth in Christ, I lie not, my conscience also bearing me witness in the Holy Ghost, that I have great heaviness and continual sorrow in my heart. For I could wish that myself were accursed from Christ for my brethren, my kinsmen according to the flesh: who are Israelites; to whom pertaineth the adoption, and the glory, and the covenants, and the giving of the law, and the service of God, and the promises; whose are the fathers, and of whom, as concerning the flesh, Christ came, who is over all, God blessed for ever. Amen.

THE preceding chapter terminates the apostle's discussion of the great doctrine of justification by faith. He had clearly proven, that there could be no justification by works, because Jews and Gentiles were both concluded under sin, the Gentile having disregarded the dictates of conscience, the law written on their hearts, and closed their eyes against the light which beams so brightly from God's glorious works; while the Jews had sinned against the clearer light of revelation, and broken even the law of Moses, by which they expected to be saved. If, therefore, there be any method of salvation for man, the apostle most conclusively argues, it must be one, not of man's devising, nor depending on human merit, but one devised by God for our benefit, and procured by the merits of another. This he calls "God's method of justification, through faith in Jesus Christ."

Now, this whole method of justification, through the merits of another, and without the deeds of the law—justification offered freely alike to Gentile and Jew, the circumcision and the uncircumcision—was a perfect novelty to the unsanctified Jew, and a thousand objections would immediately spring up in his mind against a doctrine so adverse to his prejudices as a Jew, so humbling to his pride as a man. It was a doctrine which, superseding the sacrifices of the law, and promising salvation without obedience to its ritual, seemed blasphemy against Moses and the prophets. Offering salvation to the Gentiles, many of whom believed, and denouncing eternal perdition against the Jews, most of whom rejected its proffered blessings, it seemed to reverse the whole order of God's gracious dispensations, and to wrest from the children of Abraham the glorious privileges promised to their father, merely that they might be dispensed with impious hands to the detested Gentiles; thus making void the faithfulness of God, and wasting upon dogs the children's bread. "What advantage, then," he would indignantly exclaim, "what advantage hath the Jew? and what profit is there in circumcision?" Shall the unbelief of man make void the faithfulness of God?

The apostle glances at these various objections as he passes on, but leaves the full consideration of them all, and the awful consequences connected with them to the 9th chapter, where he announces God's final rejection of the Jews for unbelief, and shows that all the promises, on which they so securely depended, were made to the spiritual, and not to the natural, seed of Abraham—that the same sovereignty which chose at first, might now, without injustice, reject them, and that this terrible rejection had been often predicted by the holy prophets.

In approaching this awful and distressing subject, the apostle exhibits all that tenderness of heart, and all that knowledge of human character, for which he is elsewhere so remarkable. In the former part of the Epistle, he has employed all the stores of his varied erudition, and all the powers of his vigorous mind, to combat their prejudices and refute their objections. But here all the deep sensibilities of his noble and affectionate nature burst forth in a torrent of the most kind and affecting expressions. Whatever obscurity may involve one or two expressions in this celebrated passage, and however critics may differ in their interpretation, it is easy to understand the general tenor of the whole, and to sympathize with the apostle's overwhelming emotions.

He was about to announce to them the disappointment of all their dearest hopes, the overthrow of all their most fondly-cherished expectations, as he looked forward to the day when Jerusalem should be laid in heaps, when God's holy temple should be defiled with impious hands, and the hundred thousand of that deluded people should perish by the invader's sword. And as he remembered that they were bone of his bone and flesh of his flesh, the children of Abraham, the chosen people, honored of God to be the depositaries of his religion, and the nation from whom his own Son sprang, would not all the feelings of the man and the Christian combine to awaken emotions of unutterable sorrow? He knew that they viewed him as an enemy, because he had told them the truth, had advocated the equal participation by the Gentiles of the blessings of salvation, and had professed to be sent of God, especially to the Gentiles. He, therefore, most solemnly assures them, as a Christian man whose conscience was enlightened by the Holy Ghost, that so far from taking pleasure in announcing the awful sentence of God against them, it filled him with perpetual grief; that, so far from cherishing any hostility against his people on account of their ill treatment, or his own peculiar vocation to the Gentile world, he could wish himself accursed from Christ, as our translation expresses it, or as it might be rendered, he could wish that he had, if consistent with God's will, been "set apart" by Christ, for the service of the Jews, as Peter was, instead of the Gentiles. It was not his want of affection for them, nor his desire to exalt the Gentiles above them, but the wise and sovereign determination of God, which led him to turn his attention to those who were lying in darkness and the shadow of death.

It has been already suggested that learned men have been much divided in the interpretation of some parts of this passage. In the dry details of verbal criticism, it can scarcely be expected that a promiscuous assembly should feel much interest, or from it derive much profit. I shall not therefore delay you by discussing, or even mentioning, the various opinions respecting the expressions translated, "I could wish that myself were accursed from Christ." I will only allude to that which is most satisfactory to my own mind, and the reasons for adopting which may be easily understood, even by those not acquainted with the original.

Men's feelings are as various as their opinions, and therefore I cannot be certain that I express the feelings of others, as well as my own, in saying, that the idea conveyed in our authorized translation appears extremely revolting and unnatural. It seems impossible, if it were even right, and wrong even if it were possible, to choose, on any conditions, to be accursed from Christ, and banished from his presence forever. We may separate, in imagination, the sufferings of the damned from burning hostility against God, but they are never separated in fact, and he who chooses hell for his residence, in reality, and not merely in imagination, chooses not only the darkness and the fire and the worm that never dies, but the sin, the pollution, the utter alienation from God and daring rebellion against his authority, which are the true spirit of the lost and the necessary qualification for their society. If then the passage will bear a different interpretation, one which is consistent with the context and perfectly natural, while it is attended with no difficulty, arising from the constitution of man's nature, or the truths elsewhere revealed, or the duties elsewhere inculcated, in the Bible, we need not hesitate to adopt it; remembering, that in inquiries of this nature, probability must be our guide, and the certainty of absolute conviction is rarely attainable.

In the Latin, Greek, and Hebrew languages, the same word which is sometimes translated "accursed" or "cursed," means originally "separated," "set apart" for any purpose. Thus in Joshua, vii. 1, the spoils were called "accursed," because they were set apart for God, devoted to his service, and the living animals among them destined to death. So in Leviticus, xxvii. 28, it is said, "every devoted thing," every *anathema*, as it is in the Greek version, the very word used in the passage before us, and in Joshua vii. 1, "is most holy unto the Lord." Here the same word, which in Joshua and in Romans is rendered "accursed," is said to be "most holy;" because holiness, as we all know, means separation, being set apart for the service of God. Now in this same chapter of Leviticus there are two words, each of which is employed to express this idea of separation, devotion to God, and each of these words is found likewise applied to St. Paul in the New Testament. The latter is applied undoubtedly to St. Paul for the purpose of expressing the fact of his being set apart to the preaching of the Gospel. In Acts xiii. 2, where Barnabas and Paul were set apart for their work and in Galatians, i. 15, where St. Paul informs us, that he was set apart from his mother's womb, and called by the grace of God; and here in the ninth chapter of Romans, we find the other applied to the same apostle. If the words, when used in the Old Testament in relation to one subject, are supposed to have the same meaning, why may they not be similarly translated when applied in the New Testament to another subject? If then the word here translated "accursed" be rendered "set apart," all difficulty and obscurity will be removed, and we see at once how natural is the assurance, which the apostle gives his brethren, that it was not his own choice, but the command of God, which sent him to the heathen; and that if left to himself, he would have chosen rather "to be set apart by Christ," the great head of the church, for the benefit of the Jews, his brethren according to the flesh.

The circumstances which the apostle afterward enumerates, in the fourth verse, are probably designed, in part, to convince the Jews, that he was not insensible to all those tender and glorious recollections which were inseparably connected with the name of Jerusalem, and the imperishable heritage of Jacob's children; and, perhaps in part, to show, that he as willingly acknowledged and appreciated, as highly as any other, the distinguished favors bestowed upon them from on high. Hence he dwells with emphasis upon the titles they possessed and the privileges they enjoyed. They were Israelites, the descendants of Jacob, called by his name, "who as a prince had power with God and prevailed;" they were adopted into the family of God and called his children, as he said to Pharaoh, Exodus, iv. 22, 23, "Israel is my son, even my first-born: let my son go, that he may serve me," and Jeremiah, xxxi. 9, "I a ma father to Israel, and Ephraim is my first-born." They possessed the glory likewise, the visible manifestation of God's presence, in the Shekinah. To them belonged the covenants made at various times with Abraham, Isaac, and Jacob; to them alone, of all the nations, had God condescended to give a written law, by the hand of Moses. On them had he bestowed a form of religious service which was acceptable to him, while others were left in darkness and often sinned most in their most solemn attempts to serve him. To them all the promises were given; to them belonged the fathers of the Jewish nation, those holy men who enjoyed such intimate intercourse with God, that they were called his friends. But above all it was in the Jewish nation that the Saviour first appeared, and of a Jewish virgin he condescended to be born. These glorious distinctions the apostle by no means denied to the Jewish people. Nay, he rejoiced in them himself, and thought it "much advantage, every way, to be born a Jew." But the height to which they were exalted only made him shudder the more at the prospect of their frightful fall. They had long rejoiced in the beams of God's cheering favor, and were soon to sink into a rayless, starless, hopeless night.

It is almost incredible how much learning and ingenuity have been unprofitably exhausted in the effort to avoid the evidence contained in the fifth verse for the real and underived divinity of our blessed Saviour. He is there called, "God over all, blessed forever."

It is obvious to the least observant reader that when we are told, in the first clause of the verse, that Christ came of the fathers according to the flesh, we naturally expect to hear, in the succeeding clause, that he was not of the fathers in some other respect. This part of the antithesis is naturally supplied, when we are told, that he is "God over all, blessed forever." This expression coincides exactly, both in the original and in the English translation, with the "supreme God." Hence we have a complete refutation here, did not its own intrinsic absurdity refute it, of the Arian hypothesis, which represents our Saviour as an inferior deity, as divine yet not very God. There we are informed that he is not only God, but supreme God, as we are told by the apostle John, "this is the true God and everlasting life."

The passage of God's Word to which our thoughts have been directed may suggest several profitable reflections. First, We may learn from the example of St. Paul the amiable and lovely nature of true Christian principle.

In whatever condition we contemplate the great apostle of the Gentiles, he seems peculiarly calculated to call forth our admiration. While standing before King Agrippa, and boldly, though in chains, proclaiming the truth of the Gospel he had espoused, we cannot but sympathize with the manly courage and intellectual energy that could meet unmoved the dangers that environed him, and admire the power of that simple but pointed eloquence which made the dissolute monarch exclaim, "Almost thou persuadest me to be a Christian." When standing on Mars' Hill, surrounded by a crowd of cavilling philosophers and superstitious people, we cannot but observe the adroit and dexterous skill with which he preached the Gospel from a text furnished by a heathen altar; and, beginning from the "unknown God" whom they blindly worshipped, made known that great and spiritual Jehovah, who has made all the nations, and in whom we "live and move and have our being." But never does he appear in a more engaging or attractive light, than when, pouring out his lamentations over his blinded countrymen, he endeavors gently to reveal to them the coming ruin, soothing their wounded pride by the recollection of their ancestral glory, and disarming their inveterate prejudices by the ardor of his overflowing affection.

How different from the conduct of many men of distinguished talents, who seem to suppose that the possession of uncommon powers, and the performance of extraordinary services, releases them from all obligation to cultivate those gentler social virtues which communicate a winning gracefulness to Christian character, and shine with a lovelier radiance when harmoniously blended with the learning that commands our respect or the genius that excites our admiration. How different, too, from the spirit of those who, in rude and unfeeling language, thunder forth their denunciations against the sinner, not remembering that we all are involved in the like condemnation, forgetting the tender lamentations of St. Paul over his blinded countrymen, and the example of Him—Paul's superior and his Master—who, as he gazed upon Jerusalem, that cruel city, reeking with the blood of murdered prophets, and then thirsting for his own, wept at the spectacle of their present thoughtlessness and the prospect of their approaching doom. Let us, my Christian friends, mingle tenderness with efforts to save dying men around us. Let the tears of our compassion water the seed that we sow. The cloud that darkly lowers and thunders loudly may pass over our heads and leave no memorial behind it but the scathed and shattered trunk which the lightning hath riven in its course. It is the gentle shower, which distils upon hill and valley, on the green grass and cultivated field, that causes man's heart to rejoice with gladness, and cheers the wearied husbandman with the prospect of an abundant harvest to reward his daily toil.

Second, The rejection of the Jews from being the people of God is an awful subject, full of terror, of warning, and instruction. The apostle could not approach the subject without stopping to pour forth his lamentations. How are the mighty fallen, how is the most fine gold become dim! Jerusalem, the city of our God, the mother of the faithful, Mount Zion, beautiful for situation, the joy of the whole earth, is as when God overthrew Sodom and Gomorrah!

They were the church of God, his chosen and peculiar people. But the sovereignty which chose them at first had determined to reject them for their sins. In vain might they plead their former privileges; these only aggravated their condemnation. Much had been given them, and of them much was required. They possessed the law, but this they had violated. They had the ordinances of God's service, but these they had so polluted by their hypocrisy that they were hateful in his sight: since we hear him saying, in the first chapter of Isaiah, "To what purpose is the multitude of your sacrifices unto me, saith the Lord, I am full, satiated with the burnt offerings of lambs and the fat of fed beasts. Bring no more vain oblations. Incense is an abomination unto me. It is iniquity, even the solemn meeting!" They had been adopted into his family, and obtained the endearing name of children; but they were wayward and disobedient children. "I have nourished and brought up children, saith the Lord, and they have rebelled against me." He was their king, but they had sought other lords to have dominion over them. Prophets had proclaimed God's truth among them, but the prophets they had put to death; and when the last messenger from heaven came down among them, him they had taken and with cruel hands had crucified and slain. Thus every privilege which they could plead as evidence of God's former love only established more incontrovertibly the certainty of his present wrath. The goodness of God had not led them to repentance, and the only alternative remaining was, that they had been treasuring up wrath against the day of wrath. Their crimes had been accumulating for centuries, till the rejection of the Saviour sealed their ruin; and the wrath which had been so long gathering above their heads was at last poured upon them to the uttermost.

We have said, that much instruction may be derived from the rejection of the Jews. We see here that the sovereignty of God, however mysterious to us in its nature, is so far intelligible in its operations that it never protects sin. The Jews were an elect people, and yet they were cut off for unbelief. If then any of us be trusting that we were once the people of God, and therefore will always belong to that favored company, while we continue in sin, we are deceived. Let it be never so certain, that you are one of God's elect, yet it cannot be more certain than the truth, that if you continue in your sins, where God and Christ are you can never come.

Let the formal and heartless professor of religion then take warning from the rejection of the Jews. Remember that thou art only a Gentile, and not of the true olive-tree. If then the true olive branches were broken off, "because of unbelief they were broken off, and thou standest by faith; be not high-minded but fear." The Lord's jealousy burneth hottest nearest to his throne. He cannot be deceived, he will not be mocked. "To the wicked, God saith, What hast thou to do, to declare my statutes, or that thou shouldst take my covenants in thy mouth?" Thy services are all an abomination, thy prayers are mockery, thine outward profession is hateful in his sight. Thou movest amidst Christians, as if a dead and putrid corpse should rise from its grave, and stalk forth amidst living men, only the more revolting for its human form, and its horrid mimicry of real life.

The church of God, as a whole and in all its parts, may well take warning from God's dealings with his ancient people. God will not endure corruption in his church. He will hide his face. He will abandon her to her enemies, and if, after many reproofs, she shall still remain unamended, he will give her up forever. Say not, "The temple of the Lord, the temple of the Lord, the temple of the Lord are we." God can erect another temple, and call another people, who will worship him more spiritually, and serve him more faithfully. "Though thou wert the signet on his right hand," as was said of Coniah, the son of Jehoiakim, "though thou wert the signet on his right hand, yet he would pluck thee thence." Say not, What will become of the glory of the Lord. He can promote his glory in your condemnation, as well as in your salvation. "He hath made even the wicked, against the day of his power." How could religion exist if Jerusalem were destroyed? might the Jew reason. Will not the heathen triumph? Yes, but in the midst of their triumph God is raising up a people to serve him, from among their own families and friends. The Roman eagle is soaring high over Jerusalem. The Roman torch is firing its sacred temple, and, as the conflagration rapidly extends, and the broad sheets of flame burst from its dizzy summit, and curl upward to the sky, terribly magnificent, the shout of pagan triumph is heard, above the clash of armor and the shrieks of the dying, to proclaim that the God of Abraham has lost his power to save. "But why do the heathen rage, and the Gentiles imagine a vain thing. He that sitteth in the heavens shall laugh, the Almighty shall hold them in derision." She that persecuted the prophets is fallen, and prophecy is fulfilled; she that rejected the Saviour is in ruins, and thus we know that the son of man has come to establish his kingdom upon earth; a kingdom which shall extend beyond the limits of the Roman empire, and take in all nations. The mistress of the world shall soon own his mild dominion, and on the walls of the seven-hilled city shall be planted the standard of the cross. The temple hath fallen, within whose narrow walls the worshippers of a single nation were wont to pay their vows, and present their offerings; but another has risen more glorious far, whose broad foundation is the great globe itself, whose garniture is the handy-work of God, and within whose spacious walls are gathered the unnumbered millions of God's elect, from every nation under heaven, bringing incense and a pure offering, a holy and a spiritual worship, approaching to the throne of the majesty on high, not with the blood of bulls and goats, but with the precious blood of the Son of God.

VI.

THE QUESTION AND ITS ANSWER.

ACTS, xvi. 30.—"Sirs, What must I do to be saved?"

ABOUT the year of our Lord 53 or 54, two obscure, unknown travellers arrived at Philippi, one of the principal cities of Macedonia. They had travelled far. Having embarked at Antioch in Syria, and passed by a circuitous route over sea and land, they had reached, at length, this celebrated city, where the Asiatic foreigners for the first time placed their feet on European soil. By tracing their course over the map, you will find that their route lay through many of the scenes rendered familiar to our boyhood by the history and fables of antiquity—the soft waters of the Ægean, the mild climate of the East, along the voluptuous shores of Asia Minor, and amidst the fertile and luxurious islands of the adjacent sea—over countries where the mighty conquerors of old fought their battles, and won their renown, and the shadowy heroes of an earlier and fabulous age performed their prodigies of valor. And their fortunes were as various, and changed as rapidly as the scenes through which they passed. At one time hooted by the rabble, at another caressed by the great; now worshipped as deities, now hissed and stoned by vagabonds; now assaulted by the populace with the insane fury of a fanatical mob; now seized by magistrates as disturbers of the peace, rudely rebuked, cruelly scourged, condemned, imprisoned. And now these friendless wanderers, safe from the dangers of the sea and the fury of persecutors, "from the noise of the waves and the tumult of the people," have reached a strange city on another continent. Is it that they may seek an end to their wanderings, find repose from labors, refuge from sufferings and foes ? Ah, if that had been their object, Christian friends, what would you and I now have been ? The history of the world would probably have been reversed, and the dark night of idolatrous superstition still have rested on the nations.

Philippi had received, before, many a distinguished, many a royal visitant. Repaired and beautified by Philip of Macedon, colonized subsequently by Julius Cæsar, rendered famous above all by that memorable battle in which Rome's liberties received their last death-blow from her own children, and the hand of Brutus that struck down the tyrant in the capitol, was turned in despair upon himself. But signalized as she was by great events and illustrious visitors, it may be doubted, whether, of all the mighty received within her walls—from the youthful prince of Macedon to that prototype of all demagogues and tyrants, the wily and supple Cæsar, and that last relic of Roman virtue and greatness, the stern incorruptible Brutus—there had ever approached a man who could bear comparison with that unknown Jew, with bald head and eagle eye and diminutive frame, who passed, at first unnoticed, along the streets of Philippi. There is we grant no universal test of greatness. But if we measure the compass of this man's mind by the largeness of his views or the elevation of his character, by the vastness of his designs or their magnificent accomplishment, by the benefits he conferred upon mankind or the influence he has wielded over the opinions and destiny of the race through successive countries and in distant lands ; whatever it may be that we most admire, whether dazzling splendor of bold and vigorous imagery, or burning ardor of deep and intense emotion, or the inexorable logic of close and compact reasoning, or all these harmoniously combined and wielded by a manly eloquence, which, whether we judge from the effects produced, or specimens still remaining, must be considered almost perfect in its kind ; in whatever light we may view the apostle, he must be acknowledged to possess all the distinguishing attributes of real greatness.

Oh, ye enthusiastic admirers of human greatness, who fall

down in thoughtless adoration before it, when its record is blood, and its monuments pyramids of human skulls; ye worshippers of the great manslayers of the world, who wail and shriek over the battle-field, and then erect an altar to the demon of the fight—come, behold a man, in genius as brilliant, as rich in accomplishments, far more comprehensive in his schemes, who, to splendor of intellect, added the sublimity of moral excellence; grasp, if you can, the stupendous plan that filled and expanded his soul—nothing less than to revolutionize the whole moral and social condition of mankind, and to send abroad the spirit of a new life through all its families. Follow him, as he speeds his way on this amazing errand, passing from city to city, from land to land, meeting reproach, derision, persecution, all unmoved, perilling his life by sea and land, baring his bosom to the storm, his back to the scourge, offering his limbs to fetters, his body to the cross, and after he had fought for years the battles of mankind, and subjugated whole nations to the truth, going down to the grave with the shout of victory on his tongue; a victory stained by no human blood except his own, and leaving a name revered through successive generations, by millions who never heard the name of Cæsar, or of Alexander, with a glory ever widening and brightening, as the progress of civilization and religion increases the numbers of those who can understand and appreciate real greatness of the highest order.

Such was the man that lay that night in chains at Philippi, thrust away into the innermost prison, in the darkest dungeon, with the vilest culprits, his feet pinned to the floor, his back gashed with wounds by the lead of the merciless scourge. Did he repine at his condition, rail at the ingratitude and wickedness of men, and sadly abandon his high mission? Far otherwise. At midnight the prisoners hear strange sounds for that prison-house, not a voice of wailing or blasphemy, but glad praises of the Most High; and soon far other sounds shall burst upon their ears, for the God of hosts has heard the prayer of his servants, and sent his angel to relieve them; and the earth trembles at his approach, the prison walls totter, the doors fly open, fetters burst loose. Well might the agitated jailer exclaim, amid these manifestations of the presence and power of the Almighty, "What must I do to be saved?"

Startled at midnight from his slumbers, by these fearful indications of the present and angry God, he springs forth pale and trembling from his couch, and, falling at the feet of the apostles, earnestly exclaims, "Sirs, what must I do to be saved?" Never did there fall from human lips a more solemn or important question; never burst from agonized bosom of man, rent by anxious and conflicting emotions, inquiry of more fearful and tremendous import. Indeed, it is the question of questions, the great question for every man that has a soul to be saved or lost. It is a question which only man can ask and answer. Brutes have no souls to save. Angels are already saved. Devils are already damned. It must be answered soon; or it will be answered too late, by the last trumpet, by the wailings of the damned, amidst the fire of Tophet, the shrieks, imprecations, and blasphemies of lost spirits. To be honestly asked, deeply, solemnly pondered, profoundly studied, faithfully, affectionately answered—oh, well might the loftiest intellect of man turn aside from all human speculations, and gather up its brightened and invigorated powers, and concentrate all in one burning focus on this high question, the question of transcendent and immeasurable interest. To comprehend it, if possible, in all its bearings, in all its height, length, breadth, and depth, and urge it home upon dying sinners with all the solemn fervor of one himself sweeping along with them to judgment, with prayers and entreaties and many tears, is the duty of every minister of God. For of all the innumerable questions which, from the foundation of the world, have agitated the minds of men, and called forth the mightiest energies and fiercest conflicts in the senate and the field, there is none so vast in its grandeur and importance, there is none which sweeps over so boundless a field of thought, involves such mighty interests, is followed by such stupendous consequences, bears with it such appalling responsibilities, and so appeals to the hopes and fears of every erring and dying man.

For, remember it is the salvation of the soul. And to you I appeal, O man most steeped in sensuality and worldliness, most maddened with love of money or of honor, if only one gleam of rationality remains! I ask of you, if in the whole circle of human interests, the whole compass of human thought, there can be any thing to be compared with this? What questions and interests on which statesmen debate, and heroes fight, and philosophers reason, can be compared with this? Suppose all for which they contend granted you, that the glory of all combined rested on you, the laurels of a hundred victories on your head, the sceptre of universal empire in your hand, the splendor of exalted genius and learning around you, applause attending your steps, everywhere the mysteries of nature unveiled, all knowledge yours—what will all avail if your soul be not saved? If the wrath of God hang darkly over you, what are the smiles of man, of millions? Of what avail are those large capacities, rich endowments, mighty powers of thought and feeling, if they be only made fitter subjects of condemnation, mightier piles for eternal burning? And now permit me to warn you, that the awful probability is, your soul will be lost; that it is already in imminent peril, and chiefly from insensibility.

But perhaps your reply to all this will be, that you see no danger! We seize your own objection, and tell you that this insensibility to the danger is the most fearful token of your coming damnation. Something must be done, and you are doing nothing, and will do nothing. If the Gospel be hid, it is hid to those who are lost. Heaven is a prize for which we must run, a crown for which we must fight, and yet you stand idly indolent all the day long. This deadly insensibility is the worst symptom. Could the physician rouse the patient from that lethargy, he were safe. But that sleep is the sleep of death. Could we but waken you to a sense of your misery and ruin, there were some hope. But all our efforts are vain: Sabbath after Sabbath, month after month, you sit in God's house, beneath warnings and invitations, and heed not. All the interests of immortality are at stake; life is wearing away, death hurrying on, judgment just at hand; yet all is safe with you. We tell you of an angry God, of a fiery perdition, of endless torments, and you sit as if these were an idle tale. Nay, as if to add insult to past sin, you come into God's own house to brave his anger. Did you see the physician turn mournfully away from that dying patient? He is sinking into delirium, and dreams that all is safe. Living in the government of a holy God, and habitually sinning—yet safe; feeding on his bounty, and spurning his hand—yet safe; his eye fixed on you, his presence around you—yet safe; his sword suspended over you, judgment pronounced, denunciation uttered—yet safe; his power pledged—yet safe. Ah! young man, that flowery path is dangerous. It leads to death. But ah! the sinner will be safe when the bolts of his prison-house have shut him in; will be safe, where no Christians annoy; safe where no Spirit, no Gospel, no hope intrudes; and when he shall be lodged there, damned spirits shall raise their shout of exultation, and say safe, safe, forever safe! Oh! horrible safety!

But who is he that stands before us there, amidst the solemn stillness of this midnight hour; with these words of anguish on his lips, and this unspeakable terror in his heart. We have not the story of his life, nor the record of his death. His birth and burial, lineage, station, and fortunes, family, friends, hopes, fears, enjoyments, sufferings, disasters, successes, are alike unknown. Of all that he thought, felt, purposed, desired, or achieved, there is no memorial. What are all these in the estimate of the Almighty? Only a dim and shadowy form is seen rising above the waste of ages. A mysterious voice is heard amidst the silence of centuries. It is the form and voice of a man like ourselves, with a guilty conscience and a deathless spirit, and all the fearful elements of our fallen but immortal nature, crying out, in the agony of his soul, "What must I do to be saved?"

Never did more important question burst from lips of man, never did question receive a more direct, simple, or satisfactory reply, "Believe on the Lord Jesus Christ, and thou shalt be saved." You can do nothing of yourselves, can make no atonement for past sin, work no deliverance from its future power. Salvation is not an achievement but a gift, not of works but of grace, offered freely for your acceptance, not to be purchased by your merit. Christ is our justification, and Christ our sanctification; Christ without and Christ within us. Christ without, the object of our adoring love, becoming, in that very act of believing adoration, the Christ within, "the hope of glory." The Christ without, removing the guilt of sin; the Christ within, subduing by his presence its controlling power, and freeing us from its pollution.

Christ is the light of the world. Wouldst thou be saved from the darkness of spiritual death? Let the eye of faith be opened to receive that light; let day dawn, and the day-star arise upon thy soul, and that midnight blackness shall vanish away. It needs no will, no agency, no work of thine to give it efficacy. It works by its own inherent energy, and seeks no aid from man. Let but the eye of faith be open to receive it, and by its own mysterious power and adaptation to thy nature, the grandeur and glory of a universe, before invisible, shall burst in all their glad, living reality upon thee.

Christ is the bread of heaven. No work or effort of thine own will give thee nourishment, or add vital power to this food. Let it only be received within thy system; it will blend with all the elements of thy being; become mysteriously part and portion of thyself; mingle with the whole flowing circulation; reach each part and function, and be found a real living power in them all.

Christ is the great physician and sovereign remedy for the disease of sin. What shall you do to be saved from this deadly malady? No power, will, effort of thine own; no spasmodic agitation of all the elements within thee, would give it healing efficacy. It works by an efficacy all its own. Let it be received within thee; each diseased action is arrested; each suspended function restored; the warm blood flows in glad currents through every vein and artery, and from each gland and duct and capillary vessel, through ten thousand channels, is distilled perpetually a nameless joy.

Now faith is the "open eye;" not the object, nor the light which reveals the object, but the avenue through which light streams in upon the soul. It does not create light or objects; yet were the avenue closed, both would for us be as though they existed not. Hence it has all the mystery of a new creation, as, when the blind man first beholds the light of day, a new universe springs into existence all around him.

Faith is neither food that nourishes, nor the remedy that heals, but only the organ that receives them both, and brings them in living contact with the system. Light, food, remedy, all are without—objective. They need no aid of ours to give them existence or efficacy; they need only the open eye, the recipient organ, the living contact, to reveal and exercise their appropriate efficacy. "Believe on the Lord Jesus Christ, and thou shalt be saved."

Consider first the sublime simplicity of this answer. This simple grandeur characterizes all God's works. Man, uncertain of his ends, and limited in resources, multiplies his instrumentalities, employs complicated apparatus, cumbrous machinery, a circuitous process. God, sure of the result, moves directly toward his object, and accomplishes the largest results by the simplest agencies: by the combination of a few simple elements produces all that infinite variety of forms, hues, and properties which we behold in nature: by one single law, that stupendous harmony in the movements of the worlds above. Gaze on those ten thousand worlds that glitter in our nocturnal heavens; look through the telescope, till those thousands are converted into millions, and nebulæ after nebulæ are resolved into increasing millions; watch the planets in their varying positions, comets in their eccentric career, then ask what rare combination of forces, what intricate and complicated apparatus keeps each in its appropriate place, brings each at its appointed season. Through all that vast domain one simple and majestic law presides. The law of gravitation retains planets and comets in their orbits, and guides the sun in his flaming path through space.

And when the great apostle lifts his eye to that glorious

galaxy of worthies, shining most brightly in the darkest night of affliction, and points us to their radiant career, as they move serenely on, "subduing kingdoms, working righteousness, stopping the mouths of lions, quenching the violence of fire, valiant in fight, turning to flight the armies of the aliens"—what, we may ask, impelled them onward in their brilliant career, and sustained them amidst surrounding perils? "Was not this their victory—even faith."

When Luther threw down the gauntlet to pope and emperor, and stood before the diet, sole advocate of a condemned and accursed faith; when he fearlessly exclaimed, "Though there were as many devils at Worms as there are tiles on the houses, I would go;" when Chalmers more recently marched calmly forth at the head of Scotland's free church (four hundred men), leaving behind them congregations, homes, each earthly comfort, for "testimony of Jesus," it was faith that impelled and sustained them all. And all those mighty men who in every age have stamped deep upon their generation the impression of their character, and lived in perpetual conflict, have been men of faith, have walked with calm and assured step amidst unseen realities, as amidst the visible, palpable things of the world around. The broad sky above was not a more real canopy, than the unseen and overshadowing majesty of God; nor could the solid earth beneath give firmer footing than the unfailing promise of God. They gazed, with steadfast eye, deep down into the abyss of woe, till all human torture had lost its terrors; walked amidst the glories and bliss of God's paradise alone, till all earthly splendor was stripped of its power to charm; fought face to face in actual warfare with powers of darkness, and issuing from closet to pulpit, fresh from solemn meditations, victorious from terrible conflicts, their words of exhortation were like a voice from heaven, their tones of warning like the trump of God.

And we remark, in passing, that the necessity and value of faith are not confined to religion. The law which operates in yonder farther heavens, operates on the surface of the earth. The same law which shapes the orbit of the planet, bends the curve of the descending stone thrown by a school-boy's hand. Objects, sphere, direction, are different, the general principle is the same. "It is impossible, without faith, to please God," says the Bible. Without faith it is impossible to achieve any thing for the good of man, or even to continue our own existence for a day. It is faith that nerves the patriot's arm, faith in his country's destiny, in the triumph of right: faith that sustains the enthusiastic ardor of pursuit: faith in the distant and unseen, which vividly portrays in the coming future the harvest that shall reward all present toil. And those men of destiny, the Napoleons and Cæsars of the world, was it not faith in themselves, in their own powers and fortune, that gave such superhuman energy to their genius? Even the present Emperor, we are told, never doubted, from earliest infancy, or in greatest peril, that he should one day wear the imperial diadem of France. And what is each anticipation of the future, and each preparation made for ourselves or others, our expectation of to-morrow, even, but an exercise of faith in the constancy of nature's laws, and the regularity of nature's course?

Here, then, we have the great principle pervading the whole of the divine administration. We have a present temporal interest at stake, that cannot be secured without the exercise of faith in the laws of natural government, which passes beyond the sphere of sense and reasoning, grasps the future firmly, and gives to the distant and unseen all the power of visible and palpable realities. If we have an eternal interest to secure, is it unreasonable to suppose that this may demand a corresponding faith in the laws and facts of moral government, and that it brings its motives and elements from that higher world and future existence?

2d. Faith, simple in its nature, is manifold in its operations and manifestations. This has perplexed the minds of theologians, and started many questions as to the doctrine of salvation by faith *alone*. Is it faith united with love, obedience, prayer, hope? I answer, these are only varied manifestations of one and the same principle of faith. It is faith which loves, hopes, adores, obeys. Present in all, pervading all, vivifying all, the grand essential element in all. We behold the same in nature all around us and are not perplexed—perpetual change of form, while the substance remains the same. Water flowing in the stream, congealing into ice, the spray that curls above the cataract, the mist that hangs in the mountain's brow, white clouds piled upon the horizon or floating over the sky, the black thunder-cloud that sweeps careering before the tempest—all these are water still. Nay—to borrow in part an illustration from an ancient father—pervading all nature, it is red in the rose, purple in the violet, white in the lily, green in the growing grass, and in the great bow of heaven reflects in gorgeous coloring every variety of hue. It is an opinion toward which all modern discovery is rapidly converging, that the mild light of day, the gentle electricity diffused unseen and unfelt through all nature, the fire that bursts from the volcano, and the lightning that flashes from the sky, are all a single element in various manifestations, and reaching farther still into distant worlds, that when suns are kindled up, or suns go out, it is due to the presence or absence of this simple element.

Even so we say faith is the light of knowledge, the warmth of love, the ardor of zeal, the gentle radiance that sheds a quiet beauty over the ordinary Christian life, and the deep, inward fire, glowing in the bosom, which ever moves the great heroes of truth, and lifts them in their mountain grandeur and granite strength high above their fellows. Nay, faith is the Christian's life. He lives by faith, walks by faith, by faith wrestles with principalities and powers. In all his battles with the powers of darkness, faith supplies the shield and wields the sword. Faith adores an unseen God, hopes for an unseen heaven. Faith unites to an unseen Saviour.

3d. This vital union with the Saviour is the grand essential characteristic of Christian faith, which not only constitutes it the sinew and substance of all Christian virtues, but the ground at once of our justification and sanctification: makes Christ our wisdom, righteousness, sanctification, and redemption. It is strange that this essential characteristic has been so much overlooked by Christian theologians, and that men of high authority, bewildered by a misty metaphysics, should have sought to lower this sublimest mystery in the Christian life, this greatest fact in Christian consciousness, to the level of an ordinary exercise of the human understanding. "Faith," they argue, "is only another name for belief;" belief is a word that expresses a well-known act of the understanding in view of evidence. Christian faith in Christ, therefore, they conclude, is the same in nature as belief in any other fact or facts—concerning Cæsar, Napoleon, Alexander. I cannot stay now to analyze this fanfaronade of folly. Perhaps it would be difficult to collect, in so small a compass, more of folly and heresy than is contained in this stereotyped phraseology, now crystallized, and almost consecrated in so many of the schools. Suffice it to say, that it is contradicted by the whole tenor of the Bible and its specific language on this very subject; and that it is also contradicted by all true philosophy.

VII.

THE EXCELLENCY OF THE KNOWLEDGE OF CHRIST.

1 Cor. ii. 2.—"For I determined not to know any thing among you, save Jesus Christ, and him crucified."

We follow man from the cradle to the grave, observe the gradual development of all his powers, the smiling innocence and waking intellect of the child, the rude sports of the boy, the impetuous passion of the man, till his energies are enfeebled, his faculties begin to fail, and he at last disappears from our view. The curtain drops, the actor passes away, he is seen no more; but what is behind the scenes? Thus generation passes away after generation, and where are they? The dead who have gone before us, where are they? We have heard of their deeds of valor, or read their works of immortal genius, or witnessed their works of benevolence and love, or mingled in all the sweet intercourse of social life along with them; and now, where are they? That eye which, even when turned on empty space, beamed bright with intelligence, is it quenched forever? That heart, which throbbed high with generous love for God and man, shall it beat no more? That smile, which beamed with divine benevolence, and shed happiness along its path, is it chilled in the coldness of eternal death. That whole mass of living and moving, and feeling beings, who in successive generations have filled the scenes of this world's history, do they live again, or "lie in cold abstraction, and there rot?"

It is here that our inquiries become really important, and our solicitude painfully intense, when the question concerns the happiness of incalculable millions, multiplied by an infinity of years. Yet it is precisely here that all human knowledge fails us, all human speculation is at fault. Thus, we examine nature in its mightiest masses and its minutest particles; we observe its wonderful machinery and its beneficent operations, but where is the moving spirit? We perceive its dead and mute materialism, but where is that mysterious and fearful Spirit who first called it into bèing, gave the first impulse to its movements, and still sits on high and presides supremely over all its operations? And what are his character and relations to us? Does he look with indolent or gloomy indifference on the course of human affairs? Does he malignantly rejoice in the suffering of the race, or does he sit with the calm and awful dignity, the pure and untarnished uprightness of the supreme and omniscient Judge, scrutinizing all human actions, and awarding to each its own moral retributions?

And this great universe, in which we live and of which we form a part, so vast in its extent, so wonderful in its structure, so connected in its parts, and yet so separate, so remote, and yet so mutually dependent—What is it, and why? Is it an enigma and a riddle, or is there throughout the whole, some one great common principle uniting all in one bond of universal harmony, and leading all to the accomplishment of some supreme and universal object. And do the beings in other parts of God's dominions feel an interest in us? Is there a bond of moral sympathy, powerful as that which binds the eternal universe together, extending throughout this magnificent creation, uniting God's moral universe into one family of brethren, under one Father's care.

Over all these questions of deepest interest and sublime import, reason casts but a faint and feeble light. Into this region of grandeur and mystery and wonder it may not enter. It may stand indeed on the borders of that land, and gaze wistfully over, with dim and doubtful vision, uncertain if the shapes it beholds are forms of light, or spirits of darkness, or creations of fancy. In the Gospel alone can these problems be solved.

I. It is Christ that has brought life and immortality to light, and the knowledge he gives is most delightful and sublime. It is the revelation of his grace which has dispelled the darkness and dimness that enveloped our sky, and has made all things bright and clear to our view. Over the grave it has cast a glory, over nature a charm; in man it has discovered a dignity and in the universe a harmony unknown before. The sun of righteousness has arisen, the mists which obscured our vision are dispersed, and the whole scene lies spread out in loveliness and grandeur beneath his pure and heavenly light. Could one of those unfortunate beings, whose senses have been locked up from the hour of birth in darkness and deep night, be suddenly visited by the full, clear light of heaven, lift up his delighted eyes upon this glorious earth, and this broad, starry sky, behold the ten thousand forms of loveliness and hues of beauty around him, and that glorious and majestic world of light above him, pouring forth from his throne of kingly exaltation, with sovereign munificence, light, life, and loveliness on this inferior globe, it would be to him no longer that old world he had so imperfectly learned before, but as a new creation sprung fresh from its Creator's hand, and endowed with new properties of beauty and of grandeur.

Even so is it with the Christian. A regenerating spirit has brooded over the waters, and a new creation has sprung up beneath his influence—"Old things have passed away and all things have become new." To him all things now assume new and nobler attributes. The broad arch of heaven and the green garniture of earth, the deep majestic ocean and the everlasting hills, the music of the grove and the beauty of the valley—in all of these "he sees a hand you cannot see, he hears a voice you cannot hear." But especially in regard to man, in all that concerns his origin and his nature, his duty and his destiny, his views have taken a higher range, his sentiments have assumed a loftier and holier tone. Man is no longer the child of clay, and the sport of chance, but the heir of immortality—a citizen of heaven. His desires, boundless as infinity, now find an appropriate object. His faculties, large by nature, and capable of unlimited expansion, obtain a suitable theatre for their exercise and development. Those desires, no longer limited by earth and sense, rising, expanding, glowing in the pure atmosphere of heavenly truth, find their most dignified employment, their most exalted gratification. Those faculties, enlarging with the objects they embrace, and grasping still vaster at each felt enlargement, secure full scope for their liveliest and healthiest exercise, in that wide field of lofty contemplation opened up in the Bible, where the soul walks forth with delight, as on its native soil, with God and angels, and redeemed spirits for its companions. All around is stamped with the impress of the Infinite and Eternal.

The whole universe is now our Father's house, where we may forever gaze on his reflected glory, exalted, humbled, and refreshed by the delightful manifestation. On all around we behold the footsteps of the Deity. This earth is the cradle, the nursery of immortal beings. Here angels minister. Here God shows forth his wonders. Here Christ died. Every spot is holy, for the Lord is here. Oh, what a theme is this!—theme to employ an angel's tongue—theme to enkindle a seraph's soul of fire, where the mind labors beneath the vastness of its own conceptions, and the tongue falters to express what the mind, alas! too feebly conceives; where the thoughts, rolling onward, become vast, vague, and fearful as that immensity in which they rove.

Oh, mother! that babe upon your bosom is no longer the feeble, helpless thing that you imagine. It is an angel in the bud. That man of multiplied afflictions, tossing from side to side upon his couch of woe, visited by the neglect or scorn of the proud and gay around him, and presenting to the eye of benevolent observation the most melancholy of earthly spectacles, shall rise above these scenes of darkness. And from the lonely inclosure, where so many decaying forms are laid, where the wild grass waves luxuriant over broken sepulchres, shall spring forth new forms of beauty and glory—angelic beauty, unfading glory.

Go with me now through the whole range of human science, and where shall we find aught at once so delightful and so sublime; aught that sheds over the world a light at once so steady, so cheerful, and so glorious, that so enlarges the mind and purifies the heart, that so glorifies the Creator, and at once humbles and exalts the creature? Have we not well said that this Christian knowledge is the most delightful and sublime? Let us proceed then to our second proposition, which is, that—

II. The most useful and necessary knowledge is that which is found in the Gospel of Christ. All knowledge is valuable, even that which serves to amuse a vacant hour, or gratify a momentary curiosity. But who would compare the amusement of an hour with the interests of a life-time, the curiosity of a moment with the weightiest concerns of families and nations. What concerns the body's comfort is important; but what is this to the soul's high interest—the duration of a day to the long lapse of interminable ages? Children waste their anxieties on the trifles of the present moment; wiser men look forward to the exigencies of future life; the wisest take in the whole interests of a life which shall not end. The knowledge of ancient navigators served their purposes, when only a few miles from shore. They had noticed a few rocks, and promontories, and observed a few well-known stars; and when the sky was serene, and the sea tranquil, and the tall mountains seen proudly lifting their heads in the distance, or the low beach in the blue line skirting the horizon, they could boldly and safely prosecute their narrow trades, but when far out at sea, with naught in view but the wild waste of wäters spreading far and wide around, or when the dense fog enveloped their bark, or the storm lashed ocean into fury, their knowledge failed—failed in their hour of peril, and left them to wander aimless and hopeless over the illimitable waters—to perish by hunger, or dash a fearful wreck upon some unknown shore. Their knowledge, though limited, was useful, but how much more useful that of modern times, when the compass points the way, and man sails securely in the darkest night, and over the farthest ocean, as in the clear light of day, in full view of his native shore.

Even so it is with the knowledge of religion. This is life's real compass amidst its storms and darkness, this points ever to the only haven of rest, and, over a tempestuous ocean, guides to an unseen land of glory and repose. But, not only did the invention of the compass lead to the discovery of unknown lands, it changed all the relations of commerce, and operated on society in all its interests and in every region. Wealth, intelligence, civilization, freedom, were diffused widely through its instrumentality, and the Gospel has been borne to untold millions, who otherwise had never heard its tones of mercy. So religion has not confined its influence to our future destiny, but has gently diffused it through all our social and personal relations, and is really a blessing to society, as to the individual. Let him who doubts it compare ancient with modern morals; the purity of domestic Christian life with the licentiousness and debauchery prevalent among the ancients; let him visit those cities half excavated from the lava which covered and preserved them, and providentially offering the contrast to our eyes, where the licentious Italian blushes for his more corrupt predecessors, as he gazes on scenes which modesty may not dare to describe. Let him compare the pure domestic bliss and household virtues of our own favored land with the pollutions which now prevail in those nations and cities where the Saviour is not known or is rejected. Thus may he learn to acknowledge how incalculable is the benefit bestowed by the Gospel on society in all its relations, political, social, and moral.

There is much, however, that is useful, and yet not indispensable; much that adorns and dignifies human life, which yet is not essential to human comfort; and of the greater part of those accomplishments which are so much prized and so eagerly sought after in society around us, it must, at last, be said, that, however gracefully they may sit upon the polished and refined, they have little beneficial influence upon human happiness or human virtue. With a clear head and a quiet conscience, one can do very well without them.

But the knowledge of Jesus Christ is absolutely indispensable. It has this pre-eminence above all other knowledge, that none other will supply its place; that in no condition of life, under no peculiarity of circumstances, with no singularity of genius or character, can it be safely neglected. To the deeply reflecting and speculative mind it is necessary, as the termination of its doubts, as the solutions of those perplexing problems which have long agitated and disturbed it; to the miserable it is necessary, as the solace of his affliction, as the only support beneath the burden which has long overwhelmed him; to one conscious of guilt it is necessary, as the only method of escape from the upbraidings of an awakened conscience; and to all, as the only hope of salvation from the wrath to come.

It will be necessary to individuals, to families, to human society, as long as purity and gentleness and love are essential to human happiness, as long as glory to God in the highest is intimately and indissolubly connected with "peace on earth, and good will among men." What would be this earth, if there were naught beside! if the blue arch of heaven no longer spanned the globe, if the stars without number no longer glittered in our sky, if the sun no longer sent down his benignant beams to cheer our darkness, nor the clouds their moisture to fertilize our valleys? Even thus would it be if there were no heaven above for the immortal spirit, if no kindly influences came down from that far-off world, to purify and elevate our race. Oh, what would be earth, if earth were all!

It is a truth which can never be too deeply pondered, too deeply engraven on our hearts, that no human knowledge can satisfy the soul. Thy philosophy may know all systems. Thy history may extend from the commencement of the globe, and descend with minutest accuracy to the present moment. Thy mathematics may include all that is known of number and quantity, in all their abstruse inquiries, and all their practical applications, but what is all this to thee, if thy soul be not satisfied? The soul is of a higher nature, and there is, within, a restless longing after higher and better knowledge, and sooner shall that soul itself be annihilated than thou canst eradicate thence this surest mark of its immortal nature. There is but one thing needful, to know the one true and living God, and Jesus Christ his only Son, whom to know is life eternal. Without this, all other knowledge is useless. Thou mayest be deeply learned in all that physicians have discovered through centuries of labor. But, alas! what will it profit? Thy body perhaps is healed, but thy soul is diseased—diseased with a deadly malady, which preys inwardly upon the vitals, and will soon break out in the darkest symptoms of eternal death! Thine estate may be secured by the learning of a skilful attorney, but what will it profit thee, thou hast no inheritance in heaven. Thou art a child of wrath, a son of perdition, an heir to the agonies that cannot be endured, yet may not pass away. At death all other knowledge fails. Will your philosophy, your medicine, your law pass on with you into heaven? Alas! what subtlety can deceive, what eloquence persuade the heart-searching and Omniscient One? What skill of man, what medicine of the shops can heal or alleviate the torments of a soul in ruin?

Then it is that this knowledge is most useful. After guiding through life it attends you in death, and in that hour when flesh and heart shall fail, it will be the strength of your heart and your portion forever. Oh, in that hour how vain is earthly wisdom, how precious the knowledge of Jesus Christ, and him crucified; how fearful to hear him say, "Depart from me, I never knew you." Observe that it is the knowledge of Christ crucified that the apostle so highly prizes, as a mediator between God and man, as an atoning sacrifice for sin, as a great high-priest, who has shed his own blood for us, and entered into the holiest of holies on our behalf. It is not merely a sentimental admiration of his exalted and beautiful morality, but a cordial acceptance of his atonement for sin. It is not as a model, but as a Saviour, that we must know him. It is not merely the glorified, but the crucified Redeemer. It is to love his Gospel, not only when greeted with the hallelujahs of the multitude, but likewise when saluted with the cry of "*Crucify him, crucify him.*" Ah, my brethren, it is easy to know Christ when all are crying "Blessed is he that cometh in the name of the Lord;" but when the question is scornfully, fiercely put, "Art thou not one of this man's disciples?" how many of us are prone to say, "I know not the man"?

But this is not the knowledge of which the apostle speaks so enthusiastically. "Gratitude," it has been finely said, "is the memory of the heart," and the definition is as philosophically just as it is poetically beautiful. Even so would we say, "Religion is the knowledge of the heart." To know Jesus Christ is not merely to have heard of him, to talk of him, to have read the history of his life and the story of his death. It is to know him as a friend, as an intimate and daily companion, as our comfort in sorrow, as our light in darkness, our joy in affliction, our guide, our director, our exceeding great reward.

It is not an uncommon circumstance for us to associate for months and even for years with an individual whom we cannot understand, whom we do not know, while we often mingle in a society where we are ourselves perpetually misunderstood. The reason is there is no sympathy, no community of character and feeling between us. The man of lofty character and pure and elevated feelings is an enigma to those of an opposite description. They have no conception of his feelings because they have nothing responsive within themselves. But when we meet with one of feelings corresponding to our own, how soon, and how intimately do we know him; each feeling, each thought, is immediately understood, nay, almost anticipated before expressed. We feel that we have access to his inmost soul, that it is but the reflection of our own. Now it is this intimacy of knowledge, which springs from true affection, from a community of feeling and character, to which the Apostle John alludes when he says, "Our fellowship is with the Father and the Son and the Spirit." To which the Saviour refers when he says, "If any man love me, I and my Father will come and make our abode with him."

Professing Christian, knowest thou nothing of this intimate intercourse, this near communion, this hidden life? Then must we say, in all sincerity, thou knowest nothing of the matter. Thou hast at best only touched the hem of the Saviour's garment. Thou hast not leaned on his bosom. Thou knowest him only as they knew him who first welcomed him as a monarch, and then crucified him as a malefactor. But how shall this divine and heavenly knowledge be attained? There is no strength of the human intellect which can master it. There is no elevation of human genius which can reach it. There is no accumulation of human learning which can approach it. "It is not of the earth, earthly. It is the wisdom that descendeth from above." It is high, you cannot attain unto it. You cannot pile Pelion upon Ossa, Alps upon Alps, one acquirement upon another, it is all in vain. He who would pluck fruit from the tree of life must ascend on the wings of faith, and be buoyed up by the mighty spirit of the Lord. It is by humble prayer, and faithful study of God's word, attended by his illuminating spirit, that man attains to the wisdom of the just.

O ye young and ardent minds, confident in your strength, and sanguine in your expectations, learn to be fools, that ye may become wise; to be humble, that ye may be exalted. How shall the blind man comprehend the glories of the world around him till a power from on high shall unlock the doors of vision, and let in upon him the light of heaven? How shall the deaf man understand the melody of sound till an almighty hand shall touch the organ of hearing, and a divine voice shall say, "Ephphatha, be thou opened"? How shall man by wisdom find out the Almighty?

And now may I be permitted to address a single word to the numerous youths whom I behold around me? Though unknown to many of you in person, yet have I been often present with you in spirit; and though separated by mountains, continents, and oceans, my heart hath yearned after you as the heart of a mother toward her first-born. 'Twas not so much that I desired to engage with you in those social studies which I have loved from earliest childhood, but it was that I hoped to mingle with human science something diviner far; that the foundation of solid learning might bear a superstructure reaching upward to the skies; that I might add my feeble testimony to that of the great cloud of witnesses for the superiority of the Gospel. Be assured, my beloved, that wherever you may wander, if not dazzled by splendor, nor awed by authority, nor misled by fashion, the conviction must ever deepen on your mind, that the fear of the Lord is the only true wisdom, and that of all earthly spectacles the most melancholy is presented when learning and genius are divorced from piety, when gigantic intellect, clothed with almost superhuman learning, and urged on by towering pride, attempts to scale the battlements of heaven, and, failing in the effort, lies crushed beneath the weight of its own massive armor, and convulsed by the throes of its own perverted energies.

VIII.

PAUL VINDICATED FROM THE CHARGE OF MADNESS.

ACTS, xxvi. 24, 25.—"And as he thus spake for himself, Festus said with a loud voice, Paul, thou art beside thyself; much learning doth make thee mad. But he said, I am not mad, most noble Festus; but speak forth the words of truth and soberness."

IF an individual, in some strange paroxysm of perverted ambition, should aspire after the reputation of the most egregious folly, and desire to be known and proclaimed among his fellow-men as the completest madman of his age, what course should he pursue to attain most certainly his object? Should he devise some new scheme of folly, stranger and more preposterous than all which had preceded it, by which man could fritter away more surely the noble powers which God has bestowed upon him in the most heartless and frivolous amusements? Should he invent some theory in morals, or some system of religion, more monstrous and revolting than any which the human imagination, in its wildest reveries has yet conceived, or the human heart in its deepest pollution has yet embraced?

If he understood at all the nature of man, far different would be his scheme. There is no frivolity so absurd or stupid, that it is not freely indulged and gravely defended by many who profess to be wise. There is no theory in matter, mind, or morals, so strangely and ludicrously inconsistent, so self-contradictory and suicidal, that it has not received the sanction of grave philosophers, and the stamp of highest wisdom. Even those who denied the existence of the objects of their inquiry, and destroyed at one fell stroke all matter, mind, and morals, were considered the profoundest in wisdom. To doubt was considered the beginning and the end of reasoning, and the sceptical philosophy was enthroned in the admiration of mankind. It is not then by being pre-eminently absurd, or pre-eminently frivolous, that he could ever attain the desired reputation. But he need not despair. Let him reverse the process, and his object is accomplished. Let him regulate his life according to the principles of the purest and truest reason. Let his thoughts ascend .to a higher region, and take a wider sweep, than those of the men around him. Exalted as he is, to a higher intellectual eminence, and looking far away over a more extensive horizon, let his feelings, his character, and his conduct all partake of a similar exaltation, and be guided by a spirit and moulded to a fashion for which others feel no sympathy, because they have no comprehension. For such a man as this, whatever might be his sphere of action or field of thought, the common mass would only feel contempt or pity. And whether he propounded some far-seen truth in politics, or some deeply-pondered principle in the philosophy of the mind, or some rule of action deeply laid in man's constitution and relations to the universe, or some wide and comprehensive view of God's creation and moral government—all this would only be fresh evidence to them of an unbalanced mind, roving vigorously, perhaps, but almost blindly in an ideal world.

It is obvious that if any man were endowed with a new sense which opened before him qualities unseen and unknown to other men, the whole of his language and conduct might be entirely different from that of other men, and moving thus in a new world, and influenced by new views, he might seem to them the subject of some strange disorder. And thus too it is easy to conceive how the individual to whom we have alluded, living in a new world of thought open to higher influences, and guided by more exalted views, might act upon principles and cherish opinions utterly incomprehensible to those around; and, while directed by the highest wisdom, might appear the victim of the grossest folly, because the wisdom which he cultivated was far above, and, as the Psalmist happily expresses it, "out of sight."

When Columbus first announced to the inhabitants of Europe the existence of that new world that lay far away in the distant west, beyond the waters of an untried and unmeasured ocean, and avowed his determination to visit that undiscovered land, and reveal its unknown wonders and hidden wealth to the astonished nations, he was considered the wildest dreamer of his age, perhaps the most extravagant and visionary speculator of any day. He travelled over Europe in the prosecution of his magnificent scheme; he passed from city to city, and from court to court, but was everywhere met with the same cool and contemptuous derision. The philosopher smiled and scarcely deigned to argue, the witling jested, and the man of influence and power listened with impatient astonishment to a scheme so full of certain danger, and so remote from probable success; and it was not till after years of unwearied labor, and most cruel mockings, that he obtained a feeble and ill-appointed fleet, to embark in the greatest of earthly enterprises. When Newton first removed the veil which concealed many of the mysteries of nature, and announced to mankind the vastness of the material universe, and the simplicity of the laws by which its various parts are bound together, and their complicated movements harmoniously directed, the views which he unfolded were too vast for the philosophers of the day, and many denounced, as idle and visionary theories, the sober results of mathematical calculation.

We ought not then to be surprised, that when the Apostle Paul went forth among mankind to tell of that invisible, whence no voyager has ever yet returned to make known his discoveries, and to proclaim those riches and that glory which no eye has seen and no ear has heard and no heart has been able to conceive, he should be often heard with careless incredulity, and his annunciations treated as the wild extravagancies of an overheated brain. Nothing, says a scoffing sceptic, could be more visionary than the attempt to reform mankind; yet this was the very enterprise in which the apostle had embarked.

Other philosophers had travelled, that they might gain instruction: he that he might communicate knowledge. Others had visited foreign lands, that they might study the laws and manners of mankind, and from the collected wisdom of nations add something to their own stores: he went forth to proclaim that wisdom which is not of the earth, earthy, but descended from above, to make known the laws and the government of Him who sits in presiding dignity over all worlds, and on whose high award depend alike the destinies of men and angels. And in the prosecution of this high design, there was no danger which he did not meet, no suffering which he did not endure: he saw death in all its shapes, and scorned them all. There was no city celebrated for its learning, its vices, or its wealth, which he did not visit; and though he labored with an energy that could not be wearied, and argued with a force that could not be resisted, and poured forth, on every topic that he touched, a torrent of the most convincing and persuasive eloquence, yet, wherever he directed his steps, he was met with the same rude insults, and bitterly derided as a fanatic, a babbler, and a fool.

A stranger once appeared in Athens. He came not to linger amidst the shades of the Academy, or to muse on the departed genius of Plato. He paused not to admire the monuments of human art, to gaze upon the works of Phidias and Praxiteles, those amazing productions of creative genius which have secured to their authors the immortality they designed to confer on others. He only saw that they were wholly given to idolatry; he only noticed that strange altar erected to the unknown God. And now the crowd of lively and inquisitive Athenians has gathered around him, and as they move up toward the Areopagus, each is whispering to his friend, "What will this babbler say?" The gay and superficial Epicurean leads on the attack, and assures him that pleasure is the chief good of man, and that the gods repose in tranquil dignity far "above the stir and smoke of the dim spot that we call earth," indifferent alike to human conduct and human happiness. The stern and haughty Stoic largely prates of human wisdom and human dignity, assures him that happiness and misery are equally indifferent, and that the wise man is superior to the fates, and even independent of the gods; darkly hinting all the while the uncertainty of the future being, and the absurdity of expecting a state of future rewards and punishments.

And now this stranger is standing on Mars Hill, the messenger of peace in the temple of the god of war, and, with the native dignity of an upright and manly intellect, he spurns away from him all the jargon of the schools, and brushes off the cobwebs of sophistry which Grecian subtilty had woven. He enters not the labyrinth of their endless disputations, but marches on with steady and assured step to the great object of his mission, and announces, in brief and energetic language, the great and sublime truths of religion, which all their systems neglected or denied. He proclaimed to the idolatrous crowd the one true and living God, who made heaven and earth and all things that are therein, and shows from one of their own poets the folly of worshipping wood and stone for gods, since we ourselves are the offspring of a spiritual and omnipresent God. He teaches the Epicurean the presiding and ever-present providence of God, in whom we live and move and have our being, and to the haughty Stoic puffed with imaginary virtue, and doubting about a future state of being, he teaches the necessity of repentance toward God, and points him forward to that day of righteous and terrible revelations, when God will judge the world in righteousness by that man whom he hath ordained. But the simple majesty of these great truths had no attraction whatever for the minds of the common mass, immersed as they were in the absurdities and the sensuality of paganism, or of the philosophers, lost as they were in the mazes of their minute and subtile disquisitions, and with one accord they began to mock when they heard of the resurrection of the dead.

Thus to be the sport at once of the wise and the foolish, of the ignorant and the learned, is perhaps the severest trial which a proud and ardent spirit can endure; and if ever there was a man whose native sensibility would writhe beneath such an infliction, whose impetuous temper would rise up and indignantly repel it, that man was the Apostle Paul. But if he felt it as a man, as an apostle he despised it all. And hence, when rudely interrupted by Festus in the midst of his appeal to the Jewish prophets, and charged with madness, he manifests no irritation, he sends back no retort, he assumes no air of fanatical superiority, he fulminates no bold or bitter denunciation, but, with the temper of a saint and the politeness of a gentleman, he addresses him by his proper title, and replies with a simple negative, "I am not mad, most noble Festus."

And here it may be well to remark how decided and how bitter is the opposition of man's nature against the truth of God. When the Saviour of men was to be crucified, Pilate and Herod forgot their ancient enmity, and united to accomplish his destruction. The Pharisees and Sadducees were always arrayed in bitterest hostility against each other, yet would ever unite to assault and to entangle our Redeemer. And so we see the various sects of Grecian philosophers. Though engaged in perpetual wranglings with each other, and warfare violent in the inverse proportion to the importance of the matters in debate, they could suspend their mutual hostilities for a season, that Epicurean and Stoic and Peripatetic in solid phalanx might march to the assault upon the new religion. Each saw the folly of all systems except their own, and each felt their own condemned along with others by the truth of God. And thus we see it is at the present day. All men perceive the faults and follies of all except themselves, yet all unite in urging the charge of madness against the serious and consistent servant of their Lord. The Jew despised and abhorred the idolatry of heathenism; and the heathen looked with equal aversion and contempt on the narrow and bigoted spirit of the Jews; while both united in cruel mockings and bitter persecutions against that divine and perfect system before which the idolatry of heathenism was soon to disappear, and the bigotry of the Jewish system was to be lost in the largeness of a more exalted and expansive philanthropy. The tenants of a lunatic asylum, though each unconscious of his own malady, often perceive the madness of their fellow-sufferers. You may probably remember the anecdote of one who pointed out to a visitor the madness of a brother lunatic. He was asked to state the evidence of his madness, and replied, "He fancies himself to be John the Baptist." How do you know that he is not John the Baptist? "Because I am well acquainted with the Baptist," and then claimed for himself the name and the attributes of the Redeemer. But of all the tenants of Bedlam, none seems more strangely and hopelessly irrational to those disordered minds than the skilful physician or the watchful keeper, who would heal their diseases and restrain their madness.

And even thus do we find it among that large and restless crowd who are hurrying to and fro with anxious steps in pursuit of imaginary and unreal good. The man of business wonders at the man of pleasure, and can scarcely excuse madness which barters away all future health, respectability, and comfort for a momentary gratification. But he forgets at once his arithmetic and his wisdom when he comes to calculate the whole profits of his business. He had gained the world, but lost his soul. The philosophic statesman thinks all conquerors madmen, from Macedonia's madman to the Swede, while the man of literary taste beholds only madness in all schemes of public ambition, and thinks that popular applause, whether won in the senate or the field, scarcely rewards the toil that would attain it. And thus is the charge of folly handed around from man to man among us: each wondering at the madness of mankind, while he and a chosen few are guided by the principles of real wisdom.

Now, suppose that a man of perfect wisdom were introduced into this Bedlam, that the principles of pure and unmixed truth and reason were exemplified in all his conduct and all his opinions, would not the madness of all be rebuked by his actions and his character, and would not all unite in charging upon him the folly which existed only among themselves? Let us not wonder that the Saviour of the world was said to have a devil and to be mad; or that those of his disciples who follow in his footsteps partake of his reproach. And let us observe how ingeniously the enemies of Christ can accommodate their charge of madness to the circumstances of the case. Is Paul mad?—it is from learning: is Peter mad?—it is from ignorance; and thus it is with us. To refute the charge of madness we point to the men who have stood foremost on every field of noble thought and lofty conduct, and show that they were Christians. We may point to a Newton, beyond all controversy, the mightiest mind of ancient or of modern times, who saw by intuition what others learned by slow and laborious study, and walked with confident and steady step over the new and wondrous fields of discovery, where others grow dizzy in the attempt to follow him; who lifted the veil from nature and revealed a new universe to our astonished gaze, and returning from such dazzling and magnificent speculations, with the docility of childhood and the humility of real genius, gave to the Word of God the same honest attention, and the intense and reverential study that he had bestowed upon His works. But they tell us that Newton was so dazzled by the magnificence of his discoveries that he could not accurately discern the truth on other subjects, and that he who was so great in the philosophy of matter, was not, after all, so deeply versed in the philosophy of mind and morals. We turn to Locke, the prince of modern metaphysicians; but metaphysicians, they say, are always misty. We turn to Bacon, the founder of all modern science, the teacher of all modern philosophers; to Milton, the greatest of all modern poets; to Hale, the reformer of English law, and Grotius, the founder of the laws of nations; to Washington, the greatest of modern patriots, and Wilberforce, the purest of modern statesmen, and most distinguished of practical philanthropists. But all these were mad, mad from too much learning or too little, from too much intercourse with men, or too close confinement to books. Their philosophy was too shallow or too deep; their fancy too lively or too dull; their reasoning too subtle or too undistinguishing!

Now, it is the easiest of all possible arguments against the truth of the Gospel, or a practical obedience to its precepts, to denounce it all as madness, but certainly, to a reflecting mind, it is of all the least convincing. Was the apostle mad when he preferred the pure and exalted morality of the New Testament to the debasing and polluting systems of heathenism? Was he mad when he preferred the Jehovah of the Bible to the Jupiter of paganism? When he adopted the belief of one eternal, immutable, omnipresent, and holy Creator, and rejected that popular mythology which peopled heaven, earth, and hell, and sea and sky, with lords many and gods many—the creations of poetical fancy—impure, revengeful, weak, rivalling the worst of men in horrid crimes, and scarcely surpassing the mightiest in power? Was he mad when he neglected the philosophy of his day, where the idlest questions were discussed with the greatest warmth; and men, professing to be wise, became fools, piling high doubt upon doubt, until the existence of God and the immortality of the soul were buried under the heaps they had raised? Was he mad when he cherished, with fondest affection, that hope of immortality, which, more than all besides, exalts our nature above the beasts that perish, cheers virtue onward in its path of duty, and sheds around man's darkest hour the brightness of a glory which shall never fade away? Was he mad when he preferred the simple beauty of the Gospel to the traditions of the Jewish elders, by which they had obscured their law? When he believed the predictions of the prophet who so long before had foretold the coming of the Saviour, his sufferings, and his resurrection, was he mad because he did not disobey the heavenly vision, but finding that which prophecy had foretold and miracle had confirmed to his senses, he testified "both to small and great, saying no other things than those which the prophets and Moses did say should come"? And are we mad, my Christian brethren, because we live according to the precepts of the Saviour, and cherish the hopes which he has kindled, and mercifully placed before us?

I believe there is a God that ruleth in the heavens, whose

eyes behold, whose eyelids try, the children of men; a God whose holiness is without spot, and his power without bounds. Am I a madman, then, when I seek to obtain his favor, and avoid his coming wrath; when I consecrate to his service the powers which his goodness and mercy have given at first, and still continue for my welfare? I look within and I find myself endowed with capacities of enjoyment and suffering which are not of this world. I perceive hopes which dart forward into eternity, and fears that hurry onward to the bar of God. I feel a longing after immortality, a stirring as if of some divinity within me, a grasping after something infinite and eternal, vague aspirations after a peace which passeth understanding, which this world can never bestow: a joy ineffable and full of glory. I feel that to such high powers belongs a corresponding destiny. Am I a madman, then, when I aim to reach the destiny before me, to fulfil the high design of my existence, to employ the powers which God has given, according to the precepts of his holy word? I have a soul to save. I have a heaven to secure. I have before me an immortality of joy or woe. I lie under a fearful responsibility. Interests too large for human comprehension, too enduring for human calculation, vast as the value of the soul, and durable as its long existence, depend upon my conduct. Will you call me mad if I stir myself up to lay hold on the magnitude of the work before me, if I gird up the loins of my understanding, if I summon every power to the great undertaking, if I look coldly upon worldly pleasures and worldly honors, if absorbed in the great business of eternity I have no leisure for the frivolities of time, no relish for its light and unsubstantial enjoyments? When the wine sparkles in the cup, and the music floats by in full and voluptuous swell, and the dance goes gayly and merrily on, am I mad if I suppose there is some other employment more worthy of a rational and immortal being, if I cast my thoughts onward to the songs and the melody of heaven, and think of the groans and agonies which ascend with the smoke of their torment from the bottomless pit? Am I mad when I use the world as not abusing it, and looking upward to the invisible and eternal one, live as a stranger and a pilgrim here? No, he is not a madman who thus lives, and thus prepares to die. But *he* is mad who, in all the light of the Gospel, closes his eyes against it all; who, with the glad news of salvation sounding in his ears, lives as if he had no ears to hear or heart to understand.

I knew a young man once, I say not where, but well I knew him, with talents of the highest order, and an education completely to develop them all. With a mind keenly sensitive to beauty of every kind, a taste developed in early life, he soon possessed a relish for the ancient classics. The language of antiquity became almost as his mother tongue, and the poets and orators and historians of Greece and Rome as familiar to his boyhood as the writers of the English language. With admiration for the great men of antiquity, he imbibed their love of glory, their restless, burning, insatiable ambition, and along with the sensitiveness of genius he had its love of high excitement, and was a voluptuary, now in literature, now in sensual indulgence. He was early touched by the Spirit of God, and brought to see his sinfulness and danger, but struggled long and boldly struggled against its heavenly influences. God's spirit will not always strive, and, like ten thousand others, he was left to the madness of his own mind and the hardness of his own heart. He sought relief in scepticism, as others seek it in spirits, and finding it an opiate, forgot it was a poison. He read and read again all the sceptical authors of our language. He dived deeper into the stream of pleasure, and, now dreaming of philosophy, and now longing after glory, and now running after indulgence, he passed from youth to manhood, and when I last conversed with him he told me with a bitter smile that his character answered to that of the sceptic described by Johnson in his *Rambler*, who had doubted all that was good and true and lovely, till he had alienated all friendship and lost all love, and was severed from all the sympathies and affections of human life. He is still alive, and, in the city where he now resides, fills a most conspicuous station in the public mind. He may yet live to be great, for his talents are uncommon, and his ambition boundless. He may rise to be the wonder and envy of all around him, but he cannot be happy. And should one hereafter meet him in the full tide of his success, midway in his career of anticipated glory—though thousands should hang with rapture on his lips, and senates should yield to the power of his eloquence—and in the language of honest truth tell him he was mad, his own heart, in the bitterness of its anguish, would too sadly confirm the truth of the charge. For, alas! all his high endowments have been perverted, his precious privileges misimproved, the fond expectations of devoted Christian friends all disappointed, the fair promise of his youth all blighted, and though the rains may descend, and the sun may shine, and the dew may fall, yet will they never revive again. And without a miracle of mercy, the bitter, burning curse of God must pursue him on through life, and soon the applause of men must be exchanged for that indignation and everlasting contempt which must be the portion of the sinner's cup forever. If there be madness in the world, is there not madness here?

But suppose the picture to be reversed, and instead of those gigantic powers urged on to wild and irregular action by the fitful stimulus of unsanctified passions, you perceive the same large capacities calmly, gradually, yet surely developing themselves under the mild influence of gospel truth, adding each day fresh knowledge to its stores, and new virtue to adorn its character, pressing forward with the settled energy of Christian resolution toward the highest perfection of its nature, and consecrating to Him who gave them all, the faculties thus enlarged and strengthened, while the blessed power of a pervading moral principle is diffused throughout to purify and elevate and harmonize the whole. And oh! if this be a spectacle which might call forth the approbation of angels, and excite even the reverence of mankind, it is when genius is thus allied to piety, the highest intellectual and highest moral worth happily united, and the most exalted powers devoted to the noblest purposes. On such a one we gaze with admiration, even when we do not imitate. And as we stand by his grave and remember his virtues, we cannot but feel how blessed is the wisdom of true religion, and anxiously wish, as did Balaam, may I die the death of the righteous, and my last end be like his.

I cannot but think that some of you are often convinced of the madness of your course. That must be a deep sleep which, during long years of sin, knows no waking. That must be, indeed, a fearful madness in which there are no lucid intervals, in which no light ever bursts in upon the darkened mind, no consciousness flashes over the soul, no solemn apprehension that all may not be right. Ah, well do I know that such an apprehension has sometimes visited each of you. O sinner! cherish it as you would your own life's blood. It is the first beam of light on your beclouded soul, the dawn of day on your benighted understanding. It is the voice of God by his word, his providence, or his Spirit, inviting you to those ways of wisdom which are ways of pleasantness, to those paths which are paths of peace. Oh, think, with shame and penitence, and wonder, on the folly of your past life. God from on high has called you to himself. The Saviour of sinners has stretched out his arms of love and pointed to his bleeding side. The Holy Spirit has offered his saving influences, and yet you have despised them all. Heaven is opened to receive you, and you heed it not. Hell gapes to engulf you, you regard it not. The thunders of the law peal over your head, the kind and tender invitations of the Gospel sound in your ears, yet all in vain. Every day may be your last, yet every day is spent in sin. Every night may prove to you the beginning of eternal darkness, but you coolly and carelessly meet its danger. Every moment is loaded with mercies, and every moment devoted to folly. The retributions of eternity are hurrying on, yet you are altogether absorbed in the pursuits of time. Your eternal destiny rests upon your own conduct and exertions, yet are you childishly wasting the hours which alone can secure your everlasting welfare. It is as if a general on whose efforts the welfare of a nation depended should waste his hours in the childish sports of the nursery while his country's destiny hung in trembling and fearful suspense. It is as if one should gather gay flowers and weave bright garlands, and sing merry songs on the very edge of a volcano, whose heaving sides and boiling crater already told that the danger was at hand, and that the hot and liquid lava should soon sweep away in its resistless torrent, man, beast, forests, cities—faint emblem of the fiery wrath which shall hereafter desolate the earth.

But what place is there for illustration or comparison ? No madness of earth is like the madness of the sinner. It is only the light of eternity which shall reveal its true character. It is only the agonies of perdition which can measure out its greatness. And through the long lapse of its revolving centuries shall be forced still more and more deeply on the soul the fearful consciousness, how great is the folly of him who has preferred the amusement of a few days on earth to the rewards of the just in heaven.

IX.

MAN'S CONDITION AS A PRODIGAL SON.

LUKE, xv. 16.—"And he would fain have filled his belly with the husks that the swine did eat."

WE have in this chapter a remarkable confirmation of the truth, "that God's ways are not as our ways, nor his thoughts as our thoughts." In the commencement of the chapter we are informed, that "then drew near unto him all the publicans and sinners for to hear him. And the Pharisees and Scribes murmured, saying: This man receiveth sinners and eateth with them." It was in reply to these illiberal and bigoted murmurers that our Saviour uttered the parable of which our text forms a part, as well as the two which immediately precede it. All of which are designed to show that, however deep the abhorrence, however scornful the contempt, which the self-righteous Pharisees might indulge toward those whom they were pleased to stigmatize as sinners, there was one, the purest and holiest of all, who cherished no such feelings. There was sympathy for them in heaven amidst all their degradation and ruin; there was joy among the angels, even over one sinner that repented.

The Pharisees, in the pride of their imaginary holiness, had learned to despise their fellow-sinners around, perhaps not more sinful than themselves; they shrank from all intercourse with them, as they avoided leprosy, as if contact were at once defilement and infection: while the Saviour, pure, immaculate, exalted as he was, "in whose sight the heavens are unclean, and who chargeth his angels with folly," received them to himself, mingled in all the intercourse of life along with them, and spent his days in laboring for their good. Now this difference of conduct and feeling is founded on a difference of character and views. Man is ever prone to isolate himself and his interests; to individualize himself; to separate himself from the great community of beings above and around him; to withdraw his thoughts from God's universe, of which he forms a part, and to which he bears, and must ever bear, most important relations; and fix them in intensest selfishness upon himself. Hence, for whatever thwarts his interest, or shocks his sensibilities, or disgusts his taste, he feels no sympathy and cherishes no regard. But God is the all-comprehending: he takes in, at once, the individual and the species, the world and the universe. He considers each one a part of the whole. He sees in the lost sheep a part of the flock, in the profligate son one of the family—in every individual, polluted and degraded as he may be, a soul that he has created.

This is one out of many cases that might be adduced to show that the superiority of the moral system which our Saviour inculcated is founded on the superior enlargedness of his views. Thus they mutually confirm each other, the grandeur of the views sustaining the authority of the moral principle founded on them, and the purity of the principle establishing the correctness of the views.

Now it is impossible that man, the limited and the finite, should found his moral and religious systems on any other views than those which are likewise limited and finite. Hence all human systems have aimed to regulate human actions on earthly principles and views, omitting those wider relations which we bear to other and higher parts of the creation. Such systems, founded on earth, can never reach the sky. They are as defective as a system of astronomy which, confining its attention to the earth, should overlook those other worlds belonging to the system, which, though immensely distant, yet revolve along with it, and influence materially its movements.

Now the Infinite and Eternal One must, from the necessity of his being, view all human character and human relations under a far different aspect from that under which they appear to man. Himself infinite and eternal, his views must bear the impress of his character. And when such a one appears to instruct and illuminate mankind, we must expect to perceive the traces of a mind thus conversant with large and universal views. And we must also expect that the relations, the principles, the motives which he reveals, shall be universal, infinite, eternal—comprehending, as he does, immensity at a glance, present to all time, pervading all space, following on the consequences of all human actions as they roll with accumulating force down to the remotest futurity, and observing the melancholy consequences of the slightest disorder, commencing in a minute part, and extending over the whole of so extensive and complicated a machinery. We must not be surprised if his instructions assume a graver and loftier tone, are urged with a solemn earnestness unknown to earthly instructors. We must not be astonished if a new and wider scene should open before us, actors of greater number, of larger stature and nobler bearing, and all lighted up with the strong clear light of eternity.

Now, the whole system of Christian truth is an illustration of these remarks. In all its most striking and characteristic parts, we behold the deep impress of the same noble and majestic mind, familiar with all large and elevated views. And we know nothing in the whole history of human composition more touching or sublime than the representation given in this parable of the origin and destiny of man, his subsequent alienation from God, the misery in which he has thus become involved, the deep interest felt in heaven for his welfare, and the kind and parental tenderness with which he is welcomed when returning from his wanderings. We all recognize in the prodigal son a picture of our own folly, and in the father's tenderness, who does not acknowledge the kind and condescending mercy of the universal maker and Father of all? Let us consider some of these topics in the order in which they have been mentioned.

I. The Origin and Destiny of Man.

What am I? And whence? And whither am I tending? The beasts that rove around and fiercely pursue their prey, or quietly feed on the green grass, or wander along the calm waters, here fulfil their destiny. Am I different from them, or only a finer materialism, more happily organized, more ingeniously constructed? Am I the highest of created intelligences? Does the ascending series close in man? Or are there other beings, pure intelligences, and ethereal spirits? "Thousands of spiritual beings may walk the earth," and people the sky, and yet they hold no intercourse with me. I see them not. I hear them not, nor are they palpable to any of my senses. And although in the hours of my lonely meditations I seem to hold intercourse with them, and have "moments like their brightest," yet my daily associations are with the dead matter and the brute animals around me, and my nature seems more nearly allied to them than to aught that is purer and more exalted. He, the Great, the Invisible, the terrible and unknown One, shut out from all human gaze by the dazzling glory that surrounds him, and baffling all human investigation by the untold mysteries of his wonderful existence, He that filleth immensity and dwelleth in light that is inaccessible, does he look down from the throne of his exaltation with tenderness on me; or am I an incumbrance on his earth, the creature of chance, springing up like a mushroom at night, and trodden down and forgotten in the morning? Shall I lie down at last with my companions, the beasts of the field, in that long sleep that knows no waking, or is there a world where the living, feeling, and thinking elements within me shall find congenial society and suitable employments?

Such are the anxious inquiries which force themselves irresistibly on the minds of all thinking, reflecting men. Man has always been a mystery to himself, a riddle and a contradiction. There is in his composition such a mixture of high and low, of good and bad, of noble and mean, such a strange combination of opposing qualities, that some philosophers have thought that all his noble feelings were the feeble reminiscences of a previous state of being. Others have considered his body as unmixed evil, and the necessary source of all his sins. While others, again, have supposed his soul to be a fragment from a better world, forced off by some powerful and malignant demon, and imprisoned for a season in its house of clay and in this world of sin. Magnificent fiction! whose extravagance one might almost pardon for its beauty, how much superior to the dulness of modern scepticism! Who would not rather be this imprisoned spirit, faintly mindful of its origin, and struggling to attain its liberty, than that heartless, soulless thing, where all sense of virtue and purity is lost, where there is no remembrance of past innocence, and no sigh after future restoration?

But after all these anxious and fruitless speculations, here, and here only, do we find the truth: we are the children of God. Body and spirit, we are his children: he is the former of our bodies, and he is the father of our spirits. We were created in his likeness at first, "in knowledge, in righteousness, and true holiness," and, notwithstanding the ruin of the fall, part of that likeness still remains. Defaced and faded though they be, yet do there still remain some lineaments of a character which was once pure and heavenly. None is completely pure, yet none is utterly abandoned. The veriest slave to lust and sin sometimes awakes to a sense of his degradation, and longs to burst the chains that bind him. There are some gleams of light bursting irregularly forth from amidst our moral darkness. There are fragments, even amidst the ruins of our nature, which testify to the greatness of the Author, and our own original grandeur. Let us then avoid alike despondency and pride. Though children, yet are we wayward and rebellious; fallen and ruined though we be, yet are we children of the Most High: yet doth he who sitteth in heaven kindly condescend to have intercourse with us: yet doth he permit us to come unto him, and address him as "Our Father who art in heaven," and who, though he be in heaven, yet looketh down with eyes of pity and compassion on his wandering, erring children upon earth, opening wide, to receive us, the arms of a father's love, assuring us of a hearty welcome and a rich inheritance, endeavoring to reclaim us to holiness and happiness and heaven.

Let us learn to bear with and love one another. In each one there is a capacity, a susceptibility, for something high and noble. It is the perversion of these capacities, and not their utter extinction, which constitutes our sin. Let us unlearn contempt. It was not made for earth. It has no place in heaven. He whom thou despisest may hereafter be thine equal and thy friend. He is even now thy brother. Despair not of thyself; degraded as thou art, there is still a capacity for good within thee; sold as thou art to sin and Satan, it is a voluntary bondage. They are not thy rightful masters. Thou art the servant, nay, by birth the child, of God. Those self-abhorrences which make thee shrink from the society of man, that deep and dark remorse which drives thee from the mercy seat of God: these are but the convulsive struggles of thy higher nature endeavoring to cast off the shameful bondage. It is the sensibility which shows that life and hope are there. It is the pain which warns of danger and arouses to effort. That very tastelessness of all earthly pleasures, that dull satiety which follows sensual indulgences, and makes us loathe the very objects of our most ardent pursuit, that reaching after something higher and better than you have yet enjoyed—all points thee upward to thine origin and thine exalted destiny.

The very restlessness of this wayward prodigal proved that he was in a strange land, far from his father's house, far from its quiet pleasures, from its mild restraints, its plentiful, but wholesome fare, its social happiness, its accustomed and appropriate round of duties and enjoyments. But, alas! remember thy capabilities and thy actual accomplishments are altogether different things. Thine original destiny and thy present condition present the most melancholy contrast. Man was the child of God, but he has made himself a son of perdition. He was formed in the divine image, but it is so defaced and marred that scarce one feature remains by which the likeness can be discovered. He was in his father's house, but he has wandered away from that holy family, and cast off that paternal government. Great were his endowments, but they have all been perverted. Rich was his inheritance, it has all been squandered; high was his station, but it has been abandoned, and now, poor and miserable and degraded, he appears the wreck of what he was, with scarce one trace of what he might and should have been. Which leads to remark—

II. Man's alienation from God.

We are informed that the son, distrusting the goodness or the wisdom of his father, or disliking, perhaps, his authority, or anxious to assert his own independence, said, "Father, give me the portion of goods that falleth to me." And then, so soon does sin follow self-confidence, so closely is madness allied to pride, "not many days after, he gathered all together, and took a journey into a far country." When he had left his father's house, he did not pause in his immediate neighborhood, but went into a far, very far country. His father's house was the place for him. There was honor, as his father's son, a member of his family; there was safety from the wiles of designing men; there was abundance, enough and to spare; there was employment worthy of his character, and suitable to his capacities—to be about his father's business; there was wisdom to guard him against his own imprudence and folly; affection to bear with his weakness and faults; power to protect him from every foe; purity to preserve from corruption, and the soft influence of that domestic peace and love which, more than wisdom and authority and power, mould the heart and soul of man: which is itself the deepest wisdom, the holiest authority, the gentlest, but the most irresistible power. Oh, how mad is he who, bursting the bands that so gently yet powerfully bind him, and casting these cords of love recklessly away from him, wanders off into a strange land, far from his father's house, and there, forgetful of all those kind affections which centre still on him, of the gentle form which knelt beside him and taught him to repeat childhood's first simple prayer; and of that venerable face which, when the evening hour came, glowed with a holy joy, as he said, "Come let us worship God," and then commended all to the care of Him who is the father of the whole family in heaven and earth—dashes heedlessly on in his career of sensual indulgences, from folly to vice, from vice to crime, till he, who was a father's pride and a mother's joy, is the disgrace of his species. He who might have been an ornament to society sinks to the level of the brutes that perish. For observe, when he wandered away, he went not alone, he gathered all together, and wasted all. All that his father's love had given, all that his father's care had laid up in store, all his rich inheritance, his *all* was gone. Truly, "one sinner destroyeth much good." And may we not here observe a striking analogy to the course pursued by each one of us? Has not each one of us wandered away from God? First, we have laid claim to our father's property. We have felt that we were our own, that our faculties, our time, our influence, our all, are ours, to use at our pleasure. We have not desired that *he* should reign over us. Restless under the control of his perfect law, we have desired to be our own masters; ungrateful for his present favors, and his promised inheritance, we have thought his benefits no blessings, so long as his gifts were attended with an obligation, so long as the Creator and Upholder of all claims an ownership in the works of his hands, and a rightful dominion over the creatures of his power. Hence we have left the household of his love and obedience. We have wandered from his family. At first we designed, perhaps, to remove but a short distance, but, step by step, as inclination guided, or temptation seduced, or heedlessness misled, we have wandered farther and farther away, till we are indeed in a far country, at a fearful distance from God. As that wayward son wandered from the home of his childhood, no doubt, he passed with "mournful steps and slow," and often, as some recollection of infancy would cross his mind, or the sight of some familiar object, or some well-known sound would call up ten thousand images of past delight, the tear would glisten in his eye, and his bosom swell and throb with strong emotion. And as he stood upon the distant hill, whence he could catch the last glimpse of that home of purity and peace, its white smoke rising tranquilly in the air, its indistinct murmur borne, almost inaudibly, on the breeze, and the venerable form of that afflicted father still gazing anxiously after him, and praying blessings on his head, perhaps his resolution might have failed; but he gazed at his rich treasure, and he summoned his youthful pride, and joining the first wayward traveller like himself; he hastened forward, forgetting all, till there was a famine in the land.

Even so it is with you. Ah! well do I know that the first steps in sin are full of sorrow. When you first left your father's house, you did not design to abandon it forever, nor to wander far, and "many a longing, lingering look did you cast behind." You thought, perhaps, to enjoy a temporary freedom, to take your station on some eminence near at hand, whence you could gaze on one side at all the glories of the world abroad, and on the other look down upon that ancient and still respected mansion. But pride, fashion, example, ambition, pleasure, avarice have led you on till now you are far away. Alas! how far, till at last there is no fear of God before your eyes, no thought of God in your minds, no love of God in your hearts, no service of God in your lives, and for all the purposes of a real and practical influence, the case is just the same as if there were really no God that ruleth in the heavens, and takes cognizance of man. As if the dark tenets of the atheist were true, and you had no present lawgiver, and no future judge, ah! attempt not to conceal it from yourself. You have gone far away from God, far from the influence of his truth, far from the restraints of his authority, far from the holiness of his requirements, far from the obligations of his law. And you have endeavored to put God far away from you, to put from you the invitations of his love, the threatenings of his wrath, the strivings of his spirit. But though far from God, he is nigh to every one of you. Yes, there is, unseen, unfelt, a mysterious and fearful agency above, around, within you, pervading all, upholding all, controlling all, in whom you live and move and have your being. Ah, how shall you flee from that all-embracing presence, or escape that all-seeing eye, or go beyond the reach of that all-grasping, all-sustaining hand. Let us proceed then to consider:—

III. The degradation and misery, which sin has brought on man.

God is light, and when far from him, we must be in darkness. God is love, and when far from him, man is the sport of all angry and conflicting passions. God is the source of blessedness, the fountain from which do flow perpetually the streams of joy that make glad the hearts of men. When far from him our joy is an earthly current, now dashing impetuously forward, and bearing on its bosom the ruins its violence hath made, polluted by the soil over which it swept, now creeping slowly and sluggishly along, amidst the filth its torrent hath accumulated, now still and motionless, its surface glittering with the rainbow's hues, while all beneath is stagnant, putrid, pestilential. God is infinite in all his perfections, in wisdom, in holiness, in power, and in proportion as we depart from the complete symmetry of his most exalted character are we degraded in the scale of intellectual and moral excellence.

Man was, at first, formed in the image of God. The precise import of this remarkable expression, it is impossible for us now to determine. But this we know, that he was constituted lord of this lower creation, that he was God's representative on earth, endowed with high capacities of thought and feeling, capable of knowing and loving and rejoicing in God, and looking abroad with a devout and intelligent observation on the works of his hands. Perhaps we may form some estimate of his character and position by observing the purest and most exalted of our species in their happiest hours, when the heart is liveliest in its emotions, and the mind most vigorous in its action. Relieved from the cares that perplex, and the passions that agitate, man looks calmly, freely, joyously around, and diffuses over earth and sky the calm serenity of his own deeply tranquil feelings, the brightness of his own glowing thoughts. From the moments such as these we may catch some glimpse, however faint: we may form some conception, however inadequate, of man's condition in his unfallen state. Nay, do we not feel within ourselves a longing after something we do not reach: an inborn fitness for something we do not attain? Are there not transient bursts of thoughts and feelings, momentary flashes of a flame that is smothered, not extinguished, revelations of something unutterably higher, purer, lovelier, worthier, than those which occupy our lives? Is there not the deep and solemn consciousness of capabilities, far above the power of earth to employ; of infinite desires, far too large for earth to fill? How strong is the proof which these afford, that we have fallen far below our destiny and have immeasurably degraded our high capacities.

How various, how extensive, how exalted, and how pure are the sources of enjoyment placed within our reach. All nature is spread out before us in its magnificence and beauty, to observe and to enjoy. Everywhere there are springs of joy bubbling and flowing around us: in the works of God, in the society of man, in our own inmost bosom, in the services of God's sanctuary now, in the anticipation of his presence hereafter, in the study of his blessed Word, and in the joyful foretaste of its promised rewards through faith which gives present reality to future blessings and commences heaven on earth as a pledge of heaven above. Yet how little relish do we feel for such pure and exalted pleasure. How greedily do we feast on lower and sensual delights. Man *did* eat angels' food, but now he feeds on husks and grovels with swine. He has left the true sources of happiness, and his longing, aching heart now fastens upon whatever will yield a temporary relief, however low and polluting. It is said in the expressive language of the original that the prodigal son was "glued" to the people and the things of the land to which he wandered. And oh, how closely do we cling to the objects of our unworthy choice. Though convinced of their folly and sinfulness yet do we adhere to them still, though disappointed in their promised pleasantness, yet do we cling, with the energy of despair, to the delusions which have so long mocked us, though resolved, again and again, to abandon them forever, to assert the claims of our rational and immortal nature, yet do we return again as beneath the spell of some mighty fascination.

We need not allude to the drunkard, the debauchee, the abject slave of sensual appetites or fiendish passions. These are the last stage of man's degradation and misery, but all the intermediate degrees are alike devoid of genuine and rational enjoyment. Man seeks for wealth: he obtains it, but finds a vacuum which wealth cannot fill; honor, but there are necessities which titles cannot supply; pleasure, the cup is dashed untasted from the lips or drunk *desperately* up, sparkling at the brim, but at the bottom dregs and bitterness. The horse grazes quietly in his green pasture; the herds wander contentedly by the still waters; the bird wings his way joyfully through the morning air, or sweetly carols forth his cheerful song as the day declines. Why then is man anxious, restless, dissatisfied; why could not the prodigal feed as quietly as his swine? Ah, his nature was different! what was nourishment for swine was degradation and misery to him. And let me appeal to you all, and affectionately ask, if in all the ardor of your sinful pursuits, in the wildest vehemence of your young passions, have you not felt the folly and meanness of them all? Have you not felt the consciousness of something unutterably better thrill over you like the memory of some lost hour of bliss, when the stillness of the Sabbath, or the fireside of piety, or solitude and sickness have given you leisure for honest consideration, or the recollection of childhood's prayers and childhood's simple faith has recalled images of purity and bliss now gone perhaps forever?

How mean then appear all worldly passions: how exalted, how pure, how blissful the service of the Lord. The path of the righteous grows brighter and brighter to the perfect day. The way of the ungodly is not so. The way of the sinner is hard. He is going against his own conscience, and, till that power is eradicated from his bosom, vain are his efforts to be at peace in sin. He is going against his own interests, which are all on the side of holiness, against all the higher and better principles of his nature. Reason condemns his course as unwise; feeling denounces it as ungrateful and unjust. He is acting against God's authority, commandments, and power; and who can contend with Him and prosper? He has cast off that "yoke which is easy, and that burden which is light," and calls himself free, but he is the bondslave of Satan, who reigneth in the children of disobedience: in abject servitude to all the lowest or worst desires of his nature, and at their command does he meanly sacrifice peace, virtue, dignity, health, happiness, all that is dearest on earth, and his soul's salvation. Ah, it is a hard service, the service of Satan! It is a cruel bondage, the bondage to sin. Now for all this,—

IV. What is the remedy?

Your misery and degradation commenced in leaving your father's house: the only remedy is in a speedy return. I will arise, said the prodigal, and go to my father. And observe the process through which he passed:—

1st. He came to himself, felt the real misery and degradation of his state. So must you.

2d. Reflected seriously on the folly of his course: "How many hired servants of my father's have bread and to spare."

3d. He resolved, I will arise and go to my father, I will act, not lament, not despair, not wait indolently for God's mercy, but, while God is operating on me, I will act.

4th. He repented, and confessed.

5th. Observe the result.

X.

THE WORTH OF THE SOUL.

MARK, viii. 36, 37.—"For what shall it profit a man, if he shall gain the whole world, and lose his own soul? Or what shall a man give in exchange for his soul?"

THERE is no prejudice more hostile to the influences of the Gospel upon the hearts of sinners, than that one, so widely prevalent among worldly men, which represents religion as a dreamy and visionary thing, its most solemn and momentous truths as unsubstantial and impalpable abstractions, appealing only to excited passions, or a lively fancy, and having nothing to do with the plain downright every-day realities of life. Now we have been accustomed to view the matter in exactly the opposite light, and to suppose, that of all plain things, religion was the plainest, and that of the innumerable questions which agitate mankind, the questions which it proposes are at once the most eminently practical, and require for their solution the easiest and the most common of all considerations.

You are men of business. The question we propose to-day is one of prudential calculation, for prudent business men—a question of simple arithmetic, of profit and loss, in the business of your lives. It is a question for every man; a fair question in which no advantage is sought, or can be taken. It is but casting up the accounts and striking the balance. You boast of the accuracy of your calculations, and the precision with which, even in the most complicated settlement, you can attain the true result; and how in any offered speculation, however attractive or inviting, you are accustomed to try its promises by the strictest calculations, and test every delusive appearance by the simple comparison of the profit and the loss. Now it is just to such an operation that we invite you to-day. We make no appeal to your passions, or your fancy. We address your reason, your cool, dispassionate, unbiassed, calculating reason. And we ask you to tell us how much he is profited who gains the world and loses his soul; and that our decision may be the more accurate, let us consider first, What it is to gain the world; secondly, What it is to lose the soul; and thirdly, What it is to lose the soul without gaining the world.

I. What is it to gain the world?

We take it for granted at the outset, that on this one point we are agreed, that many among us are really selling their souls, and may have already sold them for the world. It is impossible, indeed, to observe for a moment the course of human affairs around us, without perceiving that of all the forms of earthly traffic this is the most universal. Of worldly productions, some trade in one article and some in another. The merchant, the farmer, the mechanic, the physician, the lawyer, each has wares of his own to dispose of, but the barter of souls is universal. There is none so poor, but he has a soul to sell; none so rich or so great, that he may not hope to increase his fortune, his power, or his fame by the barter of a gem so precious. There is no price so high that Satan will not offer, no artifice so mean that he will not stoop to use. The young sell it for vanity, and less than vanity. The old are too often already sold, and hug the chains of their dreary servitude. Some sell the soul for pleasure, and some for honor; some for money, and some for sensual indulgence; some for stupid inactivity, and some for still more stupid and beastly intoxication. Oh, the world is one great market-house where souls are trafficked off—are bought and sold. And it is a fearful thing indeed, to stand amidst these busy and bustling crowds as they hurry to and fro in ceaseless and restless activity, with steps light and free, and countenances bright and gay, and spirits buoyant and exulting, as if they had achieved some mighty enterprise indeed: and then to reflect what shall the end of all these things be, how soon the gloom of death shall gather over this scene of folly, and the light of eternity burst in and dissipate all its delusion. Ah, there is sickness at the heart when one beholds the maniac expectant of a crown barter his rich inheritance for a gilded bauble, and then in drivelling idiocy exult in the wisdom of his purchase.

And dream not that you can escape the truth of these remarks, by saying that you have never thus bartered away your soul. This would be attempting to remedy the folly of the past by madness at the present, adding to all your other sins the deep and damning sin of hypocrisy: for thou hast not lied unto man, but unto God. Ah, wretched mockery! He that formed the eye, shall he not see? He that made the ear, shall he not hear? He that taught man knowledge, shall he not understand? And think you that he who sitteth high exalted over all, whose eyes like a flaming fire pass to and fro over the earth, beholding the evil and the good—think you, that he is so unobservant of the secrets of your heart, as not to perceive, that amidst all those busy and anxious thoughts which agitate you daily, the thought of your soul seldom or never mingles; or that amongst all the interests which lie nearest to your heart, the interests of your soul are never pondered; that amidst the incessant play of emotions and of energies which never slumber, there is no one emotion called into exercise, no one energy nerved to action by a high regard for the soul; that its interests are postponed to every other interest, its happiness jeoparded on the most trivial pretences, and this most precious treasure which God has committed to your care, is as unheeded as the merchandise which yesterday passed from your possession, and to-day has no place in your thoughts, or your regard?

Now we believe that this whole trade is an unprofitable business, that the speculation will inevitably involve you in ruin. And we think that we can prove it to your satisfaction, if you will only calmly, soberly, and dispassionately consider, reason, calculate together. And since we well know that few men are ever exactly satisfied with the result of an argument which thwarts their wishes or opposes their habitual conduct; that they are ever prone to imagine some unfairness in the premises, or in the train of reasoning; that they are beguiled to admit too much, or to demand too little; as we wish the argument of this evening, if possible, to be conclusive both as to your opinions and your practice, we willingly grant all that you can ask, and will even endeavor to aid you in your efforts to extol to the utmost the object of your desire. We care not how much you may include in your conception of the world, or how bright are the colors in which your fancy may array it, convinced as we are that there is something vaster still, before which the greatness of the world must shrink in conscious insignificance; that there is a brightness before which its glories must fade in dim eclipse, and a blackness of darkness beneath whose gloom all its imposing splendor shall be extinguished forever.

What then is the mighty acquisition you long to make, and for which you are willing to exchange your soul's salvation? You desire, perhaps, that splendid edifice, that extensive farm, that exalted station, that elegant accomplishment. Some would be quite content could they accumulate a few thousands more, and add to the weight that is now drawing down their souls; some ten thousand; some twenty thousand or fifty thousand dollars. But, alas! my friend, enlarge your desires. I would not give my soul for ten times the amount. Come then along with me, and I will show thee what thou mayest aspire to, grasp, and call thine own. Behold that noble palace, which proudly towers aloft on yonder distant hill; walk through its stately halls, glittering with gold and purple, where the astonished visitor, as each new apartment is thrown open to his gaze, is dazzled by some fresh display of royal magnificence, surpassing all that had preceded it—its princely libraries, rich in the choice productions of ancient and modern genius, where calm philosophy sits with quiet and thoughtful eye, and towering imagination luxuriates in an ideal world; and poetry, with its thoughts that breathe and words that burn; and eloquence, gently distilling like honey from the honeycomb—its collections of art, where the canvas and the marble glow with warm colors, and swell to the fine proportions of real life, and the mighty dead live again to the fancy and almost to the eye. Behold its hundred menials, its incessant festivities, its enchanting prospects by sea and land, its territories, extending far as the eye can reach, richly adorned by nature and art. Wander over its princely pleasure-grounds where art seems the minister of nature, where all that taste could desire is added to all that wealth could purchase. The productions of all climates are collected: whatever is fair to the sight, or pleasant to the smell, or luscious to the taste. This lordly heritage shall be yours. Its splendid equipage, its polished society, its gay amusements, its ever-recurring festivities, where the voice of merriment and music ever peal upon the ear and elevate the spirit and the fancy to a state of delicious but dangerous intoxication. All this shall be yours, if for it you will only give your soul. Do you hesitate?

Then ascend with me, and gaze still farther, where the vision is lost in the distance, and the horizon is seen resting on the blue hills that skirt it. All around is yours. The villages whose spires are seen just peeping from the trees, the towns whose busy streets are echoing the hum of a thriving and industrious population, the whole wide country as it spreads around with its rich pastures and its browsing herd, its valleys, its mountains, its cities, and its forests—all are yours, if you will only fall down and worship the prince of this world, in token of homage and of fealty. Do you say No? Then I offer thee a kingdom; thou shalt be one of the princes of the earth, wealth and power will I give thee, and a proud nation for thy subjects. Nay, we will ascend to the pinnacle of nature's temple, and look down on all the kingdoms of the world and all their glory. All this will I give thee, only fall down and worship. The whole world is in one scale, and only thy soul in the other. Ah, the world! it is a tempting offer! The whole world! It has too much to tempt a feeble mortal. It has lofty mountains, glorious valleys, majestic oceans, populous cities, splendid palaces, and remains of ancient art. There are paintings that overpower us, music that bewilders, power that intoxicates, pleasures that ravish. To the world belongs all that delights the fancy, captivates the sense, pleases the taste, fills the understanding, fires the imagination, misleads the heart. There is gold in its mountains, pearls and diamonds in its oceans, wonders in its bosom. That gold shall adorn thy palaces, those diamonds sparkle in thy diadem, those wonders be admired in thy cabinet. All these shall be thine and for thy use. The sun shall rise to illuminate no dominion on earth but thine. The winds of heaven shall blow to waft thy navies; the rivers flow to bear thy commerce; the rains descend to fertilize thy soil; and the millions of the earth shall live to do thee homage, with bended knee and ready service and obsequious devotion.

There was once a man who seemed almost destined to realize this dream of universal dominion. The ruler of the most learned and polished nation of the globe, at a time when refinement and learning were almost universally diffused, his capital the centre at once of attraction and of influence for all the earth, where learning and society reciprocally improved each other; learning imparting to society a portion of its own calm dignity, and society giving to learning its own fine polish. Himself the child of a revolution which shook the world, he walked forth over its surface as the embodied spirit of that revolution from which he sprang, to subvert and change and modify all that he touched. His generals were princes, his subjects kings. Feared by the rulers, and worshipped by the populace of Europe, he had passed from nation to nation, spoiling as he went. Whatever was most precious in modern or ancient art, he gathered from the cities of Italy and Germany; from Rome and Florence and Venice, from Dresden and Berlin, to adorn the galleries and halls of the Tuileries and the Louvre. How inconceivably dazzling must have been the splendor of such a court, where genius and learning and power and magnificence and beauty, all united to cast a witchery and an enchantment over the scene. Yet he was master of only a small portion of the world. The pillar he erected to himself in Paris, and on whose lofty summit his own statue stands proudly pre-eminent, is made only of cannon taken in the German wars, and overlooks only a single city. But thou shalt possess the whole. All its wealth, its elegance, its arts, its power, shall be thine. Its literature shall all centre in thy capital. Its poetry, its oratory, its music, shall delight to proclaim thy praises; and looking far and wide, over sea and land, in the pride of thy heart, thou shalt say all this is mine.

Now I say not how soon splendor loses its charm, how the diadem often rests on an uneasy brow, and the purple covers an aching heart, how satiety turns to disgust, and flattery only calls forth contempt, and how the native feelings of a man would often spurn away the animals that fawn and cringe and flatter at his feet. Nor need I say how the anxieties and disquietudes and dangers of such a government would destroy the tranquillity of life; nor how conscience would bring its charges, and disease its agonies, and death claim at last his reluctant victim. Of all these I say nothing. Let thy life flow on in peace and quiet, calm and glorious as a summer evening's sun. When the sun goeth down it will rise again; but when man goeth to his long home there is no return. The sun which shone upon his birth has shone upon his funeral, and still shines upon his grave—but where is he? The seasons revolve and the year looks gay, but where is he who was once the gayest and merriest of all? The world's machinery still moves on, but where is he, the skilful and the mighty one, who gave the impulse to its movements and guided and controlled and regulated all? A few short months his menials are arrayed in black, and there is all the mockery of unreal woe; and again those halls resound with the dance, the music, and the jest. But where is he? The grave is his home; corruption his brother; the worm his companion. The dust has returned to dust. The spirit has gone to judgment. He sowed to the flesh, and reaped corruption. He sowed to the wind, and reaped the whirlwind. He gained the world, and lost his soul.

II. What is it to lose the soul?

1st. It is to lose that which gives the world all its power to charm. It is to lose all beauty and magnificence, all glory and excellence. It is to lose all you love or desire, for all takes its value from the soul. The soul being lost, all is lost. Not merely is it a negative, but a positive loss: not privation only, but actual self-torture. Recall to your memory any of those scenes from which men usually receive the most intense delight—some glorious landscape where we gaze in mute astonishment on all the magnificence of nature—as standing on the high walls of some city of the Swiss, with its glorious valleys spreading far as the eye can reach, and covered with the cattle from a thousand hills, its lakes glittering in the sunbeams, its steep declivities adorned with luxuriant foliage, and variegated with the bright hues of the grape; its giant mountains lifting their heads on high and clothed with the accumulated snows of ages; so glorious, so bright, so pure and stainless, that they seem to be the habitations of heaven, the temples of the sky, the palaces of angels, the dwelling-place of God. Or select some other scene where you may dwell with fond remembrance on the endearments of domestic life, and gaze with rapturous delight around that little circle of which you are yourself the life and centre, "where heart meets heart reciprocally warm," and every eye beams with kindness and love on every other. Or, let it be your joy to act upon the stormy theatre of public business, where all is life and passion and intense excitement, and man meets man in stern and bitter rivalry, to struggle together for the palm of power or of fame.

Now, however lofty, or however ecstatic may be those emotions which swell and heave within our bosoms when thus gazing on the magnificence of nature's scenery, or the quiet enjoyments of domestic life, or the mighty exhibitions of intellectual power on the great arena, where the interests of nations are debated; we ask you to consider for a moment, what it is that communicates its interests to all that you behold. Were the sun blotted out from the sky, and the pall of darkness spread over all earthly things, all their attractions would be gone. All might exist in itself as it existed before; but to you it would exist in vain; for the light which made it visible to your eye, which spread over it the hues of beauty, and gave it the loveliness or the sublimity of its proportions, would have disappeared.

But the sun might shine on in his glory, and nature might smile beneath his beams, and the hearts of men might rejoice around; and this would all be naught to you, if the eye had lost its vision, and the ear its hearing. What would be to you the smile of friendship, or the voice of affection, if wherever the sightless eyeballs turned they rolled in vain, and the strained ear could catch no accent from the lips it once delighted to listen to? That eye might be uninjured, that ear might still retain unimpaired its delicate and ingenious organization, each exactly adapted to convey from the world without its appropriate sensations. But what would this avail, if there were no living and feeling spirit within to receive the notices thus conveyed through the avenues of the senses, and to pour forth on the dead and lifeless materialism without a portion of its own vitality and spirit and warmth? You might walk abroad over this fair earth, and your eyes might be turned upward toward this glorious sky, and by the power of some artificial galvanism might you be made to perform (perhaps) many of the offices and to exhibit many of the appearances of a living and feeling and intelligent being; yet would you move only like a corpse amidst the society of busy and bustling men—having no part in their joys or their sorrows, their hopes or their fears. No rapture could ever thrill along your nerves, or expand your bosom, or pour its full warm tide along your throbbing arteries.

Think then that of all you love most dearly, and prize most highly, the soul is the essence. It is the source of all your enjoyments in the past, and all your anticipations for the future; and remember, that to these the soul imparts all their power to communicate delight. The soul is indeed the man, and to lose the soul, is to lose himself; it is to lose his all.

How foolish then is your speculation. How mad is the game you are playing, who thoughtlessly and lightly are casting away your souls, that you may gain the world. It is as if one should pluck out his eyes, that he might increase the pleasures of vision; or mangle his ears, to increase the delights of melody; or amputate his limbs, for the purpose of relishing more keenly the pleasures of some favorite sport.

But the soul may be lost without being annihilated. There may be a perversion of its powers, without their destruction. And this perversion may be as much more fearful than its annihilation, as the infliction of positive torture is more terrible than the simple privation of enjoyment. To put out the eye would be to annihilate all the beauty of the visible creation. But it might be so diseased, that every ray of light which fell upon the inflamed and swollen eyeballs would send a shudder of agony through the whole system; or so deranged in its organization, that, like a burning-glass, it would concentrate all the rays of light into one fiery focus upon the optic nerve, scorching and consuming it, while the tortured brain was boiling and seething and maddening with the flame. Thus it is, that all the blessings of God's providence may be turned into curses; and the gifts of his hand, if perverted from their proper use, may be converted into the instruments of his wrath, till every avenue for feeling becomes an avenue for woe.

And thus may the soul itself, that noble instrument of thought and recipient of pleasure, be so lost in sin, so wander from the great end of its creation, that its immortal faculties shall be the ever-living and ever-enlarging source of a misery as vast as its own amazing powers; as eternal as its own ever-enduring existence. That imagination which is now the mirror of the universe, giving back the images of all that is great and glorious and lovely in creation, and diffusing the brightness of its own joyous existence on all around, may become the abode of all dark and hateful thoughts, haunted by the most fearful and terrific spectres, cursed with a creative power, ever restlessly active, and prolific only in horrors—those mighty energies turned away from their appropriate objects, which alone could yield them healthful exercise and nourishment, turning madly inward on themselves, and crushed by their own convulsive struggles until they writhe beneath their own self-inflicted tortures; like that reptile of the East, which in the madness of its venom drives its sting into its own body, and sinks, and sickens, and blackens, and bursts, and dies, beneath the poison which its own fangs have supplied.

But, 2d. The loss of the soul is its eternal loss in hell. The perdition of the soul in hell! Ah, what a fearful thought is this—which pushes far away beyond the limits assigned to human knowledge into a land of darkness, of deep darkness, like the shadow of death, and ranges wildly there amidst images of gloomy horror. What is it? Ah, no eye hath seen, no ear hath heard, no language could describe, no heart conceive the fearful secrets of that world of woe. No messenger has returned to bear the tidings of what he witnessed there. No voice has issued from that world of ruin, laden with intolerable woe to tell us of the agonies which Divine justice can inflict, and immortal spirits nerved and strengthened by Almighty power are able to endure. Yet, as we have some beams from heaven, we have likewise some faint echoes from hell. Ah! there are fearful depths in human nature; sometimes broken up and laid bare to our view, to make us observe and shudder and beware. When some dark spirit rent by mighty passion, blackened by secret crimes, haunted by terrific recollections, in an hour of hopeless remorse, or in the death-bed agony, reveals his deeds of darkness, despairs of pardoning mercy, writhes beneath the tortures of anticipated wrath, wrestles like a strong man against the foe that torments him, till the mind, crushed by its own convulsive throes, drives on through life like a dismantled wreck, urged furiously forward by demon powers, or bursts madly from its feeble tenement, exclaiming: Lost! lost! lost forever! Ah, that wandering eye, that flushed cheek, that burning forehead; that lip curled in agony, that brow now knit in grim defiance, now quailing in gloomy terror, all bring us to an abyss of horror, where reason falters, and the blood curdles as we gaze.

And now that restless eye is fixed, and the strained eyeballs glare upon some object of his hatred, or his terror, and he points you to the damned spirits that torment him, and tells you that troops of devils are waiting to hurry him away, and asks if you cannot see the hell that is already burning in his bosom. And he tosses and writhes beneath the anguish of its flames, and gnashes his teeth in fury, and curses God, and curses all human kind, and curses his own soul, and dies! Oh! if this be the foretaste, what is the reality? "If this be done in the green tree, what will be done in the dry?" If this be earth, what then is hell?

What is a damned spirit? We are told (but oh, how faint is language!) we are told of a worm that never dieth; and we have seen even on earth the commencement of its gnawings, the writhings of the victim under its first sting. But there, oh, there—it shall gnaw, deep into the heart; and gnaw, and gnaw, and gnaw forever! We are told of a fire that is not quenched. We have seen it kindled here. The first flashes of its lurid flame we have shuddered to behold. We have seen the first agonies; we have heard the first groans of the slow consuming victim. But there, it shall rage and glow and devour forever. The pile thereof is fire and much wood; and the spirit of the Lord, like a stream of brimstone, doth kindle it forever. For, saith the Lord, "A fire is kindled in mine anger, and it shall burn to the lowest hell, and it shall consume the earth, and set on fire the foundations of the mountains." Ah, who of you can dwell with devouring flames? Who can lie down in everlasting burnings? We are told of a blackness of darkness. Its gloomy clouds we saw gathering here. But they shall thicken and blacken and darken forever, till they settle down in one huge mass upon the soul; penetrated by no beam of light, gilded by no ray of hope—but growling fierce thunder over the sinner's head, and flashing forth lurid lightnings. And remember that this shall be the portion of him, who in gaining the world loses his own soul.

Thou mayest gain the world for a short time; but the loss

of the soul is for eternity, eternity! Mysterious and fearful thought! How often have I tried to penetrate thy depths, and form some faint conception of thy wonders, till my mind, overwhelmed by thy greatness, would sink back beneath the hopeless effort! How much lies hidden in thy bosom of fearful and tremendous import to the sons of men! Oh, what is eternity? An eternity of woe! Go ask that unhappy wretch who has sunk from a Gospel land to the pit of perdition, and he will tell you there is no language of earth, that can convey the thought. Go to that dark and haughty spirit, scarred with the thunders of Almighty vengeance, confined under chains of darkness to the judgment of the great day, and as he rises to your view and tosses on those fiery billows, ask him, what is an eternity of woe? And he will say, there is no term in the vocabulary of hell which can at all express its meaning; that if all its bitterness were distilled into one drop, and all its anguish concentrated into one keen pang, and all its groans collected into one loud expression of woe, and all its fires kindled up, to give it burning energy and power, yet it could never tell half the horrors of eternity. Oh, on whatever the air of eternity breathes, it assumes a new magnitude. Its men become spirits; its days are centuries; its units are millions. Its joys swell into raptures. Its pains burn into madness. There is no progress there; no change, no past, no future: all is one eternal now. Here weeping endures for a night, but joy comes in the morning. There, no morning ever breaks upon a night that hangs its dreary curtains around the sinner's couch of flame forever. Here as we toss restlessly from side to side upon our sleepless pillow, and long for the morning light, and cry out, Watchman, what of the night? Watchman, what of the night? We hear the answer: The morning cometh and also the night. But there no friendly voice proclaims the approach of day; but from each wailing companion in torment comes the dread assurance,—The night of eternity rolls on: slowly, heavily, unchangeably, darkly. The night of eternity rolls on. *The night of eternity rolls on.*

XI.

THE LOVE OF THE WORLD.

1 JOHN, ii. 15.—"Love not the world, neither the things of the world."

THERE is in every human bosom some great and absorbing passion, and there is some object on which that passion fixes. It may lie for a season almost dormant in the bosom, unnoticed by the world, and, perhaps, unknown to him who unconsciously indulges it. It may be modified by circumstances, and even suspended in its operation for a time, while some other passion occupies its place. Yet when these circumstances are removed, and the mind reverts to its natural state, this passion re-appears and resumes its wonted dominion. It is not the same indeed in every individual, nor in the same individual at every period of his life. The objects which delight us now, may hereafter be exchanged for others, more interesting in themselves, or more congenial with our maturer judgment. The passions that now agitate and move us, may be succeeded by other passions called forth by other objects. But there will always be a passion to control us and an object at which that passion aims, and it will be true of each one of us, at every moment of his future life, as it has been at every period of his past existence, that there is some object on which his affections are supremely fixed, and which forms the sources of his highest happiness.

And from the very nature of things it must be so. The mind is essentially active, and it must have some object on which to employ its activities. The affections are constantly going forth to find some object around which they may cling, and if it were possible that any human being could be entirely dissevered from every present object of regard, and find in the whole world beside no other on which his faculties might fasten, the world would be to him a desolation and a wilderness. Existence would be a curse, the soul itself a dreary and vacant solitude, and the keenest anguish that has ever tortured the nerves or sickened the heart of man would be preferred before the dull vacuity, the motionless and dead stagnation of such an existence.

Now the objects on which the men of this world have fixed their affections, are all worldly objects, and upon them are they most intently and closely fastened. From these they derive their highest happiness, and to these are they supremely devoted. They may abandon one object, but it is only to pursue another. They may renounce one passion, it is only to substitute another in its place, and in all the changes of their purposes and characters on earth, the same great truth is evident, that the world and the things of the world form their portion and their hope. The man of ambition may become the man of learning. The man of wealth or the man of sensual pleasure, may be wearied with the bustle and contention of public business, and seek in the privacy of domestic life the quiet and happiness he had elsewhere sought in vain. He may engage in the pursuits of science, or rejoice in the sublimity and beauty of nature's scenery, and in the stillness of his calm retreat, surrounded by all that is grand and ennobling, and far from the noise and tumult of the world without, he may enjoy the luxury of a purer and more tranquil happiness, and look back with pity and astonishment at the objects that once engrossed his attention. And thus having renounced one of the world's pursuits, he may imagine that he has renounced the world itself, while all his thoughts have centred upon worldly objects, and all his heart's devotion has been offered up at the shrine of idolatry.

Now it is this supreme devotion to the world against which we object and against which the apostle has raised his warning voice in the language of our text. It is not that the eye of man rests with delight on all that is beautiful, or magnificent in nature. It is not that the heart of man swells even into rapture, in the sweet intercourse of social life, and reposes with undoubting confidence on the bosom of his friend. It is not that the soul of man, ever actively inquisitive, loves to expatiate freely over every field of knowledge. Nor is it even that he indulges the inferior desires of his nature and receives with gladness those gifts of providence which are kindly offered. It is to none of these that we object. But it is that while we enjoy the gifts, we forget the Giver; that we love the creature more than the Creator, and that thus this world, which God has clothed with so much beauty and loveliness for our use, on every part of which he has poured in such rich profusion the bounties of his providence, and stamped the evidence of his existence and his presence, instead of leading us up to him as the Creator and Preserver of all, has only served to shut out God entirely from our thoughts, and involved us in all the guilt and all the folly of a practical idolatry.

It was the peculiar genius of the heathen mythology, that it personified every object of external nature, and deified every passion of the human mind. To these imaginary deities, it builded temples and consecrated priests. To them the sculptor, the painter, and the poet were used to devote the finest specimens of their art; and the highest efforts of human genius were employed to cast a brilliancy and a glory over the basest of human passions. Now this idolatry is more obvious and palpable; but is it more real than our own? It is not the building of the temple, nor the offering of the sacrifice, nor the bending of the knee, nor the solemn mummery of their idle superstition, which gives to their idolatry its most hateful and disgusting character. It is because the soul partakes in the idolatry; transfers to the objects of its worship the regard which is due to God alone. When the man of ambition thus engages with restless ardor in the pursuit of worldly distinction; when he sacrifices to the acquisition of this ideal god his health, his happiness, and his virtue, and makes this the object of his daily thoughts and nightly aspirations, is not his idolatry as glaring, as gross, as if in the spirit of paganism he had formed a golden image of the Goddess of Fame, had elevated it to some conspicuous place in his stately mansion, and repaired thither morning, evening, and at mid-day to offer up his sacrifices and his prayers?

Now it is with every other object of worldly regard as it is with the objects of worldly ambition. Wealth, pleasure, ease, and social enjoyment, all, when the heart's affections are intensely and supremely fixed upon them, usurp the place of God in the soul, and cast off his rightful authority. And therefore it is that we say unto you, in the language of our text, "Love not the world, neither the things of the world," for the love of the world is idolatry. We may build no temple, we may offer no victim, we may burn no incense, and yet may be guilty of the most hateful idolatry. We may be ourselves the living temples, and the victims too, and our heart's devotion be the incense on the altar. And thus may we give to our false gods an adoration, more decided and sincere than that of heathenism itself, and yield to them that peculiar homage which is claimed by Jehovah as his own undoubted right. Is it strange then that the Bible should so often warn us against the love of the world? That he who is jealous of his honor, and will not give his glory to another, should solemnly denounce the friend of the world as the enemy of God? And is it not right that his indignation should be kindled, and his wrath should burn even to the deepest hell, when looking on a world like this, so signalized by his goodness and mercy, on which he has lavished the riches of his power and his wisdom, and his grace, he beholds the hearts of its guilty inhabitants utterly alienated from him; and that surrounded as they are by his blessings and upheld as they are by his power, in the full and vigorous play of all their faculties, and luxuriating as they do in the bounties which his beneficence has supplied, there is yet no practical recognition of his hand in them; there is no returning tide of warm emotion toward the great fountain of blessings; but the strong affections of the human heart, and the active energies of the human mind are turned altogether from the Creator, and fixed on the creatures of his hand?

We are often shocked at the follies and cruelties of paganism. Behold that crowd of haggard and emaciated beings of every age and sex, dragging their wearied limbs along over the heated sands, beneath a burning Eastern sun. Many of their comrades have fallen since they left their homes, even now one and another of their band is sinking to the ground, overcome by hunger and fatigue, and the jackals and wild dogs of the desert are rushing on their prey, to riot in the luxury of living food. There is one who measures the weary miles of his long, long pilgrimage by the length of his own body laid along the plain, while all around him is whitened by the bones of his predecessors, and the hungry animals which have fed upon their flesh, are now growling over their bones, or crunching them beneath their tusks; while one and another, near at hand, has left his scanty meal, and watches with greedy and glaring eyes, the moment when another victim shall sink to the earth to rise no more. Such is the crowd of pilgrims that gather around the car of Juggernaut. And surely it is a spectacle to move a heart of stone.

But is there nothing in the pilgrimage of human life which we behold every day around us, that might serve equally to arouse our indignation and our pity? How many of our youth daily enter on the pursuit of pleasure, wandering far from their father's house, forgetting all a father's solemn warnings, and all a mother's tender and beseeching love. How many beasts of prey in human form beset their pathway. Are there no wrecks of wasted fortunes, and ruined characters, and health forever gone, strewed along their course? And when the close of life comes on, who would not rather perish as do the worshippers of Juggernaut, whose every limb is crushed at once, and every bone is ground to powder by the ponderous car, than linger out a tedious existence, which poverty, and disease, and ignominy have rendered hopelessly miserable, while conscience, with her scorpion lash, stings the soul to madness? And who would not rather stand before the throne of God at last, the poor deluded idolater, who, knowing no other God, had given his life an atonement for his sins, than as the worshipper of pleasure, or the worshipper of fashion, or the worshipper of gold, or the worshipper of fame, who, knowing the true God, had cast off his rightful supremacy, and knowing the only Mediator, had trampled under foot the blood of his atonement?

Is there nothing bloody and revolting in that idolatry of honor, and of office, which seems to have seized upon the whole of our country's population? Do we not often hear the voice of stern defiance inviting to the field of mortal combat? Do not rational and immortal beings shed their heart's blood at the dagger's point, and offer up this shocking oblation at the shrine of popular applause? And shall such an idolatry as this, be practised unblushingly in our land? Shall this abomination of desolation stand even at the door of the sanctuary, speaking great swelling words of vanity, and shall no voice of stern rebuke and deep denunciation issue from its sacred portals? Then is the spirit of our office gone, and, like the priests of old, we have bowed down before Moloch, and are partakers in the blood shed in the horrid worship. No, my brethren, until this abomination is swept from the land, the mild spirit of Christianity can never prevail. But it will soon be swept away by the breath of an enlightened and purified public sentiment; and the gathering thunders of a nation's loud and righteous indignation shall burst over the head of him who sheds his neighbor's blood, whether it be over so much pelf as one could grasp in his hand, or so much wind as he could not grasp at all.

Having thus shown that the love of the world is idolatry, and that therefore we should not love the world, I proceed now to show, *that the love of the world necessarily prevents the attainment of the true Christian character.*

Many professing Christians are perpetually employed in the vain effort to reconcile the service of God with the service of Satan, and the love of the world with the love of God. They have been told, indeed, in God's holy Word, that no man can serve two masters; no man can love God and mammon. And, although they partly believe the assertion, yet they consider it a hard saying, because they cannot understand *how* the love of the world is destructive of the true Christian character. Now to such, it might save a world of useless disappointment and trouble, could we only convince them that there is an absurdity in the very object at which they are aiming, a glaring and palpable contradiction in the whole scheme of their lives. There is a constant tendency, my brethren, to lower the standard of Christian character; to deface that line of separation which divides the church from the world. But if there be any design in Christianity whatever, if any thing was proposed to be accomplished by the revelation of God's will to man, by the mediation and death of his Son; by all that wonderful array of miracles and prophecies by which his mission was announced at first, and afterward attested; if in all this, there be any design at all worthy of the magnificent machinery employed to effect it, this design is to produce a mighty revolution in the character of man; to repair the ruins of the fall, and to elevate him to the highest state of moral excellence of which his nature is susceptible.

The method by which this object is accomplished is not an arbitrary method, but one exactly conformable to the whole nature of man. He is not transported at once by Almighty power into some new world of holiness and peace, where no sin, or trial, or temptation, or sorrow could approach him; but he is left in a world where he is exposed to every danger; he is left to fight and struggle with innumerable foes; his state is a state of probation; and if ever he attains the character of the righteous, or enjoys their reward, it is through a long process of the severest moral discipline. Now this process is begun and completed upon earth. And the character it is designed to form, is likewise begun and completed here. And the character of the real Christian as portrayed in the Bible, is widely different from that exhibited in daily life around us. It is a holy and elevated character. His thoughts are fixed on some great and worthy object, and he is pressing forward with determined resolution to attain it. He has embarked in a mighty enterprise. He has engaged in a fearful warfare. Absorbed in the magnitude of his own great undertaking, and confiding in Him who is able to give the victory, he disregards alike the dangers and allurements that surround him; and summoning all his powers as for some high achievement, he tramples the world beneath his feet, and walks amidst all its attractions and all its noisy vanities as a stranger and pilgrim upon the earth, as seeing Him who is invisible. The example of his Saviour is that which he endeavors to imitate; the same universal and disinterested love to man; the same humble and holy obedience to God; the same active self-devotion to the work he has to do. These are the dispositions he is required to cultivate. He is to be daily transformed into the likeness of his Saviour upon earth, and to be completely like Him in heaven when he shall see Him as he is. As a soldier of the cross he is to wage a perpetual warfare against every wrong appetite and passion. As a combatant for more than an Olympic crown, he is to strain every nerve in the contest, and by long and painful self-denial, is to prepare for the victory. The arena on which he contends is elevated. The interest which attends him is intense. The spectators are invisible and holy spirits. And God himself is to give the crown of glory.

Such is the character of the true Christian as given in the Bible, and such is the discipline through which he must pass before he can obtain the object of his wishes. And does not such a representation commend itself at once to the conscience and the reason of every reflecting man? Is it possible that he could consider for a moment those large endowments and high capabilities with which he has been gifted—possessing a mind that wanders through eternity and thinks and feels unutterable things, in dignity and intelligence a little lower than the angels, and made at first in the image of God himself—without feeling that some higher destiny lies within his reach, and some higher duties devolve upon him even here, than to live a slave of appetite and passion, and waste on inferior objects the whole energies of an immortal spirit? Now if such be the character required in the Gospel, how can it be formed and preserved without constant communion with high and holy objects? We all know that our minds receive their coloring from the objects with which they are conversant, and are moulded to the form and likeness of whatever they embrace. They will expand to the largest, and contract to the smallest dimensions. Hence the man whose habitual associates are vicious and corrupt, who accustoms his mind to be familiar with objects, or even thoughts which are impure or debasing, becomes utterly degraded and polluted by such associations. While he who opens his mind to larger views and better influences, who loves the society of holy men and dwells with solemn pleasure on the wonderful truths of revelation, feels his own spirit refreshed, expanded, exalted by such a contemplation; and daily, as he becomes more familiar with objects and society such as these, will he exhibit more prominently in his walk and conversation that heavenly elevation of character which they naturally impart.

Hence we are said to be sanctified by the truth, because the contemplation of the objects revealed in God's Word of truth naturally purifies the mind. While we gaze upon the Saviour's character, though we see him now through a glass darkly, yet, beholding his glory, we are transformed into the same image from glory to glory, even as by the Spirit of the Lord. And when we reach his presence on high, "we shall be like him, for we shall see him as he is." The glories of his character shall attract our constant gaze, and wrapt in perpetual admiration, we shall be assimilated rapidly to what we admire. And in proportion as we hold communion with him on earth shall we transfer to ourselves the lineaments of his character. It is not a mere occasional contemplation of religious truth which will give to the mind a religious character. Nor is it a mere occasional withdrawal of the thoughts from worldly objects which can break off from the soul the shackles of its bondage. Whatever is the object of our highest regard, and our most frequent thoughts, decides our character, stamps its image and superscription on the soul, and us for its own. A thousand other objects may attract our attention, a thousand other feelings may pass over the mind, but they leave no deep, abiding impression there.

If the world, therefore, be the object of our highest regard, no transient religious feelings, however sincere and exalted, can at all influence our real character. A thousand raptures, ecstasies, and joys and lamentations and thanksgivings and confessions may pass through our minds and fall from our lips, and the charge of worldliness may be against our character, and the curse of worldliness cling to all our doings, and even those feeble efforts which we sometimes make to think and feel on heavenly subjects, and on which we found our hopes of heavenly felicity, instead of turning back the current of our worldly feelings, may serve only to show the violence of the torrent that overwhelms us, and the feebleness of our own vain and ineffectual resistance.

All the blessings which this world can bestow are transient. "The world passeth away, and the lust thereof," says the apostle; "but he that doeth the will of God, abideth forever." It is this that stamps vanity on all earthly blessings. However certain we may be of obtaining them, however much we may rejoice in their acquisition, yet we know that their duration is short, and that the time hasteneth on when we shall take no pleasure in them. Let the young man rejoice in his youth. Let the strong man glory in his strength. Let the man of genius, and the man of learning, and the man of power, and the man of wealth, each plume himself on his superiority above his fellows; and as the eyes of all around are fixed upon him, and the gratulations of an admiring crowd meet him at every step, let him drink in all the pleasure which can flow from such a source. Let no drop of bitterness mingle with his cup of enjoyment. Let no rivalry obstruct his career. Let no envy depreciate his merit. Let no malice blacken his fair fame. Let him stand forth, by the united suffrage of mankind, on the proud eminence of an undoubted superiority. Has he beheld with grief the splendid edifice of some wealthier citizen, rising and towering far above his humbler dwelling? let there arise as by magic from the earth one loftier still, around which shall bloom and twine the loveliest flowers of every land, while the dews of heaven shall fall more plentifully, and the breath of the morning shall fan it more softly, and the evening zephyrs shall murmur more gently around it. Has he listened till he wept to the subduing strains of an eloquence he could not hope to rival? let there come down upon him the power of an inspiration which shall raise his fancy to a nobler flight, and expand his mind to a larger comprehension, and attune his voice to a more bewitching melody, and let eloquence distil from his lips like honey from the honeycomb. And to the honors which he meets abroad, let us add all the enjoyments of domestic life. Let his home be the habitation of love, and around his hospitable board let there ever be gathered a select band of enlightened and social friends; while he who stood the foremost in every public enterprise, and gathered the admiration of public crowds around him, is too the centre of every private circle, and gains a still higher testimony to his private virtues and social worth.

But what will all this profit if it will not last? Those social circles shall be broken up. The youth and beauty which once crowded those festive halls shall go down to dark forgetfulness. Even he who was the life and centre of those gay assemblies shall join the nations of the dead. That tongue of eloquence shall be mute in death. That eye of fire shall be quenched in darkness. That lofty palace shall crumble to the earth, and the very name of its possessor shall perish among men. Then is there nothing left to man but "to lie down in cold obstruction and to rot?" Yes, while the dust is returning to dust again, the "spirit is going to God who gave it." A new world shall then open on our view. New scenes shall burst on our astonished vision. Our disembodied spirits shall enter on new and untried modes of existence, and, freed from the manacles of flesh, shall swell into larger capacities both of enjoyment and suffering. Nor eye hath seen, nor ear hath heard, nor hath it entered into the heart of man to conceive, the glory which is here prepared for those that love God.

It is to this world of glory and blessedness that I would point you to-day. I would invite you to partake of its glory which never fades, to abide in its mansions of eternal rest, to seek that holiness without which you cannot enjoy it, and to bow before that Sovereign who fills it with his presence. And yet to many I know that my invitation will be vain. The love of the present evil world hath blinded your minds, and hardened your hearts against the Gospel. The lovers of this world seem bound to it by some strange spell. The power of some secret fascination seems to have charmed all their faculties, until the voice of reason and experience, as well as the voice of God, falls unheeded on their ears. In spite of all that we have known ourselves, and heard from others, we still believe that the world is a satisfying portion. We listen to its promises, and with eager expectation grasp its unsubstantial pleasures. There is none so stupid as not to perceive in his moments of serious reflection that it is all delusion, but it is a sweet delusion, and he willingly resigns himself again to its soothing influence. There is none who has not been sometimes rudely awakened from his dream of worldly happiness to gaze upon the reality of truth. But he soon composes himself softly to his repose, enjoys the same visions, pursues the same shadows, clasps the same phantom forms to his bosom, starts from his slumbers, finds it all a dream, and sleeps again. And this is the business of life, the employment of those threescore years and ten bestowed on rational and immortal beings, for the purpose of securing everlasting happiness. Nothing could show more plainly the extent of that moral derangement, which has passed upon every individual of our species, or which exhibits more affectingly the nature of that fearful bondage, wherein the prince of this world has enslaved his infatuated votaries. Against such a delusion human reasoning and human eloquence are employed in vain. None but the Spirit of God can reach a case so desperate. Nothing less than the Almighty power can break the deep slumbers of the spiritual death. It is in humble dependence on this divine assistance that I will now invite your attention, my dying fellow sinners, to a few plain and serious considerations.

Consider then, in the first place, how many millions of men there are now in the world pursuing the same expectations of worldly happiness, of wealth, of distinction, health, and long life, and inquire honestly of your own mind, how many of all these will ever attain the object at which they aim; how many will be cut off in the midst of all their schemes, and called to the bar of God; how many will linger through a long life of poverty; how many will fall short of that distinction after which they aspire, or that wealth they anticipate, and pine away in the agony of disappointed hope, or writhe under the gnawings of self-devouring envy, or wither under the consciousness of neglected worth. Of the eight hundred millions now upon the earth, how many do you suppose will attain even a moderate portion of that worldly happiness they expect? And even among the most successful, who will attain the half that he anticipates? What reason then have you to expect a dispensation from the common lot, and success in all your wishes, while others fail? Consider again, how many men have lived since the creation of the world, in the six thousand years that are past. We are lost in endeavoring to think of their numbers. Millions piled on millions fail to make the mighty sum. But when we endeavor to think of the schemes and plans and hopes which agitated each of them in his short and busy day, what a scene of restless activity is opened before us. All this activity is now quiet in the grave. Generation after generation has passed away from the earth, and we are permitted calmly to review their conduct, and learn wisdom if we will from such a retrospection.

What then is the lesson that we learn from the experience of ages? What inscriptions do we read on the sepulchres of dead millions? Is it recorded of ambition that it always reaches its goal? Did genius always wear the crown it merited? Did hope never promise what time refused to bestow? And when all that heart could desire was attained, has the soul of man rejoiced in the mighty acquisition? Very different is the record there inscribed. It is the record of crushed hopes, of blighted prospects, of joys which bloomed but to wither, of pleasures which long eluded the grasp, and when caught at last, turned into disappointment and satiety in the embrace. Oh, would we receive instruction from the experience of our fathers, how might each successive generation become wiser than that which preceded it. But though one generation passeth away and another cometh, the fallen nature of man remaineth the same. New actors come upon the stage, but the farce of human folly, and the tragedy of human disappointment are re-enacted in wild confusion over the dust of our sleeping ancestors. But if we neglect the experience of others, why should we disregard the lessons of our own? There is not one that hears me now, who has not seen enough in the little circle of his own acquaintance, and felt enough in the secrecies of his own bosom, to convince him thoroughly that the world has no certain nor satisfying portion to bestow. There is none who has not felt the shock of disappointment, or the loathing of satiated desire. Who has not seen his brightest expectations overclouded, his most deeply cherished hopes all disappointed, his tenderest affections wounded in their tenderest point. But when all has been bestowed that the world could give, who has not felt that this is insufficient? In the wildness of mirth, in the excesses of sensual pleasure, amidst the loud applause of admiring thousands, man is not satisfied. The soul cannot feed on husks like these. Debase and brutalize it as you may, it is a spirit still, and despite all your efforts it will rise and reassert its nature and its origin. It is endowed with a capacity for enjoying God, and can never be satisfied with inferior good. And hence it is that sinners pass so tediously and painfully through the world. There is a constant struggle against all the better principles of their nature, against reason, and conscience, and the immortal spirit within them.

What a fearful struggle is this; yet it is going on within the bosom of every sinner. Yes, sinner, conceal it, deny it as you may, the thin disguise of outward merriment hides it not from the eye of man, how much less from the searching glance of an omniscient God. How foolish, then, to love the world, which after all gives no real happiness, while we reject our kind and merciful Creator, who is able to satisfy the highest desire of the soul which he has made, "in whose presence is fulness of joy, and at whose right hand are pleasures forevermore." Place yourself amidst the happiest circle of the most promising youth of both sexes. They have never yet known sorrow, or experienced disappointment. The world lies fresh and untrodden before them, and as far as the eye can reach, hope gilds the prospect with the brightest colors. One hopes for wealth, and before her mind forever rolls the splendid equipage, the costly apparel, and the elegant apartments of the rich. Another hopes for honor, and his eye brightens at the thought of the bar, and senates, and assemblies, and his own voice swelling high above the rest, and guiding the tumultuous passions of the people. Another dreams of health and youth and beauty and social comfort long-continued, and thinks this happiness enough; while another, more quiet still, pictures the still retreat, the comfortable fireside, the cheerful friend, and all the accompaniments of domestic peace. Now follow them if you can through their various fortunes in their future life. Will not youth decay? Will not beauty fade? Will not that bright eye be dimmed? Will not that manly voice be hushed in death, or enfeebled by disease, or overborne by party violence? Or who can tell the thousand misfortunes which meet them in the path of life, and bring poverty, or shame, or social misery upon them. How many commenced the career of life along with Cæsar, with the same bright hopes and the same ambitious views. A mother's fondness destined for them the same eminence, and a father's fond pride promised the same high success, and the kind voice of many an applauding friend cheered them on their way. But who among them all trod the same path of glory? And yet how dizzy was the pinnacle on which he stood at last, and how soon did that dominion end in blood, which years of toil and dangers and bold ambition had just secured. Nay, the great globe itself shall be destroyed, the elements shall melt with fervent heat, and earth's last garniture shall be its winding-sheet of flames.

And is this nothing but a scene where imagination riots and reason reels? Think you that he who made the world, cannot destroy it? Are there no instruments of wrath laid up in the great store-house of the Almighty's indignation against the day of final retribution? In the very bowels of the earth on which you tread so securely, are the hidden elements which, brought together and pent up within its shell, would melt its solid rocks, and heave its quaking mountains, and by one vast explosion shatter it to fragments. The very air you breathe, if partially decomposed, would yield a substance which taking fire from a lighted lamp, would spread a universal conflagration, and which, even when prepared by the chemist's skill, and issuing in the smallest current from his laboratory, dissolves all earths and minerals, and causes the hardest steel to blaze and sparkle like the burning brand.

Thus as God has placed in every sinner's bosom the elements and the forebodings of future misery, so has he placed in the material world around us the sources and the forewarnings of its coming dissolution. But, alas! how deaf are the men of this world to the voice which thus comes to them from the word and the works of God. They would not believe though one should rise from the dead to tell them. And therefore shall this day of the Lord come as a thief in the night. None shall be expecting it. But, as when the deluge came, the affairs of this world shall be rolling on in their accustomed course, and the current of this world's occupations, pursuits, and pleasures shall be drifting men as far away from holiness, happiness, and heaven, and impiety shall lift as bold a front as ever. The Atheist shall be proving that there is no God. The Deist shall be asking, Where is the promise of his coming? The Socinian shall be proving that the Lord of Glory is no better than a man. The youth in the ardor of his untamed passions shall be urging on his chase of pleasure; and the maiden in the pride and confidence of charms, alas! too much admired and too falsely flattered, shall be distributing around the tokens of her favor. The man of ambition shall be pressing forward in his hot career of glory; and the conqueror shall then be driving his car of triumph over prostrate nations, while the wail of oppressed millions falls unheeded on his ear. The thief shall be stealing through the twilight to seek his neighbor's goods, and the murderer shall be wiping from his brow the stains of blood, and the duellist shall be aiming his weapon at a brother's heart — when suddenly, as in the twinkling of an eye, shall be heard the trump of the archangel, and the voice of God. Lift up your heads, O ye gates, and be lifted up, ye everlasting doors, and the King of Glory shall come in. Who is this King of Glory? The Lord of hosts. He is the King of Glory. And is this he who was born in Bethlehem? Who was clothed in flesh, who was despised and spit upon, who was crucified and slain? Yes, this is he, O sinner! who died that you might live. Who shed his own precious blood on the cross for your salvation. And now he is sending you the offers of his mercy, and entreating you with condescending kindness to be reconciled to God. But then, oh, how changed. His wrath is kindled into fury, and his mercies are clean gone forever. Vain, then, are the entreaties of the sinner. No voice of mercy answers to his prayer. But from the great white throne issue forth thunderings and lightnings, and a voice which says, Because I have called and ye refused, I stretched out my hand, and no man regarded. But ye have set at naught my counsel, and would none of my reproof. I also will laugh at your calamity, and mock when your fear cometh, when your fear cometh as a desolation, and your destruction as a whirlwind. Then shall these go away into everlasting punishment, but the righteous into life eternal.

XII.

THE GROUNDS ON WHICH MEN REJECT THE GOSPEL.

LUKE, xiv. 18.—"And they all with one consent began to make excuse."

THE revelation which God has given us was made in human language, and adapted to human understanding, that it might gain an entrance into the human heart, and exert an influence over the conduct and character and destinies of man. With the same benevolent design our Heavenly Father has condescended still more to the weakness and imperfections of our nature, and has accommodated the language of his word to the circumstances and relations of daily life, and the feelings and affections which these various circumstances are calculated to excite. Thus the high truths of religion are brought down to the level of the human understanding, and urged home with more affecting power even to the hardest heart, when illustrated by the commonest occurrences of life, and appealing to all our tenderest sensibilities.

Now this is the design of the parables, so often employed in the Bible, to teach us something that is unknown, by comparing it with something that is familiarly known and with which we are every day conversant, teaching us heavenly things by comparing them with earthly things, giving us some faint idea of our relations and duties toward our fellow-creatures. And this design is most admirably accomplished by the parables of the Bible; so that the truth which is meant to be conveyed, is not only brought home more affectingly to the heart, but is represented likewise more vividly to the understanding than could possibly be done by any mere verbal representation. How instructive, and at the same time how affecting and condescending, is the language of the Bible, when God represents himself as the Father of the human race, and permits us to come unto and call him, "Our Father who art in heaven;" and who, though he be in heaven, yet looks down with pitying compassion on his wandering, erring children, and desires to reclaim them to himself, to holiness, to heaven, and everlasting happiness; opening wide to receive us the arms of a father's affection, assuring us of a father's welcome, and a rich inheritance.

It is impossible, we imagine, that any man could read, with the slightest attention, the parable of the Prodigal Son, without feeling more deeply, at the close, the wisdom and duty of repenting and turning to God, and being more thoroughly convinced than he had been before that God is willing to receive the returning prodigal. While he pictures to his mind the misery and want of the wayward child, his obstinate perseverance, his downward course, even when beggary and ruin stared him in the face, his slow repentance, his reluctant determination to return, his hesitating, lingering, doubting, trembling approach to his father's house, overwhelmed with shame, emaciated with hunger and disease, corroded by remorse, with scarce a rag to conceal his nakedness, and none to veil his sorrow and disgrace; and then beholds his father, all tenderness and love, forgetting the fall of his child, and remembering only his repentance and his distress, rushing forth at the first news of his approach, welcoming that tattered beggar to his house and to his heart, falling upon his neck, weeping, and kissing him, and with all the fondness of a father's affection, crying out, "My son was dead but is alive again, was lost but is found." We say, that no individual can read such a representation as this, if he has ever known the gushings of those warm affections which flow from father to son, and from son to father back again, and doubt for a moment that these are the real feelings of the Father of the universe to our fallen family, and that no language which the human mind has ever invented could express so forcibly as the simple parable the deep instruction it was intended to convey.

But of all those figurative representations which are employed in the Bible for the purpose of recommending the truth of God to the understandings and affections of men, there is none more frequently used than that which describes the salvation of the Gospel, as a provision for the wants and necessities of men, as food for the hungry, drink for the thirsty, a great feast richly provided and freely offered to all, a fountain of living waters, a stream which never fails, a mighty river springing from the throne of God, whose gushing waters are clear as crystal, and on its banks is the tree of life, whose leaves are for the healing of the nations. By such representations as these, the abundance of the provision, the freeness and sincerity of the invitation, and the spontaneous kindness of the provider, are forcibly displayed.

Thus, in the parable just read, we are told that a certain *rich* man, who was fully able to bear the expense and insure the abundance of the provision, prepared a *great* feast, one suitable to his wealth and station, and to the number of the guests invited, and then sent his servants to call the guests. "But they all with one consent began to make excuse." Now the conduct of the guests who were invited, is intended, no doubt, to represent the conduct of mankind, who are invited by the great king of heaven to the rich provisions of the Gospel, and yet most of them decline the gracious invitation. Let us then spend a few moments in considering, First, The strange fact that men endeavor to excuse themselves from accepting the offers of the Gospel. Secondly, Notice some of their excuses. Thirdly, The danger of thus rejecting the offers of the Gospel.

I. Let us consider the strange fact that men, almost universally, endeavor to excuse themselves from accepting the offers of the Gospel.

To one who believes, indeed, that there is a God, the most solemn and tremendous of all questions is, whether he is the friend or the enemy of man. Whether he who sits far off, in uncreated light and glory above the sky, shut out from all human gaze by the unapproachable brightness which surrounds him, and baffling all human investigation by the untold mysteries of his wonderful existence. Whether the terrible and unknown One looks down upon this world of ours with kind and pitying affection, or frowns us away from his presence as the objects of his holy indignation. This is a question which has pressed most heavily upon the minds of men, in all ages and all regions of the world, and in every condition of human society. It has been reiterated again and again, with fearful solicitude, for ages past, and is still propounded with undiminished anxiety at the present day. It has agitated, it must, at some period of his existence, agitate the bosom of every reflecting man. The philosopher has asked it, as he walked with grave and solemn tread over the halls of science, musing much and deeply. The savage asks it, as he roams over his native forests, and gazing on their wild magnificence, beholds in the works around him the traces of the great and unknown Spirit. The man of pleasure asks it, when in some hour of intermitted merriment his conscience calls up the memory of wasted hours and riotous excess, and stamps upon all his pleasures, vanity and vexation of spirit. The man of sorrow asks it, as he recounts the story of his multiplied afflictions, or tossing upon his bed of long disease, feels in his withering frame the heavy pressure of a hand more mighty than his own. The living ask it, when they behold the ravages of death around them; and the dying ask it, when the dust is returning to dust again and the spirit is going to God who gave it.

The question is one to which the human understanding, unaided by light from heaven, has never yet offered any satisfactory reply. After all our inquiries it must still remain involved in the darkest mystery, surrounded with the most perplexing doubts. We may look abroad indeed upon the mighty works of God, and see upon them all the impress of a power which is infinite and irresistible; but whether this power is indifferent, or friendly, or hostile to our race, is not revealed by the works of nature. The sun, as he shines in his glory, and the moon, as she walks in her brightness, and the thousand stars which twinkle in the sky, may tell that the hand which made them is divine: but they have no speech, nor language, to reveal the high designs of the mysterious Creator. If we observe the course of God's providence on earth, all still seems dark and inscrutable. If the happiness which is enjoyed by man, seems to prove the kindness and regard of our Creator; the misery which is spread so widely over the face of our earth, would lead us directly to the opposite conclusion. If every balmy breeze which wafts health and joy to our habitations, and every human heart which throbs with high delight, is an evidence that he who directs the wind and who formed the heat is merciful and good; then every desolating whirlwind, and every pestilential vapor, and every sob of agony, must throw a sickening uncertainty over the whole of our conclusions. And then there is the consciousness of the whisperings of that inward monitor, which points to a day of coming retribution, the fearful looking for of judgment and fiery indignation, which, like a strong man armed, lays hold of every human bosom, and, struggle and wrestle as we may, maintains its lodgment there, till in man's last sad extremity its triumph is completed, and the departing spirit, even before it leaves the body, feels that its destiny is fixed.

Thus it is that the mysteries of providence, and the consciousness of guilt, cast a fearful uncertainty around every question which concerns the mutual relations of God and man. We feel that there is a mysterious agency within us and around us, pervading all things, sustaining all things, in whom we live and move and have our being, a power which no wisdom can elude and no force resist; and while we remember that he is infinitely holy, the recollection of our sins must rush into our minds, and bring home upon us with redoubled interest the anxious question, "Can God be reconciled to man?" Now suppose we were informed, in the midst of this perplexity and doubt, that God himself had resolved to answer the question, and to reveal himself in his true character to the children of men; with what anxious and breathless interest would we await the expected revelation. Will he come in flaming fire to take vengeance on his enemies, clothed in the robes of justice, and armed with the thunder of Omnipotence; or will he appear in the gentleness of heavenly compassion, as the friend, and father, and Saviour of our race? Fearful indeed would be that hour of dread suspense, and scarcely less terrific than that day of righteous revelation, when the assembled families of men shall stand before the throne of the Eternal, and hear the last unchangeable decision.

But should the messenger that comes from heaven, proclaim his character as the Lord God, merciful and gracious, who delighteth not in the death of a sinner, but would rather that he should turn and live—should the message be one of unutterable love, and the messenger that bore it, his own beloved Son; how soon would we expect to find that the anxieties and fearfulness of men were converted into wondering, and adoring, and rejoicing affection, and to hear, from every family on earth, and from every human bosom, the glad songs of thanksgiving and praise to him who ruleth in heaven, and yet so kindly condescendeth to have intercourse with men. Now just such a revelation given to mankind in those very circumstances of doubt and terror, which we have feebly endeavored to describe, is that which is made in the Gospel. In this, God has still more abundantly manifested his love toward us, because he was not only willing to be reconciled to man, but to pay the price of reconciliation too; that while we were yet enemies against him, he freely delivered up his own Son, on our behalf, to die, that we might live; and now the proclamation of pardon through his blood is made to every son and daughter of Adam; and we this day beseech you, in Christ's stead, to be reconciled to God.

Yet how vainly is the Gospel proclamation made, how lightly is the Gospel message heard, how often must the minister of the Gospel take up the lamentation of the prophet and cry out in the bitterness of his soul, "Who hath believed our report?" "For they all began with one consent to make excuse."

We go to the young man in the commencement of life, who is just entering on his career of giddy pleasures and gay amusements: and we tell him that his pleasures will at last bite like a serpent, and sting like an adder; that they will pierce him through with many sorrows; that they are at best transient, uncertain, unsatisfying. We point him to those higher and better pleasures which endure forever, and fill the largest capacities of the soul, in the presence of God, where there is fulness of joy, and at his right hand, where there are pleasures forevermore. The thoughtless youth passes heedlessly along, and scarcely pauses a moment to exclaim, "I pray thee have me excused." He embarks on his voyage of pleasure; the stream wafts him smoothly along, till at last he disappears from our view; and the rainbow colors, which had caught his fancy and allured him to destruction, still overhang, in silent beauty, the dreadful cataract where his bark was crushed. He is gone, and we turn with sad solicitude to the man of middle age, who had watched with us the wild career of the unhappy youth, and shuddered at the horrid spectacle of his untimely end. He is deeply immersed in worldly cares, in the pursuit of honor, or of wealth. He acknowledges the folly of his early pleasures, and mourns the disappointment of his early hopes; but still he makes gold his confidence and fine gold his trust; or living on the breath of popular applause, and making it the god of his political idolatry, he takes the world for his portion, and gives to the god of money, or the god of fame, the tribute of his heart's devoutest adoration. But in vain do we offer to him the riches which shall never perish, the glory and honor which shall never fade. Even heaven's crowns, which shall brighten forever on seraphic brows, are unnoticed and despised in the ardor of his hot pursuit after earthly things; and impatient of the slightest delay or interruption, he replies to the most affectionate expostulation, "Really, sir, you must have me excused."

We go to the old man, just trembling on the brink of the grave, and while we sympathize with all the sorrows of his age, and mourn over the spectacle of one about to desert his all on earth, with no portion laid up in heaven; we point him back to the vanities of his life, and bid him look forward to that life above which shall never terminate, to a youth of immortal vigor, and undecaying glory, where sickness and sorrow shall flee away, and all tears shall be wiped from all eyes. But while we press upon his thoughts, the necessity of immediate preparation for a change so near at hand, and a state of such unspeakable felicity, he hears with impatience our affectionate entreaties, turns back his wishful eyes upon the world which has so long deceived him, and, with the last trembling accents of decaying nature, exclaims, "I pray thee have me excused." We turn away in melancholy disappointment, but scarce have turned away, when another messenger arrives, of sterner aspect and more severe commands. Death brooks no delay; and the last faint excuse dies away, before it can be uttered by his trembling lips.

Now thus it is, that the Gospel is carried around to all the families and all the individuals of our land. It passes from house to house, and from heart to heart, knocking at every door, and seeking an entrance, but meeting continually the same chilling and repulsive answer, "Go thy way for the present, I pray thee have me excused." How wonderful is the forbearance and long-suffering of God, in thus enduring the contradiction of sinners against himself, and mercifully repeating those gracious invitations which have been so long despised and so haughtily rejected; and how strangely foolish is the conduct of men! From what do they wish to excuse themselves? From sin? from misery? from hell? No, they freely indulge in sin; their paths are encompassed with misery, their steps take hold on hell, and lead down to perdition. They seek to avoid the favor and service of God, the approbation of a peaceful conscience, the society of the blessed in heaven, present happiness and future glory.

II. Let us, however, examine for a moment some of these grave and weighty reasons by which men endeavor to quiet their own conscience, and ward off the expostulations of others, when urged to give an immediate attention to the Gospel offers.

The first and most usual is the pressure of worldly business, the attractions of worldly pleasure, the pursuit of worldly honor, or the obligations of worldly connections. These excuses may seem to be different in character and to come from different men; but they are all the same in principle, and are founded on the settled determination to enjoy the world in some one of its various forms, and not to permit the concerns of religion to interfere at all with their worldly plans. Whether they aim at the accumulation of wealth, or the acquisition of honor, or the indulgence of ease or social feelings, the principle is the same.

The train of thought which the sinner indulges upon this subject, seems to be simply this: I live, says he, in a world which God has made, which he has richly supplied with every thing necessary to sustain my life, or minister to my enjoyment. On every thing around me are the traces of his power, the monuments of his goodness, the evidence of his presence. I am myself, indeed, but the creature of his hands. This human frame, so fearfully and wonderfully made, is the product of his power. The eye which opens with delight upon all nature, and by its delicate and skilful mechanism holds mysterious intercourse with distant worlds; the ear which delights with harmony, and listens to the language of friendship and affection; the soul which feels, and thinks, and rejoices in the kindness of social affections and the tenderness of social relations—these are all the workmanship of his skilful hand. Surrounded, as I am, with so many blessings, and endowed with such capacities for enjoying them, I am determined what I will do; I will improve, to the utmost, my short opportunity; I will indulge the body, and forget the soul; I will live like an atheist who denies a God, or like a brute that never knew one. Drink deeply of the streams of his beauty, but never look upward to the fountain from which they flow. Bury myself amidst the mute and lifeless materialism around me, while I forget the great and everlasting spirit who gave to this material creation all the beauty and all the attractions it possesses. Riot on the gifts of his providence, while I forget the giver; and use the goodness and long-suffering of God to embolden me in sin. I will harden my heart by the very means which were designed to soften it; and that the benefits of my determination may not be confined to myself, the wife whom I have taken to my bosom, the children of our mutual love, the friends of my early years, shall enjoy the benefit of my example, and reap along with me the fruits of my approaching harvest. And what shall that harvest be? Let me answer in the language of God's Word, "He that soweth to the flesh, shall reap corruption; he that soweth the wind, shall reap the whirlwind." He that endeavors to excuse himself from his duties on any of these grounds, does deliberately choose the world for his portion and reject the salvation of his soul.

But what will the world profit him if he shall lose his soul? Suppose that he succeeds in all his enterprises, even his most ardent and extravagant calculations. Let wealth flow in upon him by a thousand channels. Let honor place him upon her highest pinnacle; and in the full exercise of all his powers, with nerves that tremble not at his lofty elevation, and a mind that comprehends, in his rapid glance, the vast variety of interests committed to his care, let him look down from the station where he sits alone, upon a world all prostrate at his feet; and when man has exhausted his stock of paltry adulation, let nature yield her stores to his command; let the mountain reveal its treasure, and the sea give up her hidden wealth; let the north send in her portion and the south her tribute; let the birds of the air and the beast of the field minister, with their choicest dainties, to his palate; let the most delicious viands sparkle at his board, and the softest melody warble through his halls, and the voice of merriment and music be heard continually around his apartments; and that this spoiled child of fortune may enjoy more than man has ever yet enjoyed, or heart has ever yet conceived, let his capacities for self-indulgence be doubled, and his life prolonged to centuries—yet will the day of his probation cease. Its morning rose in beauty; its noonday dazzled us with its brightness; its night shall close in clouds and darkness. For all these things, O man! God shall call thee into judgment;

and what art thou profited who hast gained the world but lost thy soul?

Few men have the hardihood deliberately to cast off all hope of future repentance and salvation; and although there may be some in this house who have little regard for the Saviour of sinners, yet there is not one but would shudder at the thought of renouncing all hopes of an interest in his atonement. The boldest sinner, if called upon to deed away all title to eternal life, would shrink back from the proposition. If the world were offered for his soul, he would spurn the offer; and yet the very deed, that he would shudder at when proposed in words, he is daily performing, and repeating continually in the course of his short and uncertain life. How many are saying, I will put off religion to a future season; I pray thee have me excused just now? Now to put off religion is, in fact, to reject it; for all the offers of the Gospel are made at the present time. There is not, in the whole Bible, a single promise to a future repentance or conversion. "Now is the accepted time, now is the day of salvation." "To-day, if ye will hear his voice, harden not your hearts." "Boast not thyself of to-morrow," "This night thy soul may be required of thee."

Since, then, there is no promise, no offer, except to the present, he who puts off now, rejects altogether, and all his promises and hopes of future repentance and conversion are vain delusions by which he hopes to deceive others, as the great adversary has deceived his own soul. Religion is every thing, or it is nothing. The salvation of the soul is important above all things, or of no importance; and he who delays attention to these great concerns, proves by this very act, that he has no adequate conception whatever of their awful and tremendous import. For what does he plead, who asks a short delay in accepting the offered mercy? He asks permission to sin against God a little longer; to harden his heart a little more; to strengthen his evil habits still more firmly; to risk his soul's damnation a few days longer; and by pursuing such a course as this, he hopes to be prepared, in a short time, to turn unto God, and repent of his sins. Has this man even the first idea about his own condition, or the character of God; about heaven or hell?

This whole scheme of future repentance is indeed highly insulting to God, ruinous to the souls of men. It is insulting to God, because he offers salvation now, and we propose to accept it at a future time; thus saying, that the offers of God are to stand waiting at our doors, until it may please our whim or caprice to grant them admission. It is dangerous, because the insulted Majesty of Heaven will not endure the insult. "My spirit shall not always strive with man;" and when the Spirit of God has once withdrawn his divine influences, there is no other power which can regenerate the soul; the condition of the sinner is utterly hopeless, and it were better for him that a millstone had been hanged around his neck, and he had been cast into the bottomless sea. The experience of all men warns us of its danger. The path to perdition is strewn with the bones of those who have calculated on a future repentance; and of all those unhappy beings, who are now suffering the righteous displeasure of God, there is perhaps not a single one who has not often resolved on a future repentance. No man ever yet reached heaven, who did not determine to repent now. Now is the best time to repent. Are you young? Repent now, before youthful folly has hardened into aged wickedness; before the cares and troubles of the world have pre-occupied your mind, and evil habits are fastened upon you. Are you old? Repent soon, or you will never repent at all; age is the time for serious reflections; think on the world that lies before you, and is so near at hand. Are you in prosperity? Seek the Lord now: it will prepare you to meet adversity, when it comes, and what is harder still, to enjoy the world without abusing it. Are you in adversity? Then seek your Father's face, he will not cast you off, "he giveth liberally, and upbraideth not." If you have no portion on earth, lay up one in heaven.

But I cannot convert myself you say. This is the very strongest reason, why you should not rest for a moment in your present condition. If the power lay with yourself, then you might exert it at your pleasure, and delay would not be so dangerous. But now, all depends upon the will of another. His goodness alone spares your life. His spirit alone can convert your soul. He is now waiting to be gracious. But if his patience shall once be exhausted, if he shall swear in his wrath, that you shall not enter into his rest; your doom is fixed, your condition is as hopeless as that of those who already feel the agonies of the second death. Is your need of divine assistance any reason why you should not seek it? Is your need of the Holy Spirit any reason why you should not ask his divine influences? Is your perishing and ruined condition a reason why you should fold your arms in calm security, and coolly await the coming ruin? Did the man whose withered arm the Saviour healed act thus, when he was commanded to stretch out his arm, all powerless and withered by disease, did he turn to the Saviour and complain, that he had commanded him to do what he was unable to accomplish? No, he made the effort, and God gave the power. The very command to act includes the promise of ability to those who wish it. There is scarce a command in the Bible which has not a correspondent promise, and a correspondent example. Are we commanded to seek the Lord? God says, I have not said to the house of Israel, Seek ye my face in vain; and David says, Thy face, Lord, will I seek. Are we commanded to make ourselves new hearts? the Psalmist prays, "Make me a new heart, and renew a right spirit within me." And again the promise is, "I will write my law upon their hearts." If, then, the invitation is freely given, and the offer of divine assistance is fully made; if the strength, which the sinner has not in himself, may be obtained of God, the excuse which he draws from his inability to convert himself is altogether groundless.

But bad as all these excuses are; if persevered in, they will all be taken. God will force no man into heaven against his will. His service is a voluntary service, a spiritual service, and he seeketh such to serve him. "As for those men who were bidden, none of them shall taste of my supper." The prayers of sinners are often answered sooner than they expected. The profane swearer, who calls down curses on his head, often finds that his prayer is terribly answered. He prays in jest, but God never jests; he answers him in earnest. Thus the man, who is continually praying in his heart to be excused from the service and favor of God, often meets a quick and terrible reply. God says in his wrath, he is joined to his idols, let him be excused, excused now, excused forever. We see then,

III. How dangerous it is to trifle with the offers of the Gospel. If God has spoken to man, he surely must require that man should give, at least, an attentive and respectful hearing. The voice which speaks from heaven, is the voice of wisdom, the voice of authority, the voice of affection. That wisdom must not be despised; that authority must not be disregarded; that affection must not be slighted. The messenger who comes from heaven, comes loaded with a message of stupendous importance. He reveals a wonderful plan of redemption for a guilty world. So vast and important, in the view of infinite wisdom, was the scheme devised for man's salvation, that when it was to be revealed, the Son of God himself came down, attended by hosts of rejoicing angels, who announced his first arrival; and when this scheme was to be carried into its complete and final execution, this glorious Redeemer shed his blood upon the cross, the earth shook and trembled, the sun wrapped himself in sackcloth, and angels again announced his joyful resurrection.

Now, for man to turn away, in cold indifference, from this great scheme of reconciliation devised for his peculiar benefit —a plan which angels desire to look into, and the Son of God died to accomplish—for man thus to treat, with cool contempt, the most solemn doings of the Almighty, cannot but excite the divine displeasure. Hence throughout the Bible it is represented as the last and greatest of all sins, as that which does arouse the indignation of Jehovah, till it burneth to the deepest hell. Even Sodom and Gomorrah, those cities of the plain, whose pollutions cried to heaven for vengence, and brought down a fiery deluge to overwhelm them, should rise in judgment against the cities which despised the Saviour's invitations; and how, says the apostle, how shall we escape if we neglect so great salvation!

And here in the parable before us, we are told, that the Master was angry—he who had provided the feast—who had sent out his invitations—who had said, all things are ready—he was angry, and said, "None of these men who were bidden shall taste of my supper." So when the approach of the judgment is described in the Apocalypse, those who are crying to the rocks and hills to fall upon them and cover them, wish to be concealed from the wrath of the Lamb; for the great day of his wrath is come and who shall be able to stand! Mark the expression, the wrath of the Lamb—not the wrath of the lion, or the tiger, or some fierce beast of pray, whose delight is in blood and suffering, but the wrath of the Lamb—the meek, quiet, gentle, long-suffering Lamb—the Lamb of God, slain from the foundation of the world. The sinner's best friend is become his enemy, his last hope is sunk in despair. The love which long bore with him, is now turned into anger; and mercy, long despised, has seized the sword of justice. The mountain of privileges, on which the sinner stood, is now a mountain of guilt pressing him lower and lower into perdition. Oh, there is no hatred like that which springs from slighted love; there is no wrath like the wrath of the Lamb! And let us all remember that the day is coming when these excuses will be of no avail. They shall all, one day, be examined by the clear light of eternity, and undergo the searching scrutiny of the omniscient Judge. Deceive others as we may, impose on ourselves as we can, yet we cannot impose on God. In that great day of coming retribution, when the assembled families of earth shall stand before his bar, no such excuse will then be offered; but deep and solemn silence will overspread that wide assembly, and the sinner, self-condemned, shall only hear in the decision of the Judge, the confirmation of the verdict his own conscience had passed already.

XIII.

THE DUTY, ENCOURAGEMENT, AND RESPONSIBILITY ARISING FROM THE POSSESSION OF TALENTS.

LUKE, xix. 13.—"Occupy till I come." (See Matt. xxv. 14; Luke, viii., 18; Mark, iv. 25).

THE parable, of which our text forms a part, is parallel with that contained in the 25th chapter of Matthew, commencing at the 14th verse, usually called the parable of the talents. Both are designed to illustrate the same great truths by a language and an imagery strikingly analogous. In each the privileges we enjoy, the advantages and blessings we possess, are represented as coming from the hand of God, as gifts of his bounty, or rather as loans for a season, to be reclaimed at his pleasure; as loans for which he will require an interest on the day of reckoning; as advantages, which are attended by corresponding responsibilities, and to whose improvement we are invited by the kindest encouragements, from whose neglect we are warned by the most fearful threatenings. In St. Matthew, the servants are represented as trading with their talents, and here, it is said: "Occupy till I come." The term in the original means to be occupied, to be diligently, industriously, laboriously engaged. So that the requirement of our text is diligently and conscientiously to *improve* the talent, or the pound, committed to us.

We endeavored on a former occasion, from this text, to warn you against that secret atheism, which insinuates itself the more dangerously, because unobserved, into the whole current of our habitual feelings, and usurps the place and the attribute of the Creator by claiming an absolute proprietorship in his works. We endeavored to remind you of that truth, universally acknowledged, yet too generally neglected, that God is the Lord and Proprietor of all; that we are the workmanship of his hands, created by his power, and upheld by his goodness; that the fulness of the earth is his; his the large possessions of the rich, and the scanty pittance of the poor; and that, in the wide extent of his magnificent creation, there is nothing found too large for the limits of his ownership, too insignificant for the obligation of his claims. We directed your minds to the consideration of the solemn truth, that all, which we fondly call our own, is but a loan from the treasury of the Lord, to be reclaimed in its season; a loan, on which an interest will be demanded, a talent of which an improvement will be required, and pointed to that fearful day of reckoning, when the Judge himself shall be seen in the air, when the living shall be changed, and the dead raised; when the judgment shall be set and the books opened, and the whole assembled universe shall hear the last unchangeable decision. In view of all these solemn considerations it was impossible that our minds should not occasionally glance at other important consequences necessarily resulting from them — at the duties, the encouragements, and the responsibilities connected with the possession of these talents.

What was then the object of a transient glance, or casual remark, will now demand our deliberate attention,—and we propose to consider,—

1st. The duty of improving our talents.

2d. The encouragements to their improvement.

3d. The responsibilities connected with the possession of these talents.

I. The duty of improvement may be shown from the command of God and from our own best interests. The command of God carries with it a universal obligation founded on an undoubted right—a right of property, full, complete, original, clear in itself, supported by the best of titles, the original creation and continued preservation of all things. His commands are powerful and cannot be safely resisted; they are wise and good, and calculated to promote the highest welfare and permanent interests of all. These commands are much broader than is usually imagined. They embrace man's whole nature, intellectual and physical, no less than moral; as St. Paul expresses it, "his whole spirit and soul and body." They extend to the minutest circumstances of his life, to all his domestic and social relations, to his intercourse with men, as well as his duty to God; to the cultivation of the intellect and the preservation of health and the exercise of influence, as well as to purity of heart and humility of spirit. We are commanded to be diligent in business, as well as fervent in spirit, to labor in our vocation by day as well as to meditate on God's truths by night, diligently to improve each talent, to leave no moment unemployed, no opportunity unimproved, no faculty dormant, no energy relaxed.

There is utterly a delusion here, a delusion extensively prevalent, and fatal to the interests of the Gospel upon earth, which casts down the standards of Israel's host, to be trampled under foot of the Philistines, and causes the enemies of God to laugh in stern and bitter derision. It is that the commands of God extend only to the heart and life, and that if the heart be free from guile, and life unspotted in the world, the intellect may lie uncultivated, its mighty powers undeveloped, and the whole field of human knowledge left open to the enemies of God, to master its richest treasures, to wield its mighty weapons, to distort its facts, to pervert its reasoning, to direct its most powerful instrument—the press, to mould the public mind, and stamp their own impress on this young and rising nation. But be not deceived, my brethren, we have to fight with principalities, and powers, and spiritual wickedness in high places, and if there be one demand more pressing than another, if in this age of action, and tumult, and excitement, and bold inquiry, if in this land of unfettered freedom and overflowing prosperity, there be one necessity more urgent than all others, it is the demand for holy talent, it is the necessity for consecrated learning, it is that men should rise upon our soil, strong in native intellect, rich in acquired learning, filled with the Spirit of the Lord, to walk boldly forth over the whole field of human science, gathering its scattered riches, digging deep for its precious ore, and from the Babel of discordant opinions, drawing fresh materials to build up in new glory the temple of the Lord.

I mean not that meagre and conceited talent which wastes its feeble energies in placid self-contemplation; that superficial learning which, puffed with the lightness of its own materials, longs ever after self-exhibition, and grasps for popular applause; but that real genius, always unobtrusive, which aiming at higher and distant objects, spurns away from it the pettiness of an early and temporary fame, which digs deep, that its foundation may be sure, and in silence and obscurity burnishes that armor which shall one day glitter in the noonday sun, in the face of nations, and turn the tide of battle. And well do I believe there is an exalted and expansive spirit in the Gospel, which can enlarge and elevate the mind as well as purify the heart, and under whose pervading influence there shall yet spring up another race of men—giants in their days, clothed in the whole panoply of knowledge, radiant in the light of truth, whose reason, blinded by no passion, polluted by no vice, calm, transparent, pure, shall be the mirror of eternal truth, reflecting gloriously its heavenly lineaments, as the deep, majestic ocean tranquilly gives back the faithful image of the blue sky above it.

I have not forgotten the mighty efficacy of Christian intelligence directed by Christian principle, and urged on by Christian feeling, when employed in any department of inquiry or of effort. I have not forgotten that every enterprise for the benefit of the race has for centuries past been commenced and carried on and completed by Christians; that when the world was to be freed from the bondage of ecclesiastical tyranny, and the rights of conscience, and private judgment to be vindicated and rescued, it was the manly intellect and holy courage of a Christian which achieved the work; that when philosophy was to be reformed, and the very sources of all its errors detected and exposed, it was done by a Christian; and when the mind thus taught to reason was itself to be examined, its structure investigated, its operations revealed, this work was accomplished by a Christian; and when the material universe in all its vastness, and with all its wonders was to be revealed to man, it was a Christian who first comprehended the structure of the universe, who first analyzed light and calculated its motions, who first weighed the stars and taught us their distances, their magnitudes, their densities. And when this new nation was to assume its place among the people of the earth, it was a Christian, whose cool courage, and calm prudence, and deep foresight, and sterling integrity, and devout trust in God, guided us through unparalleled dangers, commanded universal confidence, and led us safely through to unexampled prosperity and glory. The world has seen but one Luther, but one Bacon, but one Newton, and but one Washington. Here then may we read in living characters what man can accomplish when urged on by the motives and sustained by the enemies of Christian principles.

As a small community we have long enjoyed the fertility of our soil, the healthiness of our situation, the peacefulness of our society, the faithful and constant preaching of God's word, and the repeated outpourings of his Spirit. What a long recital would it require merely to enumerate our blessings; how many might with joy exclaim—Here was I born again into a new life of peace and love; how many might gaze around with swelling hearts, and streaming eyes, to behold the children of their love here brought into the family of Christ! Oh, how delightful is the recollection of those days, when the Lord was indeed amongst us, when sinners were saying, "Come, let us go up to the house of the Lord," and the loud song of praise swelled rapturously high from hearts overflowing with gratitude and love! All this we feel, and yet are we prone to put away from us the conviction that we have individually a talent for which we are personally responsible. We are so constituted, that only what is remarkable attracts our attention. Hence an extraordinary providence excites our gratitude; an extraordinary delivery from imminent danger, an unexpected recovery from wasting disease, escape from some disaster which has overwhelmed many of our neighbors, directs our eyes to a hand unseen above us, which is stretched out for our defence, while the ten thousand daily blessings which flow in a perpetual stream from the same beneficent hand are unheeded, or perhaps denied.

For the same reason we are all ready to acknowledge that the man of vast erudition, or brilliant genius, or extensive influence, or mighty power, has indeed a great talent committed to his hands; and to enlarge most fluently on the corresponding duty of a diligent and conscientious improvement, while we overlook altogether the talents possessed by the great mass of mankind, and especially those intrusted to ourselves. How ready are we to exclaim: "Oh, what good I would do with all that wealth, or genius, or influence, or learning, or power! I would suppress crime; I would instruct the poor and ignorant, comfort the sick and afflicted, relieve the needy, warn the careless, rebuke the bold blasphemer, employ the whole weight of my authority, wealth, character, all my talents for the best purposes, and having much in my power, my efforts should be proportionally great; but now I have no talent, or if any, it is very small, too small to accomplish much good, or demand much cultivation. I may live without concern, however dreadful the responsibilities of others. I am excused, however strict their accountability." Now I am not disposed to deny that there is a difference in the talents committed to men. Yet this difference is not so great as many have indolently and sinfully desired to believe. The difference is usually of our own making, lies more in the improvement, than in the original gift. Those ten talents were, perhaps, originally one, and industry and care have multiplied it. Again, if you have little, this, far from being any argument for indolence or despondency, shows the greater necessity for active and energetic exertion. Your one pound may by diligence be increased to ten, by idleness may be reduced to nothing. But all have talents, far more numerous than they suppose. Consider for a moment how many you possess, and how shamefully they are neglected.

With respect to mental endowments, none who have been at all observant, can for a moment doubt that the difference is usually less in the original structure of the mind than in the subsequent cultivation; just as the health and vigor of the body, the full development and active play of all its organs, usually depend upon fresh air and wholesome food and exercise. You are perhaps inferior now to him who was once at best your equal, or on whom you once looked down with the proud feeling of conscious superiority. How do you now excuse your present inferiority. He stands perhaps at the head of his profession, while you linger far in the rear; his mind is stored with all valuable and useful knowledge, while yours is a simple vacuum, or filled with that idle and frivolous reading which only causeth to err. In all the elements of intelligent respectibility you are surpassed by your old inferior. You are astonished, you are fretted; now you swell with vanity, and now are corroded with envy; now you laugh, and now you murmur, but your feeble voice is lost in the loudness of those acclamations which proclaim him your superior. You wonder, you repine, but never reflect on the real cause, never revert to your own culpable neglect. Your hours of pleasure were for him hours of study; the lamp which burned till midnight in his apartment, illumined no scene of revelry or idle mirth, but fell upon the page of wisdom. If his health be enfeebled, it is not through sensual indulgence; if his brow be furrowed, it is with anxious thought and not with violent passions.

Oh, ye young men, who now exult in the possession of fancied talents which you think it unnecessary to improve, how keen will be those pangs of wounded pride, those stings of ill-concealed envy, which will fasten in your bosoms when you find in future life that while you slept, others labored; while you lingered on the way, others were advancing on the course, and have plucked the crown which you thought your own. And remember that you are accountable, both in the eyes of God and man, not only for what you are, but for what you might have been; not merely for the one pound given to you, but for the five or ten which you ought to have gained. Say not then: If I possessed the acquirements or the genius of such an individual I would devote them to high and noble purposes. Those acquirements are due to industry, not genius. That genius itself, is only common intelligence happily developed. Sir Isaac Newton was thought a dunce at school, and after his wonderful discoveries in after life gave this as the secret of his amazing genius, that he had "the capacity of *patient thought.*" Oh, it is fearful to look over the institutions in our land for the education of youth, and observe how many talents are buried, shamefully buried, lost to the possessor, lost to the world, lost now and forever!

It is the melancholy result of almost universal observation, that the fairest promise is often earliest blighted, the brightest genius most suddenly eclipsed. With respect to wealth, have you not more than to satisfy your reasonable wants? Is there nothing that you can spare for the cause of God and man? Because you cannot give so abundantly as the rich, will you feel yourself excused from the duty of giving at all? Have you thus learned the nature of real benevolence; have thus read the story of the widow's mite? How small a sum may aid in circulating the Word of God through distant lands, where his salvation is not known. How slight a pittance may relieve the distresses of the needy, if attended with the mild countenance and gentle tone of Christian love. And how vast is the amount which may be accumulated from the small contributions of those who have little to bestow. You have often heard it remarked that the mighty stream of British benevolence is principally supplied by the little rills which flow in from the cottages of the poor. If, however, you have nothing to bestow on others, is it not because you lavish your income in indulgence, or waste it by carelessness? Might not greater industry, or greater economy, increase your store, and a little self-denial purchase the dignified enjoyment of daily good? But oh, my friends, when I cast my eyes over this congregation; when I look abroad upon this rich and fertile land; when I remember how God has within a few years doubled almost without your agency the value of your estates, and then ask what is the improvement of these blessings? where are the thank-offerings made unto the Lord? where is the recognition of his goodness? has your gratitude increased with the multiplication of his favors? Have you more anxiously and prayerfully improved the privileges he is bestowing, or have the blessings which have descended from heaven only pressed you by their very magnitude more closely to the earth? Are you making gold and fine gold your trust, your confidence, and cast God from your thoughts because he has never ceased to think in tenderness and kindness of you?

When questions such as these are presented to your thoughts, do they come as unwelcome visitors, unwillingly entertained and speedily dismissed? Again, have you no influence to exert beneficially? Is there no circle where it may be happily employed? I mean not that meddling, dictatorial pragmatical influence, which irritates and disgusts, while it aims to guide, and makes man hate a good cause, for the faults of an injudicious advocate,—but the mighty influence of a meek and quiet spirit. Great is the power of one pious example; mighty the efficacy of the life truly devoted to the Lord! It matters not how ignorant, how young, how low—a child, a servant, may exert an influence which shall be felt to the end of the world, and throughout eternity. It is the influence of truth shining through his conduct and character. If the vessel be earthy, so much the more glorious the divine treasure which it contains. Ah, how many opportunities for exerting a holy and happy influence have we already lost! How many here have employed all their capacity and all their influence to diffuse around them an atmosphere of corruption? How many young men pollute all within their reach by their own impure conversation and wicked example, and stand amidst their fellows, not to diffuse a holy and happy influence around, but to blast and to wither all that is beautiful and lovely in youthful character, themselves meanwhile more blasted and withered than the worst, as the scorpion often dies by the venom which he has nourished for others!

Thus might I proceed to enumerate the various objects which

you prize most highly, and show that, whether enjoyed in a greater or less degree, they are all talents. Your time, your health, your energies of body and mind, your moral and social powers, your very life, your all, your opportunities of improvement, your means of happiness, *all* these are talents, committed to your hands for valuable purposes, and for whose improvement you are strictly responsible.

This leads us to remark again on the duty of improvement, that all these talents are not our own; they come from God, not as gifts, but as loans, to be reclaimed at his pleasure. All sin is practical atheism, all neglect or misimprovement of our talents is founded on the vain assumption that all we have is our own. Hence, usually the greater the gift the more neglected is the giver; the stronger and more numerous the bonds which should attach us to our Creator, the more restlessly do we endure their pressure, the more violently are they burst asunder. The very means designed to soften our hearts only make them harder, and the goodness and long-suffering of God emboldens us in sin. One looks on his farm, richly laden with the products of a fertile soil and genial climate, and says: "Behold, this is mine," forgetting that it is God alone who sends the rain and sunshine on his growing corn, and that one breath of the Lord would sweep from his large domain every living thing in which is the breath of life. Another looks with self-complacent vanity on his large acquirements, his learning, his talents, his fame, and cries aloud as the infatuated monarch of old: "Behold this great Babylon which I have built," forgetting who it is that causeth him to differ, that keeps up the full play of those active powers, and whose single word could dismiss him from the high rank which he occupies in the intelligent and rational creation, beneath the level of the brutes that graze unthinking, yet happy, by his side.

Now all this is downright atheism, the most daring and presumptuous atheism. It is shutting out God altogether from his dominions. It is casting him down from the throne of his rightful supremacy. The spirit which it breathes in whatever shape it may appear, however gracefully decked, or ingeniously veiled, is still the spirit of atheism. Oh, my friends, have we forgotten that all things are his; that every good and perfect gift cometh down from the father of lights; that of him and through him, and to him are all things, who is over all blessed forever? Do we not see him in the dispensations of his providence? do we not hear him in the voice of his works? Can we breathe the pure air of heaven; can we gaze with heartfelt bliss around our domestic circle; can we exult in the possession of our rational and intelligent existence; can we dwell amidst the manifestation of his goodness and his glory, and heedless of all we see around and feel within us, say with the fool in our hearts: There is no God?

But if there be a God, then we are his; then all is his, all things human are stamped with holiness, and consecrated to high and holy purposes. In one sense they are ours, not as gifts, but as loans; loans on which an interest is required, of which an improvement is to be made. And why, I ask you, oh, why are these talents intrusted to you? that station, that genius, that wealth, that influence, that time, those opportunities for intellectual and moral cultivation; that they may be wasted, perverted, applied to the worst purposes, or not employed at all? Why is life prolonged, that it may be wasted in indolence, or polluted by evil passions, or brutal lusts? Why is health preserved, that all its vigor may be consecrated to the service of the world and Satan? Why are the offers of mercy made, and the means of grace continued, that you may aggravate your final condemnation; that you may heap up wrath against the day of wrath; that you may fill up to fulness your cup of bitterness, and then drink it to the dregs? Why do you possess those rational and immortal powers, capable of knowing and serving and rejoicing in God? Is it that they may be dragged down from the loftiness of their upward flight and fastened to the dust on which we tread? Is it that he, who might eat of angels' food, may grovel with the swine and feed upon their husks? Believe you, that this is the design of your Creator, that those high endowments and glorious privileges are given in mockery of man? If they were given in perpetuity, it were madness thus to prostitute them. But they were only loaned for a season. You are not proprietor, as you may dream, but tenant at the will of another. They may be reclaimed at his pleasure, you know not how soon, but they will *certainly* be reclaimed. That health, which you now abuse to criminal indulgence, and utter forgetfulness of God, may soon be undermined; that wealth which you hoard with greedy avarice, and to which as unto a God, you pay your daily adoration, to which you sacrifice your conscience and sell your soul, that wealth may soon take wings and fly away. That reason, so much vaunted and so grievously abused, so long employed to apologize for sin, and to cavil against truth, may soon tremble on her throne, totter and fall. All your privileges, all your endowments may be swept away, and you may yet stand, even in this world, the melancholy monument of God's righteous judgments, bereft of all you have vaunted most, and most abused, the wreck of what you were, like the once proud oak, now leafless, branchless, lifeless, which the fire of heaven hath scathed amidst all its pride and beauty.

But if this come not soon, it must come at last. The end of our stewardship is fixed by the words of our text, "Occupy, till I come." Till I come in the judgments of my providence to strip you of all you now possess; till I come in the hour of death to burst the bonds that unite you to the earth; till I come in the great day of final retribution, to take vengeance on my enemies. And will he come, the despised, persecuted, crucified Redeemer, will he come? Yes, he will come, and every eye shall see him, and every ear shall hear him, and every knee shall bow before him, and every heart shall quail in his presence, and they that pierced him shall look upon him, and all the tribes of the earth shall wail because of him! Will he come? And oh, how will he come? He appeared once as the Babe of Bethlehem, was wrapped in swaddling clothes, and laid in a manger; no regal pomp attended his arrival; no loud acclaim of rejoicing thousands announced his near approach; but a single band of angels was heard at midnight by the solitary shepherds, and the notes of that music, which swelled softly over the distant hills of Judea, proclaimed peace on earth and good will to men.

But far different is his coming now. He comes not as a babe, but as a monarch; not as a king of wealth, but as Lord of the universe. A multitude, such as no man can number is around him, ten thousand times ten thousand attend him as he moves, and thousands of thousands proclaim his approach, and their voice is like the noise of many waters, and like the sound of mighty thunderings, as they cry aloud: "Lift up your heads, oh, ye gates, and be ye lifted up ye everlasting doors, and the King of Glory shall come in. Who is this King of Glory? the Lord of hosts, the Lord mighty in battle, he is the King of Glory." He sits on the clouds of the sky; he is borne on the wings of the wind; darkness is round about him, and thick darkness is his pavilion. Is this the man of sorrows? Is this the babe of Bethlehem? Behold, he travels in the greatness of his strength, he has trodden alone the wine-press of his wrath, his red right hand hath gotten him the victory. He is come in flaming fire to take vengeance on his enemies, clothed in the robes of justice, and armed with the thunders of Omnipotence. Hark! did you hear that sound, which swells through heaven, and reaches over the earth, and trembles through the dark caverns of the pit? Are these the tones of that soft music, which once was heard amid the mountains of Judea? No, it is the voice of the archangel, it is the trump of God, it is the summons to the judgment bar! He comes, but oh, how different is his advent from his departure? When he hung on the cross, the sun did for a season hide his head in shame, when he cried, "It is finished," and bowed his mighty head and gave up the ghost; a little while the conscious earth might shake at the foul deed by her fierce children done, and when he rose on high he bore one mortal back, the thief upon the cross, to be in paradise with him. But now at his approach, the sun is blotted out, the heavens are rent asunder, the elements melt with fervent heat; the earth, convulsed through all her kingdoms, dashes forth the affrighted dead of a thousand generations; the sea gives up her dead, and Death and Hell give up their dead. Behold they come from the north and the south, from the east and west, from every nation under heaven; from the populous city and the retired village; from the cultivated fields and the desert plain; from the monuments of the rich, and the graves of the poor. They come from the caves of the wilderness, from the darkest and most sequestered corners of the earth. They awake from the sleep of ages, they rise, they spring from the ruins of old Babylon and Nineveh, from the churches and cemeteries of modern days. They rise together, the father and the child, the husband and the wife, the pastor and the people, the murderer and the murdered, the seducer and his victim. Oh, what an assembly will be there! God will be there on the throne of his Judgment; the holy angels will be there awaiting his commands; the fiends of hell will burst forth from their dark caverns to be there; the spirits of just men made perfect will be there; the damned who have sunk from this Gospel land into darkness and eternal night, will all be there. And the conquerors of the earth will be there; and the hypocrites will be there; and the bold blasphemers, atheists, will all be there. Pilate, Herod, Judas, will be there; you and I will be there!

Shall we not arm ourselves, then, for the warfare in which we are engaged, and summon up every power for the mighty enterprise in which we are embarked? The world has reached a new era; the breath of a new spirit has been breathed upon it; a new impulse has been given to its movements; a new life is flowing through all its members, and all the elements of moral and intellectual being are tossing to and fro in cease less agitation like the waters of the mighty deep. The men of this world have caught the spirit of their age, their minds are wound up to the emergencies of the times; behold how they prepare for its conflicts, how they struggle for its prizes; what zeal, what self-denial, what boundless energy! They contend for an earthly crown, we for a heavenly. And can it be that we, with the high and commanding motives drawn from eternity bearing down upon us, shall be less energetic and vigorous than they? Less active by day, less laborious by night; less ardent in our aspirations, less patient in our self-denial? Shall we not enter along with them on every field of lofty thought and deep investigation, urging on our inquiries and pushing forward our victories; erecting no monument to our own glory, but humbly bringing all, gold, frankincense, and myrrh, whatever is costliest and most pleasant, to the feet of Jesus. Thus to aspire after the very highest attainments; thus to agonize after the complete perfection of your intellectual and moral nature—this is the spirit of the Gospel. Is it ambitious? Then who cares for words? I tell you to be ambitious, to covet earnestly the best gifts. This is ever to forget what is behind, and press on toward the mark; this is to be straitened till your work is accomplished—to endure the restlessness of a felt discomfort, while aught remains to be accomplished.

But remember, it is sacred talents, it is consecrated learning, of which I speak. Beware, lest in the ardor of your pursuit you forget the only proper object; lest you substitute the means for the end, and accumulate knowledge not to be devoted to the Lord, but for your own personal aggrandizement. And even those who have neither the opportunity nor the capacity for larger intellectual attainments, are not excluded the spirit of these remarks, for to the extent of their possible improvement they are strictly applicable to them; nor is any thing better calculated to preserve the purity, and extend the influence of the Gospel, than the general intelligence diffused through a Christian community. But this improvement of our talents is demanded as a duty, not only by the command of God, but by our own interests. Without this diligent improvement, all the high endowments, and precious privileges bestowed upon us, will be given in vain. All the advantages of nature, and all the blessings of God, will be entirely wasted. In vain is the book of nature spread out before our eyes, in vain is the volume of revelation placed in our hands, if we turn away in heedless indifference from both. In vain are all the anxieties of parents, in vain all the solicitude of friends, in vain all the efforts of instructors and pastors. Thousands are known to burst through all these barriers in their way, and rush headlong down the precipice of ruin, destroying in their course all present prospects and all future hopes, making shipwreck alike of character and faith, and alienating all human affection, as well as grieving away God's holy Spirit. By all that is solemn then, in God's authoritative command, by all that is dear in our own eternal interests, is enforced upon us the duty of improving the talents we possess. Consider next,

II. The encouragements to this improvement. What are they? The very strongest encouragement lies in the possession of these talents. It is a clear indication of God's design. There is in all his works nothing superfluous, nothing unadapted to the circumstances in which it is placed, or the uses to which it is to be applied. The dove has not the beak or talons of a vulture, nor the ox the tusks and claws of the lion. Man has not the fins and gills of the fish; nor the fish the limbs and lungs of a man. Each is adapted to the element in which he is to live, and the organs for seizing on his prey, for masticating and digesting his food, are exactly suited for the mode of life he is designed to pursue. And it is with the mind as with the body. The very structure of the moral and intellectual powers, indicates their design and use. The very circumstances in which man is placed, point out the purposes to which these powers are to be applied. Now this design cannot fail, except through our fault, through a wilful or negligent perversion of these powers. In vain would an ox attempt to fly, or any irrational creature attempt to speak or reason, because it is contrary to his whole organization, to the very design of his Creator, the end and object of his being. But man is formed for this very purpose, to know and love and serve God. He is capable of advancing in intellectual and moral cultivation, in holiness and conformity to God's image, and his whole organization, as well as the circumstances in which he is placed, and the opportunities he enjoys, proclaim this to be the end and object of his existence. As surely then, as God exists, so surely can this end be attained. Never fear then to aim at large advancements in holiness and wisdom and knowledge. Shall the huge leviathan fear to plough his own watery element, or the eagle to fly up toward the sun? Then may man fear the boldness of that voice which calls him upward to his native element, points out to him his exalted destiny, and exhorts him to fulfill it to the utmost. Let your aim be high, and your attainments shall be great, and your influence shall be wide.

Another encouragement may be found in the promise of God, confirmed as it is by our own experience and the universal analogy of his moral government on earth. The very command of God implies a corresponding promise. He is not an austere man, a hard master, a Pharaoh requiring bricks to be made, and supplying no straw for the work. He says expressly, "I have not said to the house of Israel, Seek ye my face in vain." He promises aid to human infirmity, and "as a father pitieth his children, so the Lord pitieth them that fear him." His promises are numerous, and unlimited: "Seek, and ye shall find," "Knock, and it shall be opened;" and here the command is: "Give to him that has ten talents, for to him that hath shall *more be* given." This is a universal rule in the natural and moral world. All things tend to multiply themselves. All moral qualities, good or bad; all intellectual habits, wealth, learning, influence, all tend to their own increase. Nothing is stationary; there is no perfect quiescence, but perpetual change. Growth and decay are the universal law. So in the world of grace, there is nothing stationary here. The Christian gets more grace; the sinner loses what he has, and heaps up wrath against the day of wrath. God gives as man is willing to receive. Open your mouth wide and it shall assuredly be filled. There is a mysterious union between divine and human agency. It is a gift, a free gift, an unmerited gift, and yet is its extent measured by the diligence of the recipient in improving his blessings.

III. What are our responsibilities for the improvement and application of our talents? This view gives a grave and solemn import to all of human life and human relations. Man is the servant and steward of the Lord, and all that concerns him partakes of the dignity of this high revelation. Of a steward it is expected that he be faithful. And oh, what a fearful spectacle does this world exhibit when thus considered. Look abroad, and behold the talents and blessings, the enjoyment and privileges, the means of happiness, and opportunities of improvement and usefulness bestowed on man, and think how all are wasted, abused, perverted. Oh, what a fearful reckoning there must come at last! Those men of influence and popularity, who exert their temporary importance to deceive, to injure, to corrupt the community that trusts them; those men of genius and learning, who wield the mighty powers intrusted to them for holiest purposes, that they promote immorality and sin; those rich men, who heap up gold to gratify their appetites, their vanity, or avarice; who use the good gifts of God to dishonor his name, and close their ears and harden their hearts against the cry of the needy, the ignorant and distressed. Oh, how shall they answer when the day of reckoning shall come, when all their ingenuity shall find no excuse, and all their wealth can purchase no reprieve; and instead of the adulations of a senseless crowd, shall burst upon their ears the deep execrations of those they have ruined by their example, the indignant hiss of an assembled universe.

But of those who shall tremble before the bar of God on this fearful day of reckoning, most awful is the destiny of him, who degraded his high endowments to base purposes, and used his extensive influence only to pollute and to destroy. We need not wander beyond the limits of our own age and nation to find men enough, who, gifted with a popular eloquence the most commanding and persuasive, and social qualities the most winning and attractive, have yet employed these advantages for the worst purposes; have pleased only to corrupt, and fascinated only to ruin; have held the torch of their genius on high, not to diffuse a pure and heavenly light, but to mislead all who followed, to consume all who approached. There is an instance but too well known throughout the world, and to whom, even before I mention his name, the thoughts of all will spontaneously turn. I mean that strange and wayward genius, who in the memory of us all, drew the eyes of all the world upon himself in alternate admiration, pity, and terror. He is far beyond human praise or blame, nor even if he lived, could the voice which now addresses you, ever reach him from this distant land, or add one pang to the agonies of that dark and gloomy spirit. Endowed with all the advantages of nature and fortune, by birth a noble, by education a scholar, by nature a poet, uniting in his single person all that mankind are most accustomed to admire; to what beneficent purposes might he not have devoted his amazing genius; what a holy light might he not have shed along his path; what a blessed memory might he not have left behind him, associated with all that is loveliest in domestic feelings, that is kindest in social sympathies, that is purest in moral principles. But habituated from earliest childhood to the indulgence of every passion, a sceptic without examination, a sensualist without shame, his creed was the dictate of his heart, rather than his head, and his practice was the best refutation of his principles. Intoxicated with success, dizzied with the elevation he had reached, maddened by the consciousness of intellectual power, he poured out from the gall of his own agitated spirit, the bitterness of his scornful derision on all human hopes and virtues, on all that was fairest, and loveliest, among men. After a life which was stained with almost every vice, he consecrated the last energies of a body, worn out with self-indulgence, and of a mind wrecked by ungovernable passions, to erect a monument of moral infamy, fit emblem of its author's mind, where the flashes of genius burst irregularly forth, more brilliant from surrounding desolation, and all that is revolting in brutal lusts is ingeniously veiled and rendered seductive by all that is most splendid in poetic imagery and diction. His profligacy was as great as his talents, "of which," to use the quaint language of an ancient writer, "God gave him the use, and the Devil the application." He employed the most exalted powers for the worst purposes, wielded the sword of an archangel with the malignity of a fiend, and plucked a brand from hell to set the world on fire. Oh, was not that a fearful but righteous retribution, when he, who derided all domestic peace and virtue, was himself driven out from all its enjoyment; when he who had in the very wantonness of scepticism, thrown out upon the world his gloomy doubts, found them gathering in a dark and thick cloud around his own head; when that abused understanding was wrecked by the passions it had nourished, and that feverish frame worn out by the vices it had practised, and he who had been the idol of nations, sank to the level of the lowest, became the daily companion of those whose very touch is pollution, and very name modesty may not mention.

Thus it is that even in this world the visitations of God's mercy are often converted into the visitations of his wrath; that talent after talent is given, neglected, perverted, till fortune, intellect, character, conscience, health are gone; then cast the unprofitable servant into outer darkness; there shall be wailing and gnashing of teeth.

We have seen the wicked, like the green bay-tree, lifting its summit toward heaven, extending its branches abroad over the earth, but there was rottenness at the heart while all was fair without, and now every leaf has withered, every branch dropped away, and it remains towering alone in dead and gloomy grandeur. The dews of heaven do not revive it, nor the moisture of earth nourish it. In vain does the sunshine play around its head, or the shower moisten its roots. The seasons may come and go, the winter may pass away, and the spring may bloom again and all around look beautiful and gay, but never shall it revive from that long decay. We have seen how the candle of the Lord hath shone upon the tabernacle of the ungodly, how he exulted in that light which beamed and played so gloriously around him, as if this were light of his own creation, as if these were sparks of his own kindling. Now this light is extinguished, and "he is cast into outer darkness," the darkness which reigns without the limits of that region, where the light of life and happiness is never known to beam. Oh, what is it that constitutes the light of life? All this is lost—the light of heaven, of earth, of joy, of hope, of social happiness; and the light of reason and of conscience only shines to show how just the retribution, how gloomy the flames that roll and boil around. Oh, how deep is this darkness, this outer darkness, this eclipse of all man's brightest powers, this fearful wreck of all his mightiest energies!

Those energies are not destroyed, but inverted; finding no food without, they turn inward on themselves, the gnawing of a worm that never dies, the everlasting torture of a flame that burns forever, and consumes not, yet is not quenched. That memory, once the receptacle of all knowledge, where was once stored up all that is instructive in history, or profound in philosophy, or agreeable in fiction, is now the dark depository of gloomy recollections. The ghosts of departed hours, rise up in terrible array and shriek out in terrified tones the deeds of secret sin. The conscience, once seared over with a hot iron, now regains her feeling; once lulled to repose, she now awakes and springs up with new terror from her sleep, like a strong man armed. Like a giant from his slumbers does she come, and a host of long-forgotten sins follows in her train. These are the serpents which once seduced, and now are vipers coiling in the hair, and lashes of the furies that pursue you. That imagination, once rich in images of loveliness and beauty, is now filled with all that is dark and terrible. Once it was the mirror from which was gloriously reflected all the loveliness and grandeur of earth and sky, now gloomily shadowing out its own dark destiny, and the black scenery around. Those faculties, large to embrace and vigorous to grasp, yet blind in their might, have crushed all the objects of their wild desire, and are turned in maddened energy upon themselves. As if the rabid tiger should fasten in his own flesh those weapons of destruction designed for his prey. As if the serpent, blind with venom, should sink its fangs into its own body, and coiling with aimless rage, writhe amidst the maddening pressure of its own folds, crushing each bone, bursting each sinew, rending each nerve, bloated with its own poison, weltering in its own blood; or rather like the fierce volcano rent with internal convulsion, hot with internal fires, feeding from its own bosom the flames that consume it.

Oh, say you, I believe not a hell of outward fire? What matters it, that there is no fire without, if all be flame within? The brain is the organ of feeling; what matters it, if my hand or my foot are not in the flame, but the fire is kindled in the soul, and all within is boiling, seething with the heat? Now the soul is the seat of that feeling, of which the brain is but the organ. What matters it then, if my body be not burned, but my soul is all flame, a living fire, unquenchable, blazing madly up with its own evergrowing heats! Behold that wretch, the prey of spontaneous combustion, he is not in the fire, but the fire is in him, pouring through all his veins, bursting from all his pores, parching every tendon, torturing every nerve, heating every muscle, boiling at the heart, and, like a furnace sevenfold heated, glowing at the brain. Ah, I care not for the sufferings of the body, if the soul be at ease; nor of the body, if the soul be in torment!

XIV.

THE FAITHFUL SAYING.

1 Tim. i. 15.—"This is a faithful saying, and worthy of all acceptation, that Christ Jesus came into the world to save sinners, of whom I am chief."

The old heathen were accustomed to gather around their wise and aged men, and listen with deepest reverence and profound attention to the shrewd and sagacious sayings that fell from their lips. These remarks they treasured up in their memories, and recorded for the instruction of future generations; and thus embalmed in the love and admiration of mankind, they passed down from father to son, through successive centuries; and they constitute, in reality, all that is called the wisdom of the early ages.

Many of these "sayings" we still possess, which have come down to us, venerable for their antiquity, stamped with the approbation and laden with the accumulated wisdom of successive generations,—sayings of high repute in their day, which immortalized their authors,—"golden sayings," as they were called, which were blazoned in letters of gold, and engraven on pillars of brass, and hung up on tablets, as consecrated things, in the temple of their gods. But, Oh, brethren! where among them all shall we find a saying to be compared with this,—one so full of divine instruction, of heavenly wisdom, of precious consolation, of unutterable love and condescension as this—"that Christ Jesus came into the world to save sinners?" How different from all we have ever heard before, from all we could have expected!

Another saying had come down to us from of old, even from our first father, when the voice of the Lord was heard in the garden of paradise, and when pointing to the tree of knowledge, he said, "The day thou eatest thereof, thou shalt surely die." When that fatal sin had been committed, the same awful voice was heard again in the garden, dragging the guilty and trembling transgressor from his hiding-place of shame, and saying, "Cursed is the earth for thy sake, dust thou art, and unto dust thou shalt return;" and then he was driven from the garden into an accursed world, with the blight still pursuing him to the grave, and following onward, a terrible inheritance of woe to all his posterity. Once hath God spoken, yea, twice hath he uttered his voice. Once, amidst the peaceful shades and quiet walks of paradise, and then again from the blazing top of Mount Sinai. There amidst the fire and smoke of that tremendous scene, amidst the glare of vivid lightning, and the loud thunder-crash from quaking mountain, and the wild convulsion of all the elements was uttered again, under new circumstances of overwhelming sublimity and awe, the curse original against Adam, "Cursed is every one that continueth not in all things, written in this book of the Law, to do them!" But how cursed? Hear the book of the Law. "Cursed in city, cursed in field, in thy basket and in thy store; in the fruit of thy body, and in the fruit of thy land; in thy going out, and in thy coming in." "For a fire is kindled in mine anger, and shall burn to the lowest hell, and shall consume the earth with her increase, and shall set on fire the foundations of the mountains."

From that day to this, amongst all nations of the globe, and in every age down through the long line of Adam's descendants, and through every heart of man, has resounded that fearful curse, loudly, sadly, mournfully; deepening all our sorrows, embittering all our joys, overshadowing with a black and heavy cloud the whole of human life, pursuing us down to the grave itself with relentless justice, and not even leaving us there, but entering along with its victim into the silent place of the dead; giving his very flesh and bones to rottenness and worms; and raising him again, at the last day, only to the resurrection of damnation. Each of the prophets, as he arose, took up in his day that bitter curse; and as he looked from his watch-tower abroad over the wickedness of all around him, and downward upon the sins of coming generations, sent it on in notes of judgment, deepening and loudening as they rolled, till at last, all gathered into peals of deafening thunder, and the Old Testament, which began with the primeval sin and the primeval curse, closes with a dreadful threat, that God will come again, in his anger, and "smite the whole earth with a curse." Truly, "the curse of the Lord dwelleth in the house of the wicked." And well might one of old exclaim, "Woe unto the wicked, it shall be ill with him; for the reward of his hands shall be given him."

But blessed be his holy name, if the Old Testament closes with a curse, the New Testament opens with a blessing. We have stood by the Mount that burned with fire, and was wrapped in blackness, and darkness, and tempest; and have heard the sound of the trumpet and the voice of words so terrible, that even Moses said, "I exceedingly fear, and quake." But now, behold, what is it we hear, in the darkness of the night, amidst the solitude of the distant mountains and forests of Judea, bursting from the broad sky above us, and swelling as it rolls along over hills and valleys around? "The angel of the Lord came upon them, and the glory of the Lord shone round about them, and they were sore afraid." Is it the summons to judgment, the first blast of the trumpet, that shall wake the dead? Poor shepherds, fallen children of a corrupted father, how has the guilt of that first transgression come down to all his descendants, and along with guilt, first born of sin, terror and despair! "Fear not said the angel, for behold I bring you good tidings of great joy, which shall be unto all people, for unto you is born this day in the city of David, a Saviour, which is Christ, the Lord."

This was the first note of triumph and of rapture that ever burst from the vaulted sky upon the ravished ears of men. Oh, there is sweet music in heaven; many a song of ecstasy and wonder is lifted high by angelic voices, and poured in living melody from lips of fire, or sweetly floats in celestial music from their harps of gold! But we never hear, except on this one occasion, that the joy was too full for heaven to hold, that the mighty outburst of those large and heaving emotions, that swelled and expanded angelic bosoms, poured in its gushing and overflowing abundance upon other worlds. But behold, "There was suddenly a multitude of the heavenly host;" the full chorus of the skies praising God and saying, "Glory to God in the highest, peace on earth and good will toward men." Oh, was not this a saying well worthy of every sinner's acceptance; which was thus announced with joy by the heavenly messengers, which prophets had long foretold, which the apostles of the Saviour have repeated, and our Lord himself, again and again proclaimed, in the days of his incarnation, "That Christ Jesus came into the world to save sinners?" Perhaps one will say, It is good tidings indeed—but is it true? Will he save? Can he save? For answer we refer you to his office, his person, and his character.

I. He was appointed of God for this very purpose, and was in every respect adapted to it, being richly endowed with all those attributes of Christ, and all those gifts of the Holy Ghost, necessary to the accomplishment.

This was the very purpose for which he came into the world. For it is the express and repeated testimony of the Scripture, "God sent not his Son into the world to condemn the world, but that the world through him might be saved," and again, "God so loved the world that he gave his only begotten Son, that whosoever believeth on him, should not perish, but have everlasting life." But again, "When the fulness of time was come, God sent forth his Son, made of a woman, made under the law, to *redeem* them that were under the law, that we might receive the adoption of sons." Overwhelmed with this manifestation of God's eternal love, the great apostle of love exclaims, "Behold what manner of love the Father hath bestowed upon us, that we should be called the sons of God!" And another apostle cries out, "God commendeth his love toward us in that, while we were yet sinners, Christ died for us, and now we joy in God, through our Lord Jesus Christ, by whom we have now received the atonement."

Such was the high purpose of his mission; and think you he was sent into the world upon an idle errand, without the powers and qualifications essential to success? Behold, thus saith the Lord God, by the mouth of his prophet Isaiah, xxviii. 16, "Behold, I lay in Sion," etc. "He was anointed with the oil of joy above his fellows." "God gave not the Spirit by measure unto him." "All power in heaven and earth are committed to his hands, in him dwelt all the fulness of the Godhead bodily." In his incarnation upon earth "he was the brightness of the Father's glory, and express image of his person," that fulness of him, that filleth all in all; so that "when he bringeth in the only begotten into the world, he saith, Let all the angels of God worship him. "At his appearance upon earth, "we behold his glory," says an apostle, "as the glory of the only begotten of the Father, full of grace and truth." Angels heralded his birth; the star stood in mute homage above his cradle, and when he walked abroad upon earth, superhuman majesty attended his steps; the dead heard his voice, and lived; the blind saw; the lame walked; the awed elements recognized their Lord; and his astonished disciples exclaimed: "What manner of man is this?" But if this power be thus fully adequate to all the purposes of his high mission,—his condescension, his tender sympathy, his meek and gentle love, adapted him still more remarkably to be the Saviour of sinners. We needed such a high priest, that could be touched with the feeling of our infirmities, who could have compassion on the ignorant and erring, who would not "break the bruised reed, nor quench the smoking flax;" who would lead his flock like a shepherd, gather the lambs with his arm, and carry them in his bosom, and gently lead those that are with young.

Encompassed as we are with sorrows, infirmities, and sins, how delightful, how soothing, to hear him cry aloud, "The Spirit of the Lord God is upon me, because the Lord hath anointed me to preach good tidings to the meek, to bind up the broken-hearted, to proclaim liberty to the captives, to comfort all that mourn, to give unto them beauty for ashes, the oil of joy for mourning, the garment of praise for the spirit of heaviness." Oh, brethren, what would all his power be to us, if it were not for his love! If he stood before us, clothed in the robes of justice, and armed with the terrors of Omnipotence; if the lightnings of indignation blazed from his burning eye, and thunderbolts of vengeance quivered in his red right hand; tell me, would not all this boundless power, if wielded by inexorable justice, and guided by infinite holiness and wisdom, and divorced from a love as boundless as itself, only serve to heighten the sinner's terror, and aggravate the sinner's ruin? His power might awe us, his justice alarm, his wisdom overwhelm us, his omnipresence bewilder, but it is only his love that could win, attract, soften, subdue us, soothe our anxieties, quiet our alarm, and banish our apprehensions.

To the old heathen, and to the modern sceptic, there is no God of love in the heavens. Behind the awful forms of nature, above the starry sky, and wide beyond the outer limits of the visible creation, pervading all the universe, and strangely blended with it, there is to him an awful, dark, mysterious power, who dwelleth aloof, aloft, and alone in the depths of silence and immensity, and the dark and fathomless unknown; and who, when he issues from the depths of his infinitude, to be known of men, is felt in the earthquake's shock, and heard in the tempest's moan, or seen in the quivering convulsions of nature's agony, or the wild and warring elements. Hence to them, a messenger from heaven must be a messenger of terror.

Such a messenger might well have been sent to us, whose presence would scathe the earth, and his breath destroy the nations. How different he, who came to be the Saviour of lost sinners! He assumed our nature, was born of a woman, in the silence of night, in the solitude of the stable, amongst the beasts of the stall. Thou wast born of woman, thou didst come, O Holiest! to this world of sin and gloom. And the whole history of his life corresponded to the circumstances of his birth, and proclaimed him the friend and Redeemer of sinners. "For it became him, for whom are all things, and by whom are all things, in bringing many sons unto glory, to make the captain of their salvation perfect through sufferings." Heb. ii. 10. "He hath borne our griefs, and carried our sorrows."—Isaiah, liii. 4. He cried out in his first discourse, "Blessed are the poor in spirit, for theirs is the kingdom of heaven." Again he cried aloud, "Come unto me all ye that labor and are heavy laden, and I will give you rest. Take my yoke upon you, and learn of me; for I am meek and lowly in heart, and ye shall find rest unto your souls. For my yoke is easy, and my burden is light."

He restored the widow's son, wept with Martha, healed all manner of diseases, took little children in his arms and blessed them, and just before his departure, having loved his own, loved them to the end; and gave those touching admonitions and encouragements in the Gospel of St. John, which for deep tenderness surpass all that has been left on record. But he not only assumed our nature, but for us he tasted the bitterness of death—and such a death no man could die—death embittered by every element of human agony, and superhuman horror, ignominious, prolonged, and torturing, in which he was deserted by man and abandoned by God. Yet how meekly did he drink the cup, how like a lamb led to slaughter, how fervently did he pray for his murderers, how kindly receive the dying thief!

Oh, this is the Saviour for sinners, such as we are. It is when God becomes manifest in the flesh, that he who was far off, comes unspeakably, humanly near to us; that he, who was invisible, comes forth from his concealment, and tabernacles among men. When the ineffable glory is veiled in flesh, and royal majesty stoops from its throne, then only does the sinner's heart feel reassured, rebellious feelings melt away, and he who was lost is prepared to join in the song, "Unto him that loved us and washed us from our sins in his blood, and hath made us kings and priests unto God and his Father; to him be glory and dominion for ever and ever."

II. This leads me to speak of his person and character. He is God, the mighty God, the everlasting Son of God, by whom the worlds were made. He is God over all. As such he is admirably adapted to secure salvation for the sinner. Of him the prophet Isaiah spoke in the Old Testament, "Unto us a child is born, unto us a son is given; and the government shall be upon his shoulder; and his name shall be called Wonderful, Counsellor, The Mighty God, The Everlasting Father, The Prince of Peace." Of him the apostle Paul writes to the Hebrews, saying, "For such a High Priest became us, who is holy, harmless, undefiled, separate from sinners, and made higher than the heavens. Wherefore he is able to save them to the uttermost, that come unto God by him, seeing he ever liveth to make intercession for them."

When thus considered, all his attributes swell into infinitude, —wisdom, power, love, truth,—all are boundless as his nature, all are pledged for the sinner's salvation. They are not simply acquiescing, but actively engaged, solemnly pledged, deeply committed, and that from all eternity; disposing all things for it, employing all things in it, making all things co-operate with it. "All things," says the apostle, "work together for good, to them that love God, to them who are the called according to his purpose." The Providence, Word, and Spirit of God, all work for our salvation. Salvation then is as firm as the everlasting hills—firm as the throne of God, certain and enduring as his existence. "Every word of grace is strong as that which built the skies." It is not of man, or angel, or archangel, the highest among them, but of God himself. Oh, how meagre is the religion of Unitarians! How precious is the doctrine of Jesus' Divinity! It is the central point in the religion of sinners; the foundation of our hopes, linked with every view of truth and duty. It secures an infinite atonement, and a renovated nature. Thus Christ can save from all sin, from all the pains of hell, from the curse of the violated law, and the terrors of a guilty conscience.

This law was perfect, infinitely good, and infinitely necessary for the welfare of God's universe. It was indeed a transcript of the Divine character—the law of a Divine nature and mode, in conformity to its existence, indestructable as its being. It was strict, unbending, unchangeable, high in its requirements! Sooner shall heaven and earth pass, than one jot or tittle of the law fail. This law was revealed on Mount Sinai, and written on the conscience of man; so that every denunciation which it makes, finds its deep and dreadful response there. This law violated, utters the sentence of condemnation and death. Where is safety? No blood of bulls, no sacrifice of men, no hecatomb of angels or archangels, no tears, no blood of man or beast, could give safety. But help was laid on one mighty to save—on the man of God's right hand—upon "the man who is my fellow," saith Jehovah. The law demanded righteousness, a perfect human righteousness—here is one infinite and divine. The law demanded an earthly sacrifice—behold here is the Lord from heaven. The law demands a perfect separation—behold here is one that magnifies the law, and clothes it with new dignity; gives new sanctions, and encompasses it with higher sanctity. The law says, I am satisfied. The conscience, sprinkled with the blood of the atonement, blood of the Son of God, may now enjoy peace. Here is the ark of safety. Here is the city of refuge. The Saviour calls himself the bread of life, the way and the truth and the life, the good shepherd, that giveth his life for the world. "I am the door; by me if any man enter in, he shall be saved, and shall go in and out, and find pasture." "Truly this is a faithful saying, and worthy of all acceptation, that Christ Jesus came into the world to save sinners."

XV.

THE POWER AND TRIUMPH OF THE GOSPEL.

ROM. i. 16.—"I am not ashamed of the Gospel of Christ: for it is the power of God unto Salvation to every one that believeth."

ABOUT the year of our Lord 58, a stranger appeared in Corinth, of Jewish features and Oriental attire. A man with a bald head, an eagle eye, and of diminutive stature was seated in a retired chamber in an obscure street of that magnificent metropolis with the usual writing implements of the day before him; and as the rapid words were transferred to tablet or parchment, it was easy to see that they were written in Greek characters, and retained the Greek sound, but the sentences were moulded to the Hebrew idiom, and the earnest and solemn spirit of the old Hebrew prophets breathed through every line.

Situated on a narrow isthmus, between two celebrated ports which commanded the navigation and commerce of the Ionian and Ægean seas, Corinth was then the most magnificent city of the globe; the centre of Grecian civilization, the home of luxurious refinement, the abode of wealth, splendor, and profligacy. On every side were seen temples, palaces, theatres, porticos, towering aloft in unparalleled magnificence, adorned with the graceful columns, the capitals, and bases of the Corinthian order. Pre-eminent above the rest stood the temple of the Corinthian Venus, rich with the offerings of innumerable devotees; and within its walls were gathered one thousand of the loveliest daughters of the land, consecrated to the foul service of that licentious deity Jupiter. Apollo, Minerva, and many others had their own consecrated edifices, while in each private residence and all public places of resort, wherever the eye could turn, the statues of gods and heroes met the gaze, the most exquisite productions of the great masters of Grecian art.

It was from amidst this scene of unrivalled splendor and effeminate debauchery, where the very air reeked with the foul pollution of its unmanly vices, that this unknown stranger wrote. And his letter was directed to Rome, the mistress of nations, the acknowledged metropolis of the world. And he spake out strange, bold words to those masters of mankind, in that unpolished idiom, and with that gnarled logic of his own, unheard till then by lordly or philosophic ears—but words that are ringing still in the ears of millions, and have been through all the centuries, the battle-cry of conflict and victory in every great struggle for the renovation of the race. That was an age of deep degeneracy. The manly virtues of the heroic era were no more. The lofty courage, the stern and incorruptible patriotism of the earlier republic had departed. There remained no fear of God, no confidence in man, no public honor, no domestic purity or peace. Rome sat, indeed, crowned queen of the world; conquered kings adorned her triumphs, subjugated nations crowded in myriads to the capitol, the wealth of the world poured into her lap, and along with the wealth of conquered nations came their vices too, to avenge their wrongs. Solemnity of oath lost its sacredness, the worship of God its reverence. The very existence of God, the immortality of the soul, the fundamental principles of morals, all were denied. All the bonds that bind society together, and restrain the beastly or fiendish passions of our nature, all were dissolved. If the patrician Cæsar smiled in his sleeve as he offered sacrifice to Jupiter, the philosophic Pliny derided the immortality of the soul as a vision of human pride, and knew no God but the universe.

It was manifest to all, that human society was hastening toward its dissolution. In vain did indignant patriotism denounce the unmanly vices of the age and invoke the spirit of the mighty fathers, and point to the memorials of Rome's departed greatness. He called, but there was none to answer. The spirit of Rome's dead fathers had departed forever. All ancient patriotism was gone. The Roman citizen had no country, no home, no God, no hope, no manhood. In vain did they appeal to the ancient superstition, and recall men to the temples of the gods. The very gods themselves as they stood face to face in the Pantheon, gathered from every country under heaven, were the embodiments, representatives, and patrons of the vices of every land. There was not a passion or a lust that maddens the soul or corrupts the heart, or bestializes and degrades the nature of man, that had not its living representative and exemplar there. Men called to philosophy, but called in vain. The oracle was dumb. She gave no answer, or spoke only in mockery of human virtue and human hope. What could philosophy do? She was without a God, without a conscience, without an immortality. She was mighty to destroy, but impotent to create. "Ye have taken away our gods," cried the yearning soul of many, "and what shall we do? The sweet illusions of our childhood, the beautiful mythology of our earlier days, the Jupiter of Olympus, with all his attendant deities, you have swept away, and where is the substitute?" And philosophy was dumb, or standing amidst the ruins she had made, pointed in proud defiance to a godless universe, and a hopeless annihilation. They had shrouded the sky in blackness, and wrapped earth in sackcloth, had struck the very sun from the firmament of our future hopes. They had severed the last bond that bound the soul of man to the throne of the Creator, and all the impetuous fiery passions of his nature, loosed from their last restraint, burst furiously forth to deluge the earth in wine and lust and blood. Philosophy herself, amidst the universal consternation, took refuge in Epicurean self-indulgence, or nursed herself to stoical indifference, and haughtily and gloomily muttered forth mysterious and portentous words about the great Unit, God, Pan, World, All; irresistible destiny, inevitable fate, man's re-absorption into the infinite, and loss of all personal existence, and proclaimed as the only solace for human woes, the utter extinction of man's conscious being, and his re-absorption into the infinitude of things.

It was thus manifest to all, that human society was approaching its total dissolution. There was no element in human nature which could bring deliverance or inspire hope. Amidst the universal helplessness and hopelessness of man, the great apostle speaks. It is a voice of strong assurance and of cheerful hope; it is the tone of high authority, and serene and lofty faith. It is a voice from the throne of God himself, so calm in its sublime and solemn grandeur. He proclaims that the remedy which man would not supply has come from heaven; that a divine power has descended upon earth, which with its silent but irresistible efficacy, shall go forth among the nations to mould society anew, to save the individual and renovate the race. "I am not ashamed, for it is the power of God unto salvation to all that believe!" Bold words are these, thou Galilean prophet, and boldly spoken indeed, among the sublimest in all human records, if only they be true!

But are they justified by the results? Let us test them by the facts. Let us then consider the Gospel, first in its conflict with the heathen philosophy, heathen morality, and heathen religion of the first three centuries of our era. When thrown amidst this huge and sweltering mass of licentiousness and idolatry and skepticism, did she vindicate her claim as a divine and superhuman power, penetrating by her own silent and unaided energy the entire mass, and moulding anew all its chaotic elements? In the conflict with all these antagonist powers did she come off victorious? Let us recall the nature of the conflict to be waged, the extent of the revolution to be accomplished, the number and power of her foes. The war was on either side a war of extermination. The revolution was to be universal, reaching all human relations, interests, hopes, fears, enjoyments, sufferings,—public, private, domestic, political, social, for time and for eternity. The antagonist powers ruled everywhere and everything. All human interests, prejudices, passions, all that could please the senses or dazzle the imagination, or fire the passions, or corrupt the heart; the splendors of art, the graces of poetry, fond memories of the past, ambitious hopes of the future, the sports of the boy, the graver business of the man, temples and capitol, senate and forum, crowded theatre, merry festival, the whole great structure and organization of human society, with all its relations and all its duties and its pleasures, were pervaded, imbued, steeped in the spirit of their idolatry.

When the apostles went forth to proclaim the Gospel, it met them in every form, in every quarter an omnipresent foe. It had appropriated to itself the whole domain of human life. It presided at birth, bridal, and funeral; over the deliberations of the senate, the counsels of the camp, the conflicts of the battle-field. The domestic hearth is protected by the household god, and the statues of the first fathers of the republic stand side by side with the ancestral deities. Each commonest utensil of domestic use is consecrated by the image of a god, and the maiden's chamber and the festal hall are adorned alike with statues and with paintings where the loftiest powers of human genius are employed to lend the fascination of an ideal loveliness to the grossest of human passions, and portray with inimitable grace and exquisite minuteness the infamous amours of their licentious deities. Deep into those young imaginations and susceptible hearts sunk their images, and wide through all the ramifications of society is diffused the contagious pestilence. But side by side in all that heathen society walk lust and murder, for ever, from of old, the love of pleasure and the thirst for blood have been twin sisters.

Go with me, then, to one of those scenes of public pleasure, where high-born matrons and noble maidens most love to crowd, with the teeming millions of Rome's beastly population, to glut their eyes with blood, and regale their ears with the groans of butchered thousands. Vast beyond all those other stupendous edifices which Roman wealth had erected, and Roman piety had consecrated to pleasure or to God, was the Roman circus, extending in circumference a mile, and seating within its capacious walls from two hundred and fifty to three hundred thousand spectators. Trajan, the best of the Roman emperors, grateful to the immortal gods for a glorious victory, will offer to them the most congenial thanks, and to the Roman citizens their best-loved entertainments. Images of the gods are borne in solemn procession, consuls and priests perform the sacred rites that shall hallow these deeds of blood. Ten thousand human beings, and eleven thousand beasts of prey, during four successive weeks, are butchered. And yet they cry for more, Rome's stately senators, and lovely maidens, as well as Rome's more brutal populace still thirst for blood. Think you that they will hesitate to shed the blood of those who shall denounce their idols and interrupt their sports?

Thus heathenism has laid her bloody and polluted hand on human society, in every department of private life, and claims it as her own. Government, too, is hers, and literature in all its branches. Emperors, philosophers, fanatics, magistrates, people, priests, wit, learning, genius, argument, eloquence, the tongue, the pen, the sword, all are arrayed against these restless innovators. Victim after victim falls an unresisting prey to the fury of the populace, or the zeal of magistrates. Where now is the power which shall triumph over these combined antagonists? Where the thunderbolt, before it leaps forth to its work of death; the earthquake, before it heaves the mountains and shakes the earth in its fury? Where the great powers that move the worlds along? Invisible to man. Thus is it with the Gospel, slowly, silently, irresistibly, invisible to human eye, unheard by human ear, it is moulding all things to its likeness, subduing all things by its power. A few humble hearts have felt its influence. It is to them the power of God to purify, to cheer, to elevate, to save. It passes from bosom to bosom, from village to village, whole communities receive its joyful tidings. Already in less than half a century from the crucifixion, the great central cities of the world are full of Christians. Little more than a half century has passed, and the distant provinces are crowded with converts. A philosophical Pliny writes from his province of Bithynia, perplexed, despondent, to a philosophical Trajan, complaining that the temples are deserted and there are none to buy the victims. Men will not even offer incense to the image of the emperor. A virtuous Trajan wonders at the stupid madness of these men, would spare the effusion of blood, but the law must have its course and the obstinate be executed. A philosophical Tacitus shall write, that an "immense multitude devoted to this execrable superstition," are swarming there at Rome. A sanguinary Nero, with that grim humor of his, will have some rare sport to-night. Those Christians impaled alive, and covered with pitch, shall serve as lamps and lamp-posts too, to illuminate his gardens as the imperial charioteer drives in drunken merriment around. Satiric Juvenal shall describe them as they writhe and blaze in their agony, and the streams of pitch and blood flood the earth.

But have not the fires of that persecution sent their illumination throughout the globe, and flamed down over all the centuries even to us? Strange thoughts are moving in the minds of men. The great heart of the world, long stupefied by sensuality and doubt, is awakening to new life, throbs high with hope and vague expectations. The Gospel is in the camp and the court, in the senate and palace, in the *very temple.* The gods have heard and are startled. Jupiter of the capitol has descended from his throne; Apollo of Delphi is dumb. The haughty Roman has heard it, and paused midway in his career of conquest to listen to the story of the Prince of Peace. The subtle Greek has heard it, and arrested his noisy disputations at the mysterious tidings of Jesus and the resurrection. The northern Scythian has heard it as he quaffed his mingled portions of wine and blood from a human skull, and melted at the gentle story of him who shed his own heart's blood to save his enemies. Palpably this is no partial or superficial movement. It is human society moving silently and steadily on, beneath some mysterious, unseen influence towards some distant goal. It is the sweep and the heave and the surge of the great world-ocean moved from its profoundest depths with its whole universe of waters.

We should love to dwell on the power of the Gospel as manifested in the lives of the early Christians. I know not how it may be with other men, but for myself there is nothing in all that history hath recorded, or poetry imagined, or fiction described; nothing that so moves the soul to reverence, awes it to wonder, subdues and overpowers, as the meek submission, touching tenderness, gentle love and heroism of those earlier Christians. Go read them in the pages of Neander, where a profound philosophy is chastened by a humble faith and irradiated by seraphic love. A volume is worth a library. But we must hasten on to those scenes of outward splendor, which most readily attract the gaze of men, to the culminating point, where the contest is decided, and the Gospel steps visibly forth on the theatre of human affairs as the power of God, the controlling power of the globe.

The Christian apologist had long before exultingly exclaimed, "We are but of yesterday, yet have we filled all places belonging to you; your cities, islands, castles, towns, councils, the palace, the senate, the forum. We have left you only your temples." And should the Christians withdraw in a body from the empire, its solitude and desolation would astound the world. Christians had meekly bowed their heads to the axe, and marched boldly to the gibbet and stake. Their gentle virtues had won the affections of mankind; their sublime philosophy commanded their belief; their heroic courage extorted their admiration. Persecution, satiated with blood, wearied with slaughter, appalled by the number of her victims, had given a temporary repose. The Christians issued by myriads from their retreats, crowded by thousands to their churches, bowed with enthusiastic reverence at the sepulchres of their butchered martyrs. Superstition, weary of delay, resolved to precipitate the inevitable crisis, and to stake its fortunes on the issue of one last decisive conflict. The hostile forces met near the city of Hadrianopolis. The heathen army, led by Licinius, one hundred and sixty-five thousand in number, was strongly posted and intrenched on the mountains before the city, while its front was protected by the broad and rapid stream of Hebrus. The Christian army, a third less in number, lay in the valley below; on all sides it was felt to be a conflict between the two religions for the mastery of the world.

Before the battle commenced, the hostile leaders passed down from rank to rank, firing their troops with hopes of victory. Above was seen that Roman eagle, consecrated with so many mysterious and awful rites, which had floated for centuries above their armies, and beneath whose expanded wings their conquering cohorts had marched from victory to victory over a subjugated world. Above the other was seen only that strange and significant banner, badge of suffering and shame—the cross. The speech of the heathen emperor is still on record, made to his assembled officers on the eve of battle. Amidst the gloom of a consecrated grove and in the presence of his god, he pointed to the images of their ancestral deities, beneath whose guardian care the empire had risen to glory; invoked the spirits of their dead fathers, and appealed to their pride as Roman citizens, against the followers of "that foreign thing which we now deride," whose ignominious sign was displayed in the van of their apostate armies.

The Christian leader pointed upward to that mysterious cross, memorial of him who hung there in his agony and love and in his name promised them the victory. With that name upon their lips, that banner above them, they dashed impetuously onward, through the waters of the broad and rapid stream, up the steep declivities into the camp of the foe. Miracles of prowess and success are recorded by heathen historians of that day. It is enough to know that the pagan forces fled in dismay and terror, leaving thirty-four thousand dead upon the field. The banner of the cross waved triumphant amidst the intrenchments of the foe. From this first great conflict with superstition and philosophy and power, Christianity has come off victorious. The divided empire has regained its unity, and the nations repose beneath the dominion of a Christian emperor.

But far and wide on the outer borders of the empire, hovers

a black cloud of fierce barbarians, one hundred millions, perhaps, in number, soon to burst upon it, and bury all its glory beneath that overwhelming inundation. The Gospel has subdued that effeminate civilization; can it survive the shock of this barbaric power? From the shores of the Baltic and the Danube, of the Black Sea and Borysthenes, from the forests and morasses of Scythia, from the mountains and broad tablelands of Central Asia, from the extremities of Scandinavia to the frontiers of China, nation after nation sweeps on, crushing all before it and marking its path with blood and desolation; wild nomadic tribes, weather-beaten, toil-hardened men, inured to war and carnage, with no home but their good steeds, no law but their will, no God but their sword, which they worship with mysterious rites. Their horrid worship is in forests impervious to the sun, or in subterraneous caverns, and their altars stream with human blood. Terror has united with superstition to give them an unearthly parentage; the wild witches of the desert were their fabled mothers; their fathers, those lost spirits that wander through dry places, seeking rest and finding none. Swift as the viewless wind in the depth of winter, or in the darkness of midnight, they issue from their snow-clad homes upon the fairest Roman provinces, driving the terrified inhabitants before them, and destroying all with fire and sword. If successful, they pursue their victories; if defeated, retire to their impenetrable forests and eternal snows; but whether in advance or retreat, their path is marked with smouldering ruins and pyramids of human skulls.

They have served, many of them, in Roman armies; have learned Roman tactics, and marched with their legions to victory. They have visited as soldiers or as captives the sunny South, have breathed the air of Italy, have drank the wines of Capua, have reposed beneath the groves of orange and olive, have tasted the lemon, citron, and grape, have revelled amidst the luxuries of that delicious climate, admired the stately palaces, hated the tyrannous, and despised the effeminate vices of their imperial masters. Amidst the black forests of his wintry home, the northern barbarian dreams of Italy; fires the imaginations of his wild comrades with vivid descriptions of its glories, and promises an easy victory over its degenerate inhabitants. Tribe after tribe sweeps on, is defeated, driven back, returns with more ferocious courage and reduplicated numbers. Wave after wave is broken at the base of that decaying colossus, strong even amidst the decrepitude of age. But the foundations of the great deep are broken up, the swelling inundation comes heaving on. No human power can arrest its course. The fainting legions slowly, gloomily recede, are routed, broken. The fierce barbarians pass on, and with no glitter of gold or silver or armor, no pomp of martial music, but with loud shouts of contempt and indignation, with clash of sword and shield and battle-axe, sweep away all remains of that ancient civilization.

But time would fail us to pursue this strain of thought, and tell of all the successive triumphs which the Gospel was destined to win amongst the nations of Europe, thereby vindicating itself as the mighty power of God. As it had triumphed at first over the paganism of Rome, and then withstood the successive inroads of these barbarians, gradually bringing them as willing trophies under its all powerful sway, so has it advanced from conquest unto conquest till the present hour. From this long digression, let us now return to our text, to consider the feelings of the great apostle as, conscious of his high vocation in being called of God to preach this Gospel to the Gentiles, he contemplated a visit to the imperial city, and in the opening chapter of this epistle to the Romans, exclaimed: "I am not ashamed of the Gospel of Christ."

We are so much accustomed to consider St. Paul as an apostle, that we are apt to forget that he was likewise a man. We follow him with such intense interest through the whole of his bold and brilliant career, that his name becomes associated in our minds with all the loftiest attributes of our nature, and we can hardly conceive of him as at all exposed to the common weaknesses and infirmities of the species. This is indeed the highest tribute that can be offered by mankind—the involuntary homage of the soul to transcendent worth.

But it may be doubted whether the brightness that dazzles does not also blind us; whether the very excellency which we admire, may not lead us to underrate itself. We never think of entering into the details of his character, of comparing St. Paul with other men; and thus we lose the advantage of the contrast. We never estimate his character by the common principles that regulate the conduct of mankind, and hence we seldom understand how far he is elevated above them. There is no weakness, for instance, that is more universal among mankind, than that which is mentioned in the text; and yet, so far are we from supposing that St. Paul was ever subject to its influence, we are almost astonished that he should think it necessary formally to defend himself against such an imputation. To be ashamed of opinions which we have impartially examined and honestly adopted; to be ashamed of conduct which is founded upon these principles, and is approved and even required by our own judgment and conscience, is a weakness not confined to the ignorant and thoughtless; to stand up boldly against the current of popular sentiment, and disregard alike the sneer of the wise and the hiss of the ignorant; to go forth the advocate of truth in a corrupt and degenerate age, and carry on a fearless warfare against the opinions and prejudices, the tastes and the vices of society, with no object but the welfare of mankind, and no reward but the scorn and contempt of those you wish to benefit, is to exhibit some of the finest characteristics which belong to our nature.

Indeed we cannot conceive of a spectacle more sublime and more affecting, than that which is presented by a man, who is endowed with all those higher gifts of the understanding and the heart, which would have gained the admiration and love of all around him, yet devoting all the ardor of his feelings, and all the strength of his intellect to the simple work of doing good among his fellow-men, meeting unmoved in this noble work the contempt and hatred and ingratitude of the world, standing erect, amidst the storm that beats upon him, alone and self-sustained by the inborn energies of a manly spirit. When, in the course of real history or fictitious narrative, we meet with such a character as this, we are struck with a pleasing astonishment and yield it the ready homage of our willing admiration. But in reading the life of St. Paul, what in others seems astonishing, in him appears perfectly natural. To suppose that he would act otherwise would violate all our conceptions of his character; and the mind feels a painful incongruity between its own ideas when we attempt to conceive of him as shrinking from danger or courting admiration, as palliating error or concealing the truth. This is indeed the highest encomium ever bestowed upon genius and virtue, because it is the united and unconscious verdict of friends and foes, the universal suffrage of the race. But it may serve to render more distinct, and perhaps to impress more deeply upon our minds, a general feeling of reverence for the apostle's character, if we take a brief view of those particular circumstances, which tried and exhibited this character, and especially those to which he undoubtedly referred in the text, and which required, in his own view, the solemn affirmation, "I am not ashamed of the Gospel of Christ."

If Paul had deserted the Jewish religion and attached himself to some school of Grecian philosophy, he might indeed have been branded as an apostate from the faith; but he might have consoled himself for the loss of his old friends by the increased respect of his new companions. If he had joined any existing sect of the Jews, he would have indured the hatred of his opponents; but his talents were an acquisition to be sought by every party, and would have insured the applause of his own. If agreeing with no sect of Jewish or heathen philosophers, but dissenting from them all, he had built up some splendid though unsubstantial fabric of his own, the splendor of his genius and the attraction of his eloquence would soon have placed him foremost among philosophers, and gathered around his standard an admiring crowd of followers. But he sought not the schools of Grecian or Jewish wisdom, nor did he choose for himself some high path of original or eccentric speculation. He came down to the lowest walks of humble life; he was associated with the most despised sect of a despised people. The doctrine which he received was simple though sublime, alike inimical to the pride of philosophy, the fierceness of bigotry, and the licentiousness of passion, and his teacher was regarded as a peasant and a malefactor, obscure in his birth, and covered with tenfold ignominy by a disgraceful death. If the religion which he embraced had allowed him to remain in retirement, it might not have been so painful to a mind already wearied with noise and bustle, to seek a quiet obscurity, and indulge the pleasing revery of a happy immortality. He might then have despised the world's opinions, and forgotten the contempt he did not witness. But the command of his master, and the impetuosity of his own feelings, urged him onward in his active career; he met the full torrent of the world's bitterest derision; he travelled from city to city, from country to country; and though he preached with an eloquence that was unrivalled, and argued with a closeness that was unanswerable, and labored with a zeal and patience that were almost superhuman, wherever he directed his course he was met with the same salutation; and whether he argued with the Jewish Rabbis from their own prophetic scriptures; or reasoned with the Greek philosophers from the eternal principles of nature and of truth; or testified before the Roman governor of that wondrous vision which his own eyes had witnessed, and that wondrous voice his own ears had heard; he was branded as a madman, a blasphemer, and a babbler.

Now we say not that the apostle was insensible to this accumulated load of derision and reproach, but we say that if he felt it as a man, he disregarded it as an apostle. Never did it force from him one word of despondency or irritation. The reproach of Felix, though it drew forth one of the most striking appeals in the whole history of eloquence, brought down on his own head no indignant rebuke. He once mentions, indeed, the ridicule of his enemies as "cruel mockings;" but at all times, and on all occasions, both by his actions and his language, he proved that he was not ashamed of the Gospel of Christ. It would have been indeed an interesting spectacle to see this obscure defender of an outcast sect, as he stood upon the Areopagus, and propounded to the listening crowd of philosophers and common people the strange but sublime doctrine of the resurrection of the dead; to have heard him reason against the polytheism and idolatry of a polished city, and refute the idle speculations of a vain philosophy; and when ridicule had taken the place of argument, and they who could not reason had united to laugh, who cannot sympathize with the noble sentiments that would animate the speaker as he cast his eye around upon the assembled crowd, and pitying alike the ignorance of the multitude, and the pride of the philosophers—his bosom expanded by his own high truths, and his eye kindled up with the joyful triumph they inspired—he would exclaim in the language of the text, "I am not ashamed of the Gospel of Christ."

It has sometimes been the privilege of genius, when struggling with adversity, when attacked by the venom of malice, or annoyed by the buzzings of folly, to look away through the clouds that overcast its prospects, and see in the admiration of a coming age a rich recompense for the neglect of its own. High and thrilling, no doubt, is the ecstasy that, in a moment such as this, swells the bosom of the despised and persecuted man. But, oh! when the man was lost in the prophet, and the eye of genius was lighted up with the fire of inspiration, to look down through the long lapse of succeeding ages, how rapturous must have been the high emotions of the apostle as it glanced rapidly on from century to century, and rested at last upon the bright scenes of millennial glory. Surely if there were no reward in heaven for their labors upon earth, no triumph there for those who have fought and conquered here, no crown to be placed upon the brow which throbbed so anxiously below, even then, there would be enough, in a vision such as this, to excite far higher pleasures than this world has ever yet bestowed. But when to this splendid vision of years to come is added the sure expectation of a heavenly inheritance, we need not be astonished that the apostle should declare, "I am not ashamed of the Gospel of Christ."

The apostle may be considered as asserting the natural

power or tendency of the Gospel as a system of truth to influence and save man; or as referring more directly to that divine efficiency which attended it, in converting and saving both individuals, and communities, and the whole world. In either case it was distinguished from the heathen philosophy by the fact that the latter was powerless in operating on man. Philosophy had done all it could; it had never exerted any healthful, controlling influence on human society, and on the great subject of salvation its inquiries had failed always and utterly. Of late they had been suspended in universal scepticism. They left all human obligations in doubt, and without any certain sanction. They left men's hearts and lives impure and immoral, and without a power to purify or heal. A divine revelation was therefore needed. The Gospel proved itself to be such a revelation by the certainty of its teachings, the purity of its principles, and the efficacy of its sanctions—the power of God unto salvation to every one that believeth.

XVI.

THE REMISSION OF SINS THROUGH FAITH IN CHRIST.

ACTS x. 43.—"To him give all the prophets witness, that through his name whosoever believeth in him shall receive remission of sins."

THE memory of that state of holiness and peace in which man lived before the fall is almost universally diffused among the nations of the earth. It is handed down in their traditions, it is interwoven with their religion, it is celebrated in the highest strains of poetry by their most gifted bards. And the same traditions which have preserved the sad recollection of the fall, have likewise perpetuated the joyful expectations of a mighty deliverer to come, who should more than repair the ruins of the fall, who should restore universal holiness and piety and love on earth; and the mild glories of whose approaching reign should only shine with a lovelier radiance on account of the deep gloom which should precede his appearance. Thus the Hindoos still look forward to the appearance of their god Vishnu, who is to be manifested in the flesh, to overthrow oppression, and establish virtue and happiness on earth. And all who are acquainted with the ancient classics, will remember that one of the greatest Latin poets predicts the appearance of the great deliverer, this mighty king, even in his own day, and exhausts all the imagery of his fertile mind to exalt to the utmost our conceptions of the glories of his reign and the amazing benefits he should bestow upon mankind. In different nations this expectation varied undoubtedly in accuracy and distinctness, but in some it pointed out with amazing accuracy not only the character of this deliverer and the benefits of his government, but the precise time at which he should appear. And about the time of our Saviour's birth there existed throughout the world an universal expectation of the great deliverer, the foretold in prophecy, the desire of all nations. That this expectation was universal among the Jews at the time of our Saviour's birth is evident, not only from the facts recorded in the evangelists, but from the record of their own writers, and the testimony of heathen historians.

The appearance of John the Baptist, the crowds that thronged to hear his instructions, the trembling anxiety of Herod when informed of the Redeemer's birth, the numerous pretenders who arose about that period, and promised deliverance to the misguided Israelites, the blind fanaticism with which they gathered around these false Messiahs, and still trusted for deliverance, till hewn down by the Roman cohorts—all prove that the expectation of the Jewish nation was wound up to its highest pitch, and that the appearance of their predicted Messiah was daily awaited by the confiding nation. But all possibility of doubt is removed by the express assertion of Josephus, who informs us, that their restless impatience under the Roman yoke, and their continual efforts to cast it off, arose from their expectation of the king who was to arise in Judea and extend his dominion over the world. Nor was this opinion confined to the Jewish people. We are informed by Suetonius, the Roman historian, that "there had been for a long time all over the East, a constant persuasion, that at that time, some one who should come out of Judea should obtain universal dominion." Nor was this expectation confined to the people of the East, but had extended to Rome, and taken strong hold, at a still earlier period, even on the masters of the world. Hence, Tacitus applies the prophecy to his favorite Vespasian, and this deluded prince, even pretended to work miracles at Alexandria, and long before Mark Antony had applied the same prophecy to Julius Cæsar, and urged it as a reason why he should be crowned sovereign of the Roman empire. He appealed to the Sibylline oracles at Rome, which were doubtless the fragments of traditionary prophecies scattered among the heathen, and the answer which was given by Cæsar on the same occasion, deserves to be remembered. He opposed the coronation of Cæsar, on the ground that the prophecies which foretold this mighty king, likewise foretold that he should destroy the heathen religion, and overthrow their idols. The Roman poet to whom I just alluded, and who wrote in the succeeding age, appeals to the same traditionary prophecies collected and recorded at Rome, and describes the character of the predicted king, and the happy influence of his wise administration, in language which seems to coincide almost word for word with a part of the eighth chapter of Isaiah.

We have, then, the expectation of a great deliverer diffused, like the tradition of the flood and the practice of sacrifice, throughout all nations, varying in distinctness in different countries, but most frequent in the nations least removed from the original birthplace of the human race. We find this expectation assuming a definite form, and embodied in written documents, preserved by a people who bought them originally at a high price, treated them with the greatest reverence, and, when lost by fire, supplied the loss at great trouble and expense. We find them quoted by their politicians; appealed to by their poets; and above all, these singular prophecies, preserved by a heathen and a democratic nation, predict the coming of a mighty king, the overthrow of idolatry, and the establishment of a universal kingdom of piety and peace.

Now this universality of belief cannot certainly be causeless; this amazing agreement between pretended prophecies, preserved by Jews and heathen, demands some satisfactory explanation. The only explanation of these extraordinary facts is found in the assertion of the text, that "all the prophets from the foundation of the world have testified of Christ." Prophecy was not confined to the Jewish church, it existed before it, and beyond it. Enoch, the seventh from Adam, prophesied about the latter days. Balaam's prophecy of Christ may vie in sublimity and clearness with the loftiest of the Hebrews/; and Job, the afflicted servant of God, exercised a calm and delightful confidence in his Redeemer, and foretold that in the latter days he should stand upon the earth. When man had fallen from his obedience, he was not wholly abandoned by his God, nor must we suppose that the light of divine truth was eclipsed at once amongst the nations. It departed gradually and slowly, and its last setting rays would still beam upon some man of God, exalted by pure and ardent piety above the level of the world around him. Such a man was Job, such was Melchisedec, and such perhaps were many others, whose record is with God, and whose inspired predictions, reverenced long after their death, may have been thus providentially collected, to testify collaterally to the Messiah of the Jews. But when the world was fast sinking into idolatry, and scarcely a remnant now existed of the primitive theology, God chose the family of Abraham to perpetuate the knowledge of himself, and by a supernatural providence preserved them from idolatry, and maintained the expectation of the Messiah who was to come.

The whole Jewish economy was formed with direct reference to a better dispensation. Every part directed to the Saviour. Its sacrifices, its ablutions, its temple, its services and priests were shadows of which he was the substance. Their prophecy especially was full of Christ. The testimony of Jesus, said St. John, is the spirit of prophecy. Its whole spirit and design is to testify of Christ. Nor is any prophecy of private interpretation to be interpreted alone, but in connection with others. For prophecy is a great connected system, part of the great plan of God, for gradually developing divine truth to men, commencing at the creation, and grasping in its wide embrace the interests of the church down to the end of time. Hence its earlier exhibitions are rather hints than developments, intended rather to excite and preserve hope, than to gratify curiosity. As the fulness of time approached, its revelations became clearer and clearer, resembling the progress of the sun, as he first tinges faintly the east, then brightens into day, then rises above the horizon, and rejoices like a strong man to run his race of light and glory through the sky. In the moment of deepest despondency, the promise was obscurely given, "The seed of the woman shall bruise the serpent's head," and Eve expressed at once her gratitude and her faith, when she exclaimed, on the birth of her son, "I have gotten a man from the Lord."

It was by faith in this great deliverer, that Abel offered a better sacrifice than Cain; and the pious Lamech, worn out with toils and griefs, probably referred to this hope, when he called his son Noah, that is Repose, and said, "This shall console us from our toils, and from the pain of our labors from the ground which Jehovah hath cursed." Abraham saw his day afar off, and rejoiced, and well he might rejoice, when the promise which was first given indefinitely to Eve, was confined to his own family, and it was said by the mouth of the Lord, "and in thy seed shall all the nations of the earth be blessed." The prediction became still more distinct as time rolled on, and the expiring Jacob said in the triumph of his soul, "The sceptre shall not depart from Judah, nor a lawgiver from between his feet"—or of his descendants—"till Shiloh come, and to him shall the gathering of the people be." The prophecy which had thus been gradually narrowed down, from the promise to mankind, to the family of Jacob and tribe of Judah, became still more definite, and the promise was made to the family of David, of a descendant whose kingdom should be without an end upon the throne of his father David. The place of his birth was then identified, and Bethlehem, the city of David, was pointed out as the spot which should be honored by his first appearance. And that no possibility of doubt might ever attach to a matter of such vast importance, the very time of his birth was minutely specified, the period of his death, and the punishment which should fall upon the guilty city which rejected him.

In less than four hundred and ninety years from the command to rebuild the walls of Jerusalem, by Artaxerxes Longimauus, the Messiah should appear, and in the midst of the last week or last seven years of that period, he should be cut off, but not for himself, and suddenly should come upon the city the abomination which should make it desolate. So remarkably has this prediction been fulfilled, that infidelity has mistaken prophecy for history, and charged upon the Jews the forgery of a prophecy which condemns themselves. Again, it was foretold by Malachi, that the messenger of the covenant, as the Messiah was sometimes called, should appear during the continuance of the second temple, and by Haggai, that "the desire of all nations should come and fill *that* house with glory." We all remember how distinctly the circumstances of his life are foretold by Isaiah,—"He should be a man of sorrows and acquainted with grief,"—and those of his death,—"They parted my garments among them, and cast lots upon my vesture,"—and again, "They appointed for him with the wicked his grave, but he was with a rich man after his death," and this, although he was the king of the Jews, the mighty God, the Prince of Peace.

But not only was the Messiah to appear in the fulness of time; he was likewise to introduce a new dispensation. The enlightened Jews never considered their dispensation as final, They were indeed the people of God, chosen from the midst of the nations around them, not for any merit of their own, but for the purpose of promoting God's own high designs, for perpetuating the knowledge of the only true God, and the expectation of the deliverer, who was in the fullness of time to come. Every part of their expensive and laborious ritual was designed to answer one of these purposes, to separate them from the heathen around, or to typify by their numerous sacrifices the coming of that great sacrifice who was to make an end of transgression, and bring in an everlasting righteousness.

But it was never the intention of the great Creator to confine to them alone the benefits of divine truth, or to perpetuate a system which, from its very nature, was confined within the narrow limits of a single country. The first promise which was made of a Messiah, was made to Adam, as the father of mankind, and this promise is interpreted by the Jewish Rabbins of their Messiah. Moses in predicting the future fortunes of the nation, distinctly foretold the coming of another prophet, like himself, the author of a new law, the mediator of a new covenant, the leader of a new people. The prophets spoke in language still more decisive of this coming dispensation. The covenant which was made when they came out of Egypt, was to be succeeded by a new and different covenant. That required external service; this, the homage of the heart. The law of that covenant was written on tables of stone; this, in the hearts of the people. Under that dispensation the blood of bulls and goats could only make atonement for external defilement and involuntary sins; but under this all sin was to be forgiven through the efficacy of some mightier intercession. "Behold," says the prophet Jeremiah, xxxi. 31, "behold, the days come, saith the Lord, that I will make a new covenant with the house of Israel, and with the house of Judah: not according to the covenant that I made with their fathers in the day that I took them by the hand to bring them out of the land of Egypt;" but a different one, and how different! "But this shall be the covenant that I will make with the house of Israel: After those days, saith the Lord, I will put my law in their inward parts, and write it in their hearts, and I will be their God, and they shall be my people; for I will forgive their iniquity, and I will remember their sin no more."

The only mode of remission of sin known to the law was through the sacrifices of bulls and goats; but in the Psalms we have clear intimations that this mode was in itself of no value, and was ultimately to give way to another and better one, in which the external purification of the flesh, was to be superseded by the purification of the heart, and the exercise of inward repentance and purity of heart. In the fifty-first Psalm, where David is confessing his sins before God, he says: "Thou desirest not sacrifice, else would I give it; thou delightest not in burnt offerings. The sacrifices of God are a broken spirit; a broken and a contrite heart, O God, thou wilt not despise." There were no sacrifices in the law which could atone for the crimes of murder and adultery of which David had been guilty, and yet he hopes for forgiveness; and in the fortieth Psalm, we find the ground of his confidence was in a different sacrifice under a coming dispensation. "Sacrifice and offering," says the Psalmist, "thou didst not desire; burnt offering and sin offering hast thou not required. Then said I," speaking in the language of the expected Messiah, "then said I, Lo, I come; in the volume of the book it is written of me, I delight to do thy will O my God." This will of God which the Messiah was to do, and which was thus to supersede the sacrifices of the law, was done and suffered by the Divine Redeemer when he drank the cup his Father gave him, and said, "not my will, but thine be done." The nature of this substitution is most fully expressed by the prophet Daniel, in the ninth chapter, where we are told that the Messiah should come at the end of four hundred and ninety years after the rebuilding of the temple; that he should cause the sacrifice and oblation to cease—the sacrifices of the Jewish law—but should at the same time finish transgression, make an end of sins, make a reconciliation for iniquity, and bring an everlasting righteousness.

All this was to take place in that kingdom, which the God of heaven was to set up according to the predictions of Daniel, and of course under a different dispensation from the Jewish, which was not to be set up, but already existed. In the fifty-third of Isaiah, we are told expressly how it is that remission of sins and justification was to be obtained under this new dispensation, of which the Messiah was the head and author. By the knowledge of himself shall my righteous servant justify many, for he shall bear their iniquities. Observe how plainly it is indicated that the sacrifices and offerings of the law were to be dispensed with. Under the old dispensation when the sinner brought a sin-offering to the altar, he laid his hand on the head of the victim, confessed his sins, and the punishment of sins was transferred to the victim before him. The sinner was relieved from the punishment, and the victim was said to bear it in his stead; and thus the prophet speaks of another sacrifice, better than bulls and goats, who was to bear our iniquities in his own body on the cross. But not only was the dispensation to be changed, but its ministers too. "I have sworn by myself, thou art a priest forever after the order of Melchisedec." Here we do not pause to ask who was Melchisedec, nor is it important to inquire. Here is a new priest of a new order, not of the family of Aaron, nor of the tribe of Levi, for the Messiah was to spring from Judah, of an order not inferior to that of Levi, but superior, since Levi paid tithes to this order in the loins of Abraham; not temporary like that of Levi, which was to pass away after it had answered its purpose, but a priest *forever*, after the order of Melchisedec.

Not only was the dispensation and its ministers changed, but the offerings too, for every priest must have somewhat to offer, and we are told by the prophet Daniel, "That the Messiah shall be cut off, but not for himself;" and by the prophet Isaiah, that "He was wounded for our transgressions, and bruised for our iniquities, the chastisement of our peace was upon him, and by his stripes we are healed; that we all like sheep have gone astray, and the Lord hath laid on him the iniquity of us all." But further, the dispensation introduced by the Messiah was to extend beyond the land and people of the Jews, and embrace in its wide extent the whole race of man.

Thus, in the 2d Psalm it is said, "Ask of me and I will give the heathen for thine inheritance, and the uttermost parts of the earth for thy possession." Again, Isaiah, xlix. 6, it is said of the Messiah, "I will also give thee for a light to the Gentiles, that thou mayest be my salvation unto the end of the earth." Again, lx. 1, "And the Gentiles shall come to thy light, and kings to the brightness of thy rising." And again, in the lxv. 1, "I am sought of them that asked not for me; I am found of them that sought me not. I said, Behold me, behold me, unto a nation that was not called by my name." The Jews were called by the name of Jehovah, the people of the Lord; the people to whom these invitations were to be made, were of course only Gentiles. But it is unnecessary to appeal to particular texts, to establish a position which is demonstrated by the whole tenor of Jewish Scriptures. All their ideas of the Messiah's reign supposed its universality. It was this which excited their highest feelings, and aroused their loftiest strains of poetry. They speak of a time, when the mountain of the Lord's house shall be exalted above the top of the mountains, and all nations should flow into it. When in every place pure incense shall be offered, and God will take priests out of all nations; when there shall be an altar to the Lord in Egypt, and the ark of the *former* covenant shall no more be remembered nor visited. Their hearts seem to swell with the mighty theme, and they break forth into strains of triumphant joy in contemplation. Isaiah, lx. 1, 3, "Arise, shine, for thy light is come, and the glory of the Lord is risen upon thee. The Gentiles shall come to thy light, and kings to the brightness of thy rising." And again, "the Gentiles shall see thy light, and all kings thy glory."

Nor is the incredulity of the Jews any objection to the truth of the text, for this likewise was foretold by their prophets. He was to be a stone of stumbling and rock of offence to both the houses of Israel; a gin and a snare to the inhabitants of Jerusalem. He was to be as a root out of dry ground, without form or comeliness; they were to turn away their faces in contempt or abhorrence from him, and should esteem him as smitten of God, and afflicted, as visited by God's righteous judgments for his guilt. (In thy seed shall the nations of the earth be blessed, we have seen how.)

We have thus seen a whole series of prophecies pointing through many centuries to an individual, who was to come at an appointed period 490 years from an event well known in history, and easily calculated; a person who was to bear the most contradictory offices, and reconcile in his own person the most irreconcilable predictions; who was to be a priest and a victim, a conqueror and a sufferer, a king and a servant; who should be a despised and condemned malefactor, and yet should extend his dominion beyond the nation which persecuted him, till it encompassed the world; and we see at the very time appointed an individual appearing who reconciled in his own person all these apparent contradictions, and real difficulties, in the most natural way. We have a system commencing earlier than all profane history, avowedly looking forward to, and predicting the appearance of, this extraordinary individual, who was to establish a new dispensation founded on, yet different from it, the same in principle yet more fully developed, predicting its reception by the Gentiles, and rejection by the Jews, and immediately on his appearance we find the Jewish temple destroyed, the people scattered, their ceremonies forcibly discontinued, the very distinction of their tribes lost; and besides all this, it is now 1800 years since these things happened. Are all these strange coincidences the result of chance? Is this world of evidence built up by the fortuitous concourse of floating atoms? If, then, the truth which is confirmed by the miracles and resurrection of the Saviour, be likewise established by the united testimony of the prophets, we see how firm is the ground of our confidence, and how boldly we may come to a throne of Divine grace, seeking the remission of our sins through faith in his name.

I. Let us learn from this subject first, the sovereignty of God in bestowing his benefits on man. By the sovereignty of God we do not mean that blind and arbitrary wilfulness, which acts without a motive or principle of action. There is no such sovereignty with God, for although all his works are known unto him from the foundation of the world, yet are they all done in perfect wisdom. But we mean that wise and holy government of God over all creatures and all events, which directs all, guides all, controls all, according to the counsel of his own will, and that will regulated by reasons and principles which are necessarily inscrutable to man, embracing as they do all worlds, and reaching forward into eternity. Infidels have objected to the Jewish Scriptures, because they represent the Father of all as bestowing peculiar benefits on a single people, thus transferring to the Creator our limited and contracted views, and bringing the odious imputation of partiality against his wise administration. To this it might be sufficient to reply, that possibly the governor of the universe may observe relations and act on principles which are not obvious to our feeble understanding, and that his wisdom may see weighty reasons for bestowing blessings on one nation, which he withholds with perfect propriety from another. But we are not left to conjecture on such a subject. All experience and all history prove that it not only may be, but actually is the mode of God's administration on earth. How different are the benefits bestowed upon one nation from those conferred upon another. One enjoys the light of science, the blessings of liberty, all the advantages of civilization, while a fertile soil diffuses plenty over the land, and a genial atmosphere gives health to enjoy it, filling men's hearts with joy and gladness. To another all these circumstances are reversed. Despotic power, with ruthless hand, has borne down the first aspirations after freedom, and crushed beneath its iron tread the most cherished hopes of future improvement. A gloomy superstition has overshadowed the people, or a stupid ignorance; contented, motionless, stagnant, the inheritance of ages descends from father to son in unchangeable succession. Pestilence breathes in the air, glows in the sun, radiates from the earth; or a land cursed of God with barrenness, yields scanty sustenance to a few scattered and miserable inhabitants. Such is the diversity of natural blessings which God in his providence bestows upon man, and yet we arraign not his wisdom or his goodness; how then shall we object to a similar diversity in the distribution of his spiritual blessings? If one nation has been exalted over another in freedom, in civilization, in knowledge, in social comfort, in all that gives dignity or happiness to man, why may not another enjoy similar exaltations in all those religious privileges, which add still more to his moral worth, and exert a mightier influence over his final destiny?

This we consider a sufficient reply to all that infidelity has urged on this subject, either in the way of argument, or in the way of ridicule. But there are Christians likewise, who are opposed to the doctrine of God's absolute and uncontrollable sovereignty over his creatures, because they have been taught to consider it as arbitrary and tyrannical. To such we might plead, not only the administration, not only of God's natural, but likewise of his spiritual government on earth. Had the Jew no advantages above the heathen? Have we no advantages above the Jews of old? Do we not live under a clearer light, a brighter and better dispensation? Did not the prophet look forward with longing eyes to the days of Christian blessedness, and long to see them? Now to whom do we owe these superior blessings, and to whom did the Jews owe the privileges they enjoyed? Why were you born in a Christian land, under the full light of Gospel days, while hundreds of millions are born, and live, and die without having one true conception of God or one offer of salvation through the only Mediator? Why were the angels passed by when they had fallen? Why did the Saviour take upon him the seed of Abraham, and not the nature of angels? Why are you a man, and not a brute or an angel? To all these questions the only answer is in the language of God's Word, "Even so, Father, for so it seemed good in thy sight." We know his goodness, we know his wisdom, and therefore we believe that all his ways are ways of righteousness and truth. We do not stop to fathom what is unfathomable; we do not pause to investigate what is inscrutable; but rejoicing in God, we leave all in his hands, and say, the Judge of all the earth will do right. This is the doctrine of God's sovereignty, so much traduced, so little understood, taught in his Word and in his works, in the dealings of his providence, and in the whole economy of his grace; interwoven with every devout feeling toward God, and every true conception of his character; without which religion is but a name, and apparent piety, however ardent, is but a revolting mixture of atheism and fanaticism.

II. Let us consider next the greatness of the blessing offered us in the Gospel—the remission of sins. There are many who nauseate the whole tenor and style of the Bible communications, because it contains so much about sin. They would be much better pleased if its pages were wholly filled with glowing descriptions of the greatness and benevolence and majesty of God, and the kind and amiable affections which adorn the character of mankind, than to be perpetually annoyed with the repetition of the truth, that men are sinners, and that the holiness of God cannot look upon sin with the slightest toleration. But surely if God speak at all to man, he must address him as a sinner; nor can the inhabitants of this rebellious province expect that language of mild approval, and unmingled tenderness which would characterize a proclamation to his loyal subjects. If he speak at all, he must speak of sin; and what a mercy that he speaks of its remission; that he reveals a scheme devised by infinite wisdom, executed by infinite power, offered by infinite love, and urged with infinite tenderness and condescension, a method by which God can be just and yet justify the sinner.

Sin violates the law of God which is pledged to punish it; insults the holiness of God, whose purity abhors it; rebels against his authority, which must be exerted to repress it; destroys the happiness of his creatures, which must ever be the object of his watchful care. When the angels left their allegiance, the penalty of violated law fell upon their heads. They were sunk hopelessly and irrecoverably from the heights of bliss into the depths of perdition, and the righteous indignation of God has reserved them under chains of darkness to the judgment of the great day. Well may we then rejoice when sin is the subject of his message to our world, that it is the remission of sin which forms the burden of that revelation. It was this which formed the subject of the first great promise to mankind, and this was the object of all God's subsequent providential dealings with our race; to this the whole ceremonial of the law, to this all the predictions of the prophets pointed. For this the thousand victims bled on Jewish altars, and for this the Son of God came down to shed his blood upon the cross. It was this the angels celebrated when they announced our Lord's appearance upon earth, and into this great mystery we are informed they still strive to search with all the ardor of unsatisfied desire, with all the delight of adoring admiration. Nay, they are gladly employed as ministering spirits, in promoting this great scheme of reconciliation; and when one soul has returned to God, and obtained the remission of his sins, those happy spirits tune their harps afresh, and a new song of praise and adoration resounds through the courts of heaven.

Is it possible, then, that any of us should consider the remission of his sins as a matter of small importance? Would he, whose mighty mind takes in the vast concerns of this great creation, have lavished so much of his wisdom and his grace upon a matter of small importance? Would he have foretold it in prophecy and prefigured it in types; would he have caused the events of kingdoms and empires to conspire for its promotion; would he have made it the only subject of his only communication with mankind; would he have employed the holiest and mightiest of his servants, even those that dwell in his presence, and burn around his throne to announce and promote it; would he have sent his son to reveal, to recommend, to seal it with his blood, if it were a matter which man might safely treat with cool indifference or haughty contempt? Would he whose smallest works are replete with wisdom, while the greatest of them dazzle and overwhelm our feebleness in the effort to comprehend them, on all whose doings is the stamp of the infinite and the eternal; would he challenge all principalities and powers to behold his manifold wisdom in the scheme for the remission of sins, if there were nothing in the purpose for which this scheme was devised, that was worthy of him who devised, and of those whom it was designed to benefit? No, my friends, it was worthy of God to offer, and worthy of man to accept. It is only after our sins are remitted, that we can have peace with God, and access to our Father's presence. By nature we are children of wrath. We are condemned already, and the sentence of God's law still hangs over us, ready to be executed. We are the enemies of God, and he is the enemy of the sinner. All his attributes are arrayed in fearful hostility against him. His justice cannot spare the condemned criminal; his holiness cannot endure the polluted sinner. His very mercy cries for vengeance upon him, whose obstinate rebellion wages war against all that is holy and happy in the whole creation. To estimate fully the value of the blessing which is offered in the remission of sins, we must calculate the extent of all which it presents, and all which it bestows. It can only be measured by the greatness of the torments from which it relieves us, and the vastness of that exceeding and immeasurable glory to which it exalts us. To comprehend it fully we must understand all that man can suffer, and all that God can inflict. We must measure the duration of eternity, and know the meaning of those agonies which have no measure and no end; of the worm that never dies, and the fire that is not quenched; of that blackness of darkness which is forever and forever; of that Tophet which is ordained of old, and the wrath of the Lord like a stream of brimstone doth kindle it forever. This we shall never do, till the history of this world is finished; till the number of the redeemed is completed; till the happy have enjoyed all that immortal spirits can enjoy, and the damned have suffered all that undying spirits can endure, when reserved to high endurance by Almighty power.

If there were no remission of sins, then the law of God still cries out for the punishment of every sinner. Then the long and bright company of saints, who have marched through much tribulation to the kingdom of heaven, must be driven from the seats of blessedness. Then all who will hereafter join that happy host, must be debarred from heaven. Then all man's long, long generations are marching to perdition. Then prepare the shroud for the hopes of mankind, and let eternal gloom settle down upon the nations, for the fierceness of God's fiery wrath is still unquenched against the sinner, and though heaven and earth should pass away, not one jot or one tittle shall pass from the law till all be fulfilled. No stain shall tarnish the perfect purity of heaven, though the race of man should be multiplied by itself, and every individual should die unpardoned. The happiness of the few on earth would be purchased too dearly at the expense of God's holy government and the untold millions of his obedient subjects.

III. Let us observe, thirdly, the folly and inexcusableness of the sinner, in not seeking the remission of his sins. If the benefits offered in the Gospel were small in themselves, they would scarcely deserve the anxious efforts of the sinner to obtain them. If they were encompassed with insuperable difficulties, we might lament his failure, but could scarcely blame it. If he were required to enter on some doubtful or dangerous enterprise, the degree of danger and uncertainty would palliate if not excuse his aversion to the work. If the offer of remission which comes to him in the Gospel were of uncertain evidence, then he might pass it by as an idle tale, and treat it as the dream of an enthusiast, or the fabrication of an impostor. But none of these suppositions are true. The evidence is full and satisfactory, founded on the most undoubted miracles, and the surest prophecies. The offer is sincere and free, the terms are simple and easy, the benefits incalculably great. But the very simplicity and easiness of the duty, furnish grounds for neglecting it. If some great thing had been required of us; had we been required to endure some shocking laceration, to make some distant pilgrimage, to work out in any way some righteousness of our own, no doubt we should be pleased. But when the easiest of all things is offered to us, salvation through the merits of another; when the simplest of all things is proposed to us, to accept willingly what is offered freely, straightway we are offended. Like the Syrian general we despise the directions of the prophet, and refuse to believe that there is efficacy in the fountain which is opened in Israel for sin and uncleanness. But, oh, will it not add tenfold to the anguish of the sinner in eternal torments, to remember how easy was the way to heaven, if he had only desired to travel it; that the word was nigh him, even in his mouth, and in his heart; that the fruits of eternal life were placed within his reach, so that he need only have stretched forth his hand and ate and lived forever. Again, if the mercy offered us were small, we might neglect it amidst the pressure of other urgent business; and if it were lost at last, it might be compensated by some other gain, or might occasion only a momentary sigh.

But the blessing offered us is, as we have endeavored to show, incalculably great. It affects the whole of our existence. If lost, no other gain will repair the loss. It will not call for a momentary sigh and then be forgotten forever, but the memory of its loss and of the inexcusable folly which occasioned it, will harass the soul throughout all eternity. Perhaps of all the lamentations which are raised in the pit of darkness, this will not be the least, that they have foolishly cast away the highest privileges, and trampled under foot the choicest blessings; have proved false to their own best interests, and with suicidal hand have dangered their own highest hopes. Is not this the meaning of that wail of agony which reverberates forever around the prison-house of despair? "The harvest is past, the summer is ended and gone, and my soul is not saved!" I had once a harvest where I might have gathered the fruits of eternal life, but that harvest is past to return no more. I had once a summer when the beams of God's favor illuminated my path, but that summer is ended and gone, and yet my soul is not saved. It is not so much what I am, as what I might have been that annoys my soul. The gloomy horrors of my present condition might perhaps be borne, if it were not for that image of the past, which, like a spectre, still haunts me in the cavern of despair; that image of the past, reflected from my crushed and shattered spirit, which the more it is crushed and shattered, but multiplies the more the hateful vision.

XVII.

THE EXPANSIVE BENEVOLENCE OF THE GOSPEL.

MATT. xiii. 38.—"The field is the world."

IT is the beauty of the Saviour's parables, that they spring spontaneously and naturally from the circumstances amidst which he spoke, and are best illustrated from the scenery and individuals around. At the time when that series of parables was spoken, of which our text forms a part, he was sitting, the apostle informs us, in a ship on the lake of Tiberias. Behind him was the sea itself, around him the boats of the fishermen, who resorted thither to procure their sustenance from its waters; before him a mighty crowd, who had gathered from every village and city of Judea to hear him; while far as eye could reach, extended wide and fertile fields, which husbandmen were preparing to receive the grain. And there sat he, the messenger from heaven, "who spake as never man spake;" the sea behind him, the sky above him, immortal souls before him! What wonder that he should behold a deep and spiritual significance in the scene, and lead his disciples to meditate a nobler husbandry they had to pursue; their seed, God's blessed truth; their field of labor, the wide world of man.

It is thus that wherever the Saviour is, a new sublimity overspreads the scene, and in every word that he utters, we find the evidence of the same large and capacious mind, embracing all mankind in its regard, and comprehending all time in its survey.

I. Permit us, then, without further introduction, and imitating the simple and familiar illustration of our Saviour, to remark first, that the world is God's field. It was his by the clearest, strongest, most indisputable of all titles,—original creation, and continued preservation of all things; for "of him, and through him, and to him, are all things, who is over all, God blessed forever." "The earth is the Lord's, and the fullness thereof, the world and they that dwell therein. For he hath founded it upon the seas, and established it upon the floods." Psa. xxiv. 1, 2. It is his to possess, and to govern. "He spread abroad the heavens by his power, and laid the foundations of the earth;" by day clothes it with light as with a garment, by night it reposes beneath the shadow of his wings. He pours over it all hues of beauty, stamps upon it all features of grandeur, causes rain to descend, the sun to shine, dews to fall, maketh the out-goings of the morning and evening to rejoice, causing the cup of our blessing to overflow, giving us life and health, and all things richly to enjoy, sending fruitful seasons, filling our hearts with joy and gladness.

He is the former of our bodies, the Father of our spirits; in him we live and move and have our being. "Oh, come, let us worship and bow down, let us kneel before the Lord our Maker, for he hath made us and not we ourselves, for we are the sheep of his pasture, the people of his hand." We are his to possess, and his to govern. True, there is a prince of the power of the air, a spirit that reigneth in the children of disobedience. Long hath he waved his dark sceptre above the nations; his dark banner hath long floated in defiance, with its dismal folds darkening the earth. His throne is founded in tears, in blood, but his dominion is an usurped dominion, and soon must pass away. Its death-blow is already struck, and it is tottering to the fall. "For I beheld Satan," says the Saviour exultingly, "fall like lightning from heaven," so suddenly, so vividly, so rapidly, so irrecoverably, from such a height to such an abyss.

Man, too, dared to claim the world as *his*, to possess, to govern, to pervert, to pollute, to scourge, to erase God's image and superscription from it, and stamp instead his own vile mark of vassalage. He hath trodden proudly on earth as a subjugated thing, but earth hath opened wide her jaws to devour him;

and he who but yesterday seemed by his nod to shake the spheres, to-day lies cold in her embrace, food for her worms. He hath called himself in his madness, "Lord of the seas;" but the sea doth spurn his dominion. Behold his masts shiver in the wind, his navies are crushed amidst the waves, and he sinks to rise again, when the Lord of the sea shall call him. Surely man, with all his pomp and pride, walketh in a vain show, surely he is altogether vanity.

Thinkest thou, poor sinner, because thou hast rebelled against his authority, that it is overthrown; because thou hast wandered far from him, that thou hast escaped beyond the limits of his government, the observation of his eye, beyond the reach of his arm, the grasp of his all-embracing presence? Thou hast spurned his authority; like Cain, hast fled from his presence; burst his bonds, and cast off his cords; yet, in thy deepest pollution, thy wildest rebellion, thy farthest wanderings, the eye of a master rested on thee, and the voice of supreme authority was heard, commanding thee to return. Ah, whither shalt thou go from his spirit, whither flee from his presence? Wouldest thou take the wings of the morning, and dwell in the uttermost parts of earth? the hand thou spurnest must uphold thy flight, the presence thou wouldst shun surrounds thee even there. That morning light in its onward flight hath visited many a land; go with it, and in all, the presiding and governing God is there. It hath blushed on eastern sky, brightened the distant horizon, penetrated mountain forest, and gleamed in the vale below, from land to land hurrying, and now is glittering on western sea. It hath glanced in its course on mosque and minaret, on Christian church and heathen temple, on tower and dome, palace of king, mansion of noble, hovel of poverty, entered that high apartment and startled the lordly slumberer from his dreams. It hath glanced through the low lattice, and hath fallen cheeringly on the pallid face of disease. It hath beamed upon that countenance lighted up with faith of the mother interceding with God for her prodigal son. It hath visited earth as an angel of love, spreading her mantle of beauty over sea and land, and awaking the nations to a new existence of activity and joy; and wherever it has gone, on whatever field of grandeur or of loveliness it may have shone, the Omnipresent Deity was there, there in his power to govern, there in his goodness to bless. For the world is a field for the manifestation of his divine perfections, and on this field has he lavished, in boundless profusion, the riches of his wisdom and power and love.

It is a wide field, yet wander where you may the footsteps of the Deity are ever visible, visible in the beauty he hath poured over nature, visible in the provision he hath made for man, and in the wonders his power hath created. Oh, what a field is this which God hath chosen as the theatre for the display of his glorious perfections, a field where the flowers of paradise might bloom and cluster with fruits of heaven! Alas, that sin hath entered so fair a field, to ravage and desolate it, to mar its loveliness, and turn its sweetest joys into fruits of bitterness! Alas, that Satan hath entered it to glut his appetite for misery, his malignant hatred against God and holiness, and converted the garden of the Lord into a nursery of demons. Human passions, fiery and malignant, have made it a field for their mad career, with whirlwind violence sweeping wildly over it, blasting and withering as they pass, and marking it with tears and blood. Ambition hath made it a field of rivalry and avarice, a field of cruel extortion; sensuality, a field of brutal lust; jealousy, of hatred and revenge; and altogether a field of carnage, a perfect Aceldama.

Oh, brethren, when you look abroad over the earth, and see how men and devils, in their very wantonness, have marred this fair field, do you not sometimes exclaim with the Psalmist, Hath God forgotten, are his mercies clean gone forever? Amidst the disquietude of thy spirit, turn away from the deeds of man to meditate on the works of God. Behold the supremacy of his ever-present agency. On the battle-field, amidst the dying and the dead, his laws are not suspended. Man does his worst, but nature remains unaltered; the flowers bloom as lovely still amidst mangled corpses, and the stars shine quietly on, over heaps of slain. God still continues to manifest his goodness and wisdom, despite the sinfulness of man, and foils the rage of Satan. For this world has been for centuries the theatre of a conflict, more terrific and more sublime than any which the mighty men of earth have waged, when they deluged the land with blood, and shook the seas with the roar of their artillery. It is a mighty contest, waged by spiritual and superior beings, for sovereignty over the souls of men and supremacy in this field.

It is in *this* fearful conflict, that this world has become the field of God's most amazing manifestations. He may elsewhere have built up greater wonders, and pencilled brighter beauties, and in the hearts of living inhabitants, as well as in material scenery on the surface, may have exhibited to the eye of intelligent observation a far more attractive and imposing spectacle. But in the fall and redemption of this world, there is something of far deeper and more enduring interest than in all the grandeur of the material creation. It is to the universe what Palestine is to our earth, a land of holy wonders. It is the Thermopylæ of the moral universe, where the great battle has been fought, and the victory won, and the triumph proclaimed, and the Captain of our salvation, by shedding his own blood, has wrought an eternal deliverance for his people. Here then the world is his by a new, more sacred, and more solemn title, a title sealed with blood, the blood of his Son. And think you, shall he not see of the travail of his soul and be satisfied, perfectly satisfied? Hath he purchased it at a price so costly, merely that he might cast it away in indifference, or yield it to his foes? "As I live, saith the Lord, every knee shall bow, and every tongue confess. The knowledge of the Lord shall cover the earth, as the waters cover the great deep. Every valley shall be exalted, every mountain and hill shall be brought low; crooked places shall be made straight, and rough places smooth, and the glory of the Lord shall be revealed, and all flesh shall see it together, for the mouth of the Lord hath spoken it." Unless prophecy be false, *the world will be reclaimed.* Oh, brethren, had we not seen it, could we have believed that this very field—where God hath stooped to manifest the boundlessness of his own high and eternal attributes; where on every thing around are stamped in characters of light, visible and palpable to all, the revelations of his existence and awful presence—human folly hath chosen as the theatre for the display of human greatness; that amidst these monuments of his power, in this majestic temple, which the hand of the Almighty hath erected for his worship, and from every part of which, as from a living Shekinah of light and love, are ever streaming forth the radiations of his glory, before God and angels and devils—man would dare to step forth in the pride of imaginary power, and do deeds of devilishness, which wrap the earth in sackcloth, and veil the sky in blackness, and call down thunderbolts of wrath!

II. But consider, secondly, that this world is also *our* field. Our Master's field is ours. It is his to create, to uphold, to possess, to govern, to redeem, and, by its redemption, to manifest most illustriously his glory. It is *ours*, to occupy in the Master's name, and cultivate to the Master's glory, and subdue to the Master's service; and what employment could be more elevated, what destiny more glorious than this, to be co-workers with God in the salvation of such a world? But remember it is not a *couch* for repose, or a *throne* for exaltation, but a *field* for labor. Lift up your eyes. Behold how wide the field, how precious the harvest, how great the desolations sin hath wrought! Call up, if possible, before your minds all the sins and miseries that from creation downward have defaced and polluted the world; the sighs of suffering innocence, the groans of the oppressed, who had none to deliver, the innocent blood shed from the days of righteous Abel downward. Calculate the victims whom war hath hurried into eternity. Let them pass before your eyes, the host of desolate widows and weeping orphans, whom the bloody cruelty of man hath robbed of a protector. See how the tide of the world's population has swept on, wave after wave in rapid succession, and each wave stained with blood, and mingled with bitter tears. Conceive the misery of a single soul, whom scepticism hath robbed of all future hope, or superstition hath wrapt in an eternal gloom, or idolatry hath degraded to the level of a brute, or wild excess of appetite and passion hath inflamed to the fury of a fiend. Rather conceive the condition of a soul where all these various elements of misery are struggling together for the mastery, aggravating each the horrors of the other, and adding to their combined results the terrible anguish of uncertainty, then multiply these horrors by six hundred millions, and you will form some conception of the misery which in each successive generation sin is spreading over the world; and shall this last forever? In the name of bleeding and suffering millions, in the name of humanity and religion, in the name of the living God, we answer—No. There is balm in Gilead, a physician there, a remedy for human disorders, a panacea for human woes. We will rise and bear it to our brethren, wherever there is misery to be relieved, or ignorance to be enlightened, or pollution to be purified, or sin to be forgiven; wherever man exists with his weakness and woes, there we will penetrate with the light of the Gospel in our hands, and the faith and love of the Gospel in our hearts. Oh, brethren, that was a fine thought of the heathen poet: "I am a man, and nothing human is foreign to me." But what are the interests for which in a moment of pathetic enthusiasm he felt such deep sensibility, in comparison with those higher enduring interests which the Gospel has revealed? Those interests are of a body soon to crumble; these are the interests of a soul which, when empires had passed away, and worlds crumbled, would be just commencing an existence; whose progressive advancements in joy or woe, numbers could not calculate, and only eternity could measure out. But where shall we find the spirit that is large enough to embrace a world, and bold enough to dare all, and endure all, for the welfare of others? It is found only in the Gospel of the Saviour.

Here is the grand announcement made, that the field is the world. On every page of this wonderful book, the Bible, we find the impress of the same large and capacious mind, embracing all mankind in its regards, and comprehending all time in its survey. Its charity is as wide as the world; its philanthropy, overleaping all national boundaries, expansive as our race. Man, at best a minute and narrow-minded creature, engrossed with his own petty pursuits, anxieties, and cares, seldom looks abroad on the miseries of his race; or if some tale of sorrow excite a momentary comparison, gives sparingly out of his abundance, and returns with quiet self-complacency to his accustomed enjoyments. The statesmen and philosophers of old confined their sympathies to the limits of their own country, and even in its boundaries looked with contemptuous pity on the poor and ignorant. But to enlighten the ignorant, to purify the polluted, to relieve the wretched, to civilize the barbarous, and humanize the beastly of other lands, practically to sympathize with human suffering, wherever it may be found, and to know no luxury so great as that of doing good—such exalted principles of action as these were unknown to man, till taught by him whose life and death were their most glorious exemplification.

There is sometimes indeed among worldly men, a sort of poetic sensibility, which weeps and sighs, and is most wonderfully pathetical; and amidst the luxury of this pleasing sentimentalism, you might deem them the most heroic philanthropists of their day. But this philanthropy soon evaporates in eloquence and tears. Hence in the whole history of modern benevolence, you will not find a single scheme requiring for its accomplishment a bold, self-sacrificing disinterestedness, which has not been devised by Christian zeal, and executed by Christian courage. Nay, we most confidently assert, that in every great and beneficial revolution, which has passed on human society, in the opinions and conditions of men, in every mighty battle fought for the welfare of our race, the blood that has been shed was the blood of Christian martyrs; the men who pioneered the cause, and the men who carried on the cause, and by their labors and sufferings brought it to a triumphant issue, were men versed in the doctrines and imbued with the spirit of the Gospel. Need I refer for proof to the establishment of Christianity, to the Reformation, to the abolition of the slave-trade, or the mighty work of modern missions, while the infidel philosopher sat securely in his study, and laughed to scorn the fanatical folly which dared such dangers, with such remote prospect of success.

In their commencement, modern missions were derided as chimerical, impracticable, and their failure predicted as certain. Philosophers laughed and theorized; Christians schemed, Christians went to work, wept and prayed and labored, and now behold the result. In every quarter of the globe missions have been established; in fifty-six languages the Bible and other books have been printed and read; civilization has followed in the train of religion with the smiling cottage, the quiet fireside, the cultivated farm; and thus, while guiding to heaven, has Christianity been found diffusing blessings along man's pathway on earth.

Now we say that this is all because Christianity has introduced a new principle of action, a new motive for human conduct, new stimulus for human energies; a stimulus so strong that it can raise the tone of human feeling far above the level of our daily and selfish anxieties and pursuits, and urge it on to mightier enterprises for the good of the species. It is the profound remark of Madame de Stael in the ablest of all her works, a remark founded on an extensive and thorough examination of history, that no mighty influence has ever been exerted over human destiny, no great revolution produced in human affairs, without the influence of enthusiasm. Not that wild and disordered passion which perverts the faculties, but that divine and noble ardor, which in pursuit of a great object, elevates the soul above the every-day weakness and bitterness of life; above the appetites that debase, and passions that seduce, and anxieties that perplex, and dangers that alarm mankind, and makes it master of the circumstances of which others are the slaves.

Such was the enthusiasm of glory among the Romans; such the enthusiasm of learning at its first revival in Europe; such the spirit of primitive Christians, when men went exulting to the stake or the cross; and such must be the temper inspired by any system, which is to lay strong hold on the minds of men, and is destined to become universal.

Such is the spirit of the Gospel, self-denying, self-consecrating, self-sacrificing, of Him who came into the world not to be ministered unto, but to minister, and "to give his life a ransom for many;" of Him who said, "I have a work to do, and how am I straitened till it be accomplished;" of that Apostle who said, "I count not my life dear, so that I might finish my course with joy, and testify the Gospel of the grace of God;" of the holy martyrs, of the noble reformers, of the modern missionaries, of every Christian in whose bosom reigns that "spirit of Christ without which none can be his."

And here, brethren, we do fear there is utterly a delusion amongst you; that many of you console yourselves with the thought, that the missionary, the pastor, the theological student perhaps, ought to cherish and to manifest this spirit of entire consecration; but that for yourselves, a lower standard of religion will surely suffice. But what is the teaching of the inspired Apostle? "None of us liveth to himself, and none dieth to himself; whether we live, we live unto the Lord; or whether we die, we die unto the Lord: whether we live therefore or die, we are the Lord's." "Now I beseech you brethren, offer your bodies and spirits a living sacrifice unto God." "Ye are not your own, but bought with a price, therefore glorify God with your bodies and spirits which are God's." Oh no, there is no easier religion for you; the same salvation is offered, the same motives presented, the same crown prepared, the same cross to be borne. Are your talents more limited? then consecrate more unreservedly what you have. It was he with one talent who alone was lost. We need this spirit of self-consecration as much for its influence at home, as for its mighty operation abroad. We need the stimulus of some great enterprise, to wake up the slumbering energies of the church; the power of some noble and exalted principle to expel the frivolous spirit of the world. Oh, were its influence felt only amongst us, how unspeakably blessed might be the

15*

results on ourselves, on our families, on the many youth who resort hither from year to year!

Could there issue from this place only, one hundred young men, ten annually for ten successive years, whose souls were burning with the love of the Saviour, whose spirits were awake to the magnitude of the great work before them, whose minds were indeed cast on the circle of the earth, and their thoughts glowing with fire sent down from heaven, what wonders might they not effect, with the blessing of God on their labors. They might revolutionize a nation, they might shake a continent, their influence be felt and their voice be heard around the globe. Why may this not be? It is because your own influence, example, and worldly spirit render them worldly, ambitious, and vain. They breathe a polluted atmosphere, and all their vital energies are palsied, and thus many congregations that shall pine beneath their ministry, the heathen whom they might have saved, the world for which they ought to have labored, all will rise up in judgment against you at the last day.

XVIII.

THE PROVINCE OF FAITH.

JOHN xiv. 1.—"Ye believe in God, believe also in me."

THERE is an audacious spirit of speculation, frivolous and flippant, superficial and yet presumptuous, which refuses to believe aught that it cannot comprehend and perfectly explain. There is an humble piety, ignorant and contracted, ever trembling for the Ark, like a man groping his way amidst the twilight with a priceless treasure, which is startled at the approach of imaginary dangers, shrinks from the light that would unmask its foes and reveal their weakness, and in its terror loses its grasp upon the very truths which a manlier courage had successfully defended, and whose inestimable value alone had excited its groundless fears.

If there be anything on earth of value surpassing all human calculation, it is a firm and assured faith. The strongest thing on the broad earth is a man of faith. There is nothing sublimer beneath the skies. Beneath him is the Rock of Ages; above him is the deep heaven of heavens, in its solemn and illimitable grandeur; around him the awful majesty of God; within him a serene and celestial joy. He walks the earth with a different step from other men. He is going to another country, even an heavenly. Dangers cannot awe him. Temptations cannot seduce him; for the love of Christ doth constrain him, and crowns of glory, unseen by others, are bright before him. The arms of everlasting love encircle him. Angelic hosts encamp around him. Fires cannot consume him; the sword cannot slay him; for he bears a charmed life, and, even here, is invulnerable and immortal till his work be done. As heir of all things life is his, death is his, heaven is his, earth is his, God and Christ are his. No wonder, then, that faith should have performed those prodigies of valor and power recorded in the eleventh chapter of the Epistle to the Hebrews; and left those bright examples, which the Apostle has marshalled there, in compact and brilliant array; whose names fall upon our ears as the trumpet-tones of conflict and victory. Men of faith have ever been men of power. Faith! Yes, our faith—faith in God, faith in Christ, faith in all the words of God. Whatever else we neglect, let us not forget to cherish our faith; to hold fast our faith even to the end. If health, character, fortune, country, family, friends—all were gone, faith would more than supply their place.

But take from me my faith—tear from my bleeding and palpitating heart the sweetest and loftiest of all the hopes it has ever cherished—hopes which nestled amidst my childish thoughts, mingled with my boyish studies, and now, in the maturity of manhood, sweep from horizon to horizon of my existence, arching the heavens with sublimity and grandeur, and gilding the earth with beauty—rob me of my faith in that Eternal Holiness and Omnipotent Love revealed in the Scriptures—and who shall then repair the ruins of this desolated heart! Bereft of faith, I am left alone in an orphan world, without Father or friend, without guardian or guide, without God or hope, to stand amidst the shrouded forms, and spectral memories, and sepulchral monuments of hopes that can live no more.

No wonder, then, that the men of faith in every age have been men of honor; that ages of faith have been ages of lofty enterprise, of heroic daring, of sublime achievement, fruitful in blessings to the world; while ages of scepticism have been dark, dreary, and barren, passing athwart the track of human history, like the black clouds of a wintry night—now careering wildly before the fury of the storm, now drifting along, cold, sullen, silent, huge, shapeless, hiding the clear vault of heaven above, and blackening the earth with their portentous shadows.

Yet is there an audacious spirit of speculation abroad, which would rob us of our faith; and along with our faith would rob us of our happiness, our moral worth, and all our moral power. It was to rebuke this daring spirit, and at the same time to chasten and cheer the hearts of all humble and trembling believers, that our Saviour uttered the language of the text, Ye believe in God, believe also in me. If the admonition and encouragement were needed then, much more are they needed now. Ye believe in God, notwithstanding all the darkness that shrouds him from human vision, notwithstanding the unfathomable mystery that overhangs the mode of his existence and baffles at every point all human investigation. Notwithstanding all the difficulties that lie in the nature of the subject, and those which ingenious sophistry throws around it, you still hold fast to your belief in God. You cling to the fact; you stand upon the evidence; you thrust away all the plausibilities of ingenious and delusive speculations; and still believe in God.

Our Saviour's requirement is, "Believe also in me." The propositions involved in this requirement would seem to be the following: first, that the evidence in both cases is the same in kind and equal in degree; secondly, that there is nothing more difficult, more mysterious or incomprehensible, proposed by me, than you already believe; thirdly, that there is nothing more miraculous in the one case than in the other; fourthly, that believing in God as you do, you already believe in every relation, duty, and responsibility which I inculcate; fifthly, that believing in God, you are necessarily shut up to faith in me. Because there is no other refuge for a sinner from God's justice, and from everlasting despair, except by believing in me. "For I am the way, and the truth, and the life; no man cometh to the Father but by me."

I. Consider, first, the evidence. No man hath seen God at any time, or heard his voice. Invisible to human eye, unheard by human ear, impalpable to human sense, inaccessible wholly to all human scrutiny, he dwells in his own immensity, unapproachable by the gaze and incomprehensible to the understanding of man. Yet do we know his existence from the evidence of indubitable facts—facts that lie within the range of human inquiry, and from which our conclusion is legitimately drawn, with intuitive rapidity, and irresistible conviction, on the ordinary principles of human reasoning. Yet is the evidence of these facts only *human testimony*. All nature, indeed, yields her testimony, and science, through all its departments, brings me her varied contributions. And sweet to the Christian's heart and sublime is the harmony of that loud and universal response, which thus comes from nature throughout all her provinces, and testifies to the existence and attributes of the Great Creator. Yet, let us never forget, that it is on human testimony that we believe each one of these separate facts, which startle us from our indifference; and, by their combined and accumulated power, absolutely overwhelm our understandings, sweep away our doubts, and leave us only awe and wonder and adoration.

When the anatomist points you to the wonders of the human frame, the symmetry of its fair proportions, the mutual adaptation of all its parts, their harmonious combination towards one grand result—the life and health of the human being; when he leads you through all that intricate machinery of tubes and canals, by which blood is distributed through all the system; that still more intricate machinery by which nutrition is communicated to the blood, its impurities all removed, and it returned in healthful currents to stimulate the heart, and to pour again through veins and arteries, in one living torrent, giving hardness to the muscles, sensibility to the nerves, incessant, never-sleeping energy to the heart, from which it issued; when he points to the exquisite mechanism of the eye, the structure of the ear, the lungs, the hand, so admirably adapted to be the instrument of an intelligent being, so useless to all beside; when in every separate portion, and in all combined, you behold traces of a skill surpassing all human wisdom, and which all past centuries have not sufficed to exhaust by their investigations—remember, it is only *human* testimony which you have heard, and on this *human* testimony you have based your sublime and irresistible conclusion.

When the astronomer takes his adventurous journey through the skies, and returns with his prodigies of discovery; tells you of world after world as they wheel through the immensity of space; of system after system as they pass in rapid and dazzling succession; of great globes of light hung out there in the blue ether, self-poised, pursuing their eternal flight; when he shows you a whole universe apparently rushing to its ruin—planets oscillating from side to side on their axis—their orbits for a hundred centuries expanding, then contracting in apparent lawlessness—and then shows how each is poised against the other, so that all these irregularities correct themselves—how in the mighty march of the universe all things return once more to the point from which they started; and when overwhelmed by the magnitude of the scheme, and lost amidst the intricacy of its movements, you fall down in wonder and adoration before the inscrutable wisdom that formed them all at first, assigned them their magnitudes and relative positions, gave the first impulse to their movements, and still keeps up from century to century, through incalculable millions of years, the play of this wonderful machinery—remember it is on the strength of *human* testimony you accredit all these marvels.

When the geologist penetrates the abysses of the earth, and tells you of buried species piled layer above layer many fathoms deep—the sepulchres and the memorials of an earlier world; and pointing to the structure of all their parts, shows that one grand design, one stupendous purpose, one all-pervading, all-controlling, all-providing intelligence is seen through all the immeasurable cycles of the geologic ages—remember this too is only *human* testimony. They present the facts, *you draw the conclusion* only.

Now it does not signify to say, "many an humble and unlettered man believes in the existence of God without all this testimony." He believes it, because he cannot help it. It is spontaneous, intuitive, conviction from all he sees around him and feels within him. The unlettered Christian has the same inward and intuitive conviction, draws instinctively the same intuitive, and rapid, and irresistible conclusion, as to the realities of the Gospel. And here they are on a par. But I speak of that conviction which is the result of scientific investigation, and *here*, after all, their belief of all the facts is based on *human* testimony. You never, perhaps, witnessed the anatomy of a single subject; or saw a single experiment in chemistry; or gazed through a telescope; or calculated the orbit of a planet—nay, of all the distinguished scientific men on earth, how few have gazed through Lord Rosse's telescope, or observed the stars in the southern hemisphere, or performed half the analyses in chemistry; yet on the faith of *human* testimony, we credit all those prodigies of science, so remote from all the appearances of daily life. And why? Because there is no motive conceivable to induce so many men to combine in a conspiracy to deceive the world. It would subvert all the laws of evidence, reverse all the principles of human nature with which we are acquainted, while confessedly we are not acquainted with the infinite possibilities of things.

Such is the testimony for the facts of the Gospel—the miracles and resurrection of the Saviour. Nay, this is far more conclusive. Have astronomers been called to seal their testimony with their blood? Yet the apostles, and thousands besides, in the earliest ages, laid down their lives in attestation, not of opinions, but of *facts*—of miracles, repeated and various, occurring under their own eyes, appealing to their senses. What was the motive to deceive? Did they not peril all—lose all?

Do you say, we see around us now the evidences of God's agency and presence in the magnificent revolution of the seasons? We say, so it is in Christianity. We see its mighty influences on human society; we see its grand fulfilment of prophecy.

II. The evidence is equal. Are the truths proposed more

mysterious in the one case than in the other? Here let us guard, in the outset, against a natural misapprehension. We have denounced this speculation as audacious. Let us not be mistaken. We are not of the number of those who denounce *all speculation*. Men always have speculated, always will, always must, always ought to speculate. It is the natural, instinctive tendency of the human mind, the source of all our discoveries, to pass from the known fact to its unknown cause. Every man, every child has his little speculation. The very men who object against it, present their own speculations as an argument. The inquisitor thinks he may denounce all thought, reasons against the right to reason, and gives his own decisive judgment against the right of judgment. The only remedy for erroneous speculation, is to speculate aright. The only remedy for a false philosophy, said a departed father of our church, is a *true* philosophy. Our objection to this audacious speculation is, that it is false and childish, that it has not learned the first lesson of a true philosophy—the appropriate objects and true limits of human inquiry; and that it seeks to overleap the boundaries wisely assigned to all human, and, we believe, to all created intelligence, and wastes in search of unattainable knowledge the energies designed for subjects that lie within the limits of the human faculties.

The first lesson of a true philosophy is humility. Its earliest utterance, handed down to us from the father of philosophy in Greece, is an acknowledgment of total ignorance in all that relates to the ultimate nature and essential elements of things. All human reasoning terminates at last in some first principles, admitted by all, and which can be proven and explained by none. All physical inquiry lands us at last in some ultimate fact, too simple to be analyzed, too clear to be illustrated, too plain to be proven; which shines by its own self-evidencing light, and of which we can learn nothing but that it stands alone there in its inscrutable mystery. Such are all the great facts in nature to which we proudly give the name of laws.

Nay, were we endowed with senses that could penetrate

the inward structure of things, and see the particles of matter in their primordial elements, it has been proven, that still their movements would be shrouded in mystery to us, and we could know nothing but the facts. "All there is, is mystery," says the subtlest thinker of our age, "or nothing is mystery." In this sense the whole universe with all its parts is one vast mystery. The heaven and the earth, the stars as they move and shine, are all mysterious. Their motions are a mystery, their light a mystery. The flowers as they grow, the human body and human spirit separately, how mysterious, and in their union, a reduplicated mystery! What these scientific thinkers call an explanation, is but a removal of the mystery; or rather a multiplication of the mysteries to be solved. It is but the tracing of one fact, which cannot be explained, to another, or to many other facts, equally inexplicable; and then, after multiplying the mystery, crying out that it is explained. For example, you see a star millions of miles off. How do you see it, and know what it is? The explanation traces it on from fact to fact; each needs explanation; and at last, the great fact remains untouched, that the mind perceives, by some inexplicable process, the distant star. You have not approached a comprehension of the process. Such, then, is that boasting and supercilious philosophy which comes, with great swelling words of vanity, to rob us of our faith. It has not learned the first elements of true reasoning.

Thus do we see that in whatever direction we turn our thoughts, above, beneath, around, within, all is mystery—mystery in the great worlds above us, in their light and their motions—mystery in the minutest particles of matter, in their attractions and repulsions, their combinations and decomposition. In all vegetable and animal life, its nature and its origin, in the human body with all its varied functions, and the human spirit with its inscrutable powers, there is mystery. The whole universe is one great mystery—one temple of the Great Invisible, whose mysteries we cannot penetrate, where the learned and the ignorant alike can only stand and wonder and adore—with a wonder the more profound, and an adoration the more devout and reverential, as truth after truth bursts upon the awed understanding, and reveals to human ignorance fresh glimpses of that immensity which sweeps boundlessly away beyond the reach of man's investigation. "I am but a little child," said he, who first fathomed those spheres hitherto unfathomable, and converted those sparkling ornaments of our night into worlds of immeasurable glory, "I am but a little child, standing on the shore of the great ocean of truth, and gathering a few pebbles to show to my companions." What that pebble is to the ocean on whose shore it lies, to the globe which holds that ocean in its bosom, to the sun which holds that globe in its orbit, to the universe in which that sun itself, with all its attendant worlds, is but a point invisible—such is this whole universe to the immensity of God. What, then, must be the mystery of his nature! Surely the man who has received the idea of a God, who has analyzed it into all its component elements, who has grasped in it all its vast proportions—surely he has already accepted the greatest of all conceivable mysteries; and nothing more remains which can baffle the keenness of his sagacious scrutiny, or revolt the delicacy of his all-embracing faith.

For, tell me, what is your conception of a God? God is a spirit. But what is a spirit? It has no parts or proportions; it has no form or magnitude; it has no dimensions or color. There is nothing in the whole universe around which resembles it, nothing analogous to it, nothing to aid us in forming a conception of it. But, you say, the spirit is that which feels, and thinks, and hopes, and fears—that which is capable of all these various emotions, and remains unchanged amidst the fugitive variety of its changing states. You tell me what it *does*. I ask you what it *is?* And I ask in vain. For he who has studied it the longest and the most profoundly, will be the last to venture a reply. Its phenomena I know; for of these I am conscious. But that mysterious essence, of which these phenomena are the varied manifestation, and shrouding which they yet appear to reveal—what is that? "What is the soul?" once asked a thoughtful inquirer of his friend. "I know nothing of it," was the reply, "except that it is immaterial and immortal." "Let us ask Fontenelle," rejoined the inquirer. "Ah," said he, "he is the last man in the world to ask; for he has too much sense to know anything more about it than you or I."

It has been from my earliest boyhood, the employment and the pleasure of my life, to seek to fathom, if possible, this mystery of man's immaterial spirit, and to comprehend something of its nature; but after all my reflections, and all the investigations of others, the conviction has become every day the profounder and the more intense, of that unfathomable mystery which must forever encompass a deathless spirit. A simple, primitive conception, it declines the scrutiny of the senses, eludes the grasp of the imagination, defies the analysis of logic; and when you question it, its only answer is, that which its great Author gave—"I am that I am." It stands alone, grand, solemn, peculiar, shrouded in its own impenetrable mystery.

But God, you say, is the great First Cause, the great Creative Spirit. But what is creation? When did he create? How did he create? Can you describe the process? Here, too, all earthly analogies fail us. The mechanic, indeed, may hew his timber into form, may mould it into beauty, and polish it to brightness. The sculptor, by a yet superior skill, may take the rude marble from the quarry, and shape it into the dead resemblance of a living man. Nay, by the strange magic of his art, he may breathe an illusive reality over the whole, may give to the form all the grace of beauty, and to the brow the majesty of genius, till the love of the mighty dead shall live again to the imagination and almost to the eye. But these have the materials on which they operate, the instruments with which they work. Here, however, there are no instruments or materials with which, and on which, to begin the work of creation. Do you say, he called all things out of nothing? But what is nothing? Has it any existence? And if it had, were all things contained from eternity in its bosom, to leap forth into being at his Omnipotent fiat? View it in whatever form you may—cast it into any form of human expression—shape it to any mould of thought—it is, at last, a primitive, indefinable conception, too simple to be analyzed, too peculiar to be illustrated from any other source. It remains, and ever must remain, an original, isolated, sublime reality, to be accepted on its own appropriate evidence as an inexplicable fact.

But God is a spirit, infinite, immutable, eternal, omniscient, omnipresent, almighty. If, then, it is so difficult to form any conception of a finite spirit like our own, how does the difficulty increase, and the perplexities multiply, when you project your conception of a spirit into infinity, expand it over eternity, diffuse it through immensity; and thus add to its inherent difficulties, every other element most incommensurable with the powers of the human understanding. Eternity—what is the eternity of God? Will you first tell us, what is time? All past ages, with their combined powers of investigation, have sought to give the answer, and have sought in vain. "Time," says the latest transcendental philosopher, "is nothing in things themselves, or in events, or in their relations. Time is a form of human thought." "Time," says the most subtle thinker who has written in the English language for half a century, "Time is nothing in things or in events; time is the relation of priority and succession between events." That is equivalent to saying—time is time. Most luminously spoken! Surely wisdom will die with the luminaries of our benighted race! "Time," it is said, "is the relation of priority and succession in events." But what is a relation? Can you define it? The subtlest analyst of human thought in our country has exhausted all his ingenuity in the effort, and by universal admission has most signally failed.

But if it be so difficult to tell what time is, what shall we say of eternity? Here modern science, with all her multiplied discoveries, comes to our assistance; but comes in vain. In vain do we strive to clamber upward, step by step, on that ladder of ascent, which reaches from heaven to earth, and from earth back to heaven, whose lowest round is upon the earth, while its summit rests upon the throne of the Eternal, and is lost to our view amidst the invisibilities of that awful throne. Reason reels beneath the weight of her own stupendous discoveries, and imagination falters on wearied wing, as she expatiates amidst those millions of ages, which, when multiplied by other millions, are not the sum, but the commencement of eternity. Our brief year, and still briefer day, are measured out by annual and diurnal revolutions of the earth. Five hundred of our years would scarce suffice to measure the period of revolution, in its eccentric orbit of one of our best-known comets. One thousand of our years would be but a single year in the distant planet of our own little system. Eighteen hundred millions of years is the period assigned by the greatest astronomers of our day for the revolution of our sun, in its amazing orbit around its distant centre, in the farthest heavens. But in vain do we add millions upon millions, and multiply these again by other millions, in the effort to grasp eternity. In vain do we summon to our aid all the powers of calculation, and let imagination loose, to rise from summit to summit in this sublime and perilous ascent. For, after all, this is not eternity. That sun began to shine. These revolutions are not of eternity. And when the soul of man, of higher and nobler elements than the sun himself, and destined for a far more magnificent career, sweeps backward in thought beyond the hour when suns began to shine, behold she stands amidst eternity. Behind her are the ages of the eternity past; before her is the eternity of ages yet to come. Around, above, beneath, on every side, stretches far away, in its silent and solemn grandeur, the immensity which is the dwelling-place of God. No sun, no stars of light, no moon, no day, no night, no revolutions of the spheres are here. No voice or form of man, or angel, is seen or heard amid the void and voiceless infinite.

Who can comprehend this immensity! Our modern science expands our views, and elevates our conceptions, and seems to invite us to the effort. But it is only to show us the nothingness of man, in comparison with the infinitude of God. The smallest of those intervals, with which our astronomy is conversant, stretches immeasurably beyond our utmost powers of conception, leaving us to wonder that our geometry can demonstrate what our imagination cannot grasp. One hundred millions of miles is about the interval which separates us from our sun. One thousand times that distance will not bring us to the last-discovered planet of our little system. When we attempt to ascertain the distance of one of those fixed stars, that are visible by millions, in our sky, we find that the diameter of the earth's orbit around the sun—two hundred millions of miles in length—is too short for the base-line of such a measurement; that the lines, drawn from each extremity of this prodigious length, run up into each other, and the angle they inclose absolutely vanishes, as if they issued from a single point. Now, transport yourself in imagination to such a star as this. As you pass onward and upward, the moon soon fades, the planets disappear, the sun diminishes, grows dim, twinkles as a bright spot in the distant heavens. A new firmament is now above your head. New constellations shed their radiance on your pathway. The order of these lower heavens is reversed. Suns revolve around suns in gorgeous magnificence, and pour their radiance on your head, where all the colors of the rainbow meet, in varied combination, as if the broad arch of heaven were one perpetual memorial of love and safety, sent from the Father of lights to his unfallen offspring.

Astronomers, who have looked through the best constructed of our modern telescopes, assure us that the first emotion of all beholders is one wild gush of ecstacy and wonder, mounting up to almost delirious joy, and subsiding finally into a calm and solemn exaltation of soul, awed by the surpassing grandeur of the scene, yet expanded and elevated by the very grandeur that subdues and overwhelms. Standing now in one of those uppermost worlds, with the keener vision and superior instruments which they may enjoy, let us sweep the whole heaven of heavens in one rapid and magnificent survey. Yet far beyond the reach of eye or telescope, beyond the range of angel vision or angel flight, stretches illimitably on the immensity of God's creation, with new families of worlds, new forms of existence, new sources of enjoyment, new methods of administration, new firmaments of glory, each separate, yet all united; formed by one wisdom, upheld by one power, pervaded by one presence, subordinated to one high purpose, and ultimately, in one grand result, guided by one supreme intelligence. Stupendous eternity! Infinite complexity! Oh, the depths of the riches, both of the wisdom and knowledge of God! How unsearchable are his judgments, and his ways past finding out! Lo! these are parts of his ways; yet how faint is the whisper we have heard of him. But the full thunder of his power, who can understand? Canst thou then, by searching, find out God; canst thou find out the Almighty to perfection? Behold, it is higher than heaven; what canst thou know? It is deeper than hell; what canst thou do? The measure thereof is wider than the earth, and broader than the sea. Lift up your eyes on high; and behold, who hath created these things; that bringeth out their host by number. He calleth them all by name; by reason of the greatness of his might; for that he is strong in power, not one faileth. He sitteth on the circle of the earth; and hath measured the ocean in the hollow of his hand; and hath meted out the heavens with a span; and comprehended the dust of the earth in a measure; and weighed the mountains in scales, and the hills in a balance. To whom then will ye liken me, or shall I be equal, saith the Holy One? Gird up thyself now like a man, and answer me. When I laid the foundations of the earth, where wast thou? When I stretched out the heavens over emptiness, and hung the earth on nothing; when the morning stars sang together, and the sons of God shouted for joy; when I shut up the sea with doors, and set bars and bolts, and said, thus far shalt thou come, and no farther; and here shall thy proud waves be stayed. Canst thou bind the sweet influences of Pleiades; or loose the bands of Orion? Canst thou bring forth Mazzaroth in his season; or canst thou guide Arcturus with his sons? Hast thou an arm like God? Canst thou thunder with a voice like his? Be still then, and know that I am God. Before the mountains were brought forth, or ever thou hadst formed the earth and the world, even from everlasting to everlasting, thou art God. They shall perish, but thou remainest. They shall all wax old, as doth a garment, and as a vesture shalt thou fold them up; and they shall be changed. But thou art the same; from eternity to eternity, still unchanged; without variableness or shadow of turning, the first and the last, the beginning and the end, the omniscient, the omnipresent, the Almighty. Oh, whither shall I go from thy Spirit; or whither shall I flee from thy presence? If I ascend up into heaven; thou art there. If I make my bed in hell; behold thou art there. If I take the wings of the morning, and dwell in the uttermost parts of the sea; even there shall thy hand lead me, and thy right hand shall hold me. If I say, surely the darkness shall cover me; even the night shall be light about me. The darkness and the light are both alike to thee. Thou hast beset me before, and behind, and laid thine hand upon me.

Well might the inspired psalmist exclaim, "Such knowledge is too wonderful for me; it is high, I cannot attain unto it." And who can comprehend the height, or the depth, or the length, or the breadth, of these amazing attributes—the omniscience that includes things that are not, as well as things that are, all things that shall be, and might be, as well as those that have been—a being that is present alike through all time, and all space—through all time, without having any relation to time, and all space, without relation to space—present at every moment of time and each point in space, not by a distribution of his powers, but in the absolute totality of all his amazing attributes, in the full intensity of his whole undivided essence, lavishing all the resources of his eternal wisdom and almighty power, as truly when he gilds the wing of an insect, or pencils the leaflet of a flower, as when he creates an angel, kindles a sun, or upholds the universe.

Ye believe in God; believe also in me. If ye believe in God, as manifested in the works of creation; believe in him likewise as manifested in the person of his Son. Do you ask me to explain the nature and mode of that connection which exists between the infinite Creator, and a finite being, the mystery of an Incarnate God? I answer most cheerfully, if you will explain the nature of that relation which he bears to all around. Know you not that he is present, most intimately, vitally, essentially present, in a most mysterious and inscrutable manner, to all that lives, to all that is? He is present in the hidden elements of matter, present in all the operations of mind; present, not as a dead abstraction, but as a living power, pervading all, sustaining all, vivifying all, controlling, directing, limiting all. He is nearer to each one of us, than our spirit to the body which it animates; nearer than any particle of this body to the particle immediately adjoining, with an intimacy of relation for which nature has no illustration; because for it she has no parallel and no counterpart. It is the relation of the Creator to the creatures he has made, of the source of all life to life derived from him. He is present in the glowing sun, in the glittering stars, in the blossoming flowers. He rides in the whirlwind, thunders in the storm; foresees all without forcing any; reigns sovereign controller amidst the freedom of human agency, and causes the folly and madness of man, alike to accomplish his purposes of wisdom and mercy. In him we live and move and have our being. By him were all things created, and in him do all things subsist.

It is the mysterious relation which the Creator must bear to all his creatures that has led the atheist to deny the existence of a God, though the evidence of his existence is everywhere around us. And when the evidence could not be denied, the pantheist, in turn, has been led thus to make the universe a God, and all its various parts a portion of the universal Deity, attributing to the leaf that grows, and to the salt that crystallizes, the wisdom which he denies to the supreme intelligence. But if there be this mysterious connection with all, why may there not be a peculiar connection, though equally inexplicable, with one? If God is intimately present, connected with, and manifest in, all his work, what is there unreasonable, or difficult to believe, in the fact that he becomes incarnate and manifest in the person of his Son? If you can believe in the God of nature, and the God of creation, notwithstanding all the difficulties and the mysteries involved in such a belief; where is the unreasonableness of believing in me as the Incarnate One, sent to redeem the world from sin; and of believing that God is in me, reconciling the world unto himself?

Do you say, I object, as unreasonable, to such a union of God and man in Christ, as constitutes identity of person. I ask, in reply, if you have solved the still greater difficulty which is presented in your own person? If the union of spirit with spirit, in harmonious combination, be a problem too difficult for the Divine omnipotence, what say you to the union of an immaterial spirit and a material body in man's nature; of a spirit absolutely one and simple, with a body whose particles are infinite in number; nay, of a spirit which remains permanently the same, with particles that are forever changing; and yet, amidst all these changes, the irresistible consciousness that there is constantly the self-same person, composed of material body, and an immaterial spirit? Will you deny your own identity? Will you deny that you have a body, or that you have a soul? How body is connected with spirit, we do not know. The fact, that they are connected, we do know and believe, however inexplicable; because of that we have sufficient evidence. How the Divine nature is connected with the human in the person of the Saviour, we do not know. This is not offered to our belief. Nor does it demand our investigation. The fact we receive, as any other fact, on the authority of testimony. There may be mystery here, if you please; but it is the mystery which belongs to all human things, overhangs all human knowledge, and is inseparable from the nature and limits of the human faculties. The real mystery is, that men, who profess to think, should be so slow to learn the first lesson in all true reasoning—the appropriate objects and real limits of human knowledge—that first dictate of sound philosophy and common sense, and earliest result of all experience, that we know, and can know, nothing of the hidden nature and essences of things—that facts in every department of inquiry, collected, observed, compared, form the basis and whole superstructure of our knowledge. This restless and prurient inquiry after the hidden essences of things, mysterious powers, occult qualities, as distinct from the facts themselves, was the peculiar folly of the ancient alchemists, and is now the antiquated relic of an exploded system, rejected by common sense, repudiated by sound philosophy, and contradicted by the uniform and universal experience of man. Let us receive the great fact of God manifested in our nature, as we receive the fact of God manifested in creation. If we believe in God, let us believe in Christ. Let us believe in Christ, even as we believe in God. "He that hath seen me," said the Saviour, "hath seen the Father. Believe me that I am in the Father, and the Father in me; or else believe me for the very works' sake."

XIX.

HOW LIFE IS TO BE IMPROVED.

PSALM XC. 12.—"So teach us to number our days, that we may apply our hearts unto wisdom."

THIS Psalm is called "A prayer of Moses, the man of God." It was probably written on the borders of Canaan, when the Jews had just finished their long and dreary wanderings through that great and terrible wilderness, and were about to enter upon the inheritance so long promised to their fathers, and so long deferred, even till the heart was sick, for the sins of their descendants. It would be difficult to conceive any circumstances more affecting than those under which this Psalm was composed. The aged and venerable servant of God had outlived all his cotemporaries. He had seen them all pursued by that fierce threat of God which, the apostle informs us, is sharper than any two-edged sword, and falling in the wilderness beneath its unseen but terrible energy. One had been swallowed up with Korah and his companions; another had been bitten by the fiery serpents, whose burning poison ran like molten lead through every vein, till every nerve was wrung with intensest agony, and every muscle was parched and withered by the heat, and the waters of life were dried up at once in the system, or oozed slowly and lingeringly and painfully away. Another has dragged his wearied limbs over the tedious pilgrimage through that trackless desert, still cheering himself with the thought of Canaan and the vain hope that the Almighty would relent; until, at last, flesh and heart have failed together, and the delusive hope on which he had so long leaned is gone, and he sinks down, exhausted and desperate, upon the sands of the hot desert.

And where is she, who had hung upon his arm that fearful night when they were thrust out from Egypt; who pressed still closer to his side, as alarm and danger threatened, and gazed so wishfully upon his manly face, to reassure her trembling spirit? Ah! who so fit to minister in his last agony, and by the gentlest consolations soothe his departed spirit, as she who was the cherished object of his earliest and tenderest affections? But long ere this her feeble frame had sunk exhausted beneath the labors and privations of their pilgrimage; and the mighty host, hardened by perpetual scenes of distress, and rendered intensely selfish by the consciousness of danger, to which they were perpetually exposed, had swept on regardless of her groans and dying. Thus it was that, one by one, they had all fallen in the wilderness, hewn down by the unseen but terrible sword of the Lord, until of all that mighty host who had marched out of Egypt, in the vigor of health and the pride of triumph, and had lifted up their voices to murmur against the Lord in the wilderness, there was none remaining; and the venerated leader and legislator of the Jews, in the decline of life, bereft of all the companions of his youth, gazed around him in desolate loneliness of heart, and stood amidst the tribes of Israel as the aged and solitary oak, leafless and branchless, and almost lifeless, amidst the strewed and shattered forest which the tempest has uprooted in its fury.

It was under circumstances such as these that the afflicted servant of the Lord composed the affecting and touching Psalm of which our text forms a part. It is a pathetic lamentation over the shortness of human life, and a prayer for grace or wisdom to improve it to the best advantage. He contrasts with the shortness of human life the eternity of God's existence. He leads us away from the contemplation of our short and transitory existence here, into the depths of that unfathomable and mysterious eternity which is the dwelling-place of God, whose ever-rolling years move on unceasingly, without beginning and without an end, reaching back immeasurably beyond the creation of these heavens and this earth, and stretching forward far beyond the period when the earth shall be dissolved by fire and the heavens shall be rolled together as a scroll, and all the magnificence and all the glory of this material creation shall disappear forever.

How humbling, and yet how salutary, is the contrast thus presented between the duration of a day on earth, and the long, long lapse of those revolving ages which measure out the immeasurable periods of eternity. And even when we gaze upon the scenes around us, how deep and solemn is the impression of the brevity of life. The sun, which day by day awakens us into new life, and pours over all around the effulgence of his glory, has rolled on for centuries as he does now, and has seen a thousand generations rising and flourishing for a season in his beams, and then sinking down into the darkness of the tomb. The green fields over which we sported in the playfulness of infancy, while life was still a blessing, and to breathe the fresh air and enjoy the clear sunshine was to be supremely happy, even these continue still unchanged, clothed in the same verdure, wearing the same cheerful smile, and stirring up in youthful minds the same ardent hopes, which leap forward unconsciously into the coming year, with the joyful anticipation of health and happiness. But where are they, the companions of our childhood and earliest youth, who loved to gaze along with us on all that is beautiful and majestic in the scenes around us, and whose elastic spirits bounded forward with all the freedom and confidence of unsuspecting youth to the enjoyments of coming years? For them no sun is bright, and no fields are beautiful; no ray of light breaks in upon the darkness of their last lonely dwelling-place; and the green grass waves in rank luxuriance unnoticed and unfelt over their silent and solitary abode. Even those frail habitations which man hath erected here, as the abode of his temporary residence, and which shall soon crumble into the dust, even they outlast our dying generation. The home of our childhood still remains; but where are they who made that home so happy, who gathered around the same cheerful hearth, knelt at the same family altar, and held high and blessed communion with us about that world of spirits to which they have now departed? That venerable form, which led our thoughts in prayer, has long since mouldered in the grave. The maternal tenderness which made our home a paradise, and the name of Mother, the sweetest, dearest, *holiest* on earth, is gone forever. The loud laugh rings in those well-known halls but to mock us in our agony. It is not the boyish merriment of the brother that we lost. That light footstep is scarcely heard as it falls in its gentle gracefulness upon the threshold. But it is not of the sister we loved. Our fathers, where are they? and the prophets, do they live forever?

Let us dwell, my brethren, let us often dwell upon the memory of the dead. "Blessed are the dead that die in the Lord;" and ever blessed and ever sacred be their memories. Holy, holy, holy, far above all earthly feelings, is that fond remembrance which lingers around the graves of the departed, which cherishes the recollection of their virtues, which dwells upon their bright example, and longs to be prepared for their society above. It exalts at once, and purifies our nature; it raises us above the world to hold communion with the skies, and forms a new link in that chain of love which binds earth to heaven, and binds the destinies of man to the throne of God. There are many of us here who have more beloved friends in heaven than on earth. And what a thought it is that they are now angels of light around the throne of God—ministering spirits to us who believe—to be the object of an angel's sympathy, an angel's love!!! Now call not this the ravings of enthusiasm; it is the sober truth of God. In the coldness and hardness of a proud scepticism, call not that a too transcendent vision, which paints the dead on earth revived in heaven. It is one of those glimpses which are sometimes given us in the Bible, of the unseen and eternal world. It is one of those beams from that unutterable and unapproachable glory which sometimes penetrate these dark and heavy clouds that overhang our existence here, flash across our pathway on earth, and startle us by the very magnificence of their revelations.

Now, although there is no truth which we are more prone to forget, there is none more importunately pressed upon our attention in the word of God, than the shortness of our lives. It is clothed in every variety of imagery which could strike the fancy or affect the heart of man. It is a vapor which disappears as soon as it is seen, a cloud which rises in a summer's sky, and suddenly vanishes away. It is like a tale that is told, passing a few short hours merrily away, and then forgotten forever. Even the frailest of those fragile things which we employ as the emblems of our mortality often survive us. The flower still blooms to remind us of the hand which planted it and the gentle heart which nurtured it with a sister's love. But she, the sweetest, the dearest, the loveliest of all, the flower of her family, is gone! The long grass waves in summer still above the head whose glossy ringlets were tossed in girlish merriment as she ran to welcome and embrace us. It is like the grass which waves luxuriantly over the field in the morning, but has fallen beneath the scythe of the mower before the night comes on. It is like the flower which blooms in the garden, and receives the admiration of each transient visitor, but is withered by the first hot blast that passes over it.

It is impossible for any of us, who have seen much of the afflictions of human life, not to realize the justice of these touching representations, and feel, as we read them, a thousand recollections rushing unbidden into the mind, and adding melancholy confirmation of their truth. And at such a time, perhaps, there are few of us who do not love to meditate, in a kind of poetic reverie, on the shortness and uncertainty of man's condition here; and while we enjoy the luxury of such a soft and pleasing sentimentalism, we almost think that we are ready to leave this world of sorrow, and go to that abode of peace, where our friends have gone before us; to lie down in that long repose where "the wicked cease from troubling and the weary are at rest." But it is greatly to be feared that with many, especially amongst the more refined and cultivated classes of society, this fine sensibility is mistaken for religious feeling, and constitutes indeed all the religion they possess.

They weep and sigh, and are most tenderly pathetic, in view of man's mortality, but soon forget it all, and no real, permanent impression has been made upon their character and life. Now this is not the improvement which we should make of the shortness of our lives. We should not treat the solemn realities of human life as we do the fictions of a poet or a novelist. We should not merely weep and sentimentalize about them, but we should take them up as solemn and practical truths, in which we have a deep and eternal interest; and if we thus consider them, then indeed may we learn lessons of the deepest and most precious wisdom.

But, observe, if we would learn this wisdom, it is to be done by application. The psalmist prays, "So teach us to number our days, that we may apply our hearts unto wisdom." All wisdom lies beneath the surface. It is a hidden treasure for which we must dig, if we would obtain it. It is not a few idle wishes, nor a few feeble efforts, which will master that wisdom that cometh from above. There must be deep, close, intense and continued application. There must be a striving to enter the kingdom of heaven. There must be an agonizing after those blessings which are offered in the Gospel. The great and solemn truths of God's Word, and the awful realities of eternity, must be treasured up in the memory, and dwelt upon in our reflections, and urged home by repeated efforts upon the heart and the conscience, even as the aspiring student pores over some massy volume, where he knows are laid up all the treasures of ancient wisdom, or some knotty problem which lies in the pathway of science, and whose solution leads on to a thousand unknown truths. How does he struggle with the obstacles in his way, and summon all his powers to carry on the contest! Though often foiled, he never despairs; he never doubts the existence of the wisdom he has not yet been able to discover; but returns repeatedly to the investigation, till at last his difficulties vanish, and his efforts are crowned with complete success. Even thus must the student of heavenly wisdom meditate by day and by night on the great truths of the Gospel, the short duration of his existence here, and the certainty of that coming retribution which awaits us all hereafter. But with all his efforts must be united prayer to God, fervent and unceasing prayer, still following the example of the psalmist in his prayer for Divine teaching.

Prayer without effort, and effort without prayer, are equally unavailing. The first neglects the agency of man, the last the agency of God. The first makes man a machine, incapable of action or feeling; the last endows him with powers which he does not possess, and attributes to him a wisdom which dwelleth only with God. Let us always pray, my brethren, as if all depended on prayer; and let us labor, as if all depended on our efforts. And let us cease to wonder that the boat which is propelled by only a single oar, does not glide smoothly and easily over the water, but is swept away by every current, and whirled in every eddy. If we would rightly improve the shortness and uncertainty of our lives, let us seriously and solemnly reflect upon the lessons of our text.

I. That we are not at our own disposal, but in the hand of a Sovereign and Almighty God. This is a truth that is admitted by all in language, but utterly renounced in all the practical affairs of life. All the schemes and plans of worldly men are formed and pursued upon the deliberate assumption of the fact that our lives are our own, and that we may employ them according to our pleasure. They are preserved and sustained, we suppose, by the laws of nature, and hence we learn to attribute to them something of the certainty and stability which we observe in the operation of those laws. Sinners fear no change. They are saying, To-morrow shall be as this day and much more abundant. They look forward far into the future. Fancy spreads its gayest coloring over the distant scene, and hope leaps forward to the anticipated happiness. But in all this there is no thought of God, there is no thought of death, there is no dream about eternity. And thus is the High and Holy One, in whose hand is our life, and from whom all our blessings flow, dispossessed of his rightful authority over our hearts and lives. We erect an idol in his place, and yield to it the supremacy over our affections, and never dream that it shall not be eternal, until God, in his wrath or his mercy, casts it down from the pedestal of its worship, and mingles it with the dust of the earth. We mourn for a time in brokenness of heart, as did the one of old, who said, "Ye have taken away our gods, and what shall we do?" But human ingenuity or human folly soon discovers a new resource, and another idol is consecrated, with other rites, and enthroned with undiminished power over our souls. And it is only when idol after idol has been torn away that we learn how uncertain is human life, and how little human happiness depends on human foresight or human wisdom.

It is this proud feeling of independence which emboldens men in their rebellion against God. Did we all feel that there is an unseen Almighty hand which sustains us at all times, an all-pervading Presence following us, surrounding us, enclosing us on all sides, dealing out to us every breath, and able by a single volition to terminate our lives, what solemnity would this diffuse around us! How humbly, how softly, how fearfully would we walk before the Lord! The antediluvians were secure in the enjoyment of life, and looked forward to hundreds of years of undisturbed indulgence, until the day when Noah entered the ark, and the deluge burst upon and swept them away. The inhabitants of Sodom were secure, even while Lot was fleeing from that guilty city to avoid the coming indignation; and many a mind was then pressing forward into the future, and contemplating large schemes of future wealth, or pleasure, or applause. And on that fearful night when the angel of the Lord passed through the land of Egypt, and slew all the first-born, from the king upon his throne to the lowest peasant in his cottage, while the sound of wailing was heard at one extremity of Egypt, the voice of merriment was resounding throughout the other; and mothers clasped their first-born infants securely to their bosoms, and fathers gazed with unsuspecting pride upon the manly form and features of their sons just ripening into manhood. How vain were their expectations! And how often have we beheld ourselves the young man cut down in the flower of his youth, and the man of restless activity or towering ambition, met in the pride of his manhood and in the midst of his career, and hewn down by the keen sword of the invisible destroyer. Let us remember, then, that the tenure of our lives is very uncertain, that they depend entirely on the will of another. And since these lives are bestowed at first by his goodness, and continued by his mercy, let us seek to propitiate his favor, let us endeavor to do his will, let us prepare to meet his final judgment.

II. Let us remember that in this short life we have a great work to do. It is this which stamps a solemn value upon human life, and communicates to every moment of our existence a portion of that vast and awful interest which belongs to eternity. Every moment of our being has an intimate connection with every other, from the first dawn of reason and moral agency, to the remotest period of that existence which has no limits beyond the grave. Our lives are made up of moments, and each as it passes away bequeaths to that which follows a portion of its own character. Hence we see—since the great business of life is to prepare for eternity—how important it is that every moment of our time should be diligently improved. For the work which we have to do is vast and important; important as the salvation of the soul, and vast as all those interests which can be comprised in eternity. This is our only probation; and all that we can ever do for ourselves, all that we can do for others, all that we can do for the cause of our blessed Saviour, must be done soon, or left undone forever. What immense concerns are crowded in upon a few short, fleeting hours. And this short space may be much shorter than we suppose. You may be forming plans for years, but this night your soul may be required of you.

The great business of life, all the vast concerns of eternity, may be compressed into a single moment, and that moment full of distraction and horror. Oh, how many thoughts of horror rush in upon the bosom of a dying sinner! There is the memory of the warnings he has received and despised, the invitations he has heard and rejected, the privileges he has enjoyed and misimproved, the time he has possessed and lost, the

Spirit he has grieved repeatedly away, the vows and covenants he has made and broken, the hopes which are now turned into despair, the life which is now darkening into death, and the offered heaven, now soon to be exchanged for a hell of deepest and bitterest agony! Think not that life is too long for the business allotted to it, or that any part may be devoted to folly or to sin. Look within you, and see how much employment you may find there; what passions to subdue, what pride to mortify, what evil desires to quell, what unbelief to overcome. Look above you to the example of our Divine Redeemer, who always went about doing good, and ask how much he expects you to do in imitation of his example. Look around you on the poor, on the miserable, on the ignorant, on the sinful: is there no sorrow which you can relieve, no ignorance you can instruct, no sin you can rebuke? Look back on your past life: is there nothing to repent of and to amend? Look forward to your future path: is there no danger to alarm your fears, no enemy to oppose your progress, no temptations to seduce your passions? Are you altogether prepared, with the whole armor of God, for the contest? Then your deliverance is near at hand, and it becomes you to dwell upon that world of glory to which you are so near.

Look away beyond the scenes which are now around you; think of the glory yet to be revealed, of the crown which is to sparkle on your brow, of the joy which is to flow in full tide over your exalted spirit, of the presence of God and all the glories of the upper sanctuary; and then think whether every moment is not well employed, and every faculty most wisely exerted, when engaged in the acquisition of a reward so rich and so unmerited. That was a wise resolution formed by one of the greatest and holiest men of modern times, when he resolved that he "would live with all his might." The expression is singular, but deeply significant. It means to fulfil the great purpose of our existence, that no power shall lie dormant, no moment be unimproved, no duty neglected, no opportunity lost. If you would live to any purpose, you must live with all your might; you must gird on the whole armor of the Gospel, and endure hardness as a good soldier of the Lord Jesus Christ. Let your night be only a season of repose from the labors of the day; and when the morning wakes you from your slumbers, let it only rouse you to other duties and other efforts. A heathen philosopher once lamented that he had lost a day when he had conferred no favor on any of his friends. And be assured that day is lost, lost never to be regained, in which you make no progress towards heaven, resist no wrong propensity and strengthen no good one, do nothing for the glory of God, for the welfare of others, your own spiritual improvement. The capacities which God has given you are great, and worthy of a noble object. The work he has placed before you is exalted, and suited to the faculties of your nature. The reward he has promised is large. The account he will demand is strict and precise. The judgment he has appointed is near at hand. The time is short. Behold, the Judge is at the door!

III. Let us learn from the shortness of life the vanity of all worldly passions. Behold that splendid procession as they sweep along, in martial triumph over the streets of the seven-hilled city, from the gates to the capitol. The streets are strewed with flowers, and the altars smoke with incense; and there, arrayed in purple, embroidered with gold, a crown of laurel on his head, a sceptre in his hand, and drawn in a gilded chariot by four milk-white horses, stands the object of this gorgeous ceremony. Before him he hears the proud swell of triumphant music; and as he is charioted along the streets of the imperial city, surrounded by captive kings, and the rich spoils of empires, and cheered by the loud acclamations of the populace, and the still louder greetings of the army who partake alike in the victory and the triumph, you may see the flush of triumph on his cheek and the swell of exulting rapture as it heaves his manly bosom. But amidst all this imposing and exalting scene there is one, who sits close at his side, and whispers gently in his ear; and that glow has faded from his cheek, and that flush has passed away from his brow, and that bright eye is fixed in grave and melancholy musing.

And what did he whisper in his ear? Did he remind him of the ruin he had wrought, of the sacked cities and desolated fields, of the ruined families, the bereaved widows and orphan children which his success had made, and tell him, in the honesty of truth, that the laurel on his brow was steeped in blood and scalding tears, and ill befitted the brow that wore it? No. He told him that he was a man, and reminded him of the mutability of human affairs, and the sad reverses of human fortune. He bade him remember his mortality, and pointed forward to that day when the glories of the world should have passed away, and victor and vanquished should lie down together in the grave, and mingle with the dust from which they sprang. And now the conqueror is forgotten in the man, and the recollection of his mortality has quelled his rising spirit, and subdued the pride and ambition which success and admiration had too certainly aroused. He surely cannot agitate his mind with schemes of wild ambition who seriously reflects how short would be the triumph of his pride, and how certain and how dreadful its termination.

Let us remember that we are soon to die, and let this moderate our desires for wealth and worldly comforts, as well as for worldly distinction. We could not be over anxious to make provision for the flesh, to gratify the lusts thereof, if we felt that all these things would be taken from us, and we ourselves called to judgment. It would teach us especially to lay aside all wrath and malice and evil-speaking. How can we hate the man who is so soon to lie with us in the silent grave, and stand with us before the tribunal of Justice? There is no eloquence like the eloquence of the grave; and the lessons which it teaches are as full of wisdom as of power. Go stand by the tomb of the great, and learn the vanity of earthly greatness. Visit the grave of the humble and obscure, and wonder at those petty distinctions in society which all terminate at death. Stand by the grave of a beloved friend, and ask if we have never wounded his feelings by unkindness, or misled his confidence by an ungodly example, and resolve that, since the living must soon be among the dead, we will more faithfully perform every duty that devolves upon us; that our consciences may be void of offence, and our affections unmingled with regret, when we gaze upon their sepulchres or recall their memories. And to stand by the grave of an enemy, is to feel the folly of all human animosities. The bitterest and deadliest foes have been softened by such a spectacle, and even wept to think that they could ever hate the poor, weak being sleeping silently in the grave before them. Such would be our feeling if we seriously reflected that all men are mortal as well as ourselves. It would produce a brotherhood of feeling towards all around us, and the bitterest hatred would soften into compassion and love, when we remembered our common origin, our common misfortunes, and our common destiny.

IV. Let us learn from the shortness of life to live for eternity. This world is not worth living for. We look not at the things which are seen, but at the things which are not seen. For the things which are seen are temporal; but the things which are not seen are eternal. We boast of our superiority to the brutes that perish, but many live very much like them. They eat, drink, build houses, and seek to gratify the senses, and leave out of view their future destiny. The great mass of mankind live with no thought of God or immortality, of heaven or hell, and of those unseen realities which lie around them on every side, and fill up the eternity which is just before them. Looking at the things which are seen and temporal, men extend their knowledge in every direction, and their dominion over nature; but every such extension of knowledge and dominion, without the Gospel, only makes the world worse and man more wretched. The only remedy is to look forward to the future, and to prepare for eternity.

Things which are seen are temporal, transitory, and evanescent. Man belongs to two worlds; one visible, tangible, palpable to all the senses, the other spiritual and eternal. By the body he is allied to the grass, to the flowers, to the forest, the animals, the very dust beneath his feet. By the soul he is allied to God and angels. God only and the soul are permanent and enduring. The grass withers, the flower fades, the forest dies. Man builds houses, and they crumble; rears families, and they perish. Great cities and empires live in ruins as memorials of decay. The very names of their builders and founders have perished. Man may build for himself the lofty mausoleum, deep-grave his name in marble or in brass, lift the graceful shaft till it pierces the sky, and place his statue on the summit. Yet shall his name perish from the memory of men, and the marble crumble as surely as his body crumbles in the dust. Nay, all the works of man's prowess and genius, the mountains and oceans, and the great globe itself, shall be dissolved, the elements shall melt with fervent heat, and the very heavens shall be rolled together as a scroll, and pass away, "But thou, O Lord, in the beginning hast laid the foundation of the earth; and the heavens are the work of thy hand. They shall perish, but thou shalt endure; and they all shall wax old as doth a garment; and as a vesture shalt thou change them, and they shall be changed; but thou art the same, and thy years shall have no end."

Consider, then, the unutterable folly, the strange and mad insanity of looking only at things which are seen and temporal, to the neglect of unseen and eternal realities of God and eternity. Suppose you dwelt on some narrow, barren, ill-watered spot, in a wretched hovel, and knew you had a broad and imperial domain elsewhere, a rich inheritance, a princely estate, reserved especially for you, and secured by a title-deed, where perpetual spring reigned, with perennial gushing streams, and fruitful fields, and fragrant flowers. Suppose that one after another of your dearest kindred and friends had gone to that inheritance before you, and were waiting there to receive and welcome you. Suppose that, in departing, they had caught a glimpse of its glories, and spoken in raptures of them—had seen cherub forms inviting you to come, and heard cherub voices of welcome there. Suppose that in favored hours, when the air was clear and the sun was bright, you had yourself caught some glimpses of its spires and walls and mountain-tops, had inhaled stray breezes, and even drunk of the waters flowing from that land. Suppose that it lay just beyond a stream not far away, directly in your path, and that you might reach it to-morrow, and enter upon the full fruition of its blessedness and glory ; and yet you give all your thoughts, your pursuits, your time, your affections to that wretched hovel and barren spot in which you dwell. This would give but a faint delineation of the folly and madness of those who are neglecting things unseen and eternal, for those which are present and temporal—who are preferring earth to heaven, time to eternity, and the mere gratification of the senses to the grand realities of God and the soul.

XX.

DOES GOD ALWAYS PUNISH SIN?

ECCL. ix. 3.—"There is one event unto all." ECCL. viii. 14.—"There is a vanity which is done upon the earth, and there be just men, unto whom it happeneth according to the work of the wicked: again there be wicked men to whom it happeneth according to the work of the righteous."

THESE words were spoken by Solomon in the hour of his temptation and unbelief. How different his feelings when, enlightened from on high, he could exclaim, "The path of the just is as the shining light, which shineth more and more unto the perfect day;" and again, "Wisdom's ways are ways of pleasantness, and all her paths are peace;" and again, "The fear of the Lord is the beginning of wisdom, and the knowledge of the Holy is understanding;" and in the close of this very book, "Let us hear the conclusion of the whole matter. Fear God and keep his commandments, for this is the whole duty of man." Yet when left in his own strength, to wrestle with the powers of darkness, and the corruptions of his own fallen nature, there was many an hour of bitter anguish, and this book of Ecclesiastes is the perfect picture of just such a mind, perplexed, bewildered, maddened even to desperation. "Therefore I hated life;" "yea, I hated all the labor I had taken under the sun." Again, "I went about to despair of all the labor which I took under the sun." He had gone to all the sources of worldly enjoyment, and found them broken cisterns, no living waters in them to slack the thirst of an immortal spirit. He tries the pleasures of sense and the pleasures of the understanding, and turns in disgust and satiety from both; they are "all vanity." He turns to society for relief, and tries the friendship of man, but there finds only ingratitude and treachery; to the love of woman, and cries out in his agony, "I find bitterer than death" the fruits of such companionship. He turns to the world without, and seeks to forget himself in his sympathy with others, and everywhere injustice, oppression, violence meet him; here he finds the same impenetrable darkness, chaotic confusion, unfathomable mystery of sin and suffering. "Moreover I saw under the sun the place of judgment, that wickedness was there." "I beheld the tears of the oppressed, and they had no comforter, and on the side of their oppressors was *power*." And he cries it is better never to have been born, "than to have seen the evil work that is done under the sun." Forgetting the gentle wisdom of his father David, whose feet had well-nigh slipped under the same temptations; forgetting that final judgment, where oppressors and oppressed shall stand together at the bar of God, and those retributions of eternity where all the wrongs of time shall be rectified; he leaps impetuously to the fearful conclusion, that there is no divine order, no supreme law on earth, no virtue or vice, right or wrong; "that man hath no pre-eminence above the beast;" that there is no better thing under the sun, than to "eat, drink, and be merry." How doth God know? Is there knowledge in the Most High?

Now, why have we this record of a conflict so terrible, the picture of a soul so tossed by storms? and why is this record placed amongst the inspired writings of the sacred Scriptures? Is it not for our instruction? Because we have the same fallen nature, the same subtle tempter, and the same practical atheism, not so distinctly expressed, but vaguely felt, and tending practically to the same sad and terrible conclusion, which emboldens men in sin, and hardens them in impenitence, and leads them to the conclusion—let us eat, drink, and be merry, for to-morrow we die.

Now, in opposition to all this, we have endeavored to show that there is a visible government of God, even here on earth —a government exercised over an apostate race, and a rebel world; a holy law which reaches the proudest rebel, lays hold of every particle of body, and each wicked passion of the soul, and makes him his own tormentor. Every suffering is punishment for sin, and over this whole wide scene of sin and sorrow may we as distinctly see the hand of God inflicting punishment on sin, and hear the voice of God denouncing judgment on the sinner, as if sentence were written in letters of light over the sky, or announced audibly from heaven. We have referred to instances where sin the most flagrant was followed by punishment swift, sure, and terrible; in which this truth is so clear and startling, that it cannot be denied or overlooked.

We visited those dark abodes of wretchedness and crime, dark, damp cellars and dismal garrets, where the outcast population of our large cities are gathered nightly for pleasure or ghastly rest; where human beings of every age and sex are huddled promiscuously together, and without decency or sense of shame; the very air reeks with pollution; and as we gazed on that sweltering mass of physical disease and moral putrefaction, we turned away in loathing and horror, and exclaimed, "The way of the transgressor is hard." "Holy art thou, Lord God Almighty; just and true are all thy ways, O King of saints!" We pointed to the crowded wards of some immense hospital, where friendless, homeless, houseless wanderers, victims and slaves of sin, were welcomed by Christian love, with every human remedy that could alleviate their self-inflicted ruin, where each countenance of wan despair, each shriek of delirious horror, each curse of blasphemy and hopeless cry for mercy, is but the voice of God's avenging justice, proclaiming the penalty of violated law. We spoke of the evils of intemperance, with all its countless horrors; so gigantic in its proportions, that it overshadows all the land; so universal, that there is not a family connection, however proud or pure, not a station so exalted or so hallowed, scarce a domestic circle so sacred that it has not penetrated, and made the noblest, brightest, dearest, best-loved—the father, son, brother—the orator, statesman, poet—victims of the fell destroyer. We spoke of war with its blood and carnage, havoc and devastation, with its millions of men in Christian lands at this moment armed and trained for mutual butchery; its millions of treasure, wrung from the abundance of the rich, and the penury of the poor, for this horrid service, and at least one half as much more destroyed in wanton fury; while the wail of the nation's anguish rises from ten thousand desolated homes, and gaunt famine follows in the track, and pestilence hovers in the air, and those the sword has spared fall, amid keener agonies and longer tortures, beneath a deadlier and more inexorable foe. Now, as we gaze upon these scenes of accumulated horror, remember sin has produced it all, and as human society moves on nearer and nearer to its destined consummation, and all the elements of good and evil gather to the last great conflict and triumph of right, we can trace the gory footsteps of the great enemy of God and man as he stamps on the desolated earth, and feel his fiery breath as he kindles these demon passions. Were these evil passions all allayed, licentiousness, intemperance, and war abolished, the wretchedness would disappear. Those millions would be devoted to bless and not to curse; to the glory of God and the good of man. The Gospel would be sent to every heathen nation; ships would be freighted with the message of salvation; the church and school-house would spring up in every neighborhood; every orphan and widow would be clothed and educated; the land would be dotted with flourishing villages, quiet hamlets, peaceful cottages; and the whole emancipated earth would rejoice, like the garden of the Lord, beneath the smile of the reconciled Father; "The mountains would shout, and the little hills rejoice on every side."

Let universal love reign, love to God and love to man, and heaven descends to earth; let sin reign, and hell is already begun.

What say you? Do you blame the holiness of God? Shall we not rather say that sin is exceeding sinful; that it is that loathsome, execrable, accursed thing God hates? Were it embodied before you to-day, in some form of horror, reeking with blood, revelling in murder, feasting on human misery, gloating over the desolation it had made, still insatiate, remorseless, whetting its glutted appetite for other victims, like hell and the grave, never saying, "It is enough," but preparing for other generations, and for all coming time, for your children and your children's children, the same seductive arts of treachery and lies, to allure them into its foul embrace, and mock them in their misery—would you not rise together as one man, and say, Let us leave business, pleasure, home; let us renounce ease, comfort, gain; and go forth at once to exterminate the monster, with his hellish brood, from the face of the earth which he has blackened and crushed by his ruthless tyranny? Then commence at once; expel him from thine own bosom,—

"Rise, touched with gratitude divine,
Turn out his enemy and thine,
That soul-destroying monster, sin,
And let the heavenly Stranger in.

But will he prove a Friend indeed?
He will: the very Friend you need;
The Friend of sinners—yes, 'tis He,
With garments dyed on Calvary."

But war is not by far the worst of human evils. It is often the bitter and terrible remedy for evils worse than itself—the surgeon's knife and cautery which extirpates the malady, and is always the symptom and result of inward desperate disease. "From whence come wars and fightings among you? Come they not hence, even of your lusts that war in your members?" Even in prosperous and peaceful times the festering canker eats at the heart of society itself, and breaks out with greater or less malignity on the surface—in gibes, taunts, scorn, defiance, cold suspicion, in sly innuendo, in whispered slander, in open denunciation, in imperative will, brooking no opposition, tolerating no dissent from its opinions. Neighbor is separated from neighbor, friend from friend, brother from brother, sisters who have lain on each other's bosom, clasped in each other's arms, amidst the sweet dreams of innocence—their children the veriest foes. Sin enters the domestic circle, and mark its havoc there—anger between husband and wife, the hasty remark, the quick, fiery reply, mutual exasperation, moody silence, smouldering fires covered, not quenched. The children catch the spirit and follow the example. Rebellion against God becomes filial disobedience; order, subordination, and love are gone. They are allies against all the world, and enemies to each other. Recklessness follows indifference; honorable names are tarnished; patrimonial estates are wasted.

The nearer we approach the seat of all this evil, the deeper we penetrate into the mysteries of the human heart, the minuter our scrutiny into the working of the machinery within, the clearer are the evidences of the awful holiness of God in inflicting punishment on sin. There is not a fibre of the body he cannot reach by his power; not a passion of the soul he cannot make the instrument of his righteous vengeance. There is not an evil passion which is not its own avenger; not a right affection which is not its own sweet, abundant, delicious reward. As the adder in its fury strikes its fangs into its own body, and swells and bursts and dies with the poison it nourished; so there is not an evil passion but inflicts its first vengeance upon the bosom that nourished it. The first distillation of bitterness is shed in the heart itself. That glare of hatred and defiance answered back, kindles new hatred. We speak not of violence and the injury it may produce, nor of regrets for the past or consequences in the future; but of that inherent bitterness which belongs to every such feeling. Of two men who hate each other, there is no question that he who hates most bitterly is most miserable; while each affection is not only a blessing to others, but to itself. Each wish of good, before reaching its object, has already shed its distillation of joy over your own soul. Each look or act of gentle sympathy or benevolence has awakened a correspondent feeling in another, and, reflected, sheds a sunny radiance over your own soul; and in this interchange of kindness, he who is first and kindest in his love is most happy. In this sense, too, is it more blessed to give than to receive. How much of heaven is there in mutual regard; of hell in mutual detestation!

Could there be a more authoritative or more terrible declaration of God's abhorrence of sin, and determination to punish it, than when he thus follows it into the very soul, and makes it inflict punishment on itself? But it does not terminate here. The billows toss long after the storm subsides. The dark passions leave their shadows on the soul, send their remorse through life. To the bad man and the good, nothing is the same. No scene in nature is the same to them. Their enjoyment in the relations of life, family, friends, wife, children, of their very food, is different. "The candle of the Lord shineth upon the tabernacles of the righteous."

The curse of God resteth on the wicked. In the light that shines from heaven, all things assume a new aspect, are sweeter, nobler, holier, more *sacred.* For sin is the *disease* of the soul; holiness is its life and health. The nameless joy of the very young, the buoyancy of the convalescent, what are they? Every thing to them overflows with joy. We cannot analyze it. Every sense, every faculty, every gland, sends its own distillation of enjoyment. So to the good man, all, *all* is sweeter; but chiefly because conscience is at peace with God. This indwelling conscience is the most direct and terrible evidence of God's primitive government. Here, God speaks directly to the man's inmost soul; tells him that suffering is punishment of sin, and that "it is right;" the law within testifies to the Lawgiver above. It speaks in the name of God and with the authority of God. It has been well called the vicegerent of God; it tells him of the justice of God, and points to the bar of God. We speak not for those who deny or have stifled conscience. If so, your misfortune is great; your sin is great. Oh, cherish conscience. It is the great fact of our being. It must be supreme over all the other faculties. Man may stifle, crush it; but it will rise again. It may be betrayed by treachery, deceived by falsehood, lulled by opiates, bewildered by sophistry. It is not destroyed. As the lion, so is conscience. The lion roars; conscience speaks; and every faculty feels its power. Even those who defy it must at last feel its power.

How good is God to endow us with a conscience—the interpreter of his law; the representative of his presence; following us from childhood on; warning, whispering, rebuking, commanding us.

How awful, too! a Sinai in each soul; a voice of God; a tribunal of God; and in the last day the verdict will be found in conscience. Oh, cherish it; listen to its lowest whispers; have it sprinkled with the blood of Christ; have it enlightened by the word of God; have it quick and sensitive to every call of duty.

[To the foregoing discourse, which was evidently left unfinished, we subjoin the following strikingly pertinent passage from another manuscript.—ED.]

We have seen, in Peter, how far a man may go in sin and yet be saved. We see, in Judas, how far a man may go in religion and yet be lost. In the one case, we see how near a man may come to the gates of heaven, and yet be cast down to hell; in the other, how far one may wander from God, how near to the verge of perdition, and yet be plucked as a brand from everlasting burning. In Peter, we see how a single infirmity, self-confidence, may leave the soul an easy prey to the powers of darkness, lead to sins which we shudder to contemplate, and cast a shadow over life. In Judas, we see how a single absorbing passion, silently, perhaps unconsciously, indulged for years, may subordinate at last all the powers of the soul, and lead to the basest treachery, the blackest ingratitude, the most atrocious crimes—to irretrievable ruin, to madness, suicide, eternal death. In Peter, we see the nature of true repentance, tears of genuine sorrow for sin flowing from a heart melted by the love of the Redeemer, and bowed in meek humility, in conscious unworthiness, and adoring wonder, in the presence of that abused and yet forgiving love. He had been "forgiven much, therefore he loved much." In Judas, we see the sorrow of the world which worketh death, the horrors of remorse, the terrors of a guilty conscience, the anguish of a soul wrapt in the blackness of despair, and hardened by a sense of sin unpardoned and divine justice unappeased. In the one, we see the sweetness of those penitential tears, the joys of pardoned sin, and the assured sense of reconciliation with God; the bounding alacrity, conscious strength, exulting courage, with which man goes forth to toils and dangers. The terror and dismay, the self-abhorrence and detestation, the lurid light flashing in upon the soul, the settled gloom, the horror of deep darkness that shrouds it, the delirious anguish wildly hurrying it on to the last extremity of guilt, the traitor's doom, and the traitor's damnation, what tongue can tell?

XXI.

THE RELIGION OF THE BIBLE NOT OPPOSED TO REASON.

ISAIAH i. 18.—"Come now, and let us reason together, saith the Lord." See 1 Sam. xii. 7. Acts xvii. 2, 24, 25. Rom. xii. 1.

ON each side of the arched gateway that leads to some noble castle, or opens upon some ancient city, may often be seen, crouching as if in mutual hostility and defiance, the grim and threatening figures of two fierce beasts of prey. Now, we have often figured to ourselves the entrance to the path of truth as thus beset, on either side, by horrid monsters; and happy is that man who so wisely selects his middle path as to pass unharmed by either. The gate of eternal life is strait; and there sits gloomy superstition, darkly bidding away from her all the enjoyments of life and spreading her funeral pall over all earthly objects; and there, on the other side, haughty scepticism, drawing a veil of blackness over all our brightest expectations, blotting out the very sun from the heaven of our hopes. Religion is a reasonable service; yet there sits fierce fanaticism, with fire and faggot, to forbid the exercise of reason; and there sits a fashionable false philosophy, with an altar for her worship, and requiring all to bow down to her as a goddess. There, too, is stupid ignorance depreciating all reasoning, and limiting all human knowledge and inquiry to the narrow boundaries of its own acquirements. And there an imaginary learning, a science falsely so called, flippant, self-conceited, exaggerates her exploits beyond all truth, and claims the whole universe as the field of her bold and boundless conquests. It will be at once our duty, wisdom, and happiness, to pursue our own calm and quiet path, equally removed from these opposing errors; and while we gratefully receive, diligently improve, and conscientiously exercise the reason God has given us, let us remember its office, its real limits, and appropriate exercise. Let us consider,

1st. The duty of exercising and cultivating our reason; and,

2d. Its extent, its limits, and its office.

I. To those in whose vocabulary piety and absurdity are convertible terms—who have always considered reason and religion as antagonist powers, arrayed in deadly conflict against each other—whose motto is, "that devotion ends where inquiry begins"—it may sound like some strange announcement when we say, that of all the books in the world the Bible most frequently inculcates, most peremptorily commands, the exercise of reason. We enter here into no minute analysis of the human mind, no nice and metaphysical distinctions between the various faculties of our intellectual nature. Every man knows he is a complex being—a body and a soul. Now, by reason in its largest sense, we mean all that distinguishes man from the animals around him—his whole intellect, as distinguished from his physical powers—the living principle within him that thinks, feels, loves and hates, hopes and fears, observes and judges, compares, reasons, and decides—that can know God and love him, understand his will and obey it; and, according to its obedience or disobedience, can measure out to itself or others approbation or censure.

We pause not to answer technical objections that might be urged. We are satisfied that this wide acceptation of the term reason is justified, not only by the language of familiar conversation, but by the usage of the best writers in our tongue, and that in the earlier stages of all language, before the invention of our nicer distinctions, it must have been universally prevalent. And now, returning to our first remark, we say that the Bible not only allows, but encourages; not only encourages, but commands, the exercise of our rational powers. Nay, this is the principal and avowed design of the

Bible; and if stricken from its pages, little would be left behind to recall man to a sense of the superiority and dignity of his rational and immortal powers; to point out their origin, their nature, their exalted destiny; to heal the diseases that enfeeble and endanger, knock off the shackles that fetter, and call forth all their energies to their noblest exercise and largest development. What new and untrodden fields of thought does it open to our aspiring powers, high as heaven, boundless as infinity; and how does it allure us to the lofty contemplation, by all that could stimulate the curiosity or arouse the imagination, and strain to their utmost all the capacities of thought and feeling! By every method does it aim to arouse us to the exercise of our reason, by precept, by example, by expostulation. If the appetites and passions are to be controlled, it is that the mind may be free for its own high employments. If the flesh is to be mortified, it is that the spirit may breathe a new life. If the outer man is to be subjugated, it is that the inner man, the nobler and immortal part, may walk forth rejoicing in the freedom of its untrammeled powers. The great and ever-recurring charge against sinners is that, immersed in sensuality, absorbed in what is visible and sensible, all the higher attributes and powers of their nature are palsied; they have no relish for rational pleasures, no capacity for their appropriate employment. It is charged against the ungodly, that "he doth not regard the works of the Lord, nor consider the operations of his hand;" and in the third verse of this chapter, the complaint against the Jews is, "Israel doth not know, my people doth not consider;" and then comes the invitation of our text, "Come, and let us reason together." Rouse up from your stupid lethargy; lay aside for a moment your sensuality, your frivolity, your self-indulgence; let reason act her part, let your immortal nature, so long abused, enslaved, debased, at length speak out; and let religion then be derided as a visionary thing, if the revelation from within answer not to the revelation from without, if reason and conscience speak and add not confirmation strong to the claims of God on your affection and obedience. The prophet Samuel, 1 Samuel xii. 7, cries out to the rebel Jews, "Stand still that I may *reason* with you before the Lord."

Indeed, it is remarkable how exclusively all the appeals of the Bible are directed to the higher powers of our nature. The prophets demonstrated by conclusive reasoning the folly of the idolatry and rebellion of the Jews. St. Paul *reasoned* with the Jews at a single place, three Sabbath days, from their Scriptures, proving that Jesus was the Christ. Acts xvii. 2. It was when he reasoned of "temperance, righteousness, and judgment to come," that Felix trembled. Nay, this we are told was his usual manner, and his Epistle to the Romans still exists, an unrivaled monument of logical skill and power, where every thought and sentence, and almost word, is knit together in strong and compact order, like some Macedonian phalanx, firm, impenetrable, shield locked in shield, shoulder braced against shoulder. And have you not observed how skillfully our Saviour would refute the Jew from his own Scriptures, and how for the admirer of Nature and rejecter of Revelation he was always ready with some illustration, fresh, apposite, beautiful, forcible, of the doctrine he inculcated—how Nature seemed to teem with illustrations and argument, and how the flowers of the valley, the trees of the forest, the birds of the air, and the clouds of the sky, would furnish some bold analogy, some mild reproof, some soothing consolation, some exercise for the intellect and the heart, some food for the souls around him? Nay, so far is reason from being represented, in the Bible, as hostile to religion, that they are ever considered as inseparable companions. Reason is the constant attendant of religion—religion the perfection of reason. Sin is only another name for folly. Religion, the synonym of wisdom, the highest wisdom, the best, purest, truest reason, aims to attain the greatest, noblest, happiest ends by the best means; looks onward and upward with widest glance to the greatest, most enduring and important results.

And here allow me one passing remark. Religion is the

highest reason, and individuals and communities, advancing in religion, are most advanced in wisdom. Hence you have never seen an individual really converted, however ignorant, or frivolous, or thoughtless, who did not immediately advance in intelligence and rationality. Among serious Christians I have never seen a vacant, senseless countenance. Again, in your efforts to advance religion, in future life, do not depend on, nor be satisfied with, sudden bursts of transient excitement. Be assured, religion is wisdom—is deep, serious, sober, calm, continued thoughtfulness. Its foundation is serious thought, solid instruction. None but a thinking, intelligent community, can long continue a truly Christian community. Again, you, who expect not to preach the Gospel, but desire to advance your country's happiness, remember that the surest foundations of a nation's welfare are laid in the depths of a nation's piety. Ignorance and vice are the bane of republics; for these religion is the only remedy. In all civilized nations she has been the pioneer of knowledge, the steady ally of freedom. It is the only principle of sufficient diffusiveness and power to pervade all classes of a wide community, to counteract the tendencies of corruption and decay inherent in every human society, and to wake up all its members to the conscious dignity of rational existence, and produce that real, practical equality without which our theories are vain. And it cannot be otherwise. If religion denounce our reason, then reason must denounce religion; and to what shall she make her appeal, to whom present her credentials, who shall examine her evidences, who shall understand her doctrines, who interpret her language, but the same reason whose exercise she is supposed to forbid? No, it cannot be. The God of nature is God of grace, the God of revelation is God of reason too. He is the God of harmony, and cannot so have mingled the elements of discord in our being, that there shall be a contradiction between the revelation from without and the revelation from within us. But, let us not deceive ourselves; there may be an apparent contradiction where there is no real one. Your reason may be enfeebled or diseased for want of healthful exercise and nourishment, blinded by prejudice, perverted by passion, stupefied, debased, brutalized by sensual indulgence. Vanity may betray; sophistry bewilder; ignorance mislead; and many of those high themes of which revelation treats, may stretch onward into a region where reason cannot follow, where she can neither affirm nor deny, but must await in silence the communication of a higher wisdom. And this leads us to inquire, in the second place,

II. What is the appropriate employment of reason in matters of religion? And here, as on the former branch of the subject, we claim no peculiar exemption for religion from the keenest scrutiny of reason. We answer fearlessly, that here her office is the same as on any other subject. The method of investigation, and the laws which regulate her inquiries, are precisely the same. They are founded in the nature of the human mind, and do not vary with the subjects to which they are applied. And what is it that the intellect of man can accomplish—what the office of reason, in any department of human inquiry? It is simply and solely this—to observe facts, to collect and arrange them, to notice their points of resemblance and difference, to classify them according to these observed relations, to give them names, and to announce these as the laws or principles of the science. According to this view, now universally adopted, man is the creator of nothing; he is only an observer, a collector, an arranger of facts. He does not stand forth as Nature's master, to square her phenomena according to his preconceived opinion or *a priori* theories, but sits as a learner at her feet, and listens to her awful revelations. He stands in the great temple of nature, to observe her varying aspects, and record them for his instruction; to listen to her varied voices—the interpreter of her language the high-priest of Nature, not the Lord.

There was once a different view of the subject, and a different method. Men built up their gorgeous systems, and wove fine-spun theories, from materials their own brains had supplied; and created a universe of their own, far different from that which God made. From the universal principles of reason, and the nature of things, they derived all truth and science. Such were the systems of alchemy, astronomy, and mental philosophy, before the days of Bacon; but these are long since exploded. Now, the philosophy of modern times and of common sense has taught us that man knows nothing except as he has learned it. There are no materials of knowledge, or prototypes of truth, laid up in his reason. But facts, learned from his own observation, or the testimony of others, variously modified, combined, and classified, form the whole structure of his knowledge.

We hope you are not wearied by this inquiry, to which our answer and conclusion must be, that the office of reason, in any science, is not to form its preconceived theories, and then reject or bend the facts; but simply to investigate the truth of facts, receiving each on its own appropriate evidence. Such is the modesty of true science. Such are the principles of all philosophical investigations. And such is the proper method of procedure in the investigation of religion. The field of inquiry is wide enough. When a system of natural science is presented, you do not reject it as inconsistent with your reason, but you ask for the facts. When these are presented, you demand the evidence for their truth. This is brought forward. You examine its separate parts—their mutual agreement—their united strength, and you yield or withhold your assent, as the preponderance of evidence may be. Are the facts conclusive? the testimony convincing? then there may be much that is mysterious, even inexplicable, in the case, and irreconcilable with your previous notions; yet you do not reject—do not even doubt its truth (that is founded on its own evidence), but you strive to remove the difficulty, reconcile the apparent contradiction; and if you fail at last, you remember your own ignorance, and determine to persevere in your inquiries, assured that while your knowledge is limited and your reasonings are fallible, facts can never deceive you, nor really contradict each other. To the doctrine of natural philosophy, that all bodies are under the influence of gravitation, it may be objected that feathers rise. To the doctrine that bodies put in motion move on forever in a straight line, it may be objected that a stone, or even a common ball, falls in a curve-line. You remember, the countryman objected to the earth's revolving around the sun, that he saw the sun every day revolving around the earth, with his own eyes. These objections are obvious, and to ignorant men appear conclusive; yet, fully understood, they only confirm more fully the several truths. You do not stop at the objection, but examine farther. One of the demonstrations of mathematics is, that two lines may approach forever and never meet. We do not reject the demonstrations, but say it carries us into a region of infinities, where we cannot follow—into subjects beyond the limits of human reason; yet its practical applications are important, and truths deduced from it most valuable.

Now, we wish you to employ, in the department of religious inquiry, the same methods of investigation which have produced such beneficial results in their application to physical science; to receive facts on their appropriate evidence; never to reject a well-supported fact, on account of objections founded, perhaps, in your ignorance; and when you get into the region of boundlessness and infinitude, to acknowledge the incompetence of your own faculties to grasp, to embrace, to wrestle with, objects of such transcendent greatness. Now, the religion of the Bible, like the astronomy of Newton, is founded on facts; and those facts you are allowed, nay, at the peril of your soul's salvation required, to investigate. It appeals to a magnificent scheme of prophecy, commencing from the fall of man, and extending in its mighty sweep, through all successive ages, down to the end of time. Is there such a scheme, or is there not? Was it predicted that "the sceptre should not depart from Judah till Shiloh came—that he should come during the second temple—the light of the Gentiles—and that to him should be the gathering of the people?" And has he come in the fullness of time? Did the Gentiles cast their idols away, and did their temples fall throughout the globe? And now is the crucified Jew worshiped as Lord of all in all civilized nations? Is Babylon fallen, the glory of the Chaldees' excellency—her proud walls levelled in the dust—her palaces the possession of owls and lizards, bitterns, and pools of water? Wild beasts of the desert howl there. The Arabian shepherd fears to pitch his tent there, and the curse of God is printed on the very dust of her ruins. Is Egypt—oppressor of God's people—the basest of the kingdoms? Is Tyre a bare rock for fishermen to spread nets? Is prophecy an epitome of history, written with a pen of brass upon the front of time? Is Jerusalem desolate? Has the plowshare swept over her—her people scattered for eighteen hundred years, the by-word and scoff of nations? Religion appeals to amazing miracles, performed by Christ, in the presence of his foes. Did they occur, or did they not? Did he raise Lazarus, or were the Jews deceived? Did he feed the five thousand with a few loaves of bread, or did they only dream so? Did he rise from the grave, or were his disciples ignorant of his person? Did they go forth with their lives in their hands, risking all, suffering all, losing all, to testify the story of his resurrection? Did thousands of the Jews and ten thousands of Gentiles believe their report? Did his religion spread in the face of power and prejudice and interest, till it covered the civilized world? These, and such facts as these, are worthy of your investigation. Their truth depends, not on any speculations or theories of yours, but on their own proper evidence. Examine for yourself, and put all history to the question.

And if the evidence be sufficient, and the facts be true, and we have indeed a revelation from God, about himself, his character and moral government, then what more has reason to do? Is it to lie down and sleep? No; the trump of God has sounded, Let it be wider awake than ever. Proportioned to the importance of the communication should be the intensity of our attention and the earnestness of our investigation. Reason has to do here what it does in every other department of thought. You question Nature, and, laying aside all your theories, you humbly receive the communications she may make. All your anxiety is, that you may understand her language aright. You question Revelation, and, renouncing all your cherished prejudices, you meekly listen to the instructions she affords. Man originates nothing—can originate nothing. In natural philosophy, he is the interpreter of Nature; in religion, the interpreter of revelation. This is not the abandonment, but the proper exercise, of reason. Nature and revelation are not opposed to each other, each being alike from God, each appealing alike to reason, and each alike demanding reason as its divinely constituted interpreter.

XXII.

CHRIST'S GRACIOUS INVITATION.

MATT. xi. 28.—"Come unto me all ye that labor and are heavy laden, and I will give you rest."

"UNTO you, O men, I call, and my voice is to the sons of men." Such is the voice of Divine wisdom in the book of Proverbs. It is in full harmony with our Saviour's gracious invitation in the text. It is a voice from heaven to earth—a loud voice, whose sound has gone forth to the ends of the world. It is the voice of authority, commanding us; of tender and condescending love, inviting us to come. Sin is an alienation and departure from God—a forsaking and wandering in enmity and rebellion farther and farther from God. But God has not forgotten to observe the wanderer. His eyes behold, his eyelids try the children of men. Looking down from his throne of exaltation upon his creatures, he sees them far away from the path of rectitude and allegiance, and going farther still, notwithstanding all his love and mercy.

Does he then leave us to ourselves? No, he sends forth a voice of warning, which, even at our distance, reaches us, and with authority commands us to return. The way of sin is foolish and dangerous. The voice of nature, of experience, of wisdom, of conscience, all have spoken, but spoken in vain. They are lost upon us and forgotten. Now the voice of God speaks with authority and power; and how good it is in God not to leave us to our ruin!

He issues his high command, "Come unto me." We have cast off his high authority; but we have not annihilated it. He still commands both in heaven and on earth; and it is a fearful thing to refuse obedience to him who speaks from heaven. The fool may say in his heart, "There is no God;" yet God reigns over him, over all creatures; his authority is independent of us and our acts. We may disobey him; but still he reigns. The danger of disobedience is vividly portrayed in the first chapter of the book of Proverbs, "Because I have called and ye refused; I have stretched out my hand and no man regarded; but ye have set at nought my counsel, and would none of my reproof; I also will laugh at your calamity; I will mock when your fear cometh; when your fear cometh as desolation, and your destruction as a whirlwind." We are still in his kingdom. Though far from him, we are not beyond the reach of his arm. His eye, his very presence encompasses us. For, says the psalmist, "If I ascend up into heaven thou art there; if I make my bed in hell, behold thou art there. If I take the wings of the morning, and dwell in the uttermost parts of the sea, even there shall thy hand lead me. If I say, surely the darkness shall cover me, even the night shall be light about me; the darkness and the light are both alike to thee." Let us then obey the voice that speaks from heaven, and say, "Lo, I come, I delight to do thy will, O God."

I. The invitation is to all. It is broad as the sea, free as the air, universal as the race. It comes from heaven to earth, from God to man, from the Saviour of sinners to the perishing. "God so loved the world that he gave his only begotten Son, that whosoever believeth in him should not perish, but have everlasting life." Christ died for sinners, the just for the unjust. He came to seek and to save that which was lost. The Gospel is likened to a great feast given by a rich man, to which all are freely invited. It is compared to a river of life. "Ho, every one that thirsteth, come ye to the waters, and he that hath no money, come ye, buy and eat; yea, come, buy wine and milk, without money and without price. Wherefore do ye spend money for that which is not bread, and your labor for that which satisfieth not? Hearken diligently unto me, and eat ye that which is good, and let your soul delight itself in fatness." And so the Saviour cried in the last day, that great day of the feast, saying, "If any man thirst, let him come unto me and drink." John vii. 37. And so it is written in the last book of the Bible, "The Spirit and the bride say, Come; and let him that heareth say, Come; and let him that is athirst come; and whosoever will, let him take the water of life freely." Prodigal son! far from thy father's house, arise and come; it is thy father's voice that calls thee, all love and tenderness and compassion, saying, Come to my house and heart, the provisions are all ready, and welcome shall greet thee here. Rebellious sinner! thou hast violated my law, despised my mercy, grieved my spirit; thou hast hardened thy heart, and stiffened thy neck; no love has softened, no wrath alarmed thee; no command, no invitation has influenced thee—but even to thee does my invitation extend; come unto me, ungrateful wanderer, come, and find life and peace. I have tried to bind thee to myself by ten thousand cords of mercy; thou hast burst them all, and gone to a fearful distance. I might well leave thee to perish in thy sins; but still do I pursue thee with commands and invitations. Across the dark and dreary gulf have I cast up a highway. Come, then, safely, boldly, and without delay; it is the king's highway.

From his own high and glorious throne did Christ come down to save us; let us then return and come to him. The invitation is urgent, and it is open to all. Come unto me, and I will give you rest. He is ready, waiting, willing to receive you, just as you are. Men usually send to another for help, but he calls you to himself, in order to give you help. He giveth liberally and upbraideth not. If earthly fathers desert and earthly friends fail you, then come to him, who is a friend that sticketh closer than a brother—come to him, the great Father, who will never leave nor forsake the soul that trusts in him. If temptation assail, or sickness distress; if persecutions arise, or storms of sorrow beat upon you, still come to him. He is high above your head, high as the heavens; yet he stoops to invite you. He is holy, and you are sinful, yet he condescends to invite you. He has long been neglected, yet he still invites. He has all the treasures of wisdom and goodness in his hands, and invites you to come and take of his benefits. Let no fear, no guilt, no ridicule deter you. Let no difficulty, no indolence delay you. Sit not still, but be up and doing. Resolve at once, if you have never before, saying, "I will arise and go to my father." Now is the accepted time; now is the day of your merciful visitation. Then delay not, but come humbly, penitently, prayerfully, submissively, earnestly; for your soul's salvation agonize to enter in. "For the kingdom of heaven suffereth violence, and the violent taketh it by force." But wherewithal shall I come? you may be ready to ask. Come in your nakedness and misery. Come without money and without price. No price is demanded of you; full atonement is already made; Jesus has paid it all—all the debt you owe. Come, then, at once, and freely—just as you are, without one plea, save that his blood has been shed for you, and you need his help. But, alas, some stop short on the way. They begin fairly, but reach not the point; they set out for the kingdom of heaven, but turn back. They are convicted of sin, but not converted. Almost persuaded to be Christians, they come to the strait gate, but finding it too strait, they refuse to enter in, and return again to the world.

II. Who are invited? The weary and heavy laden. The invitation is unlimited in its own nature; yet it is addressed especially to those who need it most, and are most apt to receive it. Hence the hungry and thirsty are invited. The very terms contain an argument. For the hungry, thirsty, weary, sinful, what can be better than food, drink, rest, and pardon? The invitation applies to all of us who are weary in our struggles after earthly good; and we are urged to come to him who is the source of all spiritual and heavenly blessings.

There was once an Eastern prince, the son of an illustrious father, who had been renowned alike for his virtues and his genius. That father had been successful both in peace and war. Brave in the field, prudent in the cabinet, at once an admired poet and a successful warrior, he was beloved at home and respected abroad. He had raised his people from an obscure and despised tribe to a prosperous and respected nation. The son of such a father, sitting on a throne thus established in the affections of the people and the respect of foreigners, this renowned prince was blessed with unusual prosperity and peace through his long reign. He was celebrated for the wisdom and the splendor of his court. His commerce extended to every known sea, and brought all foreign luxuries to his door. His native land was that of the olive, the pomegranate, and the vine, where the human passions were as luxuriant as the growth of the soil, and the means for their indulgence and gratification were fully equal to their desire. In this land of passion, on this throne of power, and with these means of indulgence, the favored son of fortune traveled the whole round of worldly pleasure. All that heart could crave or intellect could relish or sense enjoy was his. Now he pored over the page of wisdom; now he studied nature and wrote many volumes on her productions; and now he rejoiced in sensual pleasures. His court was the most voluptuous and gay; his equipages, the most splendid; his grounds, the most carefully and expensively adorned; his palaces, the most magnificent; his chariots, drawn by horses from Egypt; his gardens, redolent with the spices of Arabia; his halls, glittering with the gold of Ophir; while princes of other lands crowded to his court, to witness that wisdom of which fame spoke so loudly. Deep did he drink of every cup of pleasure; and in the ardor of his impetuous temperament, hotly did he pursue each object of his changeful desire. Now he labored intensely to accumulate and arrange the science of his age and country; and now he quaffed in maddening merriment the sparkling bowl. Now he tastefully arranged his princely pleasure-grounds, and now drank in the flattery of his obsequious court. And after thus trying all earthly pursuits, and drinking in all earthly pleasures, he turns in weariness away from them all, and in the book which records the valued results of this large experience, he gives us the conclusion of the whole matter, in one brief but significant sentence—"Vanity of vanities, all is vanity and vexation of spirit."

And who of us has not often felt, in his own wearied and jaded spirit, the sickening influence of this same conclusion? Who has not found, in his experience of life, the truth of this mournful but weighty utterance—that all the world can give is vanity and vexation of spirit? It cannot satisfy the soul nor give it rest. Behold the man so ardent in pursuit of wealth. How he wrestles and struggles for it. See how it becomes the subject of his daily thoughts and nightly aspirations. He has made gold his confidence, and fine gold his trust, and Mammon, the god of wealth, has become the god of his idolatry. He forms it not into an image; he builds no temple; he offers no sacrifice. This, indeed, is not necessary to constitute him an idolater; but his heart is the temple and the victim too. His idolatry is as real as if he made an idol, placed it in some conspicuous place, and morning and evening worshiped it—turning to his treasure as faithfully as the Jew to Jerusalem, or the Persian to the rising sun. How many of those who have devoted a long life, body and soul, to the accumulation of wealth, with every energy strung up to its intensest tension, and the strained sinews almost cracked by the effort, have felt at last that it was all vanity and vexation of spirit; that there are desires which wealth cannot satiate; wants which gold cannot supply; longings of our immortal nature which earthly riches cannot meet. How many have felt and confessed that they have spent their time for that which is not bread, and labored for that which satisfieth not. And how many, at last, would have been willing to exchange all that earth can give for the quiet and peaceful rest of the soul. "For what shall it profit a man if he gain the whole world and lose his own soul, or what shall a man give in exchange for his soul?"

Behold the man who is borne along on the full, fair breeze of popular applause, when deserted by his friends and slandered by his foes: how often, as the hot blood courses furiously through his veins, and his feverish frame sinks exhausted by over-excitement—how often does he curse the fickle populace, and bitterly denounce the corruption of the great! How often, when deserted, and misrepresented, and slandered by his fellow-men, does he mourn over that madness which sacrificed health, conscience, peace, everything, to popularity, and feel in his inmost soul that all is vanity and vexation of spirit! How gladly would he exchange all past triumphs and future prospects for that peace which has now departed from him, perhaps forever!

Thus might we pass from one worldly pursuit to another, and show that, when supremely valued, they are vanity and vexation of spirit. There is no peace, saith the Lord, to the wicked; but they are like the troubled sea when it cannot rest, whose waters cast up mire and dirt. See that white foam riding on the surface, that dark sediment rolled up from the bottom, both dashing against the strand: even such is the tempest of stormy and ungovernable human passions. It is like the dark billows of the ocean, heaved upward by the storm, now rising, towering, dashing onward in their fury, now swelling, boiling, curling from beneath, careless of all human interests, wrecking all human hopes, and engulfing in their wild roar all that is loveliest and dearest to human kind. Thus insatiable, impetuous, ungovernable, destructive, are the appetites of the wicked. For this war of nature's elements in the soul there is but one remedy—but one power on earth that can say, Peace, be still, and there shall be a calm. That remedy, that power, is found alone in the Gospel of Christ.

III. What then is the duty of every weary and heavy-laden soul? It is simple, but it is urgent. Take my yoke upon you, and learn of me; for my yoke is easy and my burden is light. It is good for man that he bear this yoke in his youth. It is far different from that which is imposed by Satan and the world. The yoke of sin is galling; its bondage is hard and cruel; its demands are ever increasing; every gratification of sinful passion only inflames desire, makes the pleasure less and less, and never says, It is enough. Sin and the world cry, Give, give, and every hour brings a new demand, until the mind and body, overstrained, become enfeebled and worn out in the pursuit of things that perish in the using.

Sin has introduced a strange conflict into the mind of man,

between his passions and his reason and conscience—the inward elements dashing and warring against each other. Conceive, if you can, of a living being so strangely constituted that all its parts are hostile to each other, every muscle playing against every other muscle; every nerve jarring against every other nerve—bones, joints, tendons, all waging perpetual war. This is the condition of man without the gospel. All inward harmony is gone. Reason and conscience grasp and strive to hold the reins; but passion dashes furiously and recklessly on. The conflict rages till conscience is destroyed, reason loses its power, and the man becomes a brute or demon. Such is the work of sin, when sin is left to run its course, unchecked by any influences of truth and virtue. Who would not wish for rescue, and for rest, from this turmoil of his own natural elements, this war of sinful appetites and passions? Who would not desire some remedy or antidote for the ruin which sin has introduced into the soul? Where then shall the soul, burdened with conscious guilt, find rest and peace?

IV. The answer can be found only in Christ. I will give you rest. Come unto me, for I am meek and lowly in heart, and ye shall find rest unto your souls. I will give true rest unto the soul, perfect rest to the agitated passions. Christ speaks, and there is a great calm; the "possessed" is in his right mind; the oil of grace is on the waters. How beautiful the sea, when the storm is over and the waters at rest—the moonbeams reposing softly on its deep bosom, or the morning sun sparkling in the light waves that play on its surface. Even so is the tranquilized spirit—tranquil on its surface, with heaven reflected in its depths. The unsettled affections, once straying from object to object, uneasy and dissatisfied, are now fixed on God. "Great peace have they, they that love thy law," says the psalmist. There is rest to the conscience, that peace of God which passeth all understanding. "Peace I leave with you," says Christ; "my peace I give unto you, not as the world giveth, give I unto you." There is rest from sin and temptation. It is begun now, but perfected in glory.

This is that eternal rest which remains for the people of God, rest from all that annoyed us here below, rest in the bosom of our God. What glorious rest! Come unto me, and you shall obtain it.

Now, is not this rest needed by all? There lives not a man who is always free from inward conflict. It may seem to be transitory; but it is nevertheless there, deep and abiding in the soul. It is in this condition of disquiet and unrest that the Saviour's invitation comes to us, and his promise meets our conscious wants. Come unto me, and I will give you rest. It is thus that he speaks to the deepest wants of our nature, and has provided relief from the crushing and cruel bondage of sin and Satan. But you must hunger and thirst after righteousness before you can be filled; you must feel the dreadful disease of your nature before the physician can heal; you must be convicted of your sin before you can be pardoned and made holy; you must feel the burden before you can desire or enjoy rest. This is the order of nature and of grace—appetite before food. All provisions are for corresponding desires. Hence all good men have been weary and heavy laden with their sins, before they came to Christ for rest. David found it so; the publican found it so; the prodigal son found it so; and so must it be with us.

XXIII.

THE NECESSITY OF REGENERATION.

JOHN iii. 3.—"Jesus answered and said unto him, Verily, verily, I say unto thee, Except a man be born again he cannot see the kingdom of God."

GOD is a spirit. His government is spiritual, his service spiritual; and they that worship him, must worship him in spirit and in truth. His law is spiritual, exceedingly broad, reaching the thoughts and intents of the heart. The kingdom of heaven is a spiritual kingdom; its employments and pleasures are all spiritual; its inhabitants are holy and happy spirits who, from their creation, have been pure intelligences, or who, once manacled in clay, have burst their fetters and risen to refined and spiritual enjoyments above. Now, we might conclude clearly from the character of God, and from his law and kingdom, that the nature of our preparation for heaven would be, in some measure, correspondent to the nature of the kingdom to be prepared for us. The birth here spoken of is a spiritual birth, an internal change, not an outward act or condition. But in the present age of free and bold inquiry, keen and searching scrutiny, when all opinions are questioned, all points assailed, we are forced to go back again to first principles; examine afresh questions which were settled years ago; and lay anew the foundations of our faith. Such questions are before us to-day, as to the nature of the new birth spoken of in the text, as a necessary preparation for heaven.

In the dark ages of Popery a dreamy mysticism prevailed, which saw strange mysteries in the sacrament. To the Lord's supper and baptism it attributed strange efficacy, instead of seeing a wise adaptation to the character of man, addressing the mind through the senses. Hence bread and wine blessed by the priest assumed new sacredness, acquired new qualities, and wrought strange wonders by a secret power; while the holy water of baptism, with virtue scarcely less amazing, wrought prodigies scarcely less miraculous. And in all ages and in all countries, Jewish, Papal, Pagan, Protestant—from the formal Pharisee to the fanatical Anabaptist; from the pilgrim to Jerusalem or Mecca, and the self-immolator at the car of Juggernaut, to the comfortable citizen who takes his easy walk or pleasant ride to the spacious church, to hear a silken sermon, on velvet cushions; from the offerer of sacrifices to the offerer of prayers; from him who washes away sin with the blood that streams from his lacerated body, to him that washes it away with flowing water—has been exhibited the same universal tendency, to substitute some outward service for the religion of the heart. Now we must be permitted to express our unfeigned astonishment; not that this is indulged as a feeling natural to the human heart, but that, in an enlightened age, in a Protestant nation, it should be avowed as a sentiment, expressed in words, formed into a system, urged as an article of faith, and boldly vindicated as a thing that may challenge investigation.

We say, it is astonishing that this should be done in a Protestant nation; because it was on this doctrine of spiritual religion—the religion of the heart as opposed to outward forms, that the great battle of the Reformation was fought; as Sir James Mackintosh well observes. This was the fundamental principle of all Protestantism. Here Luther took his stand, and laid this as the broad foundation of all moral and religious truth. Man is not justified, saved, and morally approved by God for any outward act or acts, but on the ground of inward principle or character. We say, it is astonishing that this should be done in an enlightened age; because this principle, so plainly avowed, so successfully defended, so widely diffused by Luther and his coadjutors, has been received and adopted in all our modern histories, and in all our schools of philosophy; incorporated in our very civilization and recognized as fundamental truth by all writers on moral science, whether infidel or Christian, till it has become, as it were, the common patrimony of mankind. Like the light of day, it radiates indeed from the sun; yet men enjoy its beams without reflecting on the source from which it comes.

I. The new birth is the necessary preparation of the soul for heaven. To the opinion, then, which makes it an outward rite, we object, that it is a palpable absurdity, utterly subversive of all the settled principles of morals and religion, alike abhorrent to all the teachings of revelation, and the dictates of reason. If there be any one truth on earth, more incontrovertible than all besides, sustained by the universal assent of mankind, forced on the convictions of all rational men, by its own intrinsic evidence, it is that the seat of religion is in the heart, and not in the outward man; that the Divine law is designed to regulate the moral feelings and character of man; and that, only as a moral being, is he the subject of a moral government, of reward and punishment, of approbation or censure. Hence the kingdom of God is not meat and drink, as consisting in any outward or material thing, but righteousness and peace, and joy in the Holy Ghost. For the kingdom of God, said our Saviour, is within you.

There are indeed two kingdoms--the natural, material kingdom, and a spiritual kingdom. They are as different as matter and mind; as far apart as heaven and earth. Each has its own separate laws. The body is matter, and belongs to one; the mind is spirit, and belongs to the other. Religion is not a system of material laws. It is not a system of mechanics, to regulate the play of pulleys, tendons, joints, and grooves; not a system of hydrostatics, to regulate the motion of fluids; nor a physiology, to control the operations of internal viscera, glands, and secretions; but a system of moral rules and principles, to regulate the conduct of moral agents; and of these the heart or spirit is the only proper object. The law of God passes by all these grosser elements, which are the mere instruments of the man, and not the man himself, and drives home upon the heart; there utters its voice; there stretches forth its sceptre. The eye of God, seeing not as man sees, pierces through all the outward films of the flesh, and looks deep down into the heart. If all be right within, God and the soul are satisfied.

Brethren, can it be necessary to argue such points as these? Have you forgotten that solemn call of God, "Son, give me thy heart?" Have you forgotten that earnest warning, "Keep thy heart with all diligence; for out of it are the issues of life?" Have you forgotten that indignant expostulation of our Saviour, in Mark vii. 18, "Are ye so without understanding also? Do ye not perceive, that whatsoever thing from without, entereth into the man, it cannot defile him: because it entereth not into his heart. But that which cometh out of the man, that defileth him. For, from within, out of the heart of man, proceed evil thoughts, adulteries, fornications, murders, thefts, covetousness, wickedness, deceit, lasciviousness, an evil eye, blasphemy, pride, foolishness; all these evil things come from within, and defile the man." Or have you forgotten that positive and comprehensive assertion, that "love is the fulfilling of the law." The principle is not confined to religion, but is spread over the whole field of human thought and human intercourse. In all things it is the heart we require, whether in friend or benefactor. If that be right, all is right. If that be wanting, all is wrong. We value the external act, only as it is the manifestation of the inward feeling, and the instrument of the inward man. The eye kindles, the hand stretches out its cordial salutation and hearty welcome, but all the virtue resides in the soul. These outward manifestations please us, only as they are indications of the heart within. Suppose that in any of these outward manifestations you found there was no heart. You would only abhor, with deeper detestation, the mere appearance of good-will. So all apparent kindness, if discovered to be done in hatred or parade, only chills us the more by its heartless hypocrisy. So when relieved by another's helping hand, or defended from danger by his strong arm or sword—it matters not—these are but instruments, and if no heartfelt kindness prompted the act, we can feel no pleasure in it. On the other hand, if wounded by another without design, we may feel the discomfort of physical pain, but our moral nature forbids displeasure. The disabled friend, with good wishes and warm affections, who would help us, but cannot, we value more, even in his impotence, than all the heartless favors of the great. He may have no arm to save us, no money with which to help us, yet feeling that his heart is with us, we have that which we more highly prize.

But God needs not these outward manifestations. He looks directly at the heart, knows all that is within the heart, and deals with it accordingly. Whenever, under the old or new dispensation, men confounded, mistook, or substituted the sign for the thing signified, the outward act for the inward feeling, the shadow for the substance, the shell for the kernel, He makes it the subject for the most earnest expostulation, the keenest reproofs, the deepest and most fearful denunciations. It was for this especially that the Saviour poured forth that torrent of bitterest sarcasm, and of fiercest indignation, against the Scribes and Pharisees, as hypocrites and whited sepulchres. Substituting outward washing for inward purity, they were scrupulously exact in tithing mint, anise, and cummin, while they left undone the weightier matters of the law; judgment, mercy, and faith. From the very opposite view, he praised the young ruler who on a certain occasion approached him with humility, candor, and sincerity, and said: "Thou art not far from the kingdom of heaven."

II. The opinion that the new birth consists in anything outward, or any outward action, contradicts all the representations of Scripture. It would be easy to show by a multitude of passages, all bearing on this subject, that the Scripture demands inward purity or holiness of heart. The Bible represents all outward rites and ceremonies as being but the signs and symbols of internal purification, not as substitutes for or producers of inward holiness. Especially was this the case with the rite of circumcision, and the various sacrifices of the Old Testament economy. And equally so is it with the two great ordinances of the New Testament, baptism and the

Lord's supper. Bread and wine are simply emblems to shadow forth the body and blood of Christ, which must be received by faith alone, springing from the heart of the believer. The water of baptism is but the sign of that washing of regeneration and renewing of the Holy Ghost which must be wrought in the heart of the believer. But the Jews were constantly inclined to exalt the external above the internal, substituting circumcision and sacrifice for that piety of the heart which they were intended to secure. Thus when they offered to God this mere lip-service, he spurned them indignantly away, on the ground that he required the heart, and not sacrifices and vain oblations.

We see then that regeneration is a great spiritual change, a renovation of man's whole nature and character, without which he cannot enter into life. "Marvel not that I said unto thee ye must be born again." "Except a man be born again, he cannot see the kingdom of God." The necessity for such a change in man may be argued from the nature of God, from the character of the Son of God, and from the nature of the kingdom of heaven, whose inhabitants and employments are all holy. We have seen the fallacy of that opinion, which represents the new birth as an outward rite, tracing it to its double origin, in the dreamy mysticism of the dark ages, when men saw secret and mysterious powers in holy water and consecrated bread, and in the universal disposition of unconverted man to substitute outward form for inward holiness. We have seen that the first intuitive principle of all religion is, that the seat of piety must be in the heart; and that the first great truth in all morals is, that man is the subject of moral government, in his moral and spiritual nature. We have seen how fully these principles are recognized in the Bible, which represents the outward rites of religion, not as substitutes for inward holiness, nor as producers of holiness, nor as holiness itself, but as signs, symbols, and seals of inward character.

If now any one should assert that an outward rite, as that of baptism, produces regeneration (abandoning the position that it is regeneration), this last absurdity is as great as the first, and liable to the same objection. For, as in the doctrine of transubstantiation, it attributes to water qualities and powers not before existing, and impalpable to our senses—thus making a miracle when we see no miracle. We shall not delay you by discussing, at greater length, an opinion which carries its own condemnation so obviously along with it, and which, to be refuted, needs only to be stated and clearly understood. We therefore briefly remark on this subject: First, that justification and salvation are never connected with baptism, or any other outward rite alone, but always with some inward principle. Secondly, that punishment is never threatened for the want of baptism alone, but of something else inward and spiritual. Thirdly, that there are cases, in Scripture, of some who were baptized with water and not saved, as Judas and Simon Magus; while some have received the Holy Spirit and been saved without this outward baptism, as the patriarchs and prophets, and the penitent thief on the cross. Fourthly, that it is against the whole drift and tenor of the Gospel, which represents sin as an internal disease, for which it provides an inward remedy; as a moral disorder, for which it provides a moral cure; as a deep malady of the spirit, for which it offers spiritual relief.

We have so often, and at such great length, recently spoken of the nature of true religion as the image of God on the heart and the life of God in the soul; as a transition from darkness to light and from death to life; as a new creation by the mighty power of God, that I need not delay you longer on this branch of the subject, but proceed at once to consider other points. Ye must be born again. There are many men, as we are well aware, before whose minds this whole subject lies wrapped in impenetrable mystery. Like Nicodemus, they believe Christ to be a teacher sent from God. They are won by the beauty of his pure and elevated morality, astonished at the sublimity of Divine instruction, convinced by the evidence of his stupendous miracles, and captivated by the blended dignity and gentleness, humility and grandeur of his unrivalled character.

They have witnessed the benign influence of his Gospel on society around them. They have seen it casting over the violence of angry passions the charms of its restraints, more potent than the terrors of the law, or the fetters and dungeons of despotic power. They have marked it at the bed of sickness, and in the house of mourning, breathing its own sweet serenity into the troubled bosom, kindling the pallid cheek of disease, brightening the eye of sorrow, and, by its exalted hopes, robbing death of its sting and the grave of its victory. History also has told them of still greater wonders, which it has wrought on a wider theatre, and down through the lapse of past ages, as, issuing from Judea, it went forth from country to country, visiting only to bless, civilizing barbarous tribes, banishing bloody, impure, and idolatrous superstitions, casting into new mould and pervading with new spirit all the institutions of mankind. They have seen it giving freedom to civilized government, purity to domestic life, humanity to war itself—the very sun and centre of the social system, ever beaming from heaven, and, though obscured for a season, yet bursting forth again, the source of light and warmth and life to all. All this they have known and pondered; and they regard with real respect, nay, with reverence and admiration, the author of a system so widely diffused, so powerfully influential, so admirably adapted to the condition and character of man, so replete with all blessings to the earth; and so they come with sincere interest, and with respectful deference, to inquire of this great teacher in Israel.

But behold what amazement, what hopeless perplexity and dismay they feel, when they hear the Saviour say, "Verily, verily, I say unto thee, except a man be born again, he cannot see the kingdom of God." It sounds to them like the strange language of an unknown land, like the indistinct and mysterious muttering of an unknown oracle, awful and terrific, but unintelligible; and they exclaim with Nicodemus, How can these things be?

But mark the gentleness at once and wisdom of the Saviour. He does not drive him from his presence; he does not sternly rebuke his incredulity; nor authoritatively command his belief of a proposition which his reason honestly but inconsistently rejects. But he kindly stoops to reason with him, to remove his difficulties, to relieve his scruples; and, with that quick and felicitous tact which ever distinguished him as a teacher, he seizes at once the principle of the objection, and, with the rapid glance of one to whom the whole economy of the universe was known, he refers directly to analogous cases in our daily experience, to show the futility of the objection. Nicodemus came by night. The mild air of the evening was then breathing around them, so delightful after the oppressive heat of an Eastern sun. His objection was, how can an invisible cause produce a change in human character, itself as invisible as the cause which produces it? And as they enjoyed the luxury of this cool, refreshing breeze, the Saviour directs his attention to the undoubted instance of the operation of a cause, whose origin is unknown, whose progress cannot be traced; and yet its results are most important and undeniable. That breath of air which whispers through the lattice, murmurs amidst the vines, and rustles the leaves—whence has it come, to fan your cheek and cool your brow? From the distant sea, over the mountain's top, through the lonely valley, amidst forests and groves, flowers and vineyards, it has wandered, nourishing man and beast, vegetable, tree, and flower. But who is able to trace its course and tell its wanderings? Who can explain its coming and its going? "The wind bloweth where it listeth, and thou hearest the sound thereof, but canst not tell whence it cometh, or whither it goeth. So is every one that is born of the Spirit." The argument is, if you can believe in the facts of the material world, and in the common experiences of daily life, without being able to understand all the strange and inexplicable processes connected with them; why should you be filled with wonder and incredulity, in reference to the things of the spiritual and eternal world! Believing, as you profess to do, that I am a teacher come from God, marvel not that I said unto you, Ye must be born again.

XXIV.

THE HELPLESS DEPRAVITY OF MAN.

JOB xiv. 4.—"Who can bring a clean thing out of an unclean? Not one."

THERE is an extraordinary depth, an awful solemnity, one might almost say a terrible and sublime audacity, in the views which the Bible presents of the condition of our fallen nature. It boldly approaches the subject and looks it directly in the face, in all its vast extent, and all its appalling difficulties. It denies nothing, it conceals nothing, it palliates nothing. It repudiates altogether the language of a feeling and fastidious philanthropy, of a false and fashionable and superficial philosophy, and comes forth with its own broad and sweeping annunciation of the total wreck and ruin of our nature—a ruin coeval with the origin of our race and co-extensive with all its families. It proclaims a helplessness which is co-extensive with this ruin—a helplessness as total as the ruin is complete. It tells of a "carnal mind which is enmity against God, which is not subject to the law of God, neither indeed *can be;*" of a "natural man that receiveth not the things of the spirit of God, neither can he know them, because they are spiritually discerned."

The great Physician does not shrink from probing the wound to the bottom. He passes from the outward symptoms to the deep-seated inward malady, from the transient manifestation to the central and permanent source of ruin, and lays bare the foul disease which is festering amidst the vitals, in all its revolting and hideous malignity. He traces it up to its origin in that first sin of the first man, the head and representative of our race, which brought death into the world and all our woe. "As by one man sin entered into the world, and death by sin, so death hath passed upon all men, because all have sinned." He tells us of that moral pestilence which, descending from this first man through successive generations, has reached the whole of his posterity; of the deadly virus of sin which has entered our system, and now mingles with our whole circulation, flows in the veins, throbs in the arteries, beats at the heart, flashes in the eyes, burns in the brain, and reaching every faculty and every element of our being, has poisoned and polluted all: till the understanding is shrouded in darkness, and the affections are seduced from their allegiance to God. Amidst the wild uproar of the tumultuous and insurgent passions, amidst the blackness of this moral midnight, reason is dethroned, and conscience silenced, and the will subjugated; and every faculty and power of our fallen nature is mustered beneath the standard of a high-handed rebellion against God, and assumes the attitude of a proud defiance.

There is, we know, a puerile and Pelagian philosophy which is the reverse of all this. It sees only upon earth individual men and individual actions. It isolates individual man from the race of which he is a member, and individual action from the whole course and current of his acts and feelings. It would wrench out the individual man from all his relations to the species to which he belongs, and the individual act from the whole life of which it is a part, and from that inward and permanent source and principle of action, of which it is only the external and transient manifestation. On this we remark, in passing, that it professes to be a philosophy, and yet denies itself in the very terms of its annunciation. There can be no philosophy of isolated beings or isolated acts. It is of the very essence of philosophy that it seeks to mount up to higher principles, to discover universal laws. It is based upon the instinctive conviction, that there is a stupendous unity in God's universe, a mighty purpose and a comprehensive plan, which embraces not only atoms but worlds, not only individuals but species; that binds together these atoms into a world, these individuals into a species, all participants of the same nature, subject to the same laws, heirs of the same glorious or fearful destiny, with a common ruin and a common remedy.

Again, it solves the mystery of human depravity, by multiplying that mystery indefinitely, by all the millions multiplied by other millions of all past and future generations of mankind. It is in each a separate and ever-recurring mystery. Again, it explains the origin of evil, the darkest problem that overshadows and perplexes human reason, by gravely assuring us that each act of sin originates itself. Such is not the philosophy of the Bible, or of common sense. Both assure us that the man, by the very law of his birth which constitutes him man, inherits the nature of his race; that the outward act is only the expression of the inward principle; that the inward emotion, desire, passion, however transient, springs from a principle, a character, a nature, which long outlasts these fugitive emotions, and which, when they are past and forgotten, will originate other similar emotions by a process and a power as mysterious indeed, yet as certain as that which insures that the peach-tree, though now stripped of its leaves and fruit, will produce, on the return of spring, not plums or acorns, but its ordinary fruit; and that the serpent, now stiff with the cold of winter, will awake in the spring with the serpent's venom and the serpent's spite, the serpent's glittering skin and the serpent's fiery eye.

Should any one object to this, let him object to the whole course of nature. His controversy is not with revelation, but with nature, and we leave him to settle it with the God of nature. Throughout all creation like produces like, whether in the animal or vegetable world. The dove does not issue from the eagle's egg, the fish from the serpent, the lamb from the tiger's dam, nor the poisonous berry from the fruitful vine. The young eagle may be hatched beneath the domestic fowl, and trained amidst her timid brood; yet it is an eagle still, with the eagle's hooked beak, the eagle's talons, and the eagle's love for blood, with the eagle's eye of fire and the eagle's pinions, born to soar above the clouds, to make its home upon the mountain-top, and seek its prey amongst the weaker inhabitants of the forest. The young tiger, before it has lapped its tongue in blood, has still the tiger's tusks and the tiger's claws, the tiger's keen scent and ravenous appetite for flesh, which in after-life wakes it from the gentlest slumbers to bound forward in pursuit of prey. Extract the viper's fang and its bag of poison, it is a viper still, with the serpent's coil, the serpent's hiss, its tendency to strike, and the whole serpent-nature diffused throughout its frame. The poisonous shrub, even before it has expanded into bloom or ripened into fruit, has its poisonous nature; and, in its earliest germ, while invisible to man, contains the causes and the elements, yet undeveloped, which insure the future product—elements and causes mysterious and inscrutable to man, to which, in our ignorance, we give the name of nature. Nor is there anything *peculiarly mysterious* here. It is only that universal mystery which enshrouds all the ultimate facts in creation, and constitutes the boundary of all human knowledge. We know nothing of any causes directly; we only know them from their effects; and with all our supposed knowledge of the external world around us, we only know that it is the cause, the unknown cause, of our various sensations. The sweetness and the color of the rose are to us the unknown causes of our sensations; and when we ask why the rose is fragrant, or the stone falls to the ground, our only answer is alike in either case, Because such is its nature, such is the inscrutable law of its being. No being can change its own nature; and if there be in man a depraved and corrupted nature, "Who," says Job, "can bring a clean thing out of an unclean?"

First. Can education? Can education, even in its utmost perfection, based on a perfect knowledge of all the laws and elements of the human mind? In the most successful efforts, it is only one human mind operating on another. The subject, agent, and instruments are only the same laws of mind. It originates nothing, creates nothing. Great is the power of education in moulding human character; equal indeed to that of man in fashioning external nature; and the limits of its agency are precisely the same. In all the mightiest changes produced by human science, directed by human ingenuity, no particle of matter is created. The machinist, in the most wonderful and successful efforts of his skill, employs only the known laws and powers of matter. The chemist, in the rarest and most beautiful productions of his science, in all his combinations and decompositions, even when new results come forth unobserved and unparalleled before, has still employed only the existing elements and existing laws of matter. He may bring those elements into new relations; and new susceptibilities, hitherto unsuspected, may be developed; but those susceptibilities were not then first created; though latent, they existed long before. The steam-car, as it sweeps on its rapid and resistless course, is propelled, not by any new-created power or element, but by the expansive power of steam.

As in matter, so is it in mind. The revolutions which have been produced by the agency of man in the aspect of external nature, prodigious as they are, are rivalled and surpassed by the mightier influence of mind on mind in education. Ignorance has been enlightened by knowledge, weakness matured into strength, rudeness polished into refinement, debasing superstition exchanged for a calm philosophy, whole nations of barbarians elevated to the dignity of enlightened freemen. But here, too, we are limited in our agency to the materials on which we operate, the laws and elements already existing in the soul of man. We cannot add to the human frame a single limb, organ, or muscle; not a gland, even the minutest, nor the flimsiest tissue. Nor can we add to the human mind a single susceptibility or power, a single capacity of thought, of feeling, or of action. We may strengthen what is weak by exercise and healthy nutriment; we may expand, enlarge, develop what otherwise might have remained inactive. We may whet the intellect to logical acuteness, or expand it into breadth and comprehension. We may rouse the imagination to a loftier and bolder flight, and store it with images of beauty or of grandeur. We may cultivate the gentler and more benevolent affections, and thus shed a sweeter grace over all the walks of social and domestic life. All this we may do; but we can add no new element to the soul of man; and if there be by nature no principle of holiness there, education cannot implant it. Holiness is a life, a spiritual life, the life of God in the soul. Combine and organize those dead elements as we may, spiritual life we cannot infuse. All the elements that constitute the human body lie scattered everywhere around us—in the earth on which we stand, the air we breathe, and the water which we drink. Yet, if all were gathered and combined in perfect organization, though nature might supply the dead materials, all nature and all human power could not supply the life. So in that sublime vision of Ezekiel, as he wandered through that valley of desolation, and beheld the multitude of dry bones whitening there, though bone leaped to its fellow at the voice of the prophet, and the joints united in perfect articulation, and muscle and sinew and vein and artery, and every particle and every element had taken its appropriate place, yet the bodies lay there before him a ghastly congregation of the dead, till the breath of the Lord came down, with its life-giving power, and those corpses stood up as living men.

All human history, for near six thousand years, has been one vast and varied experiment on the power of education to renovate the race. The mightiest intellects, through these successive centuries, have employed all the resources of their genius—by the tongue, the pen, and the press—to improve and reform mankind. They have produced consummate generals, profound philosophers, gifted orators, and admirable poets—but not one man of God. Human nature has still remained, in all its essential elements, unchanged—worldly, sensual, godless; no tendency to evil eradicated, no element of holiness infused. Education cannot renovate the nature of man, cannot bring a clean thing out of an unclean.

Let us not be supposed, however, to underrate the value of Christian education. Great is the efficacy of truly Christian instruction, the power of Christian example, of that gentle piety which diffuses its hallowed radiance over all around. Precious beyond all thought and all expression are those seeds of truth which are early implanted in the infant mind. But let us not forget that this efficacy is connected with God's promised grace; that these germs of truth must be quickened into life by the dews of heaven, and the life-giving beams of the Sun of righteousness. I remember, in my early youth, to have heard a lady of distinguished family and great intelligence say: "I have no fear that my sons will go astray, they have been too well educated!" Beloved brethren, God is jealous of his honor, and will not give his glory to another. He will not bear that we should substitute our instruction for his grace. The very last and least of his redeemed people shall be shouted home with "Grace, grace unto it;" and when one of our loved ones is really brought home to God, with streaming eyes and grateful hearts we must acknowledge, as of the lowest of people, that it is a miracle of grace. "It is the Lord's work, and marvellous in our eyes."

Secondly. Can eloquence "bring a clean thing out of an unclean?" There are tones of the human voice that vibrate to the inmost soul of man, and awaken echoes there that had slumbered from our birth, thoughts and feelings, susceptibilities and powers, hitherto unknown. There are words which, when "fitly spoken," in appropriate combination, thrill along every fibre of the human heart, and, as by some strange intellectual chemistry, summon the hidden elements there into new and often startling results. Great is the power of eloquence! There is not a chord of the human heart which it cannot touch, not a passion which it cannot arouse or lull. But how can it touch a chord that is not there? There are men who, with magic power, can sweep that instrument of a thousand strings—the heart of man—and draw forth from each some tone responsive. But if the noblest of them all, that which ascends and is linked to the throne of God, and vibrates to the melodies of eternity, hang broken and tuneless there; if one mightier than he has dashed athwart it his fiery finger, and snapped it, who shall awaken its lost harmonies?

XXV.

THE MINISTRY OF THE GOSPEL.

1 Cor. ii. 3.—"And I was with you in weakness, and in fear, and in much trembling."

"He has sold his birthright for a mess of pottage." Such was the profane and impious sneer, the contemptuous and almost blasphemous exclamation of a distinguished lawyer and politician, on hearing of the intended consecration to the work of the ministry of a beloved Christian brother, now gone to his reward, who devoted the ardor of early youth and the prime of a vigorous manhood, with uncommon eloquence and success, to the proclamation of the Gospel; who has left behind him a long memorial in the hearts of multitudes converted by his ministry, and added to every grace that could adorn the Christian gentleman, every power of persuasion and pathos that could signalize the consummate orator. "He has sold his birthright for a mess of pottage. Had he builded upon his father's name, and his father's exalted reputation, and pursued his father's profession, he might have erected a monument of fame to himself, and have perpetuated the honor of his family."

Such are generally the opinions, the feelings, and the language of worldly men in regard to the ministry of the Gospel; and not very different from this may be the feelings of some amongst ourselves, who can with difficulty escape the voice of conscience, and the claims of a perishing world upon their sympathy and efforts. And, my brethren, we are glad that it is so; from our inmost soul we are glad that it is so.

We are glad that the Gospel ministry is still a self-denying and self-sacrificing work; that it has no splendors to dazzle the young and the aspiring; no emoluments to bribe the worldly and the venal; that the cross is still *a burden to be borne*—the badge of meanness in the eyes of worldly men, the object of derision and reproach, not the symbol of power or the passport to fame. It is thus that the Saviour watches over the purity of his church, and at the very threshold of the sanctuary, erects a barrier which usually prevents the entrance of those whose vanity would corrupt the purity of her doctrines, whose ambition would mar the harmony of her counsels, or whose vices would tarnish her yet unspotted reputation; thus out of transient evil, educing still enduring good, and causing alike the folly and the wrath of man most signally to advance the great purposes of God.

But how different from all this are the sentiments expressed by the author of our text—the conscious weakness, the felt unworthiness, the sacred reverence, the trembling awe in view of this high office! But who is this that yields such emphatic testimony to the Gospel ministry, as he thus shrinks and trembles in view of its transcendent dignity, its arduous duties, its sublime and overwhelming responsibilities? Is it some obscure individual ignorant of mankind, and alike unknown to them, who has lived and vegetated and died, leaving behind no memorial of his existence, no deep impression on his race; who, unused to the business and affairs of men, and living in some quiet and obscure retreat, was abashed at the stare of crowds, would tremble at the approach of danger, and sinks in conscious imbecility beneath the weight of some great enterprise? Answer me when I tell you he was such an one as Paul the aged, the servant of God, the apostle of our Lord Jesus Christ; who was in nothing behind the very chiefest of the apostles—in labors more abundant, in sufferings above measure, in gifts pre-eminent, in revelations of the spirit exalted to the third heavens, and privileged to see and to hear unutterable mysteries; in whose presence Felix trembled before the power of his argument, and Agrippa melted beneath the persuasion of his eloquence, and to whom, above all other men of ancient or of modern times, was granted this high pre-eminence, to stamp deep and broad upon the age in which he lived the impression of his character, and by his imperishable writings to guide the opinions and control the destiny of all succeeding generations. If, then, the great Apostle of the Gentiles, gifted as he was by nature, improved as he was by education, illuminated by all human learning and Divine revelation, was overwhelmed with the grandeur of this great work, and in view of the high and hallowed services of the Gospel ministry could exclaim, "I was with you in weakness and fear and great trembling;" what shall we say of those who, in our day, rush forward with thoughtless impetuosity and indecent haste into all the solemn responsibilities and arduous duties of this sacred calling? Let us consider, then, what are some of the qualifications and what the characteristics of a ministry which, amidst the emergencies of our day, and the crises just at hand, may stand forth before the world as the heralds of the Saviour, "workmen that need not be ashamed,"—in other words, a ministry adapted to our times.

I. First, then, we need a thoroughly devoted and consecrated ministry; for, consider the high and solemn sacredness of this great office. Throughout the Holy Bible the design is everywhere manifest, to diffuse an atmosphere of peculiar sacredness around the presence and immediate service of the Most High. When Moses was called to be God's messenger to Pharaoh and the deliverer of his people Israel, he was taught, by a most impressive symbol, the sacredness that belongs to the message and that should characterize the messenger. The Most High appeared to him in fire, the purest at once and the most terrible of elements, and as he approached to receive his commission, the voice of God, issuing from the burning bush, said: "Put off thy shoes from thy feet, for the place whereon thou standest is holy ground." And when in after-years, as the minister of that former dispensation, he received from the hands of God the tables of the law, the very mount on which the Almighty descended was consecrated from its summit to the base; no man or beast dare at the peril of life intrude within those consecrated limits; and even Moses, as he stood amidst the agitated elements, and upon the burning mount where the Lord himself came down with the myriads of his holy ones, exclaimed: "I do exceedingly quake and tremble." After the building of the temple, the Holy of Holies was closed throughout the year, and the visible symbol of God's presence there could only be approached after the most solemn preparation, and with the most august and imposing ceremonies by the high-priest of God; and the misguided Israelite who, in hasty zeal, put forth his hand irreverently to support the Ark, was smitten dead upon the spot. Well might the Apostle urge us, in view of these indications of a jealous God, to "serve God with reverence and godly fear, for our God is a consuming fire." But if the ministry of condemnation was glorious, how much more the ministry of salvation. These were all but the shadows of which Christ is the substance; and if the ministry and ordinances of that imperfect dispensation were guarded with such watchful jealousy, encircled with such awful sanctity, avenged with such terrific retributions, what shall we say of that better covenant of which Christ was at once the author and the object, the victim and the priest, the minister and Lord! How awful its dignity! How solemn its ordinances! How sacred its instructions! How elevated its hopes! How precious its consolations! How august its revelations! For the Gospel is a message directly from the throne of Heaven; and every minister of the Gospel, called and sent of God, is an ambassador for Christ. He stands a dying man between the living God and a world of dying men. Himself a sinner saved by grace, he stands between a Holy God and a world of sinners. Himself at best a pardoned rebel, he stands between an offended God and a world of rebels in open revolt against his government—abusing his mercy, insulting his majesty, defying his omnipotent justice. How momentous are the subjects to be discussed, how vast are the interests involved, how solemn the responsibilities incurred—solemn as the issues of the Judgment, vast as the value of the soul, and durable as its long and interminable existence! Were the thrones of all earthly empires piled high, each above the other, and all earthly crowns blended into one diadem of glory, these accumulated thrones would not reach to heaven; and what were that radiant diadem, when compared with the glory that encircles the brow of one immortal spirit amongst the millions of the saved? And were all the earthly interests of all the nations concentrated in one single person, how insignificant would all appear when weighed in the balances of the sanctuary, and calculated by the arithmetic of heaven, and measured by the duration of eternity! But the message which he bears is the message of a Saviour's love, the same which the angels came to herald, which the Lord of angels came to bear, which fell from his own heavenly lips, and beamed from his own countenance of radiant love, and was embodied in his own mysterious person, and gushed from his own bleeding bosom and bursting heart—a story of infinite pity, and infinite woe, of avenging justice and redeeming mercy. For, blessed be God that our ministry is a ministry of reconciliation, and not of condemnation; that the message we bear is one of unutterable love; that the burden of our proclamation still must be love, amazing, boundless, unfathomable love. "For God *so* loved the world that he gave his only begotten Son, that whosoever believeth on him should not perish, but have everlasting life." God was not only willing to be reconciled, but willing to pay the price of reconciliation too. When there was no eye to pity, and no arm to save, he was willing both to pity and to save the perishing.

Man brought ruin on himself by rebelling against God—man the enemy of God, and thus God made the enemy of man—a creature of clay arrayed against the Omnipotent, and thus God arrayed against him. The heavens clothed in blackness, the earth quaking in terror, conscience pealing in thunder-tones, and perdition gaping to engulf him—who is the sinner's stay? Cannot mercy plead? Can no angel intercede? Behold, there is help laid on One mighty to save.

He comes in the humility of man and the majesty of God. The arm uplifted to destroy us has fallen upon him. The sword, brandished and blazing above us, is bathed in his own blood; still are those arms outspread; that heart still beats with love; and we are commissioned to pray, to entreat, to exhaust *all* argument, and to do so in the name of God, in the name of Christ, by all that is terrible or precious in heaven or hell. Well might we tremble, when we put forth the hand to the Ark, lest we perish by the touch. Well might we shrink back from this solemn and sacred trust, but we dare not; by our solemn vows, we dare not decline it or be dismayed. The Gospel is mighty through God, and the demonstration of his spirit and power. Standing, then, as the representative of the Saviour upon earth, speaking in his great name and by his high authority, moving habitually amidst these scenes of tenderness and grandeur; how important that the minister of Christ be a man of God, imbued with the spirit and bearing the image of his Saviour!

II. The Gospel we have to preach is not an ingenious speculation, or plausible theory, or magnificent hypothesis, lending a portion of its own dazzling brilliancy to heighten the splendors of some rhetorical display; but a *fact*, a solemn and an awful *fact;* a sublime and glorious reality, wide as the world in which we live and universal as the race of man; pervading all human relations, involving all human interests, reaching upward to the throne of God, and downward to the depths of perdition, and onward through an immeasurable eternity, and in the wide sweep of its large and manifold relations, linking the destiny of man with all that is loftiest in the character and most stupendous in the energies of superhuman powers—the celestial sympathy of angels, the satanic malignity of fiends. It is a fact so vast in the range of its illimitable consequences, so appalling or so glorious in its necessary influences upon human destiny, so clear in the evidence of its indubitable certainty, so intimately blended with the whole tissue of our past and future history, that in comparison with it, all other facts are dim and vague and shadowy and insignificant. It is the fact of facts, the *great* fact in each man's history. That is no dream of the visionary enthusiast—the ruin of our race; but an awful fact, loudly proclaimed by every human conscience, faithfully re-echoed by every known tradition, broadly and palpably recorded upon every page of history, and distinctly visible upon the face of human society itself—visible even in those scattered traces of beauty and of grandeur which remain amid the ruins they cannot remedy; as we recognize the site of long-lost cities and demolished temples by the shattered remains of arches and columns and statues peeping irregularly forth from amidst the rubbish that entombs them. And the redemption of our race—is not this a blessed reality? which, chronicled amidst the annals of the sky, has already peopled heaven with millions of inhabitants, and is even now enjoyed in its felt and palpable reality as a living, present, actual salvation by millions of redeemed sinners upon earth? And all the solemn verities of our Gospel—are they not stupendous facts, that encompass us on every side, and overshadow with a serene and heavenly awe our whole earthly being? Truly, the realities of our existence surpass the prodigies of fiction. We live amidst a scene of wonders. Is not there the broad heaven, spread out above us in serene and solemn grandeur, with its millions of peopled worlds looking down silently upon us? And are there not here millions of immortal spirits around us moulding at this very hour their everlasting destinies? Is not our eternity already begun? Behold, all around is immensity, infinity, eternity. Above us are incalculable heights; beneath us unfathomable depths. Around us is vast infinity; behind us eternity past; before us eternity to come. Within us are boundless capacities for joy or woe; while ever present with us, encompassing all our ways, pervading our whole being, source of every blessing, and witness to every act and thought and feeling, is the silent and awful majesty of God. Such is the grandeur and such the sublime mystery of our condition here.

But he who would bring home these great truths to the conscience and practical conviction of another, must know them not only as a speculation, but must have felt them as a fact, in his own inward experience, as the great fact of his own history; must know them as the one central fact of human existence and human destiny, around which all others do obediently range themselves, to which all others are subordinate, and from which they all derive their only true significance. Hence, in all ages of the world, from St. Paul to Augustine, from Augustine to Luther, and onward to Bunyan and Baxter, and down to our own days, the men who have been honored of God to stamp deep upon their generation the impression of these truths, have borne about with them, in their own persons, the experimental realization of them; have known from inward experience the sad and sublime reality of things; have gazed with steady earnestness into the fires of perdition, till all human tortures were indifferent; and roved amidst the delights of paradise till all earthly splendor was insignificant; who have themselves, in the secrecy of their own bosoms, grappled in deadly conflict with the powers of darkness; and, issuing from the closet to the pulpit, fresh from these high and solemn meditations, victorious from amidst these terrific struggles, they have uttered words of exhortation which have been like a voice from heaven—their tones of warning or denunciation sounding like the trump of God. In the days of Whitfield a comedy was prepared, in which the doctrines and manner of this great prophet of his age were held up to public ridicule. Garrick was selected to represent the distinguished preacher. But this extraordinary man, accustomed to study the character he was about to represent, that he might sympathize with all his feelings, and reproduce a living similitude of the man he was to personate, entered with such enthusiasm into the spirit of this new hero of the drama, that he stood before them with all the grandeur and solemnity of a herald of the skies; the whole assembly was bathed in tears, and for once the theatre was converted into a place of penitence and prayer. When asked by a minister of the Gospel where lay the secret of his power, he replied with keen yet instructive severity: "We speak fiction as if it were truth, you speak truth as if it were the idlest fiction." May none of you, my young brethren, ever stand up in the sacred pulpit and drawl out with dull and lifeless insipidity, truths which inspire the songs of angels, and shall swell the raptures of eternity.

III. But again, these great facts, when expressed in language, and classified according to their mutual relations, constitute a grand system of doctrines, complete and harmonious, in which each truth occupies its appropriate place, and presupposes by a logical necessity all the rest, while each upon each reciprocally sheds additional illumination. "There is scarcely a bone," says Cuvier, the great naturalist, when speaking of the admirable harmony that pervades the animal economy, "there is scarcely a bone that can vary in its surfaces, in its curvatures, or in its protuberances, without a correspondent variation in all the rest," so that a skilful naturalist, from the appearance of a single bone, will often be able to determine the form of the whole skeleton to which it belonged. And the reason is obvious, because each must be adapted to those which are adjacent, and these to others still more remote, even to the extremities of the system, while all must harmoniously co-operate with one common object—the existence and welfare of the animal. Now it is even thus with the great system of Christian doctrines; each is adapted to others; all spring from one common source, and tend with harmonious precision towards one common centre—the cross of Christ and justification through faith in the great atonement there. And here, too, the scientific theologian can often easily descry in the minutest fragment of some remote or half-developed dogma, the whole large outline and full proportions of the coming error; with all its habitudes and tendencies, its bold protuberances towards open heresy, its gentle inclinations towards secret error, and all the graceful curvatures of an insidious and plausible theology. Thus, though but a single paw was exhibited at first—and that with studious caution and economical reserve—of that great "Beast of Babylon" of heterogeneous elements, half iron and half clay, which now moves rampant over the nations; yet did the wise men of England and of America at once proclaim his origin, character, and habits; confidently predict his growth and gradual development; and actually project, with photographic accuracy, a perfect delineation of the full-grown monster. Or, to drop the metaphor, the wisest and best of English and American bishops perceived at once, that Puseyism was essential Popery; that they who began by rejecting God's method of justification by faith in the blood of Christ, and substituting in its stead fasting and penances and such like human mummeries, must substitute the fathers for God's word; the authority of the church for the free exercise of private judgment; implicit faith for the manly exercise of reason; and having thus at once yielded up reason and revelation, must terminate in papal infallibility, transubstantiation, and the idolatrous worship of the saints and the immaculate Virgin Mary.

IV. But, as we have remarked before, the whole system of Gospel truth, with all its separate parts, tends towards one common object, and revolves around one common centre, that centre Christ. And just as of old the planets of our system gathered in high conjunction at his birth, and stood with mute homage and blended radiance above his cradle, even so do the several doctrines of his Word cluster with instinctive sympathy around the cross, and pour their combined effulgence there. Hence, the cross of Christ, and the great propitiation offered there, must be the theme of the Christian minister. But how can he preach an unknown Saviour? How lead to a cross whose efficacy he has never experienced? How even comprehend a system of truth, whose simplest elements have no place in his own inward experiences? Hence the necessity of a truly converted and spiritually minded ministry. Because only such a ministry can comprehend, or long outwardly maintain the fundamental doctrine of the Gospel—justification through faith in the Redeemer of lost sinners.

There was a tradition long prevalent in Scotland, and believed by many still, that when the great leader of his people, Wallace, had departed, his head was left behind, reserved for some future day of desperate emergency, with the assurance that, in the very crisis of his country's destiny—when her fainting battalions were just ready to recede, and the onset was most furious and desperate—then whoever should cast this venerated head amidst the advancing columns of her foes, with him should rest the victory. And the tradition tells us that on such a well-contested battle-field, when victory seemed already perching on the banners of the foe, and all was given up for lost, the chieftain to whom this precious relic had been confided, lifted high in view of the contending armies this immortal brow—signal of assured victory to friends, omen of terrible defeat to foes—and casting it far amidst the ranks of the hostile forces, dashed onward to the conflict. The enemy stood all aghast. From battalion to battalion, along the line of Scotland's forces, flashed the electric joy. The old battle-cry of Scotland and Wallace rang through the ranks; and like chaff before the whirlwind of their native mountains, was swept the invading army. Their dead leader gained for them a living victory. The verities of our Gospel are not tradition. The weapons of our warfare are not carnal; the Captain of our salvation is not dead, but liveth. And may we not say to you, who are soon to march forth to the battle of the world—and urge upon ourselves—that in our sorest conflicts with principalities and powers—when all earthly weapons of finest temper, of brightest polish, and of keenest edge, prove unavailing—with him shall be the victory who shall lift highest in the view of contending hosts, and bear most boldly forward in the front of battle, and farthest onward amidst the advancing battalions of our foes, the image of our living, though crucified Redeemer. The Cross! the Cross!—let this be our watchword amidst the darkness of the night. The Cross! the Cross!—be this our battle-cry when we advance to the charge, and upon the banner that waves above the sacramental host of God's elect, alike amidst disaster and success, whether it float in enduring triumph, or droop in apparent and transient defeat, let there be inscribed all over in characters of living light, the Cross, the Cross of our crucified and exalted Lord and Saviour. Christ and his cross be all our theme, though "the victories we speak be folly in the Jews' esteem, and madness to the Greek." And be assured that in that day of trial and of conflict which lies just before us—to which the many-tongued voices all around do summon God's own people; that crisis of the world's destiny now near at hand, in which the embattled powers of good and evil shall struggle together for the final victory; that day of coming darkness when the faint-hearted and the false shall flee, and for which each leader that is boldest in God's sacramental host is girding on his armor, his sword, his helmet, his battle-axe and shield, the weapons of offensive and defensive warfare all burnished for the contest—in that great day of terror in the valley of decision, the church beneath this banner shall be victorious; nay, to use the language of the Saviour himself when speaking of his advent, "shall be like the lightning which lighteneth out of the one part under heaven, and shineth unto the other part under heaven," and nothing can stay the course thereof. Like that lightning in its course, so radiant in its glory, so irresistible in its progress, pervading all that is homogeneous, shattering all that dare oppose, and speaking to all the world in the same tones of imperial majesty, shall move onward, conquering and to conquer, the doctrine of the cross, and of him who hung there in his agony and love.

This leads us to remark that we need an *energetic ministry.* There is a mild and meditative piety, a refined and literary piety, a subtle and speculative piety, and all this may answer in its place, may serve the individual purposes and save the individual soul. But for the conversion and salvation of the world we need a living, active, energetic piety. A man may do good service in the battle of the world, whether he go forth armed with spear or battle-axe, broad-sword or scimetar. We care not how bright the polish of your weapon, if only the edge be keen and the metal steel. You may stud the hilt with diamonds, or emboss it with gold of priceless value and solid workmanship, but let not the blade be rusted nor wreathe the point with flowers, and let it be wielded ever with an arm of vigor, impelled by a heart of fire.

V. But let us consider, in conclusion, the difficulties and dangers of the office. Every situation has its peculiar advantages and pleasures, as well as its difficulties and dangers. The ministry has its own pleasures and also its difficulties. I speak not of what the minister has in common with other Christians, but of those peculiar to his situation. His work is vast; the opposition to the great object of his life is constant, inveterate, and combined; and if apparent success for a time crown his efforts, still danger comes—the world flatters to mislead, seduce, and destroy. It is easy to produce superficial external changes. It is easy to mould the features to a smile, tune the voice to tenderness, and discipline the limbs to graceful motions; too easy, as is obvious to any one who has only glanced at the society, stupidly miscalled refined, to polish the exterior, while corruption is festering at the core. It is comparatively easy to imbue the mind with a moderate share of knowledge, and so regulate the appetite and passions and conduct as to lead a quiet and respectable life. This is the end of philosophy; but religion aims at something far more difficult and important—at nothing less than a radical and fundamental change in the whole character of the man. She announces this as her bold design—to renovate the individual and revolutionize society, to implant new principles in the human character, infuse new elements into human feeling and conduct; not to garnish the old sepulchre, but to erect a new temple to the Lord; not an improvement, but a new creation. Philosophy, of human origin, adapts itself to human tastes, prejudices, weaknesses, even in her efforts to do good. The weapons of her warfare are earthly, and while assaulting one passion, she seeks to strengthen herself by alliance with another; thus strengthening the principle of all sin, while she resists the individual practice, and only invigorating the root, while she lops the branches. Religion, divine in origin, is universal in her requirements. Holiness is written on her banner, and she can make no terms with sin in its inward principles or outward developments. Hence a minister, if faithful, must arouse opposition, extensive and inveterate; the world, the flesh, and the devil must be arrayed against him. For he goes forth amongst his fellow-men the avowed enemy of all they love most dearly—waging war against sin, against *all* sin, however ingeniously veiled, or gracefully decked; however plausibly defended, consecrated by custom, supported by interest, or recommended by fashion. Against sin, from the cottage to the throne, he must wage a war of extermination. Nay, if one sin be more widely prevalent, more securely intrenched, more extensively ruinous than all beside, against this, though power should protect it, and eloquence plead for it, and wealth and talent and genius and learning and popular admiration unite to encircle it with splendor, must the anathemas of the Gospel be boldly thundered forth. The sin of Herod must not go unrebuked though a dungeon and the axe be John's reward.

XXVI.

INFLUENCE OF EVIL SPIRITS.

LUKE xi. 24–26.—"When the unclean spirit is gone out of a man, he walketh through dry places, seeking rest: and finding none, he saith, I will return unto my house whence I came out.

"And when he cometh, he findeth it swept and garnished.

"Then goeth he, and taketh to him seven other spirits more wicked than himself; and they enter in, and dwell there: and the last state of that man is worse than the first."

WE shall not attempt to discuss any of the numerous questions which might be legitimately raised in regard to demoniacal possessions. That spirit should operate on spirit, is truly not more mysterious than that matter should operate on matter. The mode in which they operate and the nature of the connection between them we do not know; in either the *fact* is equally manifest, and equally intelligible in both. That spirit should operate on spirit without the intervention of bodily organization, is not more wonderful than that matter should operate on matter without the intermediate agency of spirit. Nay, that an immaterial spirit should operate upon the soul of man, spirit directly upon spirit without the aid of bodily organs, is not *more* mysterious but *less*, than that it should operate through the instrumentality of this material frame: for when you introduce the bodily organizations you have complicated the process instead of simplifying it. You have removed the mysterious phenomena to a greater distance, separated them by a wider interval, and interposed new links of connection in the successive series. But each of these material links itself involves a new mystery, and you have multiplied the mystery, instead of solving it.

the human spirit; that rouses the dormant passions, blows to a flame the latent sparks of lust; that with devilish skill enters at each avenue of the heart of man, seizes each element of his fallen nature, and wields it for his ruin. He throws around all forbidden things a brilliancy of fascination, an enchanting witchery that dazzles the imagination, bewilders the understanding, captivates the taste, and seduces the affections, until the voice of experience, of reason, of conscience, is unheard, and the whole machinery of his intellectual and moral being is unhinged. Amidst the tumultuous uproar of all the insurgent passions, amidst the wild war of the chaotic and jarring elements within him, reason is dethroned, conscience stifled, the will itself paralyzed, and the unhappy man, mastered by some strange and foreign power, is dragged at first reluctantly along, half conscious of the hellish agency that impels him, and struggling from time to time with spasmodic violence to be free. Then he yields himself a willing captive, blends his own perverted energies and his eternal destinies with those of the powers of darkness, and sweeps on madly exulting before the tempest of his passions; like the spectre-ship which the poet has described, the wildest and most terrible creation of human genius, which swept proudly careering on amidst the fury of the elements, above the billows and before the storm, beneath the broad light of day, and the solemn stillness of the starry night, urged furiously forward by demon powers.

At the period of our Saviour's appearance, it is known that the dominion of this power of evil had become almost universal. The insurrection against God and his government, which seemed destined to achieve a speedy, final, and decisive triumph, had penetrated every department of thought and effort. Over every institution, political, social, religious; over every class of human society, every relation of human life public or private, men's private actions or retired speculations; over all men's passions, affections, reasonings, this power exercised an omnipresent and omnipotent sway. Philosophy, in open and avowed revolt, denied the existence of a God and the immortality of the soul, the fundamental principles of morals, and, in the spirit of a haughty and stoical indifference threw itself over on the doctrine of a gloomy Pantheism; of laws of nature moving on forever under the guidance of a blind, crushing, inexorable necessity. The masses bowed down before gods of wood or stone, which their own hands had made, or deified the worst appetites and passions of our fallen nature. There is scarcely a brutal appetite that degrades our nature, or a fiendish passion that heats the blood or maddens the brain of man, that had not its temple, its altar, its worshipper; to these did the sculptor, the painter, the poet consecrate the noblest productions of their art; and thus were the most splendid efforts of human genius made to give a brilliancy and a glory to the basest of human passions; and over the whole broad domain of human society, in action and in thought, in philosophy, poetry, art, in ordinary life, the Prince of darkness reigned ubiquitous, with supreme control.

It was from the spirit and perhaps through the spirit that this influence reached the body. The inward ruin became outwardly visible; it was the total wreck of body and of spirit, so completely overmastered by the evil that the feeling of individual identity was lost. He was another, and yet the same; one, yet many; seven devils, and then, as the fragments of a shattered intellect multiplied variously the reflection of his consciousness, he was legion. They foamed, they rolled on the ground, they wandered in dismal solitudes, and shunned the abodes of men; amidst the tombs of the dead they lurked by day, and issued forth at night ferocious, untameable; with superhuman strength they tore away the bars of the prison-house, and burst the fetters that bound them. In such a state of things, when Satan had gained such absolute and universal control; when all human appliances were unavailing; when philosophy, literature, government, society had been subjugated and corrupted by his influence, and the few who retained some remains of sanity looked wildly around in despair upon the universal and hopeless ruin, it was manifest that some higher power was needed to prevent the total disorganization of society. The cry of the Syrophenician woman, when all that was sweetest, and dearest, and loveliest, and purest at her own domestic hearth was thus polluted, became but the echo of the universal voice of man: "Lord, have mercy on me, for my *daughter* is grievously tormented by the devil."

Now the miracles of our Saviour, as the doctrines which he

taught and the sufferings he endured, had a reference far beyond the occasion on which they were performed. In each of the diseases which he healed, there is a striking and probably a designed analogy, which spontaneously leads us from the physician of the body to the physician of the soul, from the outward disease to the inward malady of sin. In healing each he proclaims his power over the inward disease of sin, and when he cast out devils, and healed those most malignant forms of madness where Satan seemed enthroned in absolute supremacy amidst the total wreck of man's intellectual and moral nature, he vindicates his sovereignty over Satanic power in all its forms, and teaches a solemn lesson for all coming generations. When he opens the blind eye, he points us to the spiritual blindness of our fallen nature. When he heals the leper, he refers to the foul and contagious leprosy of sin; and when the demon is cast forth from the raving and foaming maniac, we spontaneously turn to society around, and behold with saddened hearts the exact and fearful parallel in the history of those who, in their hot pursuit of worldly pleasure, or worldly gain, or worldly honor, renounce all the principles of reason, disregard the lessons of experience and the warnings of conscience, insult the majesty and defy the omnipotence of God, drive a fearful traffic with the prince of darkness, and barter away an immortality of bliss for the illusive promise of a few transient and uncertain enjoyments. They summon every faculty to its highest exercise, and string every nerve to its intensest tension, for some perishable good; are shrewd, keen, alert, far-seeing in all that relates to their worldly interests; but for eternity, and all that it contains of vast and tremendous import to an immortal spirit, are the veriest madmen.

In pursuing the parallel, we remark first, in respect to the ordinary madman, that the first symptom of his madness is a strange delusion about himself, a total misconception of his character, his position, and his relations to all around. He imagines that he is some mighty potentate, lord of the earth; or, stretching his wide domain still farther, is emperor of the moon. His narrow cell is an imperial palace, his wooden stool a throne of majesty, his little rod a sceptre of royal power. The scraps of tattered finery hung around his brow are a prince's diadem, and the filthy rags that are gathered about his emaciated frame are a robe of imperial purple. He assumes the air and attitude of kings, and all around are but the members of his court, attendants on his person, subject to his authority, and await in mute awe and reverence his high commands. He is rich; the wealth of nations flows into his treasury; the gold of India and California fills his coffers. He is free, though he cannot move without the permission of his keeper, though his keeper's eye follows him at every step, and the stroke of his keeper's rod startles him again and again from his dream of folly; and when the night comes on with its deepening shadows, he is stripped of his robes of royalty, and locked in his dark cell, a naked madman, to rave in impotent fury as he dashes himself in vain against its bars of iron and its solid masonry.

Now, there is something absurdly ludicrous in this delusion of this ordinary madman, but the madness of every sinner is precisely parallel. He, too, is the prey of a similar illusion in relation to himself. He dreams that he is free and independent, yet can he not move without the permission, nay without the sustaining power and goodness, of God. He stalks abroad with lofty step and regal air and heart of pride, as if he were Lord of this lower world; yet the great eye of God is fixed in blazing majesty and consuming wrath upon him, and the great arm of God is lifted high, though unseen by him, for chastisement or vengeance, and ever and anon the strokes fall thick and fast and heavy; the startled sinner wakes for a moment from his dream of maniac folly, implores with many cries and tears forgiveness, and relapses and promises amendment, till at last the night of death comes on, the deep dark shadows of an undone eternity gather around his soul. Each shred and patch and shattered fragment of that mock righteousness in which he has arrayed himself, to hide the dark pollutions of a guilty heart, and cherish the illusions which he loved, is stripped from his trembling and naked spirit; the gloomy cell is ready to receive him; the heavy doors of that dark prison-house grate harsh thunder as they close forever on the imprisoned soul. The night of eternity rolls on; slowly, darkly, heavily, sadly, the night of eternity rolls on. No morning light shall beam upon that darkness. No ray of hope shall gild that black despair. No Lazarus shall fly with winged speed on angel-pinions from the courts above to give one drop of water to cool the parched tongue. No voice of man or angel shall proclaim the wonders of redeeming love. There is no cross in hell; no Saviour there. Madman, look round upon the prison-house, its gloomy walls, its caverns dark and deep, its fiery billows as they surge and boil and flash around thee. Hear the shriek of agony, the groan of horror, the curse of blasphemy, the wail of despair. Was it for this that you despised the sweet voice of mercy, rejected a Saviour's love, stifled conscience, grieved God's spirit, and restrained prayer?

But again, the sinner, too, thinks that he is rich—rich in all moral excellence. He hangs around his brows the tattered soiled fragments of some old cast-off heathen morality, and mounts a lofty pedestal, and thinks himself pre-eminent amongst his fellows in every attribute that should grace and dignify a man. You shall believe he is a man of principle, while he is the slave of sin, the very bond-slave of every beastly appetite and devilish passion. A man of principle! And yet there is not a tie so sacred or so tender, not an interest so paramount or dear, not a duty so solemn or so urgent, that is not sacrificed at the call of inclination; not a principle so firm that is not swept away by the strong impulse of momentary passion. There is not one duty to God or man which he has not violated in its true and deepest meaning. The very first of all those duties, and the basis of all the rest, he wholly and habitually disregards—his duty to the great Creator. There is no fear of God before his eyes, no love of God in his heart, no thought of God in his mind, no service of God in his life; and if the idea of God were blotted out from his understanding, and the name of God erased from his memory, as the thought of God is banished from his habitual reflections, and the service of God from the whole current of his daily life, there would be no darker shadow over his soul, no drearier, blanker atheism would shroud in its midnight blackness the utter desolation of his whole moral being. He does not even give to God the homage of a passing thought. God is to him but the madman's keeper. And yet the madman still cherishes the vain delusion that he believes in God, has a profound reverence for God, will never meet that God in vengeance and in judgment.

He is generous, noble, manly! Fine words are these, my friends, and full of lofty sound. But let us see. He is generous and manly, the very soul of honor! Yet he has betrayed the confidence that was reposed in him—the tender, generous, confiding love, the purest, truest, holiest on earth, which after many a broken promise still strives to trust, and, smiling through its tears, says with the parting kiss crowned with a mother's blessing, Remember, son, your promise when temptations come, and evil companions would seduce, remember your mother's Bible and your mother's God. Remember, son, remember! He is generous! And yet he can pierce with a pang bitterer than death that heart that for many a year has longed and yearned and prayed only for him, that lives only in his life; and in the long vista of future years can see no prospect to delight which is not brightened by the thought of an honorable and virtuous manhood for her cherished boy. Generous, manly! Yet he can bring down those gray hairs with sorrow to the grave; crush the only hope that could cheer amidst the infirmities of advancing life, and make the grave itself a welcome refuge from a mother's untold anguish, and a mother's shame. Surely he is generous, my friends, or is it only the delusion of a madman?

But he is a gentleman, at least, of untarnished character, and with all the virtues that adorn and grace that honorable appellation. A gentleman! And yet you shall see him wallow in shameless, beastly intoxication. Are the stupidity of an ass, and the foulness of swine, the peculiar and distinguishing characteristics of a gentleman? Surely the man is mad; an unclean devil has taken possession of him in body and in spirit. He is the same which entered into the service of old, and we have no reason to believe that they were either improved or pleased by his society. His name is legion, for he never comes alone. He is a social devil, and hosts of others follow in his train. They swarm in by every open avenue, creep slyly in through every crevice of the heart, storm and strongly garrison the citadel, then take possession of the whole. There is not an apartment of the soul which they will not occupy, no secret chamber, no dark nook or corner where foul vermin lurk unseen, but they will seize and render it tenfold fouler. They will seize the imagination and the reasoning power, rouse every passion, stimulate every appetite, take possession of body and spirit, and pervert every organ and every faculty, eye, ear, tongue, to their devilish purposes. The tongue is, according to the Psalmist, the glory of a man, the distinguishing characteristic between men and brutes. Yet go to his private apartment, hear his familiar conversation; obscenity and blasphemy form the whole staple of his talk. An unclean devil guides the swift tongue, and whets the prurient appetite, and quickens the eager ear. The maniac's laugh responds to the madman's filthy jest. The very air around him reeks with blasphemous obscenity, is pestilential, putrid. He soils the ground on which he treads; pollutes the atmosphere he breathes; there is contagion in his touch. In his presence and society every pure and generous and noble sentiment withers and dies, and the wise and good who would seek to save him, turn away at last in sadness and with loathing.

Another characteristic of the ordinary madman, is the absolute subversion of all the rational principles of human action, the total incapacity to appreciate the real importance, or estimate the relative value of things. With him the great and the small have changed places. The merest trifles swell into huge proportions, and excite the most profound emotion; while the most momentous interests, so vast that the human mind recoils in the attempt to grasp them, dwindle into insignificance. He laughs with maniac merriment where others weep; he weeps in bitter agony, and will not be consoled, where others would not even deign to smile. For all that interests the healthy mind of man, and arouses it to action, he feels the profoundest indifference. For the great living world of actual and palpable realities all around him, with its interests, its activities, its conflicts, and its destiny, he feels no sympathy. The wild and fantastic hallucinations of his own distempered brain are to him the only realities. Around him, on every side, the vast machinery of human society is moving on, the hum of human business, the conflicts of human interest, the agitation of human passions. Revolution after revolution may shake the globe. The freedom of nations, the welfare of the race, the salvation of a world, may be hanging in suspense, or hurrying on to a decisive issue. Yet what is all this to him? He stoops to gather the pebbles at his feet, and piles the straws around him into stately palaces where kings might be proud to dwell. His loud laugh rings in peals of gleeful merriment What is it for? He points to the mimic structure which has grown so magnificent beneath his skill. He sobs in irrepressible anguish. Why? An insect's wing, or a puff of air, has levelled his gorgeous building with the earth. Large possessions may be his, and wide connections, a home of purity and love where each gentle and generous affection is lavished upon him and noble hearts are wrung with anguish at each symptom of his madness. Stupendous interests may depend upon his conduct, bright may have been the promise of his early youth, and fond the hopes that cluster around him still. Yet what are all these to him? He disregards all, he spurns all, barters all, sacrifices all, to the merest trifle. Vain is each appeal to reason, to conscience, or affection. All that is most solemn, most tender, or most sacred, is matter of dead indifference, or brutal merriment, or fierce resentment, or demon hate. He is startled sometimes for a moment from his dream of folly; gazes eagerly around as one bewildered by some strange and sudden recollection of scenes long forgotten; gleams of half-intelligence flit across his countenance like sunbeams struggling through the riven thunder-cloud. We almost hope, we pray, we shudder, as we watch that changing countenance; the blackness and the tempest gather around the soul in deeper and more impenetrable gloom—the deepening shadow of a long and last total eclipse.

And have we not *often* seen the sinner *even thus*, when, startled by some solemn visitation from on high, or aroused from his life-long dream of sin by some peal of terrific denunciation from God's word, he gazes bewildered and terrified around upon the new realities that meet his astonished vision; wonders at the illusive shadows that had so long misled and mocked him; and the world recedes from his view, and eternity in all its terrific grandeur stands palpably out before him, until God, death, and immortality, a coming judgment, an undone eternity, a bleeding Saviour, and an interceding Spirit, are in all the universe the only realities for him? Oh! the keen agony of that anxious suspense, when an immortal spirit seems just awakening to a new life of intelligence, or, greater still, of faith; when the wayward prodigal hears the voice of a father's love, and comes to himself and beholds with horror his own nakedness, and foul and loathsome degradation, and says, "I will arise and go unto my Father;" and he is almost ready to depart, when suddenly a midnight darkness settles down on all his faculties. He forgets his father's house, the fond affection and tender sympathy of the family there, of angels, and spirits of just men made perfect, his own high origin and deathless destiny, and fearful responsibilities; plunges madly back into sin, and wanders like the demoniac of the Bible amidst the tombs of the *dead*, the sepulchres of buried resolutions, and murdered mercies, whose spectral apparitions start up at every step around him, to haunt and madden him *still more* by their presence.

The sinner, too, stands amidst an august and stirring scene, where all is life, activity, intense excitement, and every living agent is profoundly interested except himself. *He stands* amidst the march and the movement of a high moral administration, which sweeps boundlessly around him, reaching the outer limits of immensity itself, comprehending all time and all eternity and all worlds in its tremendous issues, where questions far more solemn, and interests more vast, than those of nations and empires are decided. As this plan moves on in its majestic evolution, our earth has become the theatre of a far mightier conflict than any which the embattled nations of the world have ever waged, when the earth shook beneath the charge of their thronged battalions, or the sea trembled beneath the roar of their artillery. Amidst the thickening interest of the scene, all created intelligences gather around to watch the progress of the vast experiment; superhuman beings mingle their immortal energies in the terrible conflict; holy angels fly with winged speed with messages of love; devils range abroad on their own hellish missions; God himself comes down and adds new grandeur to the scene by his own immediate presence; and he who is mighty to save travails in the greatness of his strength, and bears in his own body on the cross the whole burden of a world's transgressions. Satan falls like lightning from the sky, and rejoicing heralds hurry from land to land, to tell the story of this mysterious sufferer and this wonderful deliverance; and the angel with the everlasting Gospel flies midway in the heaven, bearing it onward on pinions of light, and with an arm of power, far above all human opposition, to shed its benignant radiance over all the world. The loud hosannas of earth are echoed back by angelic anthems from the sky, and the New Jerusalem comes down from heaven upon all the renovated earth; and amidst the shouts and the rapturous hallelujahs of redeemed and sanctified millions, the great drama of the world hastens to a close, and the scenes of a vast and unknown eternity unfold in their solemn grandeur before our view. Amidst the glories and terrors of this scene, the sinner stands; amidst its conflicts and its perils. Above, around, on every side, moves on this mighty scheme, and bears him onward, though unfelt by him, to his final destination. Mysterious agencies encircle him on every side. An unseen power overshadows him with its awful presence. Above him is a holy God, within him is an immortal spirit, before him is a long eternity of joy or woe; around him on every side are immortal spirits, moving onward with him to the same glorious or fearful retribution; while many a noble heart beats high with generous ardor in view of these great realities, and many a tear is dropped, and many a sigh is heaved, and many a prayer is offered, as the awed spirit bows before the throne of God, and asks that the sinner may be awakened from his madness.

There could be nothing more solemn in the universe of God. A sublime and awful earnestness is stamped on every feature and on every part of this great plan. There is a solemn earnestness in every message that issues from that great white throne, and summons back a rebellious world to its allegiance to the king. In that mysterious form where infinite pity and infinite woe are strangely blended, where eternal justice and eternal love, the extremes of divine compassion and of human suffering, mysteriously meet; in the garden and the cross; in the bloody sweat, the meek endurance, the imperial triumph; in the blackening heavens, the quaking earth, the bursting rocks, the awakening dead, there is a sad solemnity of earnestness, the solemn urgency of some high and overmastering purpose. In the martyr's dungeon and the martyr's blood, in the martyr's fiery agony and the martyr's shout of triumph, in Apostolic sufferings and Apostolic toils, their solemn warnings, their tender entreaties, their terrible denunciations; in the seraph's shout of "Glory in the Highest," in the seraph's swift obedience and adoring wonder at the cradle and the cross; in all of these is there not a deep intensity of holy earnestness, which no human language can express? And is not that a terrible earnestness of him the great enemy of souls, who, though cast down from heaven, yet, rebounding from the fall, reasserts his dominion upon earth, and through long centuries of tears and blood, though often foiled, still pursues with desperate zeal his hellish purpose, and plies his devilish stratagems to seduce and ruin the souls of men? Yet, amidst all this earnestness in heaven and earth and hell, the madman dares to trifle! He trifles in full view of Calvary, with all its awful accompaniments of sublimity and terror. He trifles with the cross and him who hung there in his agony and love; trifles with the precious blood of our redemption, with the blood of his own immortality. Nay, he dares to trifle beneath the great eye of God, and beneath his uplifted arm of omnipotent vengeance. Madman, beware! Go, mock at the lightning as it falls crash after crash upon thy doomed home, and laugh and jest above its smouldering ruins, where thy dearest ones lie buried! Go, brave the fury of the hurricane as it sweeps over sea and land, tossing forests and navies and human habitations lightly in the air, and leaving no living thing behind on its broad path of utter desolation! But trifle not with him who speeds the lightning on its errand of death, and lets loose the imprisoned elements to be his ministers of vengeance. Go, be merry, if you can, amidst the ruins of some desolate city, which the earthquake has demolished, where the mangled remains of the dying and the dead lie quivering in their gore, beneath the buildings which were once their homes, and are now their sepulchres. Go, play the buffoon there; it is but an earthly tragedy, let it be followed by an earthly farce. Human madness has invoked it, let human madness riot amid the scene with song and laugh and jest and wild delirious merriment. But there is a ruin which is not of earth—the ruin of an immortal spirit! Mock not at that. Those earthly ruins may be rebuilt once more, rise in equal beauty and perhaps in loftier grandeur than before. But for a lost spirit there is no recovery: from that ruin there is no resurrection. There is but one God, one heaven, one Saviour, one probation. God has no second Son to give if Christ be rejected. Man has no second soul to be saved if this be lost. For "the salvation of their soul is precious and it ceaseth forever."

A lost soul! What language could portray the ruin of a soul lost forever! Well might the most gifted orator of our day exclaim, as his great mind trembles beneath the overwhelming solemnity of the theme, and his own majestic language, in its rich and varied grandeur, labors vainly to convey his vivid yet inadequate conception : "What, if it be lawful to indulge the thought, what would be the funeral obsequies of a lost soul!" "Where shall we find the tears fit to be wept at such a spectacle? Or, could we realize the calamity in all its extent, what tokens of commiseration and concern would be deemed adequate to the occasion? Would it suffice for the sun to veil his light, the moon her brightness? To cover the ocean with mourning and the heavens with sackcloth? Or were the whole fabric of nature to be animated and vocal, would it be possible for her to utter a groan too deep, or a cry too piercing, to express the extent and magnitude of such a catastrophe?" * Thou mayest be thyself that ruin, and the nobler the edifice the mightier the ruin. The imperial palace of thought swept by laborious study, garnished with all the stores of learning and illuminated by brilliant genius, the stately arch, the polished shaft, the graceful column, the colossal dome, nay, the great pyramids of thought, towering up towards heaven, may lie smouldering in ashes, or crushed in ruins, vital with an intense and inextinguishable consciousness. It is no human imagination, though endowed with prophetic solemnity and grandeur, but God's own Word, which tells of those far mightier prodigies, in the heavens and the earth, those fiercer throes and agonies that shall convulse the whole frame of nature, when nature's funeral shall be tolled from the heights above, and the blackness of everlasting night shall shroud the lost soul. No human or angelic sympathy shall then avail.

But there is another characteristic of ordinary madness to which I would invite your especial attention. It is not usually the annihilation of the mind, but its perversion; not the extinction of its faculties, but their misdirection or mutilation. The maniac has often mental activity even in excess. Each inmate of a lunatic asylum readily perceives the madness of every other, though unconscious of his own.

* Hall.

You will remember the incident recorded by a gentleman who visited one of those homes of the insane. He was addressed by one of plausible demeanor, who had ingeniously foiled every effort to detect the seat of his derangement, who said to him, pointing to one of his companions in misfortune, "that man is mad." "How do you know?" was the visitor's reply. "Because he says he is John the Baptist." "But how do you know that he is not John the Baptist?" "Because," said he with infinite self-complacency, and equal contempt for the other, "I am Jesus Christ, and if he was John the Baptist he would surely know me." Thus, too, in the great *madhouse* of the world each class can perceive the madness of every other, though unconscious of their own, and are often heard to exclaim with wonder, and even with bitter indignation, against the incorrigible madness and merited suffering of mankind. The man of middle age sees nothing but the wild delirium of absolute derangement in the reckless gayety and self-indulgence of thoughtless and dissipated youth. The sedate and quiet citizen distinctly perceives the madness of those ambitious and restless spirits, whether warriors or statesmen, who have made the world mad by their contagion. The ardent and aspiring, the lovers of pleasure and of fame, return the charge of madness against the dull drudges of ordinary life, who live amidst the perpetual stagnation of the soul, without the intense excitement of any vivid pleasure, or strong impulse of any high emotion, or the broad expression of any elevated or comprehensive purpose.

And for ourselves we believe that they are right, for if there be a madness which in its stupid obstinacy transcends all other forms of human folly, it is that dull delirium of the soul, which, amidst all those elements of grandeur in the universe around, and all the corresponding susceptibilities of the soul of man; amidst the mighty interests at stake, the conflicts that are waging, and the lofty sympathies they are calling into action in a world where prophets and patriarchs and apostles and martyrs have lived and prayed and toiled and died, and noble patriots and heroes still are living, can find no object so worthy their pursuit as the accumulation of worldly wealth, or the attainment of a transitory worldly distinction. But are they not often shrewd, keen, sagacious, far-seeing in all that concerns their worldly interests, skilfully employing their own resources, and dexterously wielding the feelings and passions of other men, to accomplish the one great object of their wishes and their efforts? Very true; yet this is precisely the characteristic of the ordinary madman. He too is quick, shrewd, adroit, cunning, in the attainment of his ends. But, in the calm view of sober reason, his ends are not worth attaining. On every point save one he exhibits rare activity of mind. On this he is the victim of some strange hallucination. He reasons often with an intuitive rapidity and precision surpassing that of the trained logician, but his premises are the illusions of a distempered fancy. His conclusions would be true, but for the madness of his premises. We might admire the shrewdness, the energy, the undaunted courage, the defiance of all difficulty and danger in the prosecution of his object, were not the end desired too frivolous to enlist the sympathies, or command the approbation, of a rational and immortal being.

Thus too is it with the worldly madman. Even amidst the most dazzling exhibitions of the poet, the novelist, or the ambitious statesman, we pause to mourn that so much energy should be lavished on subjects so inferior. And the wider the range of his inquiries, the vaster the accumulation of his knowledge, the mightier the sweep of his genius as he rises in this ascending climax from step to step towards some fiery burst of oratoric passion, or to some remote conclusion which crowns the summit of some high fabric of reasoning, the more profound is our regret and wonder, that a mind formed for immortality should summon its powers to their highest exercise, and lavish its resources on any theme less than eternal and divine. He may have read all history, studied all philosophy, may be deeply versed in the science of human nature, and intimately acquainted with the mutual relations and conflicting interests of the most distant nations. He may bring light from the past to shine upon the present, and cast its radiance over the distant future; and it is precisely in such a case as this, where the greatest of earthly efforts has accomplished the greatest of earthly objects, and attained the greatest of earthly rewards, and the greatest of earthly madmen has gained the loudest eulogies from other madmen around like himself, that the madness alike of the many and the one is most distinctly manifest. He can tell you the products of a nation's soil, the value of a nation's commerce, the sources of a nation's revenue. All this he has calculated with minutest precision. But on all that concerns his immortal interests he is insane; his very arithmetic here fails him. The simplest of all problems, the most solemn, the most sublime, the most urgent, pressing every moment for a solution, and from which there is no escape, he cannot solve; he recoils in convulsive repugnance from it, scowls on it with a madman's horror and a madman's hate: "What shall a man be profited if he gain the whole world, and lose his own soul?" And now, as he is charioted along in splendor through the crowded streets of some illuminated city, cheered with the loud applause of congregated thousands, who hang with eager admiration on his lips; what is all this when viewed in the light of eternity, but the empty pageant of a maniac procession? And does not he who sits high exalted above all worlds, and comprehends all time, truly stamp the charge of madness on him, who thus casts away the celestial diadem of glory for a fading laurel, and exchanges the glad hosannas of the blessed for the wild and delirious applause of a fickle and besotted generation?

On every faculty of his nature, intellectual, emotional, and moral, is stamped the broad, indelible impress of immensity, infinity, eternity. He cannot think of time, but it swells into eternity; of space, but it expands into immensity of cause; but he rises to a first great cause of causes. His destinies too are commensurate with his powers of thought and calculation; they spontaneously overleap all the boundaries of space and time, and acknowledge no satisfying portion, but one that is infinite and eternal. The first step in his moral life is from the law upon the conscience to the legislator upon the throne. The first ray of moral light comes from the world above, and in the last hours of his earthly being, when every sense and every faculty whose appropriate theatre is earth, is failing fast, this which peculiarly links him with eternity, springs into new activity, and bounds forward instinctively and irresistibly to the bar of God and the retributions of eternity. Yet all these higher elements of his being, and their correspondent interests, he wholly disregards, and all the large provisions which eternal love has made on their behalf. To all his earthly interests, however trivial, he is wide awake, quickly sensitive, keenly sagacious. Touch his honor, his estate, his civil rights, and every faculty springs into spontaneous activity. But the interests of his soul! To these he gives not one anxious thought; postpones them to every other interest, sacrifices them on the most frivolous pretences, to the merest trifles. He quaffs with eager haste the intoxicating portion which the world offers, though he knows that the drugged draught is fever in the blood, and madness in the brain, and wild delirium. Every avenue of sense and feeling—the eye, the ear, the heart—is closed against the solemn realities around him, and he roves and raves and revels amidst the illusions of a voluntary intoxication. Heaven from on high invites him home, and her everlasting gates, on golden hinges turning, utter soft music as they open wide to welcome him at his arrival. Hell from beneath yawns wide to receive him. Ten thousand voices peal above, beneath, around, within him; from the bed of sickness, from the chamber of death, from the freshly opened grave, from the mouldering sepulchre, from the sinner's bed of remorse and despair, and the saint's couch of rapture, from the depths of his own agitated conscience, and from God's great throne on high. Yet he marches heedless on, his eyes fastened on the earth, and his heart cleaving to the dust. He weaves gay garlands, and sings merry songs, on the very verge of the abyss, which is crumbling beneath his very footstep, and gaping wide to engulf him. And when he sinks at last, his epitaph might be written *thus:* Here lies the body of one whose soul has gone to judgment. He lived like a madman, and as the fool dieth *so* he died. One momentary flash of intelligence gleamed horribly over his last hours, to reveal the ruin which it was too late to remedy, and he sank back with a groan into midnight darkness. He feared the laugh of fools, but heeded not the instructions of wisdom. He courted the approbation of men, but feared not the frown or the vengeance of God. He pampered his body, and neglected his soul; and the wealth which he spent his life to accumulate, and for which he sold his immortal spirit, is now enjoyed by others, who gayly revel in his halls, and of all his large possessions have left him only this six feet of earth, and reared this monument to perpetuate the memory of his madness. Reader, pause to drop a tear over the madman's grave, and offer a prayer for his soul. It is not yet too late. That grave, that epitaph, that history is thine. Thine that life of insensate folly; that death, that undone eternity, too, without repentance is thine own!

Another characteristic of the ordinary madman is his extravagant estimate of himself, of his powers, of his fortune, his immunity from the evils that reach common men, his superiority to the ordinary laws, and independence of the ordinary course of nature. Perils that deter other men have no terrors for him. Forces that would crush other men shall pass by him harmless. Laws that encircle other men with their omnipresent majesty and immutable sanction can never reach *him*, were not made for *him*. He mocks at the lightning and the thunderbolt. The floods and the pestilence cannot hurt him. On his behalf the laws of nature are suspended or reversed. He leaps from a window and shall not be injured. The law of gravitation shall be suspended—rather some mysterious charm encircles him at every moment to insure his safety. His puissant arm shall arrest a rail-car in full speed, or stay a falling mountain. He breathes the pestilence, and yet shall live. He drinks the deadliest poison, it shall be health and nutrition to his system. He cherishes the young adder in his bosom, yet fears not the venom or the fang of the full-grown reptile.

Just so is it with the youthful sinner. He lives and moves and breathes amidst a tainted atmosphere, where every word and thought and feeling is full of worldliness and sensuality, of ambition and hostility against God. He quaffs with eager joy the poisoned chalice which the world offers, and, amidst the fever of his delirium, dreams that the spasmodic energy of madness is the calm vigor of health, nay, the loftiest exertion of heroic courage and manly strength. He cherishes within his bosom those passions and those habits which first coil gently around his slumbering powers, then with tightening folds embrace every faculty, crushing each rising energy, and paralyzing each lofty purpose, until at last with their serpent's eye of deadly fascination, and serpent's hiss of terror, they send the serpent's venom along the whole throbbing circulation, through every vein and artery, through head and heart, and every member; and the man stands before us one bloated and hideous mass of moral putrefaction. The evil associations that ruin others shall not injure him. The habits that enslave others shall not master him. The slightest call of inclination he cannot now deny, the gentlest breath of passion he cannot now resist. But when every appetite has been inflamed by long indulgence, every passion glowing with the gathered fuel of years of sin, when all its fires are up, and all its energies in motion, and the whole train is sweeping furiously on to its destined goal, he thinks that he can in a moment arrest its mad career, and even reverse its movement. He can leap over the precipice of ruin, and pausing midway down, shall never reach the abyss below. Nay, like the madman of whom we all have read, who spurned the vulgar feat of leaping from the summit of a tower to the ground below, and embraced with eagerness the proposition to leap from the earth to the top of the tower, so the sinner imagines that he too can clear by a single bound the loftiest heights of moral excellence, and without the slow and painful progress of other men, can, by an effort of his will, be at once a wise and virtuous and happy man. Around him on every side are the bleached bones of those who have run the same mad career; and wrecks of wasted fortunes, and ruined character, and souls lost forever, are strewed along his path. They lived without God, were ruined without remedy, died without hope, were judged without mercy, and damned without deliverance.

But the laws that decide the destiny of other men, were not made for him. There is a law of God, eternal, omnipotent, immutable as any other; a law extending to our whole intellectual, physical, and moral nature, universal and irresistible, and which has no exceptions. It is the law of habit. We shall not pause to analyze this law, to explain its nature, its origin, its necessity. It establishes a terrible unity in human life; makes the past the parent of the present and the future, the boy the father of the man; and passes on to the trembling hand of the aged sinner the cup of bitterness which had been mingled by his youthful folly. It binds together by links stronger than steel the remotest boundaries of human destiny, the first dawnings of moral agency on earth, with the final issues of eternity. There is not a thought of the mind, or an act of the life, not a word that issues from the lips, or an emotion that flits across the countenance and straightway disappears, which has not left its impression on the soul, deep, permanent, indelible. You shall never be, through all eternity —*can* never be—the spirit you might have been, but for the thoughts and acts of yesterday. Sin may be forgiven, but never obliterated. The wound it has inflicted on the soul may be healed, but the scar remains. The moment just passed is gone indeed, but it is not destroyed. It has gone to mingle with the solemn ages of the eternity that is past. It has gone to bear its record to the bar of God, but it has left behind a more fearful record here. Its thoughts, passions, purposes, have mingled with all the elements of our being, have been incorporated into the very constitution of our nature, have penetrated the whole texture of our existence, and become the warp, web, and woof of our whole future life.

But if such be the dominion of habit in every department

of our nature, if it not only moulds our thoughts and actions, but the very capacity to think and act; when we ascend to the department of our moral nature it seems to be endowed with a peculiar and almost supernatural control—a control which leads us to suspect that as the body was formed for the service of the mind, and the mind was formed for the service of God, so this law of habit, when viewed in its higher and wider relations, is nothing less than the solemn utterance cf God's approbation of the right, and judicial condemnation of the wrong. Thus much at least is certain, that as it is the sweet and precious privilege of virtue ever to become more virtuous, and as the stream of life flows on to diffuse itself continually in ever-wider expansion, and profounder depths of piety; so it is the irrevocable and unmitigable curse of sin, that it must perpetuate and multiply itself, in ever accumulating hideousness and horror, must become more "exceeding sinful," must diffuse itself by an infernal contagion over all around and all within, passing from faculty to faculty, till the whole man is mastered; from the body to the mind, from the appetites to the passions, from the passions to the imagination, from the imagination to the reasoning powers and the moral sentiments, from the transient and momentary indulgence to a whole life of sin; when the memory recalls only scenes of past indulgence, the heart pants only after forbidden things, the polluted imagination, impotent to resist, riots amidst imagery of licentious joy, and every power of thought and feeling and association sweeps bounding on in the broad deep channel of habitual desire, only to swell the current they cannot stem. Resistance now is hopeless, even were it not impossible, and impossible if it were not hopeless, for the only power of resistance, *the will*, is captive. "Can the Ethiopian change his skin, or the leopard his spots?" "Then may ye also do good who are accustomed to do evil." Every sin indulged increases the power of temptation, and diminishes the power of resistance. The voice of conscience is feebler, the decisions of reason less distinct, the motives for the right present themselves more seldom, and with decreasing confidence.

The motives to the wrong rush in, in greater number and with increasing importunity, upon the enfeebled and distracted mind.

No man renounces at once all fear of God, all reverence for religion, all sense of shame, all the principles of honor. He offers first a faint resistance; then parleys and temporizes with the foe; then receives him into the citadel; then wears his gaudy silken fetters, exults in his bondage, glories in his shame; then receives reluctantly his manacles of steel, and groans beneath the burden; then madly dances to the music of his chains.

Such, then, is the law of habit, which is nothing else than the insidious power of sin—the eternal law of God and nature—the inexorable doom stamped indelibly upon its brow by the hand of the Almighty, and legible to all. It is written in the blood of millions, and yet the madman fancies that this most terrible and universal of all God's laws is suspended in regard to him; that he can defy its terrors and cast its fetters from him. The cord which binds him to the world, and holds him away from God, is composed of many a subtle and invisible strand, which habit and early association have already woven out of the elements of his fallen nature. He cannot burst from them even now; cannot even wish to be free. The fetters have reached his soul and paralyzed its power, and yet he believes that when years of sin have strengthened the cords that bind him, and enfeebled all his powers, he who could not burst the cords—and each day of sin is adding another and yet another strand—will, by an easy effort, rend asunder the cable. Each step in sin is bearing him further from God and nearer hell, and as the distance widens, the attraction of the good diminishes, and the power of evil increases its strange and dreadful fascination. And yet he madly hopes that when he has wandered for years further and further away from God and heaven, he will find himself very near the kingdom; and need only stretch forth his hand in the hour of his extremity, and knock at the door of heaven, and it shall be opened.

This leads us to consider another law of God's moral government, of which the former one is the counterpart. The one is learned from experience and reason, the other from revelation. The one lies amidst the mysteries of human agency, the other amidst the higher mysteries of the divine administration. Both may perhaps be traced upward even by us to one common principle, the mind of eternal justice. Both are exemplified on the theatre of human affairs. Both have their solemn and tremendous issues in eternity. The one tells us that if we dally with sin we shall be the slaves of sin; that if we trifle with conscience we shall not see its light, nor hear its voice, nor enjoy its influences. That voice, if stifled, shall wax feebler and feebler still, while the uproar of the passions shall be louder and louder, and the very power to hear shall become extinct. The other bears us at once amidst the realities of the unseen world of spirits; and shows us this same law transferred to the agencies of that higher supernatural administration. It tells us of a holy Spirit of God that visits the soul of man to arouse the slumbering conscience, and quicken the dull perceptions, and points to a coming judgment. And now he whispers in tones of gentlest invitation; and now he thunders of the wrath to come; and now he pours the light of a convincing demonstration on the benighted understanding; and now he reveals the beauty of holiness and the love of a dying Saviour in melting tenderness; and now he discovers to the startled sinner the dark pollutions of a soul steeped in sin.

Yet ever as this mysterious visitor is treated, will he treat the soul of man. If kindly welcomed, he will often return. If fondly cherished, he will take up his permanent abode, and make it a habitation of God, and shed abroad, over that consecrated soul, the light and peace and joy of his habitual presence. If neglected, grieved, insulted, he will depart, seldom to return, perhaps never. Now, the holy Scriptures manifestly place the turning-point, the crisis of man's salvation precisely here, amidst all the inscrutable mystery of God's eternal sovereignty. Yet manifestly in that strange union of human and divine agency, in the work of man's salvation, the whole interest of his eternity hinges upon this single question: How does he receive these visitations of God's Spirit? The whole Bible is full of this subject. Warning after warning reverberates along its pages against the slightest indignity offered to this Spirit. Exhortation after exhortation peals from prophet, evangelist, apostle, and the Saviour himself, to welcome with joy and gratitude this mysterious visitant. Example after example is adduced, in solemn and terrific array, to show how fearful is the doom of those who slight his offered influences, and grieve away his gracious presence. "My spirit shall not always strive with man," was the death-doom of the antediluvian world; and in all the wild roar of those tumultuous waters as they swept over that desolated world, or the shrieks of the perishing millions that sank beneath the billows, there was nothing half so awful as that solemn sentence. It was a God-abandoned world! deliberately cast off by God because they had grieved his Spirit. And when our Saviour stood and wept over Jerusalem, what was the burden of her condemnation? The accumulated guilt and accumulated vengeance of fifteen centuries rose above their heads, the blood of all the prophets was upon their hands, soon to be stained by the blood of the Son of God! But all this might have been forgiven. They were a God-abandoned people, given up to judicial blindness and judicial insensibility. "They knew not the day of their visitation, the things that made for their peace were hidden from their eyes." And when an individual or a race is given up finally of God, it matters little whether the fires of conflagration, or the waters of deluge are the ministers of justice, to summon them to their final account.

Around this central and decisive point in the great moral warfare of the soul, all the thunders of the Bible roll perpetually, and all the forces of the great enemy are rallied, and all his skill is concentrated there. Even he who was life and truth and love itself, who never spake but in love and tenderness for man, even he assumes an unwonted sternness, and says, "All manner of sin and blasphemy shall be forgiven unto men, but the blasphemy against the Holy Ghost shall not be forgiven unto men." It is only here that the solemn tenderness of the Bible is turned into bitterest irony. "Because I have called and ye refused; I have stretched out my hand and no man regarded. But ye have set at naught all my counsel, and would none of my reproof; I also will laugh at your calamity; I will mock when your fear cometh, when your fear cometh as desolation, and your destruction cometh as a whirlwind; when distress and anguish cometh upon you. *Then* shall they call upon me, but I will not answer; they shall seek me early, but they shall not find me; for that they hated knowledge, and did not choose the fear of the Lord; they would none of my counsel, they despised all my reproofs. *Therefore* shall they eat of the fruit of their own way, and be filled with their own devices." I know of nothing so terrible as this. It seems as if the very heavens above had become one vast gallery where every lowest whisper of human mockery was gathered up, and echoed back, in tones of stern and concentrated defiance; as if infinite patience were at length wearied out, and the last drop exhausted from the cup of God's forbearance.

Yet it is precisely here that the madman trifles most; trifles habitually, trifles daily, is trifling still. Examples are all around us. There is scarcely a man in this assembly, a youth, a child who has reached the years of moral agency, that has not experienced the visitations of that Spirit. Where are they now?—those meltings of tenderness, those tremblings of terror, that solemnity of awe, that sensibility of conscience—the falling tear, the heaving sigh, the murmured prayer for mercy? Where the convictions of Felix were, after he had said to Paul, "Go thy way for the present, at a more convenient season I will call for thee." God's grieved Spirit has departed: is it forever? One act of deliberate rejection may seal your doom. On a single moment often hangs suspended the eternal destinies of an immortal spirit. There are in the life of every human being moments big with the issues of eternity—the great landmarks of his existence, where the past all terminates, and the whole future begins anew.

But we must pass on to the next division of our subject, and here can only give hasty hints, and leave them to your own reflections.

Christ only can cast out the devil and heal the madness. All philosophy, all poetry, all literature, art, government, civilization, refinement, for sixty centuries, have been but varied devices of human ingenuity, to exorcise the demon, and relieve society from the evils he inflicted. But all in vain. They could alleviate, palliate, but not heal; could sweep and garnish the house, adorn it with all the choice productions of human art, illuminate it with the corruscations of brilliant genius, but could not restore the original and rightful occupant. The demon, startled for a season from his lair, returned to his vacant habitation with seven other devils worse than himself, and controlled for his own malignant purposes, and appropriated to his own use, and imbued with his own spirit, the very means employed to dispossess him. Sad result of all human history! In all ages and all nations it is the same. All human efforts conducted without the Gospel have not only proved failures, but have aggravated the evils they aimed to remedy. Philosophy has *always* terminated in atheism, refinement in effeminacy, art in licentiousness, freedom in anarchy, and then in despotism. "This is the moral of all human tales." This is the goal to which all schemes and experiments to elevate men, and nations withal, without the true religion have conducted them.

The sterner and loftier virtues of an earlier age are always allied to some faith in God and immortality. Increasing civilization banishes the demon of superstition, but as wise men of the world mutter their incantations over the body of society, the demon passions are aroused once more; the possessed exclaims, "Jesus I know, and Paul I know, but who are you?" And nobility, priesthood, and king, law and order, all the learning, graces, and refinements of civilized society with the very foundations of society itself, are swept away in the wild whirlwind of revolutionary passions. Even under the light of the Gospel a strange phenomenon may be observed in individuals and nations. The evil spirit may go out. His power may cease for a time. The spirit of impiety, blasphemy, licentiousness, may be exorcised for a season. The swearer may cease to swear, the bold blasphemer to revile. Yet how often does he return again—bitterer, fiercer, more numerous than before—the very spirit of infidelity, hypocrisy, and formality. Why? The house is *empty*. Christ is not there. If we would keep the demon out, every apartment of the soul must be occupied; not by metaphysical abstraction, or graceful sentimentality, or dead dogmas; but by Christ in his living efficacy.

XXVII.

THE FINAL AND UNIVERSAL TRIUMPH OF THE GOSPEL.

REV. xiv. 6.—"And I saw another angel fly in the midst of heaven, having the everlasting Gospel to preach unto them that dwell on the earth, and to every nation, and kindred, and tongue, and people."

WE shall not attempt this evening to open the book that is sealed with seven seals, to unveil the mysteries of this wonderful work, or to discuss the truth of any of those various and conflicting theories which have been advanced, in ancient or in modern times, respecting the millennium, the time of its commencement, or the harbingers that shall announce its near approach, but shall proceed directly to consider the great event predicted in our text—the universal diffusion of the Gospel—and remark:

First, the glorious *certainty* of this event. It is no remote contingency of an unfathomable future—lies not among the vague possibilities or even the higher probabilities of a coming era. We have learned it from no doubtful report, announced it on no questionable authority, have ascertained it by no circuitous or complicated process of reasoning. It is not a wild conjecture, nor is it a delusion of fancy. Oh, no! I saw it, these eyes beheld it. It was on the Isle of Patmos. I was in the spirit on the Lord's day, when wrapt in visions of the Almighty that gave my spirit strength to sweep adown the gulf of time, in full possession of all my powers, with every faculty invigorated, purified, exalted by direct communion with God, till in that high apocalyptic vision all the glories of heaven, and the whole future history of earth, lay expanded before me.

It was then that it appeared, not a shadowy phantom of a

disordered brain, but openly, boldly, visibly, palpably it stood before me a transcendent and glorious reality. How could I be deceived? It was the Gospel that I loved, and borne by an angel that I knew. His bright pathway was in the midst of heaven, and I gazed and gazed intent, delighted, till I beheld him bear it to "every nation, and kindred, and tongue, and people." I saw it with all the certainty of vision, announced it with all the authority of inspiration.

Again, it was borne onward by an angel's arm of power, on an angel's pinions of strength, with an angel's devoted love. Now, who shall resist his progress, what barrier retard his career, what energy arrest his flight? "Let the heathen rage, and the people imagine a vain thing, let the kings of the earth set themselves, and the rulers take counsel together against the Lord and against his anointed." Let all the combined powers of earth and hell array themselves against it, let them hurl their envenomed missiles, peal their loudest artillery, fulminate their bitterest denunciations, let all the arts of secret malignity and open warfare be united—yet what will it avail? Behold his luminous pathway in the midst of heaven! and far above the puny malice of his foes, from country to country, in his own sublime and serene elevation he pursues his onward career, shedding down the light and joy of the Gospel on successive generations and in distant lands. The mists of earth may obscure our vision, the clouds of the air may hide him from our view, but to the unscaled eye of him—lone exile on Patmos, as he stood on that high mount of prophetic vision, there was no pause in his flight, but it was onward, still and ever onward, onward amidst the brightness and purity of heaven, laden with everlasting blessings for all the nations of the world.

Oh, brethren, can we not elevate ourselves this evening to the height of his sublime and blessed assurance; do we need another prophet to arise and teach us, that the Gospel of this kingdom shall be preached in all the world? That no weapon forged against Zion shall prosper; that sword and spear and battle-axe shall be broken together? Has it not been so in all ages? When the angel commenced his flight, beginning at

Jerusalem, was not all human power arrayed to resist his progress; were not all human interests, prejudices, passions, leagued in open hostility against him? Magistrate, people, priest, emperor, philosopher, fanatic, wit, eloquence, argument, learning, genius, the tongue, the pen, the sword, all combined to retard his career—but in vain. The eyes of expectant nations gazed with wonder and rapture on his flight; the hearts of desponding millions welcomed the message that he bore. The very gods of the heathen, startled at his approach, grow dumb; the Apollo of Delphi withholds his oracles, and the Jupiter of the Capitol abandons his throne. From land to land the tidings fly, from mouth to mouth the message spreads. The haughty Roman, the polished Greek, the savage barbarian heard it. It was whispered in the porch and the academy, and the philosophers gathered at Areopagus to hear of Jesus and the resurrection. It has resounded amongst the hills of the eternal city, and is heard amid Cæsar's household. The eastern mystic has heard it and is startled from his dream. The northern barbarian, as he drank his draught of blood from a brother's skull, has paused to listen to the story of one who loved his enemies, and shed his own blood, an infinite atonement for sin. Strange thoughts are waking up, new hopes are kindling in the minds of men, the tremulous agitation of a new life is felt throughout the world's great mass of putrefaction, and every eye that is turned toward heaven sees that it is an angel's flight.

But shall Satan without a struggle yield his long dominion? No, let every device of cruelty and falsehood be plied to resist the progress of the Gospel. Those Christians are atheists and despisers of the gods, says the priest. Yea, and enemies of Cæsar, says the magistrate. In their midnight assemblies scenes are exhibited of licentiousness and crime, at which day would blush, says one, and in their hellish orgies they devour young children, and swear horrid oaths as they drink their young blood, says another. The gods have abandoned earth for their crimes, exclaims a third, and signs in heaven above and earth below—earthquakes, famine, and pestilence—proclaim the avenging Deity. Away with such monsters from the earth, exclaim all together, to wild beasts or the fire! The Christian martyr walks meekly to the stake. The cup his Father gives shall he not drink it? But does the angel stop his flight? Tell me, does the sun cease to shine? the stars, do they lose their brightness? is the moon turned from her orbit of glory? Are the great laws of nature reversed? is the universe of God unhinged? Blessed be God that far above, and wide beyond the circle of human passions, the theatre of human power, extend the laws of a wider and loftier jurisdiction, and that he who sitteth enthroned high above them all, has so subordinated all to his own great designs, that even the wrath of man shall accomplish the purposes of God. The violence of persecution recoils upon itself, the enormity of the charges contrasted with the purity of a spotless life, is their own perfect refutation. The Christian dies, but the undying angel pursues his own sublime and beneficent flight. And from that day to this how constant, yet how vain, have been the efforts to prevent the diffusion of the Gospel. In the days of Luther, pope and emperor and kings, a licentious aristocracy, and depraved priesthood, could not resist it. At a later period the keen swords of gay and gallant cavaliers could not suppress it. In the last century, the wit, learning, eloquence of Voltaire, Rousseau, Hume, and Gibbon, and in the present the deeper learning and more insidious wiles of German literati, have failed. And now, after the scrutiny of centuries, amidst the accumulated discoveries of modern science, now that a cautious scepticism has sifted all knowledge, and all the lights of genius and learning are intensely concentrated on it, we may fearlessly assert that the Bible stands on a prouder eminence than ever—that the angel who bears it is taking a loftier and more rapid flight.

Second. An *angelic mission* this! the diffusion of God's Word. God and angels are embarked in it. So vast is its importance, so overwhelming its grandeur, that it excites the interest and arouses the sympathies and calls forth the activities of the heavenly inhabitants. Oh, brethren, what a thought is this to confirm our faith, to rebuke our inactivity, at once to elevate and humble us. Let us not amidst our degradation and misery forget the grandeur of our high original, the sublimity of our future destiny. And is it true? Yes, it is an inexpressibly precious truth, that, fallen as we are, there is hope in our case; that though wayward children, we are children still; that we are members still of God's great and universal family of love; that though voluntary wanderers from our Father's house, yet the fondness of a Father's love yearns after us, and the tenderness of fraternal sympathy melts through all the members of that family. There is joy in heaven at the repentance of one sinner, and that joy was once heard overflowing the walls of heaven, and bursting from the sky, when they announced the Saviour's advent. "There is joy in heaven, and amongst the angels of God, over one sinner that repenteth." Brethren, all poetry can furnish nothing so touching or so beautiful as those simple words, and in the whole compass of uninspired philosophy there can nowhere be found a view at once so comprehensive and so just, of the bond that binds the remotest parts of God's moral universe together, that encircles with so mild a radiance the throne of the universal Father and universal King.

And this is no doubtful revelation, no casual or hasty glimpse of the glories too bright to be endured—not one of those flashes, intolerably bright, from that ineffable glory, which dazzle and stun us by the grandeur of their revelation. It is one of the clearest and most frequent teachings of God's Word, lies at the very foundation of the method of salvation, is interwoven with the whole fabric of God's truth. Without it, we could neither understand the ministry of angels, nor the sacrifices of his Son. "God so loved the world that he gave his only begotten Son, that whosoever believeth in him, should not perish, but have everlasting life." This was at once the measure of his love and the motive to the sacrifice. With what solemn dignity, incalculable value, imperishable grandeur does this invest the soul of man! When God would commend his love to us, he tells us of the price he paid for our ransom: and what? A whole world of matter? No. The whole material universe? Did he take his brightest angel? Did he take all matter, and offer on it all spirit? No; but he did more. He went into his own bosom, and gave his only begotten and well-beloved Son. And then he chose the princes of his household, prime-ministers from around his throne, to be the ministers and messengers of his love. What an elevated theatre have we to act upon! What a load of infamy, or crown of moral approbation, are we to receive according to our conduct or characters here! God and angels observe our conduct, God and angels are interested in our welfare. They offer us all the assistance that we need, and if we shall after this prefer the poor enjoyments of earth, how great will be our fall, how deep and awful our condemnation! All the glories of the heavenly world are laid open to our view; we have only to accept and be saved, to taste and live. If we refuse the offers so kindly made us, when the disapprobation and contempt of a holy universe, the accumulated abhorrence of all that is good and lovely in creation shall frown upon us, what will be our feelings! The church then is safe, though men oppose; there are more for us than against us. Oh, in what a world we live, with what awful grandeur encompassed on every side, linked with God and angels, tending to heaven or hell! All around us infinity and eternity, above us incalculable heights, beneath us unfathomable depths, within us capacities of unlimited enjoyment or woe, energies of fearful intensity, which, perverted or rightly directed, may bring agony or joy to ourselves or others—around on every side perishing millions. But is all heaven awake, and do we slumber? Does the angel still push his onward flight with unwearied pinion, unabated ardor, unquenched and unquenchable love; and has God given his own Son, and are we inactive, giving to this great cause the tribute of a transient thought, and an empty wish? You remember who it is that hath said, "If any man have not the spirit of Christ, he is none of his."

XXVIII.

CHRIST WEEPING OVER JERUSALEM.

LUKE, xix. 41, 42.—"And when he was come near, he beheld the city and wept over it, saying, If thou hadst known, even thou, at least in this thy day, the things which belong unto thy peace! but now they are hid from thine eyes."

THESE words were spoken on our Saviour's last solemn approach to Jerusalem. The Feast of the Passover was at hand, and already six days before were gathered the thousands of Israel, from every corner of Judea, and every region of the globe, to celebrate that solemn festival, and to record, with hymns of grateful praise, the day of the right hand of the Most High, when the first-born of Egypt perished, and with a high hand and uplifted arm the God of Jacob led forth his chosen people.

And now, as the crowds of annual visitors come up, while the thronged streets are filled with the hum of a lively and busy population, acquaintances of the past year are revived, the ready recognition, affectionate salutation, and kind inquiry circulate; but, above all, there is one of whom all inquire and all have heard. "What think you, will he come to the feast?" But he was one of spirit far different from theirs. A man of sorrows, he knew this visit was his last, that a life spent in doing good was to terminate there. That holy heart knew no evil, yet it should burst beneath the burden of the world's transgressions. The typical feast was to pass away, and he the Lamb of God to be slain, and there offered a propitiation for sin.

On his last melancholy passage he lodged at Bethany in the bosom of that pious and devoted family, where Martha ministered, and Mary sat at his feet, and Lazarus, raised from the dead, reclined at the table with his astonished guests. It was at the foot of Mount Olivet where he was wont to retire from the noise of public crowds and the malice of foes, to meditate and pray amidst its groves of palms, and figs, and olives, and vines. Already had the fame of his morals and doctrine gone abroad, and his last great miracle on Lazarus attracted universal attention. And now expectation was on tiptoe, friends awaited his glorification, foes his destruction, and the curious, excited crowd, aware of his approach, went forth to meet and welcome him. It was at the eastern descent of Mount Olivet, as it looks toward Bethany, where this throng met to escort him to Jerusalem. Here they hailed him king of Israel, welcomed him as son of David, strewed flowers and palm-branches along his path; and the full tide of joy flowed forth in those songs of exulting and rapturous praise, which the old prophets wrote in view of the Messiah's days. "And the multitudes that went before, and that followed, cried, saying, Hosanna to the son of David; blessed is he that cometh in the name of the Lord; hosanna in the highest." Matt. xxi. 9.

And now that triumphal march is moving on, and they stand on the summit of Mount Olivet—and what a prospect! It is the tallest of the mountains around, and commanded a view far and wide, of green valleys, vine-clad hills, seas, and rivers. Far in the west was the broad Mediterranean, to his right the valley of the Jordan, to the south was the Dead Sea, to his left Bethlehem, and before him Jerusalem, with her lofty towers, her splendid temple, rich with the offerings of ages, and august with its awful ceremonies, and her crowded population ready to welcome him as their long-expected king. A thousand hearts around were beating with exultation, the air was vocal with his praise, the distant mountain-tops echoed back their joy, the very rocks, we are told, were ready to break into singing, and all the trees of the forest to clap their hands for joy.

Was not that a proud day for him, the despised and derided one? The man of Nazareth was now hailed Messiah of the Jews, the son of the carpenter, the hope of Israel and salvation of the world. Surely, if innocence ever may triumph, it is when the clouds obscuring it are dispersed, and its righteousness is brought forth as the sun, and its enemies forced to yield the tribute of their applause. And he, the man of sorrows, did he not then rejoice? Was there no glow upon his cheek, no brightness in his eye? His bosom heaved indeed with an unwonted fullness, but 'twas the fullness of his anguish, and amidst all the joy and exultation of that applauding crowd the Saviour "wept." He looked down upon the city lying quietly and securely below, upon the crowd now worshipping, and soon to crucify him, and as he thought of all their privileges and abuses, of their past security, and coming doom, his heart was overwhelmed with the view of their certain and self-caused ruin, and he wept. The Saviour of sinners, the Prince of Israel, the Lord of Glory, wept. It was a city of unnumbered privileges, and he wept; of unnumbered crimes, and he wept; and weeping he exclaims, "Oh, that thou, even thou, hadst known, at least in this thy day, the things which belong unto thy peace."

Now the rules of God's government are unchangeable, and Jerusalem's fate is the type of others. Consider, 1st, Every man has a day of merciful visitation. 2d, When disregarded, the things that make for his peace shall be hid from his eyes.

I. Life is such a day. It is a solemn thing to live in God's world, to breathe his free air, tread upon his earth, be upheld by his goodness, fed on his bounty, in him to live, and move, and have our being, to have constantly around us that awful presence, and fastened upon us the keen gaze of that omniscient eye. When God breathed into man the breath of life, he made him a living soul endowed with high and immortal powers, placed before him a noble and exalted destiny, and brought on him solemn and fearful responsibilities. Now life is the time given to prepare for meeting these responsibilities, fulfilling this destiny, training these immortal powers for that higher and more glorious world, their ultimate abode. It is the infancy of man, the period of education for eternity. Oh, it is this which gives to life its solemn and momentous import—that every circumstance, however minute, has its influence on eternal destiny. Every act, word, thought, feeling, that flits over the mind or moves the heart, gives an impression which no time, no circumstances, can eradicate, but endures through eternal ages. The moment just past has gone to the bar of God, and its testimony is there recorded, but it has left behind its own deep impression stamped on the soul. You will never be, through all eternity, the exalted spirit you might have been had yesterday been wholly given to God. The past may be forgiven, but never annihilated: the wound of sin may be healed, but the scar remains, a memorial of our folly and the kindness of our good physician. A chain binds our whole being together, and its smallest link, when touched, vibrates throughout its whole extent. Is not life a solemn time, a precious time, a time of invitation, of reprieve, of visitation; every day a day of mercy, in the blessings of his providence, and the invitations of his grace.

Your life has long since been forfeited by sin; every moment it is preserved is a merciful visitation. Think of the many mercies that constitute the happy existence of a moment—how numerous, delicate, fragile, are the cords which keep in play the machinery of our lives. One cord snapped, existence is gone; one deranged, its enjoyments are fled; all diseased, its misery is intolerable. Do you remember one young as yourself, your companion and friend; his prospects were fair as yours for life and continued health and happiness, and he is gone, cut off in the midst of sin, unwarned, unprepared; and are you spared? What a merciful visitation! And now all around is calculated to call you to God: the works of his hands, the ordinances of his house, the solemn services of the Sabbath, and many turning to God. All these constitute your visitation. Give heed, then, to the things of your peace.

Consider again, that prosperity and adversity are days of visitation. Parts of life are signalized from others, and some individuals are favored with signal blessings. Some enjoy every blessing. Their cups overflow. They have no sickness, no affliction in themselves or their families. All their schemes succeed; every day adds to their wealth and respectability.

Their talents are great, their influence extensive; their joy overflows in feasting and merriment.

What is the design of God? Why that influence? To be perverted? Why those talents, that wealth? And what is their effect on you? Are you humbly filled with gratitude and love; or do you say in pride, "Behold this great Babylon which I have built?" God would win you by kindness, would draw you by cords of love as by the hands of man, would give you greater riches and pleasures. I knew one thus converted amidst surrounding infidelity, a young successful lawyer. Providence smiled, industry and talents soon brought wealth and influence, and his heart was melted. Connected by blood and marriage with some of the most distinguished scholars of Europe, and surrounded by infidel society, the goodness of the Lord led him to repentance. He took up such a cross as none of us have to bear, and sang the songs of Zion in a strange land indeed.

Now God is thus visiting you. You tremble not at his wrath, he would conquer you by love. Your indignation is excited when the thunders of Sinai are pealed in your ear. He addresses you in the language of love, every day ministering to your wants, every night watching around your couch, every moment pouring on you some fresh blessing. But will you forget your obligations and responsibilities? Then fearful will be the account, as that of the steward who began to eat and to be drunk while his lord was away. God will leave you to harden your heart, or will bring affliction on you. And I appeal to you who have been afflicted. Has not this been God's last resort, his strange work? He afflicts not willingly. Affliction is a merciful visitation; so the apostle Paul, so the Psalmist, so many have found it. This life must be viewed as connected with another. This gives prosperity and adversity their true meaning. You must see more than your pain, must see the hand that causes it, and the heart that guides the hand. Thus all the events of life form part of one great system of love, and all the threads that guide us run up into an unseen hand. Some cannot be won by kindness; the rod must be used. Success intoxicates, they must be defeated; fullness is not good for them, they must be brought to want. In the majority of cases sense and sensual things are present and urgent, and shut out eternal realities. We need solitude, retirement, leisure, to reflect, to be called back into ourselves, to commune with our own hearts and be still. What has been your experience in prosperity? What is that of the world? Without affliction men would lose one half their better earthly feelings. Are you afflicted, have you been afflicted? Then see a father's hand, kiss the rod. It is a visitation from heaven, and calls you from earth to the skies. Sanctified afflictions are the greatest blessings: unsanctified, bitter curses.

General revival of religion is also a day of visitation. There are periods in the world's history, when religion seems almost extinct, universal apathy and formality prevail in the church, worldliness and hypocrisy and heresy among ministers. Then vice prevails, and impious men bear sway, blasphemers are bold, licentiousness, sensuality, profligacy, are universal; the general atmosphere is tainted; in every book, in every society, you see irreligion diffused by the smile, or the jest, or the argument, or misrepresentation. Such was the last century, when genius, learning, wit, power, combined to extirpate the Gospel from the earth. Again, there are days when the general mind is alive and wide awake to religious and eternal truths. Many run to and fro, and knowledge is increased. Ministers are clothed with salvation, and shod with the preparation of the Gospel. It is an age of religion and religious enterprise. It pervades everything. Wherever you go, you meet Christians: at home, abroad; in high places, in low; public conveyances, everywhere. The Bible is widely diffused. In the parlors of the rich, and the cottages of the poor, religion is respected, and learning and genius consecrate their powers to defend its truths, and enforce its practical importance.

Such were the days of the Reformation, and such is our day. It is a day of visitation to the world, and blessed is he who sees it. Again: "Religion," says Luther, "is like a summer shower which falls, now here, now there." Countries where the Gospel is preached faithfully and plainly are blessed to the salvation of many. To live in such a land is to enjoy a visitation. Such is our land, and blessed are ye of the Lord.

Again, there are especial seasons of awakening and conversion in these favored lands—precious and glorious times when all conspires for the sinner's good. Man and God urge him, heaven and earth combine their influence, and the very air is filled with a palpable solemnity. None escape. The spirit operates powerfully, preaching is earnest; ministers are baptized, as it were, afresh, with spirit and power. Whole hosts enter in. How many long to see such a day, how many wonder. What a day of visitation!

But special movements on our own hearts create a day of merciful visitation. They are the beamings of that light which has come into the world. In such an age, such a land, it is impossible but that such influences must be felt. In the full career of sin, in the bustle of the world, in the noise and mirth of society, one feels them. So Herod cried out, "It is John,—John, whom I despised, imprisoned, beheaded, is risen from the dead, and mighty works do shew forth themselves in him." In retirement, in darkness, sickness, meditation, we have caught glimpses of purer and better things, when all was quiet around; in the still moonlight, in the calm sunset, when the mind, freed from its earthly cares, had time and taste for higher things. Often the stillness of the Sabbath, the voice and venerable form of some reverend father in Israel, the memory of childish days, and all the tender impressions then felt, especially of her, now no more, who watched your cradle, and taught you to lisp Christ's name, have called up tears of sympathy and penitential sorrow. Thus the mind has looked away from earth, and risen to clear and etherial views of truth; then soft and gentle, as the music of heaven, was the voice and of God calling you to the skies.

II. Consider the second truth. Now are they hidden from your eyes. If not improved, all these privileges are taken away. This is the universal testimony of Scripture: "to him that hath shall be given, but from him that hath not, shall be taken away even that which he hath." The unprofitable servant lost his one talent. So teach reason and experience. We have read of a man who on some medical theory shut out the light. You can anticipate the effect. Some fanatics tie the limbs uselessly in some position, form is destroyed, the blood does not circulate, and life is gone. Man is an active being, and must be actively engaged. There are seasons in religion, harvests for souls, decisive crises on which hang tremblingly everlasting realities. The husbandman, in the bright days of sunshine, must plough and sow, and not wait for the storm. For some of you there is to-day such a crisis. Then improve the day of your visitation. And, now, to you who will not improve the day of your visitation, what can we say? The Saviour weeps for you; kindly, affectionately, would he call you to himself, but you turn away. He knows your certain misery, and wept; and will you not weep for yourselves? Ah! in your hours of merriment you have great cause for weeping, and could one glimpse of the future burst on you, you too would weep.

The lovers of this world seem bound to it by some strange spell. The form of some secret fascination seems to have charmed their faculties until the voice of reason and experience as well as the voice of God falls unheeded on their ears. In spite of all that we have known ourselves, and heard from others, we still believe that the world is a satisfying portion; we listen to its promises, and with eager expectation grasp its unsubstantial pleasures. There is none who has not been sometimes rudely awakened from his dream of worldly happiness to gaze upon the stern reality of truth. But he soon composes himself softly to his repose, enjoys the same visions, pursues the same shadows, clasps the same phantom form to his bosom, starts from his slumbers, finds it all a dream, and sleeps again. And this is the business of life, the employment of threescore years and ten, bestowed on rational and immortal beings, for the purpose of securing everlasting happiness.

But is it all a dream? Is it true of the great and the learned and the wise, the shrewd, sagacious, calculating men of the world, that the objects they are pursuing are as unreal and unsubstantial as the veriest figments of a dream, that amidst all that restless activity which agitates unceasingly the millions of our globe, there is nothing at all more rational than the feverish excitement of a disordered brain? Yes, my friends, it is a dream, "all the wild trash of sleep, without the rest." Such is the decision of God's word, and such, we will endeavor to show, is the unbiased decision of reason. What think you of ambition, then, that noblest of worldly passions, "that last infirmity of noble minds?" Of all the restless beings that crowd our globe, and harass it with their mad designs, there is none more evidently irrational than the ambitious man. His whole life is one long pursuit and restless dream. He is perpetually haunted by visions of ideal glory which destroy his peace of mind, impair his health, and beckon him onward to some dangerous precipice, whence he falls to rise no more. Amidst the glorious delusions which swarm thickly in his sight, he dreams of universal empire, of undying fame, he grasps the sceptre of the world, and already hears the pæans of its millions, and, in the madness of the horrid dream, he thinks that men are but sheep to be slaughtered at his will, and marches forth with his armies, spreading devastation and carnage in his path. But at last he meets his doom. Heaven has decreed that even in this life injustice and crime shall often experience a dreadful retribution. The indignation of mankind is aroused against the common enemy, and ambition awakes at last upon the rock of St. Helena.

But suppose the delusion had lasted a little longer, it would still have been a dream. Suppose he had attained all that he desired and hoped for, that Europe had bowed beneath his yoke, and Asia and Africa and America extended his wide dominions, till the sun never set upon his territories, as it never did on his boundless and insatiable ambition. Even then, he must have soon awaked to a sense of the delusion. The happiness which seemed just within his reach would then have vanished, and as he grasped the object of his long desire, he would only feel the crushing energy of his own convulsive embrace. The mind, finding no employment without, would have turned in upon itself, and avenged the wrongs of a world, by the very energies which had been employed to subdue it. Of those who are engaged in the pursuit of wealth, of pleasure, how much more rational are the schemes? How vast and visionary are the expectations of success in the pursuit, how mad the anticipations of enjoyment in the possession. Of the millions upon earth, how many are expecting to be either rich or great, and of all that number how few succeed.

In view of all these things, the uncertainty of life, the certainty of death and judgment, the transitory character of all earthly pursuits, the unsatisfying nature of all earthly good—how ought you to pause and consider your ways, before the day of your merciful visitation shall be closed forever. What shall it profit a man if he shall gain the whole world and lose his own soul; or what shall a man give in exchange for his soul? The attempt to gain the world would be futile; and if you could gain it all, it would be unavailing to satisfy the wants of an immortal spirit. What can we say, what shall we do to induce you to improve the present moment as it flies, and lay hold on eternal interests? We can only set the case before you and then weep, as Christ did over Jerusalem, and commend you to God.

XXIX.

AMBASSADORS FOR CHRIST.

---

2 Cor. v. 20.—"Now then we are ambassadors for Christ, as though God did beseech you by us: we pray you, in Christ's stead, be ye reconciled to God."

The Gospel is a message from the throne of heaven, and every minister of the Gospel, called and sent of God, is an ambassador for Christ. The message which he bears is one of awful dignity, of supreme authority. It is God's proclamation of pardon, God's offer of reconciliation, to this rebellious and ruined world. The position he occupies is one of high and solemn responsibility. He stands, himself a dying man, between the living God and dying men; he stands a sinful man, between a holy God and a world of sinners; he stands a pardoned rebel, between an angry God and his offending subject.

There was once a far different messenger from heaven. He was the brightness of his Father's glory, and express image of his person; and although he left the glory which was his before the world was made, yet did the radiance of his essential divinity often beam forth through that inferior nature, in which it was enshrouded. Mild persuasion and high authority sat enthroned upon his lips, and when he spake, even his enemies unwillingly acknowledged, that he spake as never man before had spoken. But his work was soon finished, his mission soon terminated, and, after a life of sorrow and a death of agony, he soon abandoned a world that was not worthy of him, and sitteth now exalted forever at the right hand of the Majesty on high.

And now, the great work for which he became incarnate and lived and died, the message which fell from his own lovely lips, and was sealed by his own most precious blood, the great embassy from heaven to earth—great in itself but stamped with a new and imperishable dignity, by the character of him who bore it first—has been entrusted to earthen vessels—to men of like passion with ourselves. Now, also, the minister of the Gospel, as the humble representative of his Saviour, in Christ's stead and by his high authority, offers a treaty of peace, presents the terms of reconciliation. How awful are the subjects he is called to discuss, how vast the interests involved, how tremendous the consequences which may result from the neglect or the right performance of his duties. The Gospel which he preaches is the Gospel of God, and however feeble may be the instrument by whom it is proclaimed, it must prove the savor of life unto life or of death unto death to every soul of man that hears it. O brethren, what a fearful thought is this, that of all those mighty crowds that gather Sabbath after Sabbath in all the churches of our land, and sit beneath the warnings and invitations of the Gospel, of the hundreds that hear me now, there is not one that does not possess an immortal spirit, hurrying onward to the bar of God, moulding its destinies for eternity, on whom each sermon that he hears is leaving some deep impression, sealing it for eternal life, or stamping on it the dark impress of eternal death. Oh, who of us is sufficient for these things?

How tremblingly should mortal man lay his hand upon the ark of God, lest he perish by the touch! Oh, who could have dared to hope, had it been one of our early dreams, had it only mingled with the wildest, boldest, of our childish visions, that we should be ministers of God, that on us should all these high and boundless responsibilities hereafter rest, that to us should be granted, all sinful and unworthy as we are, the great privilege of standing up before a dying world and proclaiming the unsearchable riches of Christ, the great salvation of our God. How fervent and earnest would have been our prayers for divine assistance! would we not have spent our days in anxious thought, our nights in sleepless preparation? We would have improved each hour as it passed, we would have seized each opportunity before it was gone forever, we would have cultivated to the utmost the limited capacities of our nature; and, summoning all our powers for this high service, concentrating all our energies in one burning focus on this great object, would have thought it happiness enough to pour forth our full souls in one earnest, affectionate remonstrance with dying sinners, and then depart and be with God.

But, alas, the time lost can never be reclaimed, energies once wasted on the world can never be consecrated in their fulness and freshness to God, and it is only in great weakness that we can present before you the message of our King. Yet we address you in Christ's stead, by his authority; in his great name, we make the very offer which he, if present, would make you to-day. Our commission is before us, stamped with the Father's approbation, sealed by the blood of the Son. And, "he that hath ears to hear, let him hear," for we come before you on no light trivial errand, come not to comply with an empty form, not to gratify an idle curiosity, nor to furnish the amusement of an hour, but to discuss subjects of large and enduring interest, large as the soul's immortal powers, enduring as its never-ending existence. We come to urge you, most affectionately and most solemnly, to be reconciled to God. The sum and substance of our business is to show that there is a fearful controversy between God and man, and, if possible, to produce a reconciliation.

And here the difficulty meets us, on the very threshold of our subject, that you utterly deny the existence of any controversy, and, of course, the necessity of any reconciliation between God and man. You look around you, and everywhere behold the traces of infinite benevolence. All nature is calm and peaceful, the blue sky is spread out in still and solemn beauty above you, the bright sun pours its mild and cheerful radiance around you, the soft air of evening breathes gently on your brow, the warm life-blood bounds merrily from your heart, and flows in healthful currents along the arteries, where every throb is joy. You mingle in the gay society about you, and as the jest and the laugh pass around, as the dance moves merrily on, and the music sweeps by in full and voluptuous swell, you yield yourself up to the bright illusion of the scene, and say within your heart, surely there can be no danger near, no clouds and darkness to gather around that sun, no tempests to sweep across that sky, no thunderbolts that lie slumbering there, no angry God, that sitteth frowning in the heavens. Gladly would we leave you to the enjoyment of this pleasant dream, but as ambassadors for Christ, we dare not: nay, if there be, indeed, a fearful controversy between God and man, unsettled, still pending, in which all the attributes of God's nature, and all the powers of his government are arrayed in terrible hostility against the sinner, surely it becomes every reasonable creature to ascertain the fact, and prepare to meet or avoid the danger. That such a controversy exists is most clearly manifested from the language and the acts of each of the parties.

The very idea of "*reconciliation*," in our text, supposes a controversy; for if there be none, where is the need of reconciliation? Again, we are expressly told, in the Epistle to the Romans, that "the carnal mind is enmity against God," nay, so deep and inveterate is this enmity that "it is not subject to the *law of God*, neither indeed *can be*." And the Psalmist assures us, that when God looked from heaven to behold the children of men, there was none good, no not one, none that did *know* or *regard God*." The language of their heart and their conduct is that of utter evil, of bitter derision or open defiance. "Who is the Lord, that we should regard him, or the most High, that we should serve him?" "How doth the Lord know?" "Let us burst his bonds asunder, and cast his cords from us." The same idea runs through the whole New Testament, where sinners are represented "as enemies against God, by reason of evil works," "as enemies to the Cross of Christ," "as rebels against God's government, and subjects of the Prince of the Power of the air, the spirit that reigneth in the children of disobedience." On the other hand,

God is represented as "angry with the wicked every day," as "laughing their devices to scorn," as pouring down from his high throne in the heavens the bitterest derision upon their puny efforts, as arraying himself for the complete making ready his bow, preparing his arrows in his quiver, as a man of war girded up, and panting for the fight, as a lion roaring in his majesty and strength. Nay, if there be one term in language which can express more forcibly than any other, indignation, deep and deadly, if there be in all nature one image more full of terror than all besides, this term, this imagery, is selected. Epithet is piled on epithet, image heaped on image, to impress our minds with this determined anger and its awful effects. It is "indignation and wrath, tribulation and anguish," it is "vengeance and fiery indignation," it is "darkness and outer darkness," and "the blackness of darkness forever." Indeed, throughout the whole Bible we are told of a kingdom of light and of darkness, of a daring rebellion against God's government and throne, led on by a haughty and fallen Spirit, and aided by men who have joined the standard of his rebellion.

It is to overthrow this rebellion that Christ came into the world to produce a reconciliation of this controversy, on terms honorable to God and safe to man. The whole scheme of the Gospel, the whole Jewish and Christian system with all their sacrifices for sin, from the first lamb that bled on Abel's altar to the last great offering on Calvary—all are based on the assumption of such a controversy. If there be none, then the Gospel is a delusion, then all the array of types and prophecies, and miracles by which the Saviour's appearance was announced at first, and afterward attended, was a mockery. Then the death of Christ and the offers of salvation are a farce, then we are madmen and you are dupes.

But the existence of this controversy is not only revealed in the word of God, it is equally manifest from the acts of his providence and the works of his hands. It is written upon the face of human society, and engraven as with a pen of brass upon the front of nature, so that wherever man exists, or nature has been observed, the conviction has sunk deep into every human bosom, that the Creator of nature and of man had a fearful controversy with the workmanship of his hands. If not, why is the history of the world a history of woe? Why is man born in agony, why does he die amidst tears and groans? Why does the pestilence devastate earth's fairest regions? Why does famine sweep her pale nations to the grave? Why does disease in ten thousand forms still watch about our path? Why does death, standing at the door of life, stamp his pale signet on the infant's brow, and claim it as his victim? Ah,—why is the face of nature scarred as with the thunderbolts of wrath? Why does the volcano pour its liquid lava on the earth and bury in its fiery torrents the habitations of men? Why does the earthquake burst her solid rocks, and heave her quaking mountains, and, yawning wide, engulf its populous cities? Why do we still discover in earth's remotest regions the traces yet remaining of that terrible convulsion, when the fountains of the great deep were broken up, and over earth's loveliest valleys, hills, and highest mountains — over all human habitations — over all man's hopes, fears, joys, and sorrows, the wild waters of the ocean rolled along—dark, boundless, irresistible—a fit emblem of the Creator's majesty—a fit element of the Creator's wrath?

Why? But the answer is already given, we hear it in the moans of the dying infant, in the shrieks of the agonized mother, in the groans of the strong man, when in the vigor of his days he is called to struggle with his last foe. It comes from the chamber of the dying, from the grave of the dead, from the sepulchres of earth's buried millions. Down through the long lapse of centuries, it comes in tones that cannot be mistaken, loud, distinct, solemn. There is a fearful controversy between God and man. Such is the testimony of God in his Word, and in his works, and now, does the testimony of man fully correspond? Most fully, "out of thine own mouth will I condemn thee."

There is not an individual in this house who will not acknowledge that he is a sinner. Now holiness is directly, irreconcilably opposed to sin, and if God be a God of holiness, he must have a controversy with sin. Now sin is not an idle abstraction, a word without any corresponding thing. The world in which we live is a world of solemn and substantial realities, and sin is the palpable act of an accountable agent, nay, in strict propriety of speech, is really the sinner acting. Hope not, then, to escape behind the flimsy pretext that God abhors the sin, but will spare the sinner. When the executioner comes to punish murder, let the murderer beware. When God shall arise to take vengeance on sin, let the sinner tremble. Ah, at the judgment-bar your subtle distinctions will be of no avail. When heaven and earth shall flee before his face, where will your cobweb sophistry be found? And this is not the acknowledgment of a few educated under the influence of Christian instruction, it is the universal testimony of the human race, it is the voice of human nature, sounding as best it may through every channel that can give utterance to human thought or feeling—in history and in fiction, in poetry and philosophy, in all the institutions of society. It is interwoven with the structure of all known languages as if it were a necessary element of human thought. The fall of man and his final restitution, the sins of the people and the wrath of the gods, form the staple of the ancient tragedy and epic. All the philosophers admit the corruption of human nature, and even the gay and licentious Horace admits that our "sins do not permit the thunderbolts of the gods to sleep."

So deep was this conviction that every misfortune of life, and every uncommon appearance in nature, was attributed to some incensed and avenging deity. If a comet swept across the sky, or a meteor blazed through the air, or a shadow darkened the sun, whole nations trembled; and when in the dark hour of night the wintry wind howled around his dwelling, or the loud storm burst over his head, the affrighted heathen crept pale and shivering to his altar, for the infernal furies were out upon the wind, and some god had spoken in his anger from the clouds. And then, some victim must appease that wrath, some lamb, some trembling captive, some innocent babe, must bleed upon that altar, perhaps whole hecatombs must die, that the indignation of heaven may be averted. But this you say is superstition. Granted; yet every universal effect must have a cause as universal as itself. No widespread opinion prevalent through all ages and all nations, can be pure and unmixed falsehood, and beneath the monstrous and ever-changing forms of this wild superstition, is clearly visible one great, substantial, unchanging truth, distorted, if you please, degraded, yet still a truth, stamped in enduring characters upon the human mind and never to be erased, "that there is a controversy between God and man."

And does not conscience add confirmation to this truth? Why does the sick man at the approach of death look wildly in agony around, beg for a day, an hour, a single moment? Why does the prisoner, immured in his horrid dungeon, shudder at the thought of execution, and when the hour is struck, feel that this is the consummation of woe? Meet a strong man in the streets of a pestilential city, and tell him that the plague-spot is on his head and he must die, certainly, instantly die: why does the cheek bleach, and the lips quiver, and the pulse flutter, and the knees fail, and the eyes swim in dizziness, and the reason reel upon its throne? Is it not all because God has a controversy with man, and man knows that he is a sinner, and fears to stand before his God in judgment? Is it not all proof of a deep, abiding conviction of the soul as universal as our race, that there is a day of retribution in which God will judge the world in righteousness, and settle this long standing controversy with man?

Then how great is the need of reconciliation, and how urgent is the call of God who is now in Christ Jesus reconciling the world unto himself through the death of the cross! Behold, now is the accepted time, and now is the day of salvation. God has provided an atonement. God has found a ransom. God has offered terms of reconciliation, and by the preaching of the Gospel the invitation is extended to all men. "Ho! every one that thirsteth, come ye to the waters."

"Whosoever will, let him take of the water of life freely." "For God hath made him to be sin for us who knew no sin, that we might be made the righteousness of God in him." "Now then we are ambassadors for Christ, as though God did beseech you by us; we pray you, in Christ's stead, be ye reconciled to God."

THE END.

www.ingramcontent.com/pod-product-compliance
Lightning Source LLC
LaVergne TN
LVHW021321110826
845150LV00003B/632

* 9 7 8 1 4 2 5 5 5 7 1 2 6 *